RESEARCH IN ECONOMIC HISTORY

Supplement 6 • 1991

THE VITAL ONE: ESSAYS IN HONOR OF JONATHAN R.T. HUGHES

RESEARCH IN ECONOMIC HISTORY

A Research Annual

THE VITAL ONE: ESSAYS IN HONOR OF JONATHAN R.T. HUGHES

Editor: JOEL MOKYR
Departments of Economics and History
Northwestern University

SUPPLEMENT 6 • 1991

JAI PRESS INC.

Greenwich, Connecticut *London, England*

55 Old Post Road, No. 2
Greenwich, Connecticut 06830

JAI Press Ltd.
118 Pentonville Road
London N1 9JN
England

ISBN: 1-55938-150-7

Manufactured in the United States of America

CONTENTS

LIST OF CONTRIBUTORS

Edward Berkowitz
Department of History
The George Washington University

Brian Binger
Department of Economics
University of Arizona

Louis P. Cain
Department of Economics
Northwest University

Lance Davis
Department of Economics
California Institute of Technology

Robert E. Gallman
Department of Economics
The University of North Carolina
at Chapel Hill

Jack A. Goldstone
Department of Sociology
University of California, Davis

Rolf Hendriksson
Department of Economics
University of Stockholm

Elizabeth Hoffman
Department of Economics
University of Arizona

Theresa D. Hutchins
235 Orchard Place
Ridgewood, New Jersey

Eric L. Jones
Department of Economic History
LaTrobe University

William Kennedy
Department of Economic History
The London School of Economics

Gary D. Libecap — Department of Economics, University of Arizona

Kim McQuaid — Department of History, Lake Erie College

Joel Mokyr — Departments of Economics and History, Northwestern University

John Nye — Department of Economics, Washington University

Stanley Reiter — KGSM Mgr. Econ. Decision Sci., Northwestern University

Richard Szostak — Department of Economics, University of Alberta

Paul Uselding — Dean, College of Business, University of Toledo

Samuel Williamson — Department of Economics, Miami University

EDITOR'S INTRODUCTION

When I first set foot on the Northwestern Campus, on a sunny fall day in 1974, Jonathan Hughes was awaiting me in his office and took me for a long walk around campus. During our walk, he told me things about the university and about the department that nobody else would have observed, let alone shared with another. A typical detail that has stuck in my mind is his observation that the Northwestern undergraduates represented millions of dollars of investment in orthodontist work. Look around, Jon said, all perfect teeth. A small detail, perhaps, but a revealing one captured through an uncommon perceptiveness.

And that is the way it has been for the past fifteen years during which Jon and I together ran the economic history section in the economics department. We have worked together in perfect harmony against, I may add, the expectations of most of those who knew us both. As all who know him are aware, Jon is somewhat larger than life, a *sui generis* defying stereotyping. Above all, what has mattered most to me is that Jon *shares* what he has: information, insight, irreverence, iconoclasm. If over the years his influence on me has been noticeable, as more than one mutual friend has pointed out, I am proud of it. A better role model and senior colleague no scholar can imagine. This volume is a small way of saying "thank you, Jon."

This collection contains papers by a combination of Jonathan Hughes' students and colleagues. Some of those students were Jon's alone (Cain, Uselding, Kennedy, and Henriksson). Sam Williamson was indeed a Purdue Ph.D., one of the few economic historians lucky enough to come out of that long-defunct powerhouse of which Jon is so proud. McQuaid and Berkowitz were formally in Northwestern's history department but learned that crossing Deering Meadow is neither lethal nor irreversible. Others arrived later and were jointly trained by us (Szostak and Nye). As for colleagues—Lance Davis was Jon's colleague at Purdue, while Eric Jones, Betsy Hoffman, and Jack Goldstone at different times joined forces with us in building Northwestern's economic history program.

The topics of the papers all relate in some way to Jonathan Hughes' written work. This is not too hard given that Jon's written work has covered virtually every topic in economic history, from business cycle theory to entrepreneurship and his three textbooks. Government, entrepreneurship, business cycles and economic growth provide the main subject matter to the papers below. Interestingly enough, Jon's presidential address to the Economic History Association, "The Great Strike at Nushagak Station," his only essay on environmental economic history, emerges as a separate topic inspiring both Davis and Jones.

Many individuals have helped in making this volume possible. Among the contributors, Eric Jones was one of the first who approached me with the *festschrift* idea. In later stages, Louis Cain consistently provided me with excellent advice and encouragement. Paul Uselding provided some indispensable connections. Many others helped in advising me on a variety of questions and in reading and commenting on the papers, especially colleagues in both the economics and the history departments at Northwestern: Charles Calomiris, Avner Greif, Paul Huck, Jacob Metzer, Akira Motamura, Cormac Ó Gráda, and Dan Shiman in economics; Arthur McEvoy, Harold Perkin, and Bob Wiebe in history. Outside Northwestern, I would particularly like to thank Paul A. David, William N. Parker, and Kenneth Snowden. Mrs. Angie Campbell has displayed her usual virtuosity in working out endless technical details, and Martin Kearney helped to prepare the index.

Joel Mokyr
Editor

THE VITAL ONE: ESSAYS IN HONOR OF JONATHAN R.T. HUGHES

THE VITAL JONATHAN R. T. HUGHES

Louis Cain, with Stanley Reiter and Paul Uselding

vital—adj., from L. *vita*, life—of,
concerned with, or manifesting life

I

The vitality of Jonathan Roberts Tyson Hughes is apparent after a few minutes in his company. Jon was born in Wenatchee, Washington, in 1928, a member of the ninth generation of his family to live in this country. He was raised in Twin Falls, Idaho, and still relishes the outdoors. Once a varsity football player (lineman), today he is an avid walker and cross-country skier. A talented clarinetist, he toured with the Joe Martin (from Hollywood) Band following graduation from high school. Jon travelled from Twin Falls to Los Angeles to get the gig, but the band ended up doing one-night stands throughout the Northwest. This memorable experience convinced him that college was a superior alternative.

After graduating from the Utah State Agricultural College in 1950, Jon ventured to the University of Washington to begin graduate work in economics. It was there he encountered economic history, young assistant professors Douglass North and Morris D. Morris, and a fellow student named Lance Davis.

Research in Economic History, Suppl. 6, pages 1-13.

ISBN: 1-55938-150-7.

After two years in Seattle, and summer employment as an accountant at the Alaska Packers' Nushagak Station, he was named a Rhodes Scholar and accepted by The Queen's College, Oxford. In Seattle, Jon learned to perceive economic history on a large canvass, to be unafraid to make generalizations. He became, in the words of Paul Uselding, a "paradigm maker." Jon, in turn, has encouraged his students to respect those scholars willing to speculate about the unknown.

Jon took advantage of his opportunity to attend Oxford and completed his graduate work in economics, receiving a D.Phil. degree in 1955. It was nearly a singular achievement then as there had been only one successful recent D.Phil. student in economics from the United States. The standards were exacting; there was a feeling that the faculty was not anxious to award the D.Phil. degree, particularly to Americans. At Oxford, Jon attended the theory seminars of John R. (now Sir John) Hicks, Thomas (now Lord) Balogh, and Professor Paul Streeten. According to Jon, Hicks decided what everybody should do and assigned him to work under Hrothgar (now Sir John) Habakkuk. He also worked with Charles Neville Ward-Perkins.

The rules of Oxford made life difficult for D. Phil. students. As Jon has described them, supervisors in those days were forbidden to give detailed supervision to their supervisees. Following Professor Habakkuk's non-detailed advice he studied the British trade cycle of the 1850s. His initial paradigm was inspired by the two recently published volumes of Arthur Gayer, Walter Rostow, and Anna Schwartz, *The Growth and Fluctuation of the British Economy: 1790-1850*, but that paradigm did not prove fruitful. Given the rules, he went to see Hicks who suggested he contact "Robbie" Matthews at Cambridge, a young scholar Hicks described as "damn good." By return mail, Jon Hughes received the galleys of R. C. O. Matthews, *A Study in Trade Cycle History*. Matthews had solved the problems that had troubled Hughes. With great relief, Jon pushed a pile of now-superfluous manuscript off his desk into the wastebasket. As Jon wrote the final draft of his dissertation, Habakkuk pushed him to eliminate all explicit theorizing on the argument that he could still fail if there was anything in the manuscript with which someone could argue. Habakkuk's caution proved to be the path of wisdom. The final product was a detailed study of the development of the British economy which factually examined what had happened, thereby avoiding the difficulties that had prevented most U.S. economics students from receiving the Oxford D.Phil.

Jon developed an enormous respect for widely-read scholars while at Oxford. Historians who had read widely in other disciplines became the model to which Jon aspired. At the height of the "revolution" in economic history in the early 1960s, Jon reminded his students that, if his generation of economists "went to the library and started reading, it would take at least ten years to catch up with David Landes." He has been a voracious and intelligent reader and has an incredible command over this material.

It was during the Oxford years that Jon met Mary Gray Stilwell, a young Texan studying anthropology with Edward Evan Evans-Pritchard, "the Keynes of anthropology." They were married in 1953 and "lived happily ever after." A son Benjamin was born in 1960, and twin daughters Charis and Margaret were born in 1962. A series of dogs with various idiosyncracies completes the Hughes family.

In March 1955, Jon and Mary Gray returned to the states. Jon accepted a position in the Research department of the Federal Reserve Bank of New York, where he worked under the authority of Arthur Bloomfield and was associated with several other economists, including Andrew Brimmer, Stephen Clarke, Charles Coombs, Hans Dernburg, Rimmer de Vries, Edna Ehrlich, Peter Fousek, Alan Holmes, Madeline McWhinney, Lawrence Ritter, Francis Schott, and Albert Wojnilower. During these years, Jon learned how to read and interpret bureaucracies. Having written a sentence that noted a particular country's "exports fell," he was asked to rewrite it to say "exports largely ceased to rise" so as not to offend that country.

Band, business, and bureaucratic careers were left behind permanently when Jon, in the fall of 1956, accepted the call of Emmanuel Weiler to become an Assistant Professor in the Economics department of Purdue University. Weiler, who was then chairman of the department, acted on the suggestion of an assistant professor by the name of Lance Davis. A year later Jon and Mary Gray were back in New York while he spent the 1957-58 academic year as a Visiting Assistant Professor at Columbia University. Returning to Purdue, he was promoted to Associate Professor in the fall of 1958 and was appointed Professor in 1961.

At Purdue, Jon was part of one of the most dynamic young economics departments in the country. He initially shared an office with Lance Davis and then with Stanley Reiter. He shared ideas with the likes of Davis, Reiter, Edward Ames, Robert Basmann, Kirby Davidson, Thomas Dernburg (Hans' son), George Horwich, Duncan McDougall, Jim Quirk, Nathan Rosenberg, Reuben Saposnik, Vernon Smith, and the late Cliff Lloyd to mention just a few. Purdue was the institutional home of the revolution that became the "New Economic History," an episode chronicled in greater detail later in this volume. Other names from other schools are included in the list of the initial revolutionaries, yet they all travelled to Purdue to share ideas. Jon moved to Northwestern in the fall of 1966 to replace the retiring Hal Williamson. He and his close friend Stan Reiter (who arrived at Northwestern two years later) have kept the spirit that existed at Purdue alive and well.

Jon has returned to Oxford twice. He visited Nuffield College in 1962-63 as a Guggenheim Fellow, and it was during this leave that his daughters were born. Jon and Mary Gray were not expecting twins. Jon had ordered a Volkswagen Beetle to be delivered in England and shipped at year's end to the United States. Subsequently, all five Hugheses travelled with their belongings from the Port of New York to West Lafayette. In 1971-1972, Jon visited All Souls College as a Ford Foundation Faculty Fellow. During the latter year, Jon and Mary Gray built a home in the mountains of Vermont where they now spend their summers. Somehow it all makes sense that a man from the rugged mountains of the Northwest and a woman from the rolling plains of the Southwest who met in England and who work in the flat prairies of the Middlewest would choose the gentler, wooded mountains of the East as their retreat.

II

At the risk of doing Jon a great injustice, it is convenient to divide his publications into six interrelated and, often, overlapping groups. The six groups are European (predominantly English) economic history, the new economic history, entrepreneurship, the nature of government, the American economic history textbook, and autobiography. This schematization of Jon's published work is not exhaustive in breadth or depth; readers should consult the list of publications at the conclusion of this essay.

Jon's most prominent work in European economic history, the first group, is *Fluctuations in Trade, Industry, and Finance, 1850-1860* (1960). This is the published version of his dissertation. It continues to be widely cited. His first publication "The Commercial Crisis of 1857" (1956) came directly from this research, as did "1859, Entering an Age of Crisis" (1959). *Industrialization and Economic History: Theses and Conjectures* (1970) is an elaboration and extension of a course Jon first presented at Columbia University in 1957. The course represents something of a turning point in Jon's research as he began to integrate material on the United States into his presentation of European economic history. English history continues to be a major interest, but it no longer shapes his career as it did at the start. As Jon's research came to focus increasingly on these shores, his writing continually reminded us of the important role our English heritage plays in U.S. economic history.

Jon wrote two classic review essays; one was on the work of Deane and Cole which he entitled "Measuring British Economic Growth" (1964), while the other, "Henry Mayhew's London" (1969), was written when Mayhew's four-volume study of *London Labour and the London Poor* was reissued. Other essays in English economic history were written for *festschriften* honoring Sir John Hicks and Sir John Habakkuk, those most responsible for this part of his career. "Wicksell on the Facts" (1969) was contributed to the Hicks volume. It lies somewhat outside the scope of Jon's other work and embodies what he once claimed was his "only original idea." "A World Elsewhere: The Importance of Starting English" (forthcoming) is his contribution to the Habakkuk volume. It stands as a reminder that Jon has not lost sight of his debt to Oxford.

The second group of publications are those in the "New Economic History." One of the earliest works in this genre was "The First 1,945 British Steamships" (1958), coauthored with Stanley Reiter. It is difficult for those of us who are now middle-aged to remember what was involved in producing such a paper at that time. The word "keypunch" has largely disappeared from our working vocabulary. Young "cliometricians," who have fancy regression programs entered on their hard disks, may remember when the simplest regression program required a large pack of computer cards that were placed at the front of your "deck." The steamship paper is a product of an even earlier age when computer boards were wired separately for each job.

"Aspects of Quantitative Research in Economic History" (1961), coauthored with Reiter and Lance Davis, is the self-proclaimed "Purdue Manifesto" regarding quantitative work in the field. As the story goes, Stan Reiter humorously inserted the word "Cliometrics" in an early draft of this paper which was presented to the Economic History Association meetings in Philadelphia. Jon liked it. One reason it has become the term of choice surely must be that the revolution proved successful. Now well into its fourth decade, can it still be considered "new?"

Collaboration was a hallmark of the Purdue approach. Jon's comparative advantage within the group is apparent in the steamship paper, "A Dollar-Sterling Exchange, 1803-1895" (1960) with Lance Davis, and "The United States Business Cycle before 1860" (1963) with Nathan Rosenberg. These and other papers, written by the wide variety of scholars contributing to what was then "new" in economic history, were republished in *Purdue Faculty Papers in Economic History, 1956-1966* (1968).

American Economic History (1961), written with Davis and Duncan McDougall, defines this period more than any other work. This topically-arranged text developed for the first-year course required of economics students at Purdue was the textbook of the new approach. Critically hailed, it went through three editions, but it never proved as popular as chronologically-arranged books. One suspects Jon recalled this when approaching the task of writing his own chronologically-arranged text two decades later.

Of all his new economic history articles, the one which I most frequently re-read is "Fact and Theory in Economic History" (1966). This methodological paper presents Jon's point of view about the writing of economic history, new or old. It is a reminder of the care with which economic historians are expected to conjoin abstract models, empirical evidence, and documentary material to tell a good story.

The third group, entrepreneurship, is dominated by Jon's *opus classicus, The Vital Few* (1966) and the revision (1986). While it is not really "new economic history" in that it is not quantitative, Jon adopted that methodology to approach biography. The question he addressed was one that has occupied him in various guises ever since—Why did the American economy develop the way it did? As such, it was a question with great currency at the time. In *The Vital Few* he chose to emphasize the individual because, as he argued, the economy at any time is "a social artifact, the remains of the past actions, successes and failures, of individuals engaged in economic enterprise of all sorts" (p. 1). This was what led him to attempt to explain American economic development through biography. While the entrepreneurial skill of dedicated individuals is sometimes assumed, sometimes forgotten in the abstract models of economic theorists, attempts to incorporate it explicitly as an endogenous independent variable have been unsuccessful. As it became fashionable to reason that individuals did not matter, Jon used "the precision of the historian, the logic of economic analysis and the art of the biographer" (p. v) to introduce his views on the development of the U.S. economy. It was not meant as a "great man" approach to history. He identified eight (now ten) individuals as "surrogates" for others whose biographies were all too often inaccessible.

"Eight Tycoons—The Entrepreneur and American Economic Development" (1964) was an article based on the book; it was the talk Jon presented at Northwestern's recruiting seminar. "Entrepreneurship and the American Economy—A Sketch" (1979), "Entrepreneurship in the American Economy" (1979), his entry on "Entrepreneurship" in the *Dictionary of Economic History* (1980), "Arthur Cole and Entrepreneurial History" (1983), and "The Engine of History: Entrepreneurship" (forthcoming) are testimony to his continuing interest in this area. Further, he continues to offer a highly regarded course on entrepreneurship to the students of Northwestern's Kellogg Graduate School of Management.

Jon's research on what became his fourth group of publications, the nature of government, began shortly after the move to Northwestern. He continued his investigation of American economic development, but now the emphasis was on the "rules of economic behavior imposed by society." The work expanded to encompass the "overall nature of American government response to economic problems, the form of that response, and its historical development." As the programs introduced as part of the Great Society became a settled part of American life, as individuals and businesses had to accommodate an increasing government role in everyday life, Jon's research attempted to explain how it began and how it grew. The result was one large manuscript that eventually was published as two books.

The first of these books, *Social Control in the Colonial Economy* (1976), was once the lengthy introductory chapter to the portion of the original manuscript that became the second book, *The Governmental Habit: Economic Controls from Colonial Times to the Present* (1977). While this bifurcation made the material more approachable for many readers, it eliminated an important connecting link in the original manuscript. *Social Control* traced U.S. laws regarding land tenure, inheritance, labor contracts, prices, and several other economic concepts back to their English roots. These become simply a given—"a matter of pedigree,"—in *The Governmental Habit* which explained how those laws evolved following the American Revolution. The final chapter of *Social Control* strikes a chord that resonates throughout *The Governmental Habit*, "Nonmarket Control, an American Tradition." The separation of Jon's research into two books makes the nexus between law and economics that emerges in *Social Control* less clear in *The Governmental Habit*.

Both books were criticized as containing familiar material, but that familiarity is deceiving. Different critics had varying opinions about what was familiar, and some reached divergent conclusions about the books' central message, often different conclusions from that of the author. Jon's conclusion was clear: the inefficient, unplanned patchwork of controls we have today is a result of our present legal system which was adapted from the English common law by the thousands of individuals cases that have shaped U.S. precedents. Yes, it is inefficient, *but* it is evidently what our society wants. It is unlikely we collectively would prefer either a rightist approach involving greater reliance on freer markets or a leftist approach involving greater government control.

Motivating all this research was Jon's continued interest in the question of American economic development. His research into the evolution of law and economics spawned additional questions, including those that led to another collaboration with Stan Reiter, "Preface to Modelling the Regulated Economy" (1981). The two chapters on government entrepreneurs in the expanded *The Vital Few* (1986), "The Great Land Ordinances: America's Thumbprint on History" (1987), and "Public Sector Entrepreneurship" (forthcoming) reflect additional themes that emerged as part of this research.

The fifth area of publication is Jon's textbook, *American Economic History* (1983). As with any text, Jon set out to present an overview and synthesis of the American experience. It might be thought that he would attempt in this book to answer the question he first articulated in *The Vital Few* (How did the American economy develop?), but history is not so kind. Jon had to go beyond his own contributions, and he approached this task as he had his other books, by reading all the important work in American economic history. While the text is weighted toward the "new," Jon presents all the alternatives without choosing between them. While students may complain they are not sure what "really" happened, they do learn that history has few simple "truths." Jon is well aware his question remains unanswered even as the text reached its third edition.

The final group of Jon's work is easiest to characterize as those of an autobiographical nature. Perhaps the best known of these is "The Great Strike at Nushagak Station, 1951: Institutional Gridlock" (1982), his presidential address to the Economic History Association, a group in which he has been actively involved from the first days at Purdue. While it is not directly related to Jon's study of government, many of the lessons he learned about the operation of bureaucracies are woven into this piece. In addition to the *festschriften* honoring Hicks and Habakkuk, Jon has contributed to three others. "A Summing Up" (1973) is a commentary on the other essays honoring Hal Williamson. "Douglass North as a Teacher" (1982) honors the man who made a significant contribution to Jon's formal training as an economic historian. "Public Sector Entrepreneurship" (forthcoming) is his contribution to a volume honoring David Landes, a scholar whose work he has long admired. Jon's Mormon upbringing helps account for the chapter on the entrepreneurship of Brigham Young in the first edition of *The Vital Few* and the chapter on the public sector entrepreneurship of Marriner Eccles in the expanded edition. Jon's Idaho upbringing plus his interest in government help explain his interest in *The Economics of Internment* (in progress). One part of the sad story of the World War II internment of Japanese-Americans occurred outside of Twin Falls, his hometown. As a young teenager, Jon recognized he was part of history, and, as a professional, his view of history has always contained an intensely personal component. His view has also reflected a strong sense of justice. It is a view as complex and diverse as the man himself, a man who can be passionate about and easily traverse the distance between football and chamber music.

Jon's current plans for the future center around a project tentatively titled "The Climacteric of American Capitalism," a study of the evolution of American capitalism from colonial times to the twenty-first century. This work, intended to be his *magnum opus*, will make use of the lifetime of research that produced all six groups of his publications.

III

It is not editors and publishers who contribute to *festschriften*, but students and colleagues. The stimulus for any *festschrift* is a scholar's influence in his role as teacher and colleague. I can attest to both in the context of Northwestern's program in economic history. I was just beginning my dissertation when Jon came from Purdue; indeed my preliminary oral examination awaited his arrival. Paul Uselding was in a similar position. The two of us benefited from the years Jon overlapped with Hal Williamson. As the new economic history continually referred to data from, say, Victor Clark's *History of Manufacturers* and hypotheses from, say, George Rogers Taylor's *The Transportation Revolution*, those of us in the economic history seminar requested a bibliography that encompassed the old and the new. Jon threw himself into the task with an enthusiasm that proved infectious.

The experience was instructive. We realized how unread we were with respect to the works normally cited in economic history, but Jon's respect for reading and his concern about the revealed reading habits of new economic historians produced a list that included more than a few titles that seemed out of place on an economics reading list (e.g., Wilhelm Dilthey's *Pattern and Meaning in History* and W. H. Walsh's *Philosophy of History*). Through our willingness to read, Jon hoped to challenge us to think beyond the next regression, to think big. In the process, he hoped to develop and focus our creative abilities. In the almost two years we spent working our way through that list, we (unknowingly at the time) went on an odyssey that took us through Seattle and Oxford without ever leaving Evanston.

Many of the authors in this volume are former students. Most of us approached the dissertation process and Professor Jonathan Hughes with a sense of foreboding. Both Paul Uselding and I had similar experiences. We had ideas, relatively small ideas in retrospect, that might have produced interesting articles and undistinguished dissertations. The fact these were small ideas was established early in our first meeting with Jon, and, with fear and trembling, we expected him to then tear them into small pieces. What came next was a surprise. Jon turned the discussion into what these ideas could become, how the work that had gone into our proposals could be turned into important dissertations. At the start, it was Jon who asked the yet unanswerable questions, who took our topics and tied them to times and events of which we were as yet blissfully unaware. Jon and Hal Williamson made us believe we could find the answers. They also helped us sort out the central conundrum of historians—how much to read and how much to write—by being available, on a daily basis, to help shape the ideas from the previous day's reading and to focus that day's search.

Both Paul and I were enthusiastic about our work. We quickly discovered the questions Jon had raised were important questions, often the key linkages. As we filled in more of the details, Jon became more excited, more involved. At the end of this process, we felt a sense of achievement. The process, the ability to draw on the talents and enthusiasm of the dynamic Hughes and the gentle Williamson, promoted self-confidence as well as competence. Nonetheless, we knew our dissertations would have turned out quite differently were it not for Jon. I have continued to benefit from discussing my work with him.

A few years after I graduated, Eric Jones joined the Northwestern faculty. Eric, who had visited at Purdue, proved a wonderful complement to Jon. With Hal's retirement, the seminar moved into Jon and Eric's living rooms. Jon cheerfully served up store-bought chocolate-coated marshmallow cookies with the same panache with which Eric offered his wife Sylvia's homemade torts and scones. While Jon and Eric had read many of the same books and articles, they took great delight in locating a critical citation with which the other was unfamiliar. Each privately expressed the belief the other must spend the better part of the night reading. Jon quietly maintained his fervent interest in sports. Eric took great delight in the work of Monty Python and others of that ilk. When Joel Mokyr joined the department, he proved to share Eric's addiction to Monty Python, references to which continue apace. In brief, Northwestern has been a joyful, humorous, rigorous place to become immersed in economic history.

Jon's sense of humor holds a special fondness for irony and paradox, both of which occupy prominent places in his writing style. Thus, in *The Vital Few*, Henry Ford is described as "the great multimillionaire hick from Michigan going to tell the Kaiser to call off the dogs" (p. 306). Sometimes the intended results are not humorous. *The Governmental Habit* is an excellent example of this. Nonmarket control is discussed as part of the solution in the late nineteenth century and as part of the problem in the late twentieth century; efficient politics may prove to be inefficient economics. Even here, however, Jon is looking at the world with the eye of the humorist, not the eye of the cynic. It is the eye of one who searches to find people in their full humanity. It is a trait that comes across clearly in the classroom and in seminars. Jon especially enjoys quirky, human moments of economic irrationality that prove history was not lived by androids programmed to behave according to rational market principles. Jon is a perceptive reporter of the human condition, one who has developed successfully both essential traits of an economic historian. He is a social scientist and a humanist.

During the Vietnam years, colleges undertook a critical self-examination of their mission. At Northwestern this was accompanied by a great deal of student pressure to make curriculum changes. "Relevant" became a much-used word from the physical and intellectual barricades the students erected, but few bothered to address the question of "to what?" Jon considered these barricades to be destructive, but, unlike other faculty who held this opinion, Jon did not turn on the students who casually spouted "two-bit" Marxism. His response was to offer a seminar on "American Radicalism," to have would-be radicals learn from those of a similar mind who had a reasoned opinion about the American economy. Jon prodded them to read the works of Henry George, Thorstein Veblen, and others, then to write papers. In the end, these students produced work of which they (and Jon) were proud. The course was nationally honored for innovative teaching.

In 1978, I returned to Northwestern as a Visiting Associate Professor. Eric Jones had just left for La Trobe University, and I was asked to offer one of his old courses. I was an imperfect substitute at best, but Jon helped me through it. I also taught the advanced graduate course in "Topics in Economic History," and thereby became responsible for a portion of the seminar which I had continued to attend while teaching at Loyola University of Chicago. Joel's basement replaced Eric's living room. Homemade torts and scones disappeared, but the ambience remained as before. Jon and Joel welcomed me into the planning as a colleague and have done so ever since. In 1988 I returned to Northwestern as a Visiting Professor. It has been gratifying to rediscover that the sense of intellectual stimulation, pleasure, and comraderie I associate with the seminar does indeed exist throughout the week.

It is in this spirit that Jon's students and colleagues come together to honor him. We are grateful for his admonition to read widely and think broadly, for his friendly encouragement, for his creativity and his vitality. We are grateful for the vital role Jon Hughes has played in our lives.

REFERENCES

Books

Fluctuations in Trade, Industry and Finance. Oxford: The Clarendon Press, 1960.

American Economic History (in collaboration with Lance Davis and Duncan McDougall). Homewood, IL: Irwin and Company, 1961, 1965, 1969.

The Vital Few–American Economic Progress and Its Protagonists, Boston: Houghton Mifflin, 1966. Paperback edition, New York: Bantam Books, Matrix edition, 1967, and New York: Oxford University Press, Galaxy Edition, 1973.

Industrialization and Economic History: Theses and Conjectures. New York: McGraw-Hill, 1970.

Social Control and the Colonial Economy, Charlottesville, VA: University Press of Virginia, 1976.

The Governmental Habit: Economic Controls from Colonial Times to the Present. New York: Basic Books, 1977.

American Economic History. Glenview, IL: Scott, Foresman, 1983, 1987, 1990.

The Vital Few: The Entrepreneur and American Economic Progress. New York: Oxford University Press, Galaxy Books, Expanded edition, 1986.

The Economics of Internment (in preparation).

The Climacteric of American Capitalism (presently a glint in the mind of its creator).

Articles

"The Commercial Crisis of 1857," *Oxford Economic Papers* (April 1956).

"The Canadian Dollar Premium," *Business Scope* (May 1957).

"Financing the British War Effort," *Journal of Economic History* (June 1958) (a review article).

"Foreign Trade and Balanced Growth," *American Economic Review* (May 1958).

"The First 1,945 British Steamships," *Journal of the American Statistical Association* (June 1958) (in collaboration with Stanley Reiter).

1859, Entering an Age of Crisis. Bloomington, IN: Indiana University Press, 1959 (a chapter on the British economy).

"A Dollar-Sterling Exchange, 1803-1895," *Economic History Review* (August 1960) (in collaboration with Lance Davis).

"Aspects of Quantitative Research in Economic History," *Journal of Economic History* (March 1961) (in collaboration with Stanley Reiter and Lance Davis).

"The United States Business Cycle Before 1860," *Economic History Review* (August 1963) (in collaboration with Nathan Rosenberg).

"Measuring British Economic Growth," *Journal of Economic History* (March 1964).

"Eight Tycoons—The Entrepreneur and American Economic Development," *Explorations in Entrepreneurial History* (Spring 1964).

"Fact and Theory in Economic History," *Explorations in Entrepreneurial History* (Winter 1966).

"Bank of England Reserve Policy," *Journal of Economic History* (March 1967).

"Economic Aspects of Industrialization," *International Encyclopedia of the Social Sciences* (1968).

"Wicksell on the Facts," *Value, Capital and Growth: Essays in Honor of Sir John Hicks*, edited by J.N. Wolfe. Edinburgh: Edinburgh University Press, 1968.

Purdue Faculty Papers in Economic History, 1956-1866, Homewood, IL: Richard Irwin, 1968 (contains reprints of eight of these papers).

"Henry Mayhew's London," *Journal of Economic History* (June 1969) (a review article).

"Economic Growth and Change, How and Why," *Journal of Interdisciplinary History* (Spring 1971) (a review article).

"Is the New Economic History and Export Product?" in *Essays on a Mature Economy*, edited by D.N. McCloskey. London: Methuen, 1971.

"The New Economic History, Collected, Integrated and Explained," *Explorations in Economic History* (Fall 1972) (a review article).

"A Summing Up," in *Business Enterprise and Economic Change: Essays in Honor of Harold F. Williamson*, edited by L. P. Cain and P. J. Uselding. Kent, OH: Kent State University Press, 1973.

"Krooss on Executive Opinion," *Journal of Economic History* (March, 1976).

"Transference and Development of Constraints Upon Economic Activity," in *Research in Economic History*, vol. 1, edited by P.J. Uselding. Greenwich, CT: JAI Press, 1976.

"What Difference Did the Beginning Make?" *American Economic Review, Papers and Proceedings* (January 1977).

"Government and the Economy—The Long View," *Modernization and Change* (1978).

"Is American Capitalism Dead?" *Business and Economic History*, 2nd series, vol. 7 (1979).

"The Roots of Regulation—The New Deal," in *Regulation Atmosphere of Crisis*, edited by G. Walton. Greenwich, CT: JAI Press, 1979.

"Entrepreneurship and the American Economy—A Sketch," in *Research in Economic History*, vol. 3, edited by P.J. Uselding. Greenwich, CT: JAI Press, 1979.

"Walt Rostow's Brave New World," *Inquiry*, 1(23) (November 13, 1979).

"Expectations About the Public Sector—An Historical Perspective," *Proceedings of the Carnegie-Mellon–Miami Law School Seminar on Growth of the Public Sector* (no date).

"Tax Revolts," *National Tax Journal* (June 1979).

"Entrepreneurship in the American Economy," *Libertarian Review* (Winter 1979).

"Entrepreneurship," *Dictionary of Economic History*. Boston: Little, Brown, 1980.

"Preface to Modelling the Regulated Economy," special supplement on Social Choice, *Hofstra University Law Review* (Summer 1981) (in collaboration with Stanley Reiter).

"Professor Hobsbawm on the Evolution of Modern Capitalism," in *Essays in Contemporary Fields of Economics*, edited by G. Horwich and J. Quirk. West Lafayette, IN: Purdue University Press, 1981.

"The Great Strike at Nushagak Station, 1951: Institutional Gridlock," *Journal of Economic History* (March, 1982).

"Douglass North as a Teacher," in *Explorations in the New Economic History*, edited by R. Ransom, R. Sutch, and G. Walton, New York: Academic Press, 1982.

"Arthur Cole and Entrepreneurial History," *Business and Economic History*, 2nd Series, vol. 12 (1983).

"The 1930s Again," in *Money and Crisis*. New York: Ballentine, 1984.

"Comment on Dornbusch and Frenkel," in *A Retrospective on the Classical Gold Standard 1821-1931*, edited by M. Bordo and A.J. Schwartz. Chicago: University of Chicago Press, 1984.

"Long Run Growth and Development," in *Energy and the Southwest Economy*. Federal Reserve Bank of Dallas, 1986.

"The Great Land Ordinances: America's Thumbprint on History," in *Essays on the Economy of the Old Northwest*, edited by D. Klingaman and R. Vedder. Athens: Ohio University Press, 1987.

"Variations on a Theme: Long-Term Growth of Government," *Journal of Financial Services Research* (1989).
"American Economic History: The European Connection," in *Perspectives on the History of Economic Thought*, edited by D. Moggridge. London: Edward Elgar (1990).
"Cycles in Regulation?" (forthcoming in a volume edited by Vernon Ruttan).
"A World Elsewhere: The Importance of Starting English," in *Essays in Honor of Sir John Habakkuk*, edited by F.M.L. Thompson. Oxford: The Clarendon Press (forthcoming).
"Public Sector Entrepreneurship," *Essays in Honor of David Landes*. Cambridge: Harvard University Press.
"Great Basin Kingdom After Thirty Years" (forthcoming).
"The Engine of History: Entrepreneurship" (forthcoming).

THE HISTORY OF CLIOMETRICS

Samuel H. Williamson

WHAT IS KLĪ-Ö-MET'RIKS, n. SINGULAR?

What is Cliometrics besides being what Cliometricians do?[1] Answers range from "historical economics," "economics of history," "econometric history," and "'new' economic history." As good a definition as any was written by Jon Hughes and his two collaborators at Purdue, Lance Davis and Stan Reiter, and was the statement that introduced the term for the first time in print in the December 1960 issue of the *Journal of Economic History*.

> In brief, the logical structure necessary to make historical reconstructions from the surviving debris of past economic life essentially involves ideas of history, economics and statistics. The offspring of such an act of inter-disciplinary miscegenation calls for a name worthy of it; at Purdue the resulting discipline has been labeled "Cliometrics" (Davis, Hughes, and Reiter, 1960, p. 540).

The word is a nickname that stuck and has become too difficult to shake. It was coined by Reiter, who is not a historian, but a mathematical economist and who, while collaborating with Lance and Jon, was "musing" about for a word that described the quantitative economic history work they were

Research in Economic History, Suppl. 6, pages 15-31.

ISBN: 1-55938-150-7.

discussing.[2] What he did was to join the muse of history—Clio—and the suffix "metrics" from the word econometrics and they defined the term in that article.

It should be noted that the expression "new" economic history was the name adopted for the field for many years.[3] The expression was coined in the same article as cliometrics, however, it was not the intent of those authors to push *either* name.[4] During this time "new" economic history was *jokingly* referred to as cliometrics. Predictably the "new" became not so new and that definition has lost its usefulness, while the joke has now become the name.

Cliometric work and the term itself came under attack early and often. M.L. Burstein (1964), in a book review, made the following statement that prompted a defense of the term by Jon.

> The Dismal Science grinds the Muse of story into a handful of dust. Economic historians, some vulgarians among whom call themselves cliometricians, sift this dust into binds, into economic boxes, specifically analogous to mathematical symbols suggested by the structure of economic theory (p. 56).

Jon's (1965) response was to explain

> Burstein refers to the members of the Cliometrics Society (a purely informal group of social drinkers) as "vulgarians" (p. 56). Since the word "cliometrics" has now entered the language—several times—may I say a few words in its defense? The word came originally from the fevered imagination of my colleague, S. Reiter, who had a hand in three of the original papers produced using data-processing methods in Economic History. . . . If there is a better, short, word to describe what has since become a burgeoning industry, we would consider it. However, our intentions toward Clio were and are nothing if not honorable, and deserve not the sobriquet "vulgar" (p.154).

Over the years the term has evolved: a good current definition is that Cliometrics is the application of economic theory and quantitative techniques to describe and explain historical economic events. Cliometricians often use large data sets that historians have regarded as unusable, uninteresting or irrelevant for describing the past. Cliometricians are apt to make deductive statements about why a particular economic event has take place, where the more traditional economic historian is more interested in describing what happened. There are possibly better words for what the field has become, but the term has stuck with its current meaning and the field with its name.[5]

WAS CLIOMETRICS A REVOLUTION?

Just as some have said there was no Industrial Revolution, but a gradual transformation, it could be said that the Cliometrics Revolution was only a continuation of the style of work that others (although not necessarily economic historians) had been doing before. Davis et al. (1960) state "while the qualitative stream in the discipline has usually been larger, there has been from earliest times a significant and respectable flow of quantitative work." No less a revolutionary, Robert Fogel (1963) took pains to note the legacy of earlier work that the "new" economic historians were building on, when he said: "economic history has always harbored scholars with a keen interest in the application of theory and statistics to historical problems. The new economic history is the contemporary continuation of this theoretical-quantitative tradition."

However, to those in the field during the late fifties and early sixties, there clearly was a "new" economic history that was sending the old guard running for cover as the cliometric brigade was calling for nothing less than a total rewrite of the field. To quote Douglass C. North (1963) from a note in the *American Economic Review*,

> A revolution is taking place in economic history in the United States. It is being initiated by a new generation of economic historians who are both skeptical of traditional interpretations of the U.S. economic history and convinced that a new economic history must be firmly grounded in sound statistical data. Even a cursory examination of accepted "truths" of the U.S. economic history suggests that many of them are inconsistent with elementary economic analysis and have never been subject to—and would not survive—testing with statistical data (pp. 128-129).

In his presidential address to the Economic History Association, David Landes (1978) recounted the view from the other side:

> while not rejecting measurement and quantitative analysis out of hand, as did many of the noneconomic historians (how, after all, could one banish numbers from economic history?), they argued that the new cliometrics was a meretricious novelty, unscientific in its procedures, faulty in its logic, limited in its applicability by the spottiness of the historical record and by the complexity and ambiguity of historical change. But they said this more in the privacy of their homes and classrooms than in the public prints, for (I think it is now fair to say) most of them were too intimidated by the New Economic History to challenge it to open combat. They could not understand some of the new work. Sometimes they could not even read it. In their hearts they knew what was right, but they had to keep it in their hearts. Many of them withdrew into a kind of internal exile within the profession (pp. 4-5).

In retrospect, the revolution was not so much what was happening, but in *what* arena. Hughes (1985), in his speech to the World Congress of Cliometrics, stated:

> One has to remember that mainstream Economic History in the early 1950's was largely innocent of overt uses of theory and quantitative techniques. So Cliometrics was seen by some to be a conspiracy of young technicians against respectable scholarship. I don't mean that such work had not been done in the field. As has been said many times, Cliometrics was a revolution just waiting to happen. Much work of our sort had already been done, and was being done, but not by those who presided over the field called Economic History,

> our rightful place in the universe of scholarship. The question concerned our work being accepted by those who called themselves economic historians (p. 2).

WHEN WAS THE CLIOMETRICS REVOLUTION?

During the post-World War II period several cliometric type works were being done. For the most part they were not being published in the *Journal of Economic History*, and were regarded as applications that happened to use historical data.[7]

More use of quantitative and theoretical tools in economic history had been called for since the field began.[8] It was, however, in the mid-1950s that a group of younger economic historians began to invade the field with their new bag of tools. They came not to use historical evidence to test economic theory, but to use theory to analyze historical questions. Part of the timing of the field was due to newly available computers that could analyze data sets that had been impossible to deal with before. "The First 1,945 British Steamships" by Hughes and Reiter (1958) was one of the earliest cliometric works and is methodologically noteworthy as it was the first to use computers in economic history.[9]

As will be discussed below, the transformation of the field of economics also played a role. However, in a very non-cliometric type explanation, it must be pointed out that at this time three individuals had an important influence: Doug North, and two who were not regarded as cliometricians themselves, Simon Kuznets and Alexander Gerschenkron.[10] With a few notable exceptions, most American cliometricians studied with these three men or their students. Kuznets, at Johns Hopkins, influenced a generation of scholars to the better measurement of historical economic variables to explain economic growth. Both North, at the University of Washington, and Gerschenkron, at Harvard, were known to have active workshops where rigorous economic hypotheses of historical events were heatedly debated. Both Hughes and Davis were among North's first students.

It was only a matter of time before the journals of the field would publish more of this new work. In 1955, John Meyers took over *Explorations in Entrepreneurial History*, which became the first outlet within the field for the work of the cliometricians. In 1960, North and William Parker became the editors of *The Journal of Economic History*. An important date in the field was the 1957 joint sessions of the Economic History Association and the NBER Conference on Income and Wealth. It is clear that this was a significant meeting where several important papers were presented.[11] Much of the NBER Conference was devoted to better measurement and historical analysis of the long-term economic variables. It was strongly influenced by the empirical work of Kuznets, Mitchell, and Burns, and theoretical models of the Harrod-Domar type.

Two papers on methodology were presented at the Economic History sessions: "The Interrelation of Theory and Economic History" by W.W. Rostow (1957) and "Economic Theory, Statistical Inference, and Economic History" by Meyer and Alfred Conrad (1957). Rostow seems to wonder about how theory is useful in explaining growth (a bit introspectively, considering his famous book was to come in less than three years). He does not give any clear prescriptions and at one point asks, "Are we to conclude, then, that of the nature of their professions the economic theorist and the economic historian are doomed to work different sides of a street so wide that it is hardly worth shouting across?" (p. 516).

Meyer and Conrad were more specific and prescriptive. They called for the tools of scientific inference to be applied to economic historiography. They stated that hypotheses could be presented as behavioral equations, such as $X = a + bY + e$, and thus, "one can encompass deterministic or systematic factors and unique or unsystematic factors within a single and also consistent model." Meyer and Conrad argued that most of economic history at that time was concerned about e, the random error term, that is, the unique events that would now be called "shocks."[12] What was needed was more concern with the rest of the equation, or the systematic factors that explained behavior in normal times. Both papers drew little attention at the meeting.

A second paper by Conrad and Meyer (1958), titled "The Economics of Slavery in the AnteBellum South," was an example of the new method they proposed, and caused quite a stir.[13] The conclusions of this work were only mildly controversial, as they basically were seconding the conclusions that Kenneth Stampp (1956), a historian, had reached in his book *The Peculiar Institution* which had been published the year before.

It was their method, however, that was regarded as revolutionary. Instead of directly examining the motives of slave holders or reviewing the accounts of particular plantations, they approached the problem as one would any investment problem—that is, how would you decide to invest in a new piece of capital that had a depreciation rate, maintenance cost, and a probability of becoming obsolete? And when might it be profitable to sell it? They looked at historical data on cotton yields, average life span of slaves, prices of inputs and output, and concluded that owning slaves was a sensible investment. This paper was the spark that ignited a flood of cliometric work and controversy on the economics of slavery for the next twenty years.

The revolution sparked considerable debate on methodology during the latter half of the 1960s. Much of this debate was published in a book edited by Ralph Andreano (1970) titled *The New Economic History: Recent Papers on Methodology*. One of the articles reprinted in this volume was by one of the most vocal critics of cliometrics, Fritz Redlich (1968) who defined much of the work as *ante*-historical research, and called its practitioners "counterfactualists." He did not dismiss the work, but classified it as social-science and not historical thinking. His main concern was what role theory should play. For example, Albert Fishlow and Fogel differing on the social saving of railroads by 3:1 is irreconcilable to a historian, but only an issue about which model and assumptions are correct to the cliometrician. Theory was the master of the research, it was not history. He was not preaching to totally deaf ears as Hughes (1966) had made much the same point to some extent two years earlier in his article "Fact and Theory in Economic History."

THE PURDUE SEMINARS

The birth of the Cliometrics Conference was a small meeting at Purdue in December 1960. Perhaps a dozen attended to discuss six papers. Those attending all agree that the most memorable part of that first meeting was the performance of Bob Fogel, a newcomer to the rest of the group. Explaining the social saving of the railroads, Fogel started talking in the morning and was still going late in the afternoon. Later in the conference he and Bill Parker were wrestling on a point, and a graduate student was dispatched to the library to find the relevant fact. A style of working hard combined with informal socializing was set at this meeting (one that has been preserved ever since). There was no organization, and as Jon said, it was "a purely informal group of social drinkers."

The meetings continued at Purdue for eight more winters with many other memorable events. Many recall the third meeting where, after a lengthy debate on a paper by Eugene Genovese, the issue turned on the average weight of hogs—the discussion evolved into the question of how one weighed a hog in the early nineteenth century. The meeting in 1967 was also memorable—this time because of the weather. Lafayette became ice and snow bound with most of the participants unable to leave for up to three or four days after the conference ended. Others never made it, such as Peter Temin who was stuck in O'Hare airport for three days. It is not surprising that the meetings are now in May.

THE CHICAGO AMERICAN ECONOMIC ASSOCIATION MEETINGS IN DECEMBER 1964

Perhaps the point when, as Andy Warhol would have said, "Cliometrics had its 15 minutes of fame" was at the AEA meetings in Chicago in 1964. Parker had put together a program titled "Economic History: Its Contribution to Economic Education, Research, and Policy." Papers were given by North, Fogel, Barry Supple, Richard Easterlin, Robert Gallman, and Rondo Cameron. Evsey Domar and R.A. Gordon were the discussants.

I was a graduate student at Purdue at the time and had been fed a diet of cliometrics for three years by then; it was no more controversial to me than money and banking. So I was very surprised when I wandered into the session to find a room filled with at least 200 people listening to what I thought was "old hat." The discussion was intense, as were the questions from the floor.

That session clearly indicated that there was a strong interest in what was going on in those annual Purdue meetings. The "New" Economic History was the hot topic. The point was brought home to me further at that time because, partly since Davis was on leave that year, Hughes asked me and fellow graduates students Jim Rae and John Legler to help run the fifth Cliometrics Conference that coming February at Purdue.

Somehow many of the principals of the group knew this, so I, a mere graduate student, was stopped in the hall by Gallman to tell me, "You really should invite Professor X to the conference, he is very upset that he did not get an invitation." A few minutes later, Gene Smolensky came to me with another suggestion. It had become important to be at the Purdue Conference.

WHY A CLIOMETRICS REVOLUTION?

The Cliometric Revolution was only one part of fundamental and long-lasting conflicts taking place in the general field of economics. In the beginning, questions about the causes of economic growth and the development of economic institutions had all come under the umbrella of economic history.[14] In addition, before Keynes, there had been a fairly strong connection between economic history and business cycle theory, as can be easily seen by reading the work of Schumpeter and others.

During the post-war period, economic theory began crowding out what is now called institutional economics. Graduate programs in economics were dropping their language requirements and emphasizing theory, a paradigm that was copied from physics—rigorous models to be tested with sophisticated statistical techniques. Keynesian Economics had pushed the field of business cycles to the sidelines and created the field of macroeconomics which was concerned with monetary and fiscal policy. Traditional economic history was regarded as one of the most nonrigorous parts of the field, and was being dropped from many graduate departments.

The questions of the field still attracted the study of scholars, but they were approaching it from several new avenues—including those outside the "traditional" economic history profession. The newly trained Keynesian theorists defined economic growth as increases in output per capita, measured by national income statistics, and explained by mathematical models of factors of production and saving rates. The question of what caused industrialization in the past evolved into how to encourage industrialization in the present, and how to help the less developed countries of the day. In 1960, Rostow published his famous *The Stages of Economic Growth* which was presented as a proposed model of economic development using historical evidence to support his contentions.

About the same time that Cliometrics was causing waves, there was also much discussion of whether economic historians should become a branch of the Economic Growth (and Development) field. Carter Goodrich (1960) focused on this question at his introduction to the session of 1960 Economic History Meetings where Davis, Hughes, and Reiter were explaining cliometrics. At that time both "Economic Growth" and modern quantitative methods (i.e., cliometrics) were regarded as challengers to traditional economic history.

In the end, the first created its own field, economic development, while the latter, cliometrics, took over much of the mainstream of (American) economic history. In the process much of the traditional economic history retreated into business history and history departments, and cliometrics may have helped save economic history in (many) economics departments.

Students from these new graduate programs who came to economic history were interested in applying their quantitative and theoretical tools. It may not be that they were disdaining the methods of old, but that they did not know better (or should I say "any other way").

> They seemed to understand little of the methods and motives of the old-time fact men in economic history, and went to work rewriting economic history, revising much of the older interpretation, but also pushing the old framework aside altogether and producing entirely new information by new methods, statistical techniques, and data processing (Hughes, 1966, p. 80).

Unlike their (younger) professors who were trained in both old and new techniques, this new group did not have a choice to make. They cast their lot with the new. Growth theory and cliometrics were the new.

According to Alexander Field (1987), the rapid success of cliometricians was helped by external factors that included the general change in the demand for economists and the demographics of the time. The post-World War II period was one of rising educational aspirations and enrollments. This was first fueled by the GI Bill and then by economic prosperity in the 1960s. The recognition that a college education was becoming a "must" to get ahead coincided with the impending arrival of the baby boom at the college level.

Most states were responding with large increases in their higher education budgets, the building of new universities, and increases in their spending on staffing. Added to this, economists were finding work in the nonacademic areas as they had never done before.

The choice of economic history for a graduate student in an economics department had become "another" applied field where the time from matriculation to dissertation could be expected to be the same as other concentrations. No more being told "go off to the library and read for a year and come back for another assignment." And the newly minted Cliometricians could easily find work in the rapidly expanding economics departments. They could talk the language of their colleagues. But there was a cost, as discussed below.

HISTORY OF THE CLIOMETRICS CONFERENCES

The conferences at Purdue organizers were Davis and Hughes, with help from Duncan McDougall and later on, Nathan Rosenberg. Purdue had received a grant from the Ford Foundation and Reiter had received some of that money to sponsor a workshop in mathematical economics.[15] Davis and Hughes liked the format of the math group and felt that quantitative economic history was equally deserving. Thus the first Clio meetings were financed and patterned in the same form as the mathematical economics group.[16]

The Conference continued annually at Purdue throughout the sixties. During this time, it was called "The Purdue Conference on the Application of Economic Theory and Quantitative Techniques to Problems of History," or shortened to "The Purdue Economic History Conference." Informally, it was called "The Purdue Cliometrics Society."[17] After the first few years, Fogel became involved in the funding by raising a matching grant from the Mathematical Social Science Board, while the other half was paid by Purdue's Krannert School.

By 1969, all the original founders had left; Hughes went to Northwestern, McDougall went to Kansas, Davis left for Cal Tech, and Rosenberg was visiting at Harvard and soon moved to Wisconsin. Purdue had tried to replace them by hiring Joe Swanson, Lewis Solmon, and Jim Shepherd, but by 1969 only Shepherd was left and both Kansas (Tom Weiss and McDougall) and Wisconsin (Andreano and Jeffrey Williamson) had expressed an interest in taking over the Conference.

The decision was to go to Wisconsin, which at the time had a large and active group in both economics and history departments. The first sessions were organized by Andreano and Williamson, who were later joined by Peter Lindert. By this time it was being financed by the National Science Foundation (NSF). Other economic historians in residence during this period were Claudia Goldin, Rosenberg, Smolensky, Cameron, and John Bowman in economics, and Alan Bogue, Eric Lampard, Diane Lindstrom, Morton Rothstein, David Herlihy, and Sella in history (only Andreano, Bogue, Lindstrom, and Sella are still there).

By 1979, the Wisconsin group thought it a good idea to have a change and Donald McCloskey took over the Conference and moved it to the University of Chicago. When he took a job at the University of Iowa in 1981, Clio went with him. McCloskey and I ran the Conference for the three years from 1981 to 1983, and in 1984 it moved to Miami University.[18]

THE FIRST WORLD CONGRESS

At this point, it seemed appropriate to promote an international meeting so that scholars from outside North America could come and interact with our group. It was decided to have a World Congress in the Spring of 1985 at Northwestern University because Joel Mokyr offered to be co-organizer with McCloskey and me, its location near Chicago's airport would reduce costs, and one of the "godfathers" of the field, Hughes, was there. There were 90 participants, with some 20 from overseas. The Congress lasted three days instead of the usual two and we experimented with our first poster session. It was decided that the Congress was quite successful and that we would have another in four years.[19] In 1983 The Cliometrics Society was formed and now had over 380 members world wide.

THE TOOLS AND ACCOMPLISHMENTS OF THE FIELD

It would be impossible to give here an extensive summary of what Cliometrics has accomplished in its 30-year span. It is also unnecessary because there are several other works that have (for example, see McCloskey, 1987; Crafts, 1987; Davis and Engerman, 1986; Field, 1987). I will give a short summary here.

There are several avenues that cliometricians have taken. First, is *better numbers*. With the advent of the computer, it became possible to answer the question, "How much?" Instead of comments such as "vital factors" or "it-is-difficult to exaggerate-the-importance-of," cliometricians were deflating metaphors with statements such as "there were exactly 1,945 steamships," or "profits were from 8 to 12 percent." It took the romance out of history, replaced by concrete and, almost, "scientific" answers.

Besides their habit of quantifying anything for which numbers could be found, cliometricians also were fond of *inferring numbers* that could not be found. For example, in order to understand if the South was self-sufficient in food in the Antebellum period it was necessary to know at what weight hogs were being slaughtered. Because records of weights were not available, information on feeding habits were used to compute indirectly how much hogs could have weighed. In another example, instead of looking at the account books of nineteenth-century midwest farmers, the question of whether it was profitable to buy a reaper was approached by looking at the relative cost of hand versus machine harvesting on a hypothetical average sized farm.

Cliometricians began using *economic and accounting theory* to change the focus of arguments that have raged in history for years. By rephrasing a question it is often possible to look for a more definitive answer. Controversies have just as often been widened as solved, but the argument has become more rigorous. One of the most common innovations of early cliometric work was the application of price theory. As North (1965) pointed out, in all the debates about the burden of the Navigation Acts, a cliometrician was the first to consider what the elasticities of demand may have been.

Cliometricians became masters at the use of the *counterfactual hypothesis*. A counterfactual is an attempt to measure the significance of an event by pretending it never happened and asking how the world would have been different. Fogel did exactly that with the railroads in the United States, and concluded that by use of canals and wagons the economy would have been set back only a couple of years. Others have used this technique to measure the cost of the Civil War, the costs and benefits to the American Colonies of remaining part of the British Empire, and the impact of New Deal fiscal policies.

As the toolbox of economists has grown, so has the application of theoretical and quantitative techniques to historical questions. The possibility of market imperfections is being used to explain agricultural organization in the post-Bellum U.S. South and in twentieth-century China. The theory of efficiency wages is being applied to the dynamics of nineteenth- and twentieth-century labor markets. Translog production functions have been applied to the question of the relative labor-saving bias of technology between the United States and Britain. General equilibrium models have been applied to a large number of questions from how income distribution changed in both the United States and Britain to who bore the cost of the Corn Laws.

The field has touched every question imaginable. A bibliography of the field, currently being compiled, contains 4,500 citations of essays and books published in the area between 1957 and 1980.

CLIOMETRICS AT MIDDLE AGE

The acceptance of Cliometrics has had its costs. Within economics departments, cliometricians have fought to have equal status with "other" applied fields. We claim to be equally capable of teaching an applied econometrics course and of using NSF money wisely. Unfortunately, economic history has become regarded as only another applied field—no longer one of the three legs of Schumpeter's stool, but another field that it would be nice to have (if the Department could afford it).

When it comes time for promotion and tenure, the rest of an economics department may not appreciate the difficulties of working in the archives, or for that matter even working in a library, the cliometrician's work is judged on the basis of what the rest of the department knows—the theory and quantitative tests used.

What is clearly missed in these comparisons is the important distinction between *the economic historian* and other applied economists. To be an economic historian, the cliometrician must learn the tools of history, geography, demography, languages, and so forth. This is in addition to being able to talk the language of their economist colleagues.

The "old" economic historian was never expected to run a regression, but was supposed to "know the story" of the past. The cliometrician is expected to do both—know the past *and* to be able to model and test explanations about it. If the model is sloppy, the economists are critical, and if the history is inadequate, the historians dismiss the work.

To do both well is labor intense. Under the pressures of academic life to publish as much as your competition, it is not hard to understand that cliometricians in economic departments have sometimes short changed the "story." This may partly explain some of the criticism they have received.

HOW ECONOMISTS HAVE SEEN CLIOMETRICS

Throughout the 30-year history, economists and, in particular, economic theorists, although usually encouraging their historian colleagues, have some times expressed skepticism about how much can be accomplished with (what is sometimes viewed as the narrow) cliometric techniques. At the 1957 meeting, where the Rostow and Meyer and Conrad papers were presented, the discussion as summarized by Kuznets (1957) shows their initial misgivings.

> The Economists in the group . . . were rather skeptical of the value of greater integration of economic theory and economic history, and particularly of the use of econometric models and statistical tests as suggested in the Meyer-Conrad paper. On the other hand, at least some of the economic historians . . . appeared to feel a greater need for reliance (in economic history) upon economic theory (p. 550).

By 1964, when the field was taking its turn in the spotlight, economists, such as Gordon (1965), were asking for more breadth:

> This is not yet the end of what economic history has to contribute to the education of the economist. The latter needs to know something about the pattern of institutional change over the decades and centuries, the reasons for such changed, and the ways in which such change has affected the economic relationships in which we are most interested (p. 117).

And at the session, "Economic History: A Necessary Though Not Sufficient Condition For an Economist," which was held at the 1984 American Economic Association meetings, Robert Solow (1986), commenting on (surely not the best part) some of the current cliometric work, stated:

> As I inspect some current work in economic history I have the sinking feeling that a lot looks exactly like the kind of economic analysis I have just finished caricaturing: the same integral, the same regressions, the same substitution of *t*-ratios for thought. Apart from anything else. It is no fun reading the stuff any more. Far from offering the economic theorist a widened range of perceptions, this sort of economic history gives back to the theorist the same routine gruel that the economic theorist gives the historian (p. 26).

This is not to say that Solow and other theorists do not appreciate economic history, Solow continued by saying:

> there is a clear and productive division of labor between the economist and the economic historian. The economist is concerned with making and testing models of the economic world as it now is, or as we think it is. The economic historian can ask whether this or that story rings true when applied in earlier times or other places, and, if not, why not. So the economic historian can use the tools provided by the economist. . . . In return, economic history can offer the economist a sense of the variety and flexibility of social arrangements and thus, in particular, a shot at understanding a little better the interaction of economic behavior and other social institutions (p. 28).

CONCLUSIONS

In conclusion, let me quote the last paragraph of the survey by Davis and Engerman (1986):

> Clio appears fat, happy, and sassy—but not lazy. The focus is on economic growth and welfare (both Gerschenkron and Kuznets would be happy); economic models are no longer ends in themselves but tools to direct thinking and research; institutions provide the constraints on change but they themselves have become the subject of study; and the cliometricians have discovered what more traditional historians have always known—no cliometrician is better than his sources. The victory, if victory is the right word, is nearly complete . . . . Those who met in Williamstown as well as those who braved December at Purdue should feel pleased (p. 11).

NOTES

1. The *Chambers 20th Century Dictionary* (1983) defines Cliometrics as "the application of econometrics in economic history." *The American Heritage Dictionary* (1985) defines it as: "The study of history using advanced mathematical methods of data processing and analysis."

2. In a recent conversation (June 5, 1988), Reiter said that at the time he was searching for a name for what they were doing and coined the phrase. While in graduate school he and fellow students had joked about a field "called "theometrics" which dealt with theological measurement

such as how many angels could dance on a head of a pin. While the etymology is the same the result was different.

3. For example, in 1970, Ralph Andreano was able to publish a book with the title of *The New Economic History* which was solely devoted to the methodology of the field. Also, in 1979, Susan Lee and Peter Passell published a textbook using a variation on the name.

4. "We are not suggesting in this paper that there is to be a "new" economic history which will render nonquantitive economic historians unemployed" (Davis et al., 1960, p. 10.).

5. "'Cliometrics' is too easily construed from the Greek to mean simply quantitative history, rather than the quantitative and theoretical history of economies. Quantitative political and social history, to be sure, have much in common with quantitative economic history. All the quantitative histories draw on the corresponding social sciences and expect the quantitative skills of their practitioners to match the social scientists. But quantitative economic history has different origins—in economics itself rather than history—and has different outcomes" (McCloskey, 1987, p. 13).

6. The note was prepared at the request of the editor of the *AER*.

7. The first series of *Exploration in Entrepreneurial History* however, was an important outlet for this new work. For example, John Meyer (1955) published a paper there titled "An Input-Output Approach to Evaluating the Influence of Exports on British Industrial Production In the Late 19th Century." but it was not referenced in the economic history section of the Index of Economic Journals.

8. Eli F. Heckshеř (1953) wrote an article in 1926 titled "A Plea for Theory in Economic History," where he presented several examples of how theory helped with the understanding of history. He also pointed out the value of history to theory when he said, "But no doubt the value of economic theory increases enormously when the work of historians is carried further than the stating of external facts; for its most important use refers to the choice of facts and the explanation of them." Even within the Economic History Association, the call for more theory had been heard. The following is a quote attributed to Don Kemmerer as he pleaded for more economic theory in the teaching of economic history during a panel discussion at the meetings in 1949: "texts in American economic history . . . were, whether written by economists or historians, usually deficient in analysis and interpretation. They neglected both causation and consequence" Kirkland (1949).

9. The Hughes and Reiter study was the first using computers and was done by coding the observations and entering the data on machine readable cards after which Reiter explaining the algorithm they wanted to the programmer who then physically wired a board that was installed into the computer to do the analysis.

10. By making such a list, I am of course going to exclude others. For example, although Gershenkron signed William Parker's dissertation, his main influence was Usher, thus Bill could be added as another "original." Also Moe Abramavistz, at Stanford, and Hal Williamson, at Northwestern, were producing students who were to do cliometric work before the "cliometricians" trained by the three mentioned above arrived on their faculties. Another addition could be W. W. Rostow, whose his work stimulated some of the early Cliometric debates, however his more important impact was in focusing the profession on the question of economic growth.

11. The proceedings of the NBER Conference were published in Vol. 24 of the NBER Series on Income and Wealth, a book regarded as a "must have" among Cliometricians in the sixties.

12. They did not make the distinction in this article about specification error and "regime change" which in econometric work would not be part of the random term, but, also corresponds to the more unique events that concerned traditional economic historians.

13. Some economic historians for years had been saying that slavery had been profitable and that the historians who said it would die as an institution under the weight of inefficiency were wrong. One of the inspirations for this work was a conversation at a cocktail party at Northwestern University between Williamson and Conrad. Conrad had recently arrived as a new faculty member and was reportedly looking around for a place to apply rigorous economic and statistical techniques

and Williamson recounted that when he was a student at Harvard, Professor Usher had lectured that ownership of slaves must have been profitable noting their extensive use and their positive price.

14. The following is a quote from the introduction of a popular textbook in the field: "Interest in economic history naturally centers upon the factors that make change. What are the dynamic elements in economic development? What are the conditioning circumstances that encourage or inhibit change? What forces lead to particular forms of economic institutions? Answers to questions of this type are the principal concern of the economic historian" (Williamson, 1951).

15. That group has a legacy as well and is still meeting annually as the "Midwest Mathematical Economics Association."

16. The following memo was reproduced in the December 1985 Newsletter of the Cliometric Society after John Hughes found it in his attic. The Memo was sent in September 1960 to Ron Stucky, then Associate Dean at Purdue. It is one of the memorabilia of the origins of the cliometrics conferences.

TO: Director of Quantitative Research Institute
FROM: Lance Davis and Jon Hughes
SUBJECT: Seminar in Quantitative Economic History

It has been suggested by Dean Weiler, considering recent successes of work by Purdue scholars in quantitative economic history, that we take the initiative in organizing a series of colloquia to promote on a national scale the kind of work which has been so successfully pioneered by Purdue people. We feel that such a series would consolidate Purdue's position as the leader in this country in quantitative research in economic history. The enthusiasm aroused by our paper, delivered September 10 at the Philadelphia meetings of the Economic History Association, suggests to us that the time is advantageous for our Quantitative Research Institute to move in this area.

Moreover, it is our understanding that Professor Lloyd Reynolds at Yale has recently received a considerable sum of money to establish an institute of quantitative research in Economic History and Development. Since, at this time, virtually the entire modern literature in the United States in this kind of work has originated at Purdue, we think that we are in an excellent position to sustain our lead in what is evidently becoming a rapidly growing and well financed area of research in Economics.

We would like you to consider using funds from our institute to underwrite the cost of bringing to a colloquium at Purdue this fall twelve to fifteen of the best young scholars currently working in quantitative Economic History. At your request we will submit a proposed schedule of sessions for the first colloquium, together with a list of scholars we wish to invite. It has been suggested that the first colloquium be held in late November.

17. See Hughes (1971) for a more detailed and personal account of this period.

18. The first year at Iowa was also funded by NSF, and then we received funds from the Chase Manhattan Bank and Continental Illinois. From 1984 on, the conference has again been funded by NSF.

19. The 1986 and 1988 Conferences were at Miami University, while the 1987 and 1990 Conferences were at the University of Illinois. The Second World Congress was held at Santander, Spain in 1989. The 1991 Conference will be held at Indian University.

REFERENCES

The American Heritage Dictionary: Second College Edition. (1985). Boston: Houghton Mifflin.

Andreano, R.L. (Ed.). (1970). *The New Economic History: Recent Papers on Methodology.* New York: Wiley.

Berstein, M. L. (1964). "Homer on the History of Interest Rates." *Explorations in Entrepreneurial History/Second Series*, 2(1): 56-67.

Conrad, A. H. and J. R. Meyer. (1958). "The Economics of Slavery in the Ante Bellum South." *Journal of Political Economy*, 66: 94-130.

Chambers 20th Century Dictionary. (1983). Edinburgh: W. & R. Chambers Ltd.

Crafts, N. F. R. (1987). "Cliometrics, 1971-1986: A Survey." *Journal of Applied Econometrics*, 2: 171-192.

Davis, L. E., and S. Engerman. (1986). "Clio is Alive and Well in More Places than Oxford, Ohio." *The Newsletter of the Cliometrics Society*, 1 (3).

Davis, L. E., J. R. T. Hughes, and D. McDougall. (1961). *American Economic History*. Homewood, IL: Richard D. Irwin.

Davis, L. E., J. R. T. Hughes, and S. Reiter. (1960). "Aspects of Quantitative Research in Economic History." *Journal of Economic History*, 20: 539-547.

Field, A. J. (1987). "The Future of Economic History." In *The Future of Economic History*, edited by A.J. Field. Boston: Kluwer-Nijhoff.

Fogel, R. W. (1962). "A Quantitative Approach to the Study of Railroads in American Economic Growth: A Report of Some Preliminary Findings." *Journal of Economic History*, 22: 163-197.

Fogel, R. W. (1964). "Reappraisals in American Economic History: Discussion." *American Economic Review*, 54: 377-389.

Goodrich, C. (1960). "Economic History: One Field or Two?" *Journal of Economic History*, 20: 531-538.

Gordon R. A. (1965). "Economic History: Its Contributions—Discussion" *American Economic Review*, 55: 117.

Heckscher, E. F. (1953). "A Plea for Theory in Economic History." In *Enterprise and Secular Change*, edited by F.C. Lane and J.C. Riemersma. Homewood, IL: Richard D. Irwin.

Hughes, J.R.T., and S. Reiter. (1958), "The First 1945 British Steamships." *American Statistical Journal*, III 282: 360-391.

Hughes, J. R. T. (1965). "A Note in Defense of Clio." *Explorations in Entrepreneurial History/Second Series*, 2(2): 154.

Hughes, J. R. T. (1966). "Fact and Theory in Economic History." *Explorations in Entrepreneurial History/Second Series* 3(2): 75-100.

Hughes, J. R. T. (1971). "Is the New Economic History an Export Product?" In *Essays on a Mature Economy: Britain After 1840*, edited by D.N. McCloskey. Princeton, NJ: Princeton University Press.

Hughes, J. R. T. (1985). "Cliometrics: Memories and Predictions." *The Newsletter of the Cliometrics Society* 1(1).

Kirkland, E. C. (1949). "The Place of Theory in Teaching American Economic History," *Journal of Economic History*, 8(Suppl.): 99-102.

Kuznets, S. (1957). "Summary of Discussion and Postscript." *Journal of Economic History*, 17: 545-553.

Landes, D. (1978). "On Avoiding Babel." *Journal of Economic History*, 38: 3-12.

Lee, S. P., and P. Passell. (1979).*A New Economic View of American History*. New York: W.W. Norton.

McCloskey, D. N. (1976). "Does the Past Have Useful Economics?" *Journal of Economic Literature,* 14: 434-461.

McCloskey, D. N. (1978). "The Achievements of the Cliometric School." *Journal of Economic History*, 38: 13-28.

McCloskey, D. N. (1987). *Econometric History*. London: Macmillian.

Meyer, J. R., and A. H. Conrad. (1957). "Economic Theory, Statistical Inference, and Economic History," *Journal of Economic History*, 17(4): 524-544.

Meyer, J. R. (1955). "An Input-Output Approach to Evaluating the Influence of Exports on British Industrial Production in the Late 19th Century," *Explorations in Entrepreneurial History*, 8: 12-34.

North, D. C. (1961). *The Economic Growth of the United States: 1790-1860*. Englewood Cliffs, NJ: Prentice-Hall.

North, D. C. (1963). "Quantitative Research in American Economic History." *American Economic Review*, 53: 128-130.

North, D. C. (1965). "The State of Economic History." *American Economic Review*, 55: 86-98.

Redlich, F. (1968). "Poentialities and Pitfalls in Economic History." *Explorations in Entreprenurial History/Second Series* 6(1): 93-108.

Rostow, W.W. (1957). "The Interrelation of Theory and Economic History." *The Journal of Economic History,* 17(4).

Solow, R. E. (1986). "Economics: Is Something Missing." In *Economic History and the Modern Economist*, edited by W.N. Parker. New York: Bail Blackwell.

Stampp, K. (1956). *The Peculiar Institution: Slavery in the Ante-Bellum South*. New York: Alfred A. Knopf.

Wiliamson, H. F. (Ed.). (1951). *The Growth of the American Economy*. Englewood Cliffs, NJ: Prentice-Hall.

THE FACTS ON WICKSELL ON THE FACTS:
WICKSELL AND ECONOMIC HISTORY

Rolf G.H. Henriksson

I. INTRODUCTION

In one of his most interesting papers, "Wicksell on the Facts," Hughes (1968) takes up Wicksell's attempt at resolving one of the great issues in monetary history—the development of the price level in the nineteenth century. This historical analysis was part of Wicksell's (1898) presentation of his famous contribution to monetary theory, *Geldzins und Güterpreise*, where he explained price movements as a result of deviations between the market and the natural rates of interest (see also Wicksell, 1936). Hughes' paper is primarily a contribution to the continued discourse on this historical issue and has attracted considerable attention among the participants of this debate (see, for example, Jonung, 1979).

However, as signalled by its title the paper is also a contribution to the history of economic theory. In this field the seminal writings and fascinating personality and life history of Knut Wicksell is a steady perennial.[1] The Wicksellian theme brought up by Hughes is, however, an unusual one. He has stirred not only quite placid but also somewhat murky waters. Generally, very

Research in Economic History, Suppl. 6, pages 33-50.

ISBN: 1-55938-150-7.

little has been said about the empirical analyses by Wicksell, the general view being that this is hardly the interesting and important side of his work. Furthermore, there seems to be a wide consensus that although Wicksell was quite keen on assessing the accuracy and the authenticity of singular historical and other facts, he did not have much historical sense (see Gustafsson, 1961). When compared to Cassel in this respect, Cassel comes off much better than Wicksell (see Lundberg, 1984).

Hughes does little to amend Wicksell's reputation as a low-grade historian but by putting him on record for an important, albeit short historical analysis he incites doubts about the accepted view. Was Wicksell really so unaccomplished in dealing with the past? What type of historical analyses did he carry out and how did he do them? And to be fair when passing judgement on them we naturally have to ask, why did he do them? Were they part of an attempt to test a theory or was history used in some other way? These are the questions that will be dealt with briefly in the following paper.

II. TWO PLEAS FOR HISTORY IN ECONOMICS

History for the Development of Theory

Wicksell made very few explicit and formal statements about his views on history and what role it could and should play in Economics. His most important declaration is to be found in his inaugural lecture which was published in *Ekonomisk Tidskrift* in 1904 (see Wicksell, 1958a). Addressing the question of why the science of Economics had come up with so few, if any, undisputed behavioral laws of the economic system, Wicksell suggested that one important explanation was to be found in the use of improper methods. He asserted that if Economics was ever to move ahead and reach a level of performance similar to that of the natural sciences it would have to resort to essentially the same methods as used in those sciences. Theirs was, according to Wicksell, the only scientific method, namely that of the controlled empirical experiment.

Wicksell rejected the argument that this method could not be applied in Economics. Although experiments could never be set up in the same way as in a natural science laboratory situation, many legislative measure could be seen as experiments even if there was no conscious effort to set them up with such a purpose. He even held that many events were actually the results of policy efforts which were based on precalculations which indeed amounted to the staging of an experiment: What history offered were opportunities to test theories.

In stating this position, Wicksell developed a very interesting criticism of the Younger Historical School and its leader, Schmoller. In his early and most radical statements, Schmoller had little faith in the possibility that the workings and the evolution of the economy would be governed by any economic laws. He tended to view historical studies and accumulation of historical information as a substitute for, rather than a way toward, a theoretical result. However, this early atheoretical position was replaced later on by a more moderate position where the possibility of arriving ultimately at a theory was admitted.

Schmoller's views on the possibility of economic theory were geared to a methodological position that initially rejected the *a priori* method adhered to by the classical and neoclassical economists. However, he later came to recognize that the Classical School had not been entirely unsuccessful in its approach, although he thought that they had exhausted what could be accomplished that way (Wicksell, 1958; Dopfer, 1988). In order to move on it was, according to Schmoller, necessary to use a more statistical and historical approach. However, he underlined that before expecting any theoretical results, a vast amount of empirical observations in the form of historical case studies had to be undertaken.

Although Wicksell defended the Classical School against the criticism of Schmoller, he admitted that Schmoller was sound in his empirical ambition. However, he thought that the correct empirical method in Economics was not the method of historical-statistical induction of the Historical School. Wicksell advocated the Classical School's intuitive-deductive method complemented with a second step of empirical testing. It was only in this second step of verification of the theory that Economic History and Statistics would be used systematically. The procedure to be used in setting forth the theory would on the other hand have to be subjective and impressionistic guesswork. Analogies from other sciences or walks of life outside the realm of Economics might be the key vehicles of thought.

Wicksell's position deserves a comment. Because statistical theory had not developed very far at this time, Wicksell did not even come near to developing any modern principles for statistical testing. Neither did he come close to the modern Popperian view of induction as an essentially nonlogical or even irrational type of prescientific mental operation—the inductive "leap into theory." Wicksell was more open to the old Millian view that inductions could and should be set up as a rational systematic method. He even talked about "the method of analogy" in his inaugural lecture. However, we should not infer that this was siding with Mill's attempt to set up an inductive logic (Nagel, 1950).

There is another divergence from Popper. In dicussing the testing of hypotheses Wicksell remains in the prepopperian "verification" position. This seems to be abandoned today by philosophers of science in favor of the corroboration approach of repeated falsification attempts. As noted, Wicksell never reached the modern statistical testing view which was not worked out until in the inter-war period by Neyman and Pearson. However, it is interesting to observe that Wicksell is somewhat of a precursor of the modern view of testing theory as the testing of "proffered" economic laws, a view advanced in the 1960s by Basmann (1965) and upheld also by Hughes (1966) in the New Economic History debates of that period.

History for the Application of Theory

The plea for history that Wicksell made in his inaugural address did not only concern the role history could and should play in the development of economic theory. He also made a plea for the use of history in the application of theory. The type of theory that was uppermost in Wicksell's mind in this case was what we today would call Normative or Welfare Economics. Such a theory would provide criteria for what would be considered good performance of the economy. It would help to define the goals which economic activity should serve and would thus provide a basis for criticism when these goals were not reached. The view of Wicksell was that if the economy failed to reach these goals there was then something wrong with the performance of its institutions and an economic policy of institutional reform was called for.

Here is where history comes in. Wicksell (1958a) saw "history as the best guide to progress" because it helped us "to understand the existing order of things" (p. 60). Thus it would clarify the feasability and implications of various institutional reform alternatives. The lesson of history was, according to Wicksell, that of helping us distinguish between institutional form and function. History would teach us

> how certain out-of-date institutions or social custom, which now seem completely irrational to us were once fully justified under a different set of conditions (Wicksell, 1958a, p. 60).

However, this was a rather special type of lesson. History

> rescues us from throwing away in a rash fit of reforming zeal, things which although concealed by old forms, may still be full of life and perhaps too precious to lose (Wicksell, 1958a, p. 60).

This seemingly conservative view does not rhyme well with the reputation Wicksell has of being a political radical. However, it conforms well with Wicksell's well-known concerns of safeguarding the interests of minority groups from being overrun by simple majority rule (Wicksell, 1958b). Wicksell may well be placed on the left before the universal suffrage reforms in Sweden and on the right only thereafter.

Wicksell may appropriately be labled a "functionalist." His view about the use of history in conducting institutional reform is not that of helping us see the roots of the present but rather providing a mirror of the present. Somewhat rashly, Eli F. Heckscher, who at that time subscribed to a more evolutionary view, criticized Wicksell for not recognizing the real task of economic history: the study of the evolution of past economic life (Heckscher, 1904).

The two "pleas for history" that Wicksell made in his "inaugural" obviously call for further exploration. To bring forth a more complete view of Wicksell as an historian, we need to take a look at his actual performance in research. Before we turn to his major works for such an assessment, we need, however, some further background on factors that might have determined his predispositions for dealing with history.

III. DETERMINANTS OF WICKSELL'S VIEW ON HISTORY

Wicksell's Exposure to History and Natural Science

Although Wicksell was a natural scientist with a graduate training in Mathematics and Mechanics, he was no stranger to the field of History. He was well-read in the subject like almost all university-educated people in his day. However, Wicksell's exposure to Social and Economic History came late and was related to his involvement in social and demographic issues. As this in turn led him into Economics he, of course, encountered the Historical School. He was probably influenced by their writings, although he was, as noted, averse to their methodological position. Furthermore, as part of his long struggle to find a university teaching position, he had to take a basic law degree late in life, which forced him to study the History of Law. He also kept adding to his historical knowledge throughout his life by his sheer conscientiousness in backing up his scientific results.

Yet all such exposure to History does not make anyone a historian. Wicksell's outlook remained dominated by his training in the natural sciences and Mathematics. Mathematics focused his attention on logical consistency instead of causal nexuses. It set his mind on formalizing problems, thereby reducing and simplifying them in order to arrive at solutions. This of course is not a talent wasted for studies in History but it might generate a premature search for essentials on too superficial a level in a material which may only respond to the labors of someone who approaches it with "the method of source criticism" and the willingness to subordinate himself somewhat to it with a listening ear.

Wicksell's ahistorical predisposition created by his training in Mathematics was further enhanced by his studies and research in Mechanics. A comparison with Marshall, also a mathematician, is illuminating. The fact that Wicksell did not see any Mecca of Economics in Biology but rather directed his pilgrimages to the old tombs of Archimedes, Newton, and LaPlace explains not only the divergence in their approaches in Economics but also why their views on history differed so sharply. Wicksell, whose methodological views emanated from Mechanics, naturally gravitated toward the Menger position in the great "Methodenstreit" of the 1880s, whereas Marshall showed a contrary inclination towards Schmoller. Consonant with this, Wicksell had his mind set to search for the static base—the repetitive nature—of historical events and processes while Marshall's organic view made him search for an evolutionary pattern.

Undoubtedly, Mechanics was also important in shaping Wicksell's empirical bent. Here it is interesting to note that his search for empirical regularities—"covering laws"—that might have been stimulated by Mechanics did not turn Wicksell toward the modern stochastic view of multivariate statistical theory. Wicksell had studied Mechanics in its days before modern Quantum Physics and the "laws" in the field were still stated mainly in deterministic terms. Although the "regression error term," had long appeared in Gaussian Physics, it was still, in Wicksell's days, viewed essentially as a reflection of measurement errors. Scientists naively failed to recognize the importance of erroneous conceptualizations beyond and above the errors due simply to faulty specifications of the mathematical forms of causal or functional dependencies. The "analysis of variance approach" geared to the development of experimental design techniques did not yet exist. Incidentally, this great advance occurred in Biology rather than in Physics.

Perhaps the deterministic rather than the stochastic view that was the mark of Wicksell's empirical bent should not be considered a drawback in historical research. It served to maintain and perhaps even to raise Wicksell's great respect for facts, which of course cannot be anything but beneficial to the work of a historian. But this advantage of Wicksell's natural science background should not be exaggerated. The physicist's view of facts was indeed fundamentally different from that of historians, who had made a science of how to establish the authenticity of a fact.

Perhaps more beneficial for Wicksell as a historian was the great learning he obtained in the history of the Natural Sciences. One of the pleasures of reading Wicksell is that he has such a good knowledge about and insights into the history of Mechanics and Astronomy. His habit of carefully studying the history of his research fields impacted his work in Economics with quite important results.

The "Personal Equation"

Wicksell's formal schooling and studies do not of course explain all his views of history. To an important degree, his historical vision must be seen as a result of or a part of his general views of society and outlook on life. Thus, factors in the so-called "personal equation" must have played an important role. However, it is not easy to assess such influences in the case of Wicksell. He was a very complex and contradictory character. However, it is not possible to move on without making some observations.

There are two important traits in Wicksell's character: his great polemical urge is the first. Open and vivid discussions characterized daily intercourse in the Wicksell family during his childhood. This sharpened Wicksell's critical faculties and undoubtedly strengthened his easy and skillful handling of formal Logic and Mathematics in his later career as well as his resourcefulness in mobilizing facts in support of his points.

Stubbornness was the second pervasive trait in Wicksell's character. It was symbolically expressed in one of his gymnasium achievements: He solved a problem in Physics—*How to stand steady*—and was rewarded by having the solution published in a Swedish mathematics journal (Wicksell, 1869). This particular personality trait was a source of much trouble in his life. However, his friends were generally more concerned about it than he was. But it was, of course, also an indispensable asset for him in his career in Economics. He did not start this careeer until his late thirties, and then met with many obstacles that would have been insurmountable without his great endurance. He also showed great tenacity in smaller things, which accounts for the thoroughness with which he dealt with any task.

The combined polemical urge and stubbornness made Wicksell a formidable opponent in debates. He always wanted to have the last word. He was also witty and a very good stylist. Having once thought of becoming a writer and actually tried out as a playwright, he commanded both his pen and his spoken words with great skill. This, of course, was not always good. In scientific discourse, the ends of science are served by carrying an argument to the very end, but even here such tenacity can be socially counterproductive. Certainly Cassel felt Wicksell's criticism as personally destructive for their relationship. Wicksell's stubborn "polemicism" made him powerful enemies even outside Economics and jeopardized his career.

The public's reaction to his views were of course mainly due to their content. Wicksell was not only argumentative and stubborn, he also showed great courage in taking radical stands on public issues. In this way he would often become the hero of the day in many circles, especially on the Left. But he could not be relied upon. He never made any loyalty pledges. Socialists who wanted to count him as their man did not like his quip that the capitalist was the great friend of the worker while the engineer or the inventor was the enemy.

The reasons Wicksell so often turned his public appearances into "shows" are of course beyond the scope of this paper but some minor observations should be made, as they lead up to the picture of him as a historian. Biographical accounts make it clear that at least some of his often displayed absurd radicalism can be explained by experiences in his childhood. There was first of all the premature death of his mother followed by the remarriage of his father and thereafter the death of the father. These emotional blows made

Wicksell's adolescence a difficult time for him and he ended up in what appears to have been a long and severe religious crisis. It lasted well into his university years.

Eventually his critical faculties led him out of the crisis, however. Perhaps gradually losing faith, Wicksell had turned to Theology for spiritual reinforcement. However these studies did not rescue his faith. His logical acumen and quest for empirical evidence eventually made him turn away from religion and Theology. He even became one of its most outspoken critics in Sweden. In this activity Wicksell developed into a Bible scholar of sort, and having studied both Greek and Latin and even Hebrew he was able to take on the theologians of his days almost as an equal. His main weapon, however, was that of satire. In his ridicule of the Church Wicksell excelled in teasing manners, infuriating many while sending many more into laughter.

Rational men holding the same views of religion as Wicksell could never understand why he should have devoted so much time and energy to crucifying the various absurdities of Christian faith upheld by the Church and mobilizing so many inexorable enemies. However, the fact was that Wicksell remained as religious as he ever had been. He had just changed religion. In turning his interests and attention towards social issues he met a new faith in Neomalthusianism. This utilitarian reformism became then his commitment for life. He published pamphlets and papers on neomalthusian issues in an ongoing campaign from the early 1880s until his death in 1926, seemingly without ever faltering from this second confession of his. There is no other word for this than dogmatism and dogmatism, of course, never makes a good historian.

IV. THE NEOMALTHUSIAN POSITION

Wicksell's Neomalthusianism served as a catalyst of the influences from his studies and from his personal background. It channelled his interest toward social and political issues and it focused his attention on the demographic aspect of economic change.[2]

The Neomalthusian economic theory which Wicksell had absorbed before he took up his systematic studies in Economics was that of the Classical School in its static Millian garb where the law of decreasing returns held a central place (Drysdale, 1878). However, it was bereft of many of its Ricardian attributes.[3] Mill's own rejection of the Malthusian theory of wages had broken the classical model apart and his attempt to plaster it together with the so-called "wages fund theory," which Mill himself finally recanted, could not rescue its theory of income distribution. Mill recognized this when he stated that the science of Economics entailed only general laws in the sphere of production and no general laws of distribution.

Mill had not succeeded in his attempt at a restatement of the classical theory and the palace he handed over to Wicksell was a house in ruins. However, the marginal principle discovered by the early neoclassical economists made it possible for Wicksell to fill in the vacuum in Mill's synthesis and work out a theory of factor pricing in his first major work, *Über Wert, Capital and Rente* (Wicksell, 1893, 1954).

This, Wicksell's central contribution to the great neoclassical reconstruction of the theory of income distribution was, however, based on the premise of the stationary state. It, therefore, retained the major static premise in his neomalthusian position and actually seems to have strengthened his emphasis on decreasing returns.

But this was only a temporary station in a research program that aimed eventually towards dynamics. Although Wicksell never entered very far into issues of dynamics he hit on several interesting points when approaching the question of how an optimum population should be brough about.

He apparently had been put on this dynamic track through an early analysis of emigration related to a long swing in the growth of the population (Wicksell, 1882). He later worked out the role of age structure in the formal dynamics of population change by exploring how a continuous change in the birthrate would influence the future growth of and size of population through the effect on the age distribution. In a neat diagram, Wicksell illustrated a very interesting dynamic transition path (Wicksell, 1978).

These demographic analyses made it possible for him to carry out a number of informal but interesting population forecasts. He demonstrated this ability already in the 1880s, before he started his formal work in economics, by predicting the course of emigration and the development of the population (Wicksell, 1882). Especially notable are his later suggestions about the effects on the population from the falling trend in the birthrate that had begun in the final decades of the nineteenth century (Wicksell, 1924).

Despite these interesting forays into dynamics Wicksell's basic outlook on the Swedish situation remained a static one. The reason Wicksell saw decreasing returns whereever he looked was no doubt a consequence of his static neomalthusian premise. However, this was not an unreasonable one in view of the low rate of technical change and fixed natural resource base. It prompted him to make repeated attempts to assess the optimum size of the population in Sweden. These calculations were based on the scant statistical material available and a number of bold assumptions. This made them vulnerable to criticism and they were never accepted in the population debates as a factual basis on which a population policy could be laid out. The results Wicksell had arrived at seemed too outrageous. In his early calculation in the 1880s as well as in his calculations during World War I, he arrived at estimates that indicated that at least 30 percent of the Swedish population was excessive if the optimum population criterion were to be applied.

However, Wicksell's argument that Sweden was overpopulated was also a relative one. He thought that the rate of population growth even after deduction for the outflow of emigrants was larger than the rate of resource expansion.

In this context Wicksell explored the role of emigration as a means of bringing about the optimum population size (1882, 1896). He concluded that emigration was decidely a less effective way than lowering the birthrate through contraceptive devices, which was the main point on the neomalthusian agenda. However, he recognized its immediate beneficial effect on the real wage level (Henriksson, 1969).

Wicksell's Neomalthusianism admitted no other endogenous change factor in history than the population growth mechanism. He ascribed to no theory of technological change or of institutional change that would make it possible to deal at least formally with growth and development as an endogenous process. Wicksell was indeed explicitly critical of such theories. He argued against both Hildebrand's deterministic theory of stages and Marx's theory of the development of the capitalist system. However, Wicksell did not completely shut his eyes to the basic dimension of dynamic change in history. His may actually be the very modern view of Catastrophe Theory that rejects that history can be caught correctly in a formally closed dynamic model.

Yet Wicksell still believed that there were so called "covering laws" at work in history. Indeed, in his inaugural lecture, he said that if there were no such laws there would be no history (Wicksell, 1958a). But it is very important to keep in mind that the laws he conceived of in this statement were static laws. It is possible that Wicksell, in his Laplacian broodings about stellar mechanics, meant that there could be no other "laws" in the universe than static ones. The great "cause" that turns historical "being" into "becoming" will never be pinned down to anything more than transitory disturbances in the vanishing dimensions of the great paradox of our existence.

V. WICKSELL AS AN ECONOMIC HISTORIAN

Performance in Swedish Population History

Turning to Wicksell's actual performance as an historian we may note that some of his empirical research on Sweden's demographic development, which we have already reviewed, may qualify as contributions to Historical Demography. This work was not only of practical value. As noted it provided Wicksell with the key to population dynamics. It is perhaps the best example in Wicksell's work where historical research led to theoretical insights. Here Wicksell responded to his own first plea for history in Economics: history for the development of theory.

However, this was not the sole historical yield from his neomalthusian research. We noted that Wicksell also touched on Social and Economic History in his neomalthusian writing. This work may to some extent be seen as Wicksell's abiding by his own second plea for history in Economics: as a way of promoting policy ends. However, this research, although important for the development of his own policy stance, generated few results that might be of interest outside the field of Family History. His views on the history of marriage, of prostitution, of infanticide and other themes in a neomalthusian vein may perhaps be noted in a future emancipatory history of gender. Wicksell is in these writings too far off from a Beckerian approach to find an audience among present-day economic historians.

Interpretations of the History of Swedish Taxation

Wicksell's first major historical writing after completing his neoclassical synthesis was a survey of the development of the Swedish tax system and tax burden from the seventeenth century until his own day. This was presented in several of his Swedish writings in the mid-1890s, but most interestingly also in his pioneering German work *Finanztheoretische Untersuchungen*, (1896). Here, Wicksell elaborated the theory of tax incidence and presented his now famous contribution to the field of Public Choice. Yet more than half the book is devoted to the historical survey just mentioned. Presenting such a sizable historical account in German garb in a treatise catering mainly to theoretical economists was of course to invite neglect among historians. However, it has remained "enshrined knowledge" even to economists. Although Lindahl (1958b) lauded it as a unique public choice interpretation of Swedish taxation history it has only recently attracted some attention (Hennipman, 1982).[4] This continued neglect is to a large extent the result of the rather awkward way in which Wicksell himself presented the text. His intention that the historical account was to serve as a prop for the theoretical section is only indicated in an off-stage passage in the general introduction to the treatise. The reader is left with the impression that the historical survey stands independent of the theory.[5]

Close scutiny of Wicksell's treatise as well as circumspect attention to his other writings on taxation problems at that time makes it clear that the dismissive view so far accorded his low-keyed historical survey is unwarranted. Wicksell obviously believed that it provided, if not a formal empirical test of his theories, at least illustrations of their applicability. The latter claim could appropriately be invoked for his theory about the differential incidence of taxation which did not seem to fit the Swedish case very well. However, Wicksell's elaborations of this theory indicates that he was well aware that the restrictive assumptions he employed severly reduced the explanatory power of that theory.

Wicksell's account showed that the predominant part of the tax burden in the more remote past had fallen on land. However, this was not really the result of the workings of the competitive market mechanism assumed in his theory of differential tax incidence but rather the outcome of an historical process dominated by nonmarket forces. He believed, with Adolf Wagner, that property rights were an institutional heritage little influenced by sheer economic processes.

Wicksell was more assured about the empirical support gained from Swedish history for his contribution to the theory of public choice. He held that Swedish historical evidence "provided an empirical confirmation of his thesis that the measure of justice in taxation always depended on the extent to which the various interests are represented in parliament" (Hennipman, 1982). Supporting this view was his public choice finding that the tax burden on land over time had been shunted off to the lesser landholders who were without political influence. Although markets had increasingly permeated the system they were apparently not efficient enough to load the tax burden entirely onto land rents. Instead the burden of the tax seems to have fallen increasingly on the growing army of nonpropertied classes. Wicksell took this observation as proof that reinforced his public choice argument that the burden would fall on the politically weak.

One reason why Wicksell's account of the history of taxation in Sweden gave a somewhat ineffective support to his positive theories of taxation may have been that it had initially been worked out to support his fiscal reform proposals for progressive redistributive wealth and income taxes and for a confiscatory inheritance tax. But by showing how the tax system and the tax burden had come about through an evolutionary process, the functional characteristics of which were the lack of political justice, Wicksell wanted to alert people to the fact that the inequitable situation in the present was not a God-given one but rather an institutional set-up of human making and thus something that could and should be remade. Fitted to the needs of the past, the institutional heritage failed to meet the new claims of a democratic order and being no longer functional it should be abandoned. However, while Wicksell's use of history in backing up the normative application of his theory may have aroused political emotions, it interfered with his use of history for the development of theory. Thus his second plea for history in Economics seems in the field of public finance to have intruded on his first plea.

Contributions to Monetary History

Wicksell's contributions to monetary history have to date been the ones most noted. Yet, they deserve much more attention than they have received. However, these contributions are not easily summed up because they evolved gradually. Abiding by his two pleas for history in Economics Wicksell made them part and parcel both of his attempt to find empirical support for his thinking in monetary theory and of his effort to support various policy stances on issues of monetary reform.

Central to Wicksell's views on the issues of monetary reform was his great concern for the equity effects of changes in the value of money. In his more theoretical discussions with Davidson he developed the view that a stable price level was the prime goal of monetary management. In the policy debate he became one of the most outspoken critics of the inflationary policy of the Swedish central bank during World War I (Thomas, 1936). In the postwar period, he was an advocate of returning the price level to its prewar level as a way of blotting out the inequities created by the war inflation. Because of these strong ethical views, it was natural that he supported institutional reform toward setting up a monetary system that would safeguard the stability of the price level.

In his early days he had been a defender of bimetallism as a way of insulating the value of money from the disturbances caused by fluctuations in the stocks of one or the other of the two basic money metals, gold and silver. He later on came to support a pure paper standard as the best system serving the end of price stability in a country. However, actual developments made this stand somewhat utopian. Therefore, he involved himself also in the issues of how to make the gold standard,which he actually wanted to discard, work better.

In arguing his position, Wicksell devoted much attention to the historical record. We find in his writings interesting surveys on the history of minting, banking, and so forth. By describing how monetary institutions had evolved and changed he pointed out that the workings of the monetary system was no automatic machinery but rather a matter that required policy attention. However, his most notable writings in this field are tied up with his effort to develop theory. The major accomplishment is the attempt in his 1898 treatise, discussed by Hughes and others, to rescue the Quantity Theory (Wicksell, 1898, 1936).

The background for this contribution was the empirical and historical work that had been undertaken by Tooke and Newmarch in their *History of Prices* (1838-1857). They had discovered what Keynes later called the Gibson paradox, that is, contrary to what the Quantity Theory would predict there was a positive correlation between changes in the price level and the money rate of interest.

Wicksell's famous model presented in his 1898 study appeared to resolve the Gibson paradox. This, as was observed at the beginning of this paper, was attempted by Wicksell through the historical testing of his model. He was able to show plausibly that his model could explain the developments of the price level during the nineteenth century as a result of deviations between the market rate of interest and its natural level. However, as pointed out by all the discussants, Wicksell never carried out the testing fully because he was never able to provide a measure of the deviation referred to. The natural rate of interest was conceptually a difficult thing and there was no way to gauge it directly.

Wicksell himself, however, soon became aware of the unsatisfactory empirical validity of his defense of the Quantity Theory. This led him to further queries about the workings of the gold standard which had been his test case. In Wicksell's work of 1898, the level of prices was seen as controlled via the effect that the increase in the quantity of gold temporarily exerts on the bank interest rate, and hence on the gap between the natural level for the rate of interest and the actual market rate.

His position in volume two of *Lectures*, which appeared in 1906, focused more on the direct mechanism (Wicksell, 1935). The workings of the so called "law of one price" in commodity markets indicated that the diffusion of the changes in the terms of trade of the gold producing countries had a faster effect on the commodity trading system and thus on the world price level than the diffusion working via the capital market networks. Because of this, the change in the rate of interest would lag behind the development of prices. This was a much more direct and convincing explanation of the Gibson paradox than his first explanation in the 1898 model.

This newer interpretation of the workings of the gold standard did not force Wicksell to introduce any major changes in his formal model. However, it made him open to the possibility that the causal relationships postulated were more complex than what the Quantity Theory had specified. The new complexities which were here introduced provided a fruitful starting point for later developments in theory where Wicksell himself made an interesting beginning. What interests us most here however, is that, in his theoretical development Wicksell had also made a contribution to our understanding of the working of the gold standard, that is, a contribution to Economic History.

VI. CONCLUSIONS AND FINAL WORDS

Wicksell would have been the first to yield to Heckscher's criticism that he was not recognizing the real task of Economic History, which was the account of past economic life and its development. Although Wicksell had presented two "pleas for history in economics," he never claimed to be a historian of any kind. When he wrote on historical subjects he always viewed himself as an amateur and also thought that this must by necessity be the role of an economist, pursuing essentially Historical Economics rather than Economic History proper. The writing of History in the sense of recreating and reconstructing the past should be left to the professional historian.

Wicksell knew well what the standards were. As noted earlier, he lived in an era and in a milieu where he had easy access to the inner sanctuaries of historians. He even had experience from working with archival sources and other primary material in his neomalthusian research. But in his economic-historical writings, Wicksell used mainly secondary sources and he viewed himself as a mere user of the pictures of the past provided by the real historians. He believed in the advantages to be gained from a division of labour where the task of producing Economic History should be left to the economic historian. However, he repeatedly underlined the need for economists to keep in close touch with that field. He actually admonished his younger colleagues to study history (Ohlin, 1926). However, he had in his inaugural lecture demanded that economic historians should also bend in order to meet the economists. To conduct their task properly, they had to study eonomic theory. This "plea for theory in economic history" then became the battle cry of Heckscher and there must have been at least some influence from Wicksell on him.

No account of Wicksell as a "producer" of history would be complete without mentioning his writings in the history of economic theory. Wicksell was very well-read in the classical literature but what is particularly striking is the thoroughness with which he had read it, especially Ricardo. Knowledge of the classics has never been an "ubiquity" in the economics profession but the specialization trends of recent years have made the field almost destitute of any such externality. Therefore, reading Wicksell's theoretical works carries that extra reward to a modern student.

All in all, Wicksell comes off much better than expected as an economic historian. However, this may not be the most important result of this paper. The results throw new light on Wicksell's theoretical contribution and urge us to take a closer look at his research program. They indicate in particular that there is a methodological dimension in Wicksell's work that needs to be looked into much further. Wicksell strikes the reader as very modern especially in view of the recent resurgence of "methodological realism"—once heralded strongly by Hughes back in the heyday of Cliometrics. The Wicksellian heritage seems to be opposed to "methodological instrumentalism" that has for many decades now been the strategy dominating mainstream economic discourse. But this issue has to be dealt with in another context.

ACKNOWLEDGMENTS

The author is indebted to Mr. William Wright for language assistance including discussions of content and to Mrs. Anne Marie Lindén for expert typing. Style and language was also much improved by referee comments. All remaining errors and deficiencies are, of course, my own responsibility. Financial assistance from Jacob Wallenberg Fund is gratefully acknowledged.

NOTES

1. There are several early and predominantly Swedish reviews and discussions of Wicksell's life and work, but no major surveys appeared until in the 1950s. The first is the anniversary paper by Lindahl (1958b) which appeared in Swedish in *Ekonomisk Tidskrift* (1953). Then followed the major biography by Gårdlund (1956), which, slightly amended, is available also in an English edition (Gårdlund, 1958). The most comprehensive overview and thorough exposition of Wicksell's scientific contribution in general is provided by Uhr (1960). A report from a Wicksell symposium in Lund (1977), listed in the references as the volume containing Wicksell (1978), is a good testimony of the continued interest in Wicksell both inside and outside Sweden. The publication of the Wicksell bibliography (Hedlund-Nyström, 1976) is of course a major event for continued work on Wicksell.

2. Wicksell's neomalthusian conceptualization of social issues was set out as "the two population problems" (Fong, 1976; Wicksell, 1978). The first problem concerned the analytical and measurement aspects of the optimum population size in a country. The second problem concerned how an optimum population size should be brought about. Wicksell originally published this analysis in 1901 as the introductory chapter in the first Swedish edition of Volume One (*General Theory*) of his *Lectures* (Wicksell, 1934). However, it was omitted in the second and third editions and printed as a separate booklet. The translation referred to (Wicksell, 1979) is from the first Swedish edition of this booklet which Wicksell prepared for publication while serving a jail-sentence for blasphemy. The revisions introduced into the book were, however, only empirical updatings. A second edition of this booklet, again with mainly empirical updatings by Wicksell, was published posthumously by his son in 1926, the year Wicksell died.

3. The Swedish translation of the Drysdale tract was made from the sixteenth edition. The English title was *The Elements of Social Science. Physical, Sexual and Natural Religion. An exposition of the true Cause and only cure of the three primary Social Evils: Poverty, Prostitution and Celibacy*. The first edition appeared in London 1854 and the book then went through more than thirty editions. It's fourth part was a summary of Mill's *Principles*.

4. Hennipman (1982) gives a masterly account of Wicksell's writings in Public Finance filling in much of the void existing in the English literature but there is so far no adequate rendering into English of Wicksell's historical writings in this field.

5. Why Wicksell chose to present it that way is an intriguing question. He wrote many of his contributions in this period under great time pressure but Wicksell seldom left the reader unclear about the why's of his doings. There is the surmise that he left the historical survey seemingly merely appended to the theoretical parts of the study for tactical career reasons. He aspired at that time for a professorial chair in economics and needed to proved his eligibility for it. All Swedish chairs in economis in those days were allied with fiscal law including not only its theory but also its history and any candidate for such a chair had to show proficiency in that area of jurisprudence.

REFERENCES

Basmann, R.L. (1965). "The Role of the Economic Historian in Predictive Testing of Proffered 'Economic Laws'." *Explorations in Entrepreneurial History*, Second Series 2: 159-186.

Buchanan, J. (1986). "The Constitution of Economic Policy" (*Nobel Price Lecture*). Paper presented to The Nobel Foundation, Stockholm, December 8.

Dopfer, K. (1988). "How Historical is Schmoller's Economic Theory?" *Journal of Institutional and Theoretical Economics,* 144: 552-568.

Drysdale, G. (1878). *Samhällslärans grunddrag eller fysisk, sexuell och naturlig religion*, Stockholm: Associationsboktryckeriet.

Fong, M.S. (1976). "Knut Wicksell's 'The two Population Questions.'" *History of Political Economy*, 8: 311-323.

Gustafsson, B. (1961). "Svensk ekonomisk teori. Knut Wicksell 1851-1926." *Vår Tid*, 17: 203-226.

Gårdlund, T. (1956). *Knut Wicksell. Rebell i det nya riket*. Stockholm: Bonniers.

Gårdlund, T. (1958). *The Life of Knut Wicksell*. Translated by N. Adler. Stockholm: Almqvist & Wicksell.

Heckscher, E.F. (1904). "Ekonomisk historia. Några antydningar." *Historisk Tidskrift*, 16: 167-198.

Hedlund-Nyström, T. (Ed.). (1976). *Knut Wicksells tryckta skrifter 1868-1950*. Compiled and with an introduction by E.J. Knudtzon. Lund: CWK Gleerup.

Hennipman, P. (1982). "Wicksell and Pareto: Their Relationship In the Theory of Public Finance." *History of Political Economy*, 14: 37-64.

Henriksson, R.G.H. (1969). "An Interpretation of the Significance of Emigration for the Growth of Economic Welfare in Sweden 1860-1910." Ph.D. dissertation, Northwestern University.

Henriksson, R.G.H. (1990). "Eli F. Heckscher: The Economic Historian as Economist." In *The History of Swedish Economic Thought*, edited by Bo Sandelin. London: Routledge & Kegan Paul.

Hughes, J.R.T. (1966). "Fact and Theory in Economic History." *Explorations in Entrepreneurial History*. 3 (2nd Series): 75-100.

Hughes, J.R.T. (1968). "Wicksell on the Facts: Prices and Interest Rates, 1844 to 1914." In *Value, Capital and Growth*, edited by J.N. Wolfe. Edinburgh: Edinburgh University Press.

Jonung, L. (1979). "Knut Wicksell and Gustav Cassel on Secular Movements in Prices." *Journal of Money, Credit and Banking*, ll: 165-181.

Lindahl, E., (ed.) (1958a). *Selected Papers in Economic Theory by Knut Wicksell*. London: George Allen & Unwin.

Lindahl, E. (1958b). "Knut Wicksell 1851-1926." In *Selected Papers in Economic Theory by Knut Wicksell*, edited by E. Lindahl. London: George Allen & Unwin.

Lundberg, E. (1984). *Kriserna och ekonomerna*. Malmö: Liber Förlag.

Nagel, E. (1950). *John Stuart Mill's Philosophy of Scientific Method*. New York: Hafner.

Ohlin, B. (1926). "Obituary. Knut Wicksell 1851-1926." *The Economic Journal*, 36: 503-511.

Thomas, B. (1936). *Monetary Policy and Crises. A Study of Swedish Experience*. London: George Routledge and Sons Ltd.

Tooke, T., and W. Newmarch. ([1838-1857] 1928). *A History of Prices and the State of the Circulation from 1792 to 1856*. Introduction by T.E. Gregory. London: P.S. King & Son Ltd.

Uhr, C.G. (1960). *Economic Doctrines of Knut Wicksell*. Berkeley: University of California Press.

Wicksell, K. (1869). "Sats, framställd och löst af student Knut Wicksell. Huru står man säkrast?" *Tidskrift för matematik och fysik* 1: 20-21.

Wicksell, K. (1882). *Om utvandringen, dess betydelse och orsaker*. Stockholm: Albert Bonniers Förlag.

Wicksell, K. (1893). *Über Wert, Kapital und Rente*. Jena: Verlag von Gustav Fischer.

Wicksell, K. (1896). *Finanztheoretische Untersuchungen nebst Darstellung und Kritik des Steuerwesens Schwedens*. Jena: Verlag von Gustav Fischer.

Wicksell, K. (1898). *Geldzins und Güterpreise. Eine Studie Über die Tauschwert des Geldes bestimmenden Ursachen*. Jena: Verlag von Gustav Fischer.

Wicksell, K. (1924). "Befolkningsfrågans nuvarande läge." *Tiden*, 16: 193-209.

Wicksell, K. (1934). *Lectures on Political Economy*. Volume 1: *General Theory*. Translated by E. Classen and edited by L. Robbins. London: George Routledge and Sons Ltd.

Wicksell, K. (1935). *Lecctures on Political Economy*. Volume 2: *Money*. Translated by E. Classen and edited by L. Robbins. London: George Routledge and Sons Ltd.

Wicksell, K. (1936). *Interest and Prices. A Study of the Causes regulating the Value of Money.* Translated by R.F. Kahn with an introduction by B. Ohlin. London: MacMillan.

Wicksell, K. (1953). "The Enigma of Business Cycles." Translated by C.G. Uhr. *International Economic Papers*, 3: 58-74.

Wicksell, K. (1954). *Value, Capital and Rent.* Translated by S.H. Frowein with a Foreword by G.L.S. Shackle. London: George Allen & Unwin Ltd.

Wicksell, K. (1958a). "Ends and Means in Economics." In *Selected Papers in Economic Theory by Knut Wicksell*, edited by E. Lindahl. London: George Allen & Unwin Ltd.

Wicksell, K. (1958b). "A New Principle of Just Taxation." Pp. 72-118 in *Classics in the Theory of Public Finance*, edited by R.A. Musgrave and A.T. Peacock. London: Macmillan.

Wicksell, K. (1979), "The Theory of Population, Its Composition and Changes." Translated by G. Ohlin in *The Theoretical Contributions of Knut Wicksell*, edited by S. Ström and B. Thalberg. London: MacMillan.

THE CAUSES OF LONG WAVES IN EARLY MODERN ECONOMIC HISTORY

Jack A. Goldstone

I. INTRODUCTION

Nothing, possibly, is more galling to the mature and careful historian than the appearance of a one-cause explanation of a long, complex, and tortuous sequence of historical events.

—Hughes (1968)

J.R.T. Hughes wrote those words twenty-two years ago, in examining the long cycles of price inflation and recession in Britain from 1844 to 1914. He noted that the long cycles could be explained as a combination of a "sticky" policy by the Bank of England in setting discount rates, plus structural changes in the world economy that affected the supply of real goods. Hughes pointed out that when the output of the world economy sharply changed, due to war or the rapid emergence of American production, maintaining stable prices required the Bank to adjust the money supply by setting new ceilings or floors for the discount rate. However, the Bank's policy of restricting interest rate fluctuations meant that the discount rate adjustments generally failed to fully

Research in Economic History, Suppl. 6, pages 51-92.

ISBN: 1-55938-150-7.

balance the structural shifts. By holding on to old ceilings in times of inflation, and a fixed 2 percent floor even in times of recession, the Bank failed to achieve stable prices. Instead, the inadequate adjustments produced "long waves" of inflation or recession as sticky discount rates kept money either too plentiful or too dear.

Hughes's explanation involved attention to bank policy, structural change in the economy, and the reaction of investors to those factors. In other words, it was a multi-causal explanation, invoking the interplay of structural and institutional forces. Yet historians today still too often treat the long waves of price inflation and deflation that occurred prior to 1800—that is, prior to the dominance of modern banking systems—with one-cause explanations. Although the "one" cause is a subject of dispute between monetarists who point to Spanish bullion imports, Malthusianists who stress population change, and Marxists who postulate a "crisis of world capitalism," all these explanations generally rest on a single primary factor.

This one-cause approach is particularly misplaced inasmuch as the early modern period, roughly from 1500 to 1800, indeed witnessed "a long, complex, and tortuous sequence of historical events," including massive bursts of urbanization and de-urbanization, changes in the scale of market organization and market participation, and a transformation of the patterns of overseas trade. Attention to overall population growth, or to bullion stocks, by themselves fail to bring all these changes into a coherent framework. The goal of this paper is to explain the long waves in price trends and population movements that occurred in most of Europe and Asia from 1500 to 1800. The explanation I offer, by resting on both structural changes and institutional habits, seeks to emulate the spirit of Hughes' approach, although in a different time-period and different institutional setting.

II. LONG WAVES IN EARLY MODERN ECONOMIC HISTORY

It has long been apparent that against the background of the long-term growth in population, urbanization, total output, and trade that occurred from 1500 to 1800, there have been marked cyclical fluctuations. Some of these have been on the scale of years, or of decades. Prompted by harvest variations, short-term weather catastrophes, and the incursion of epidemics, levels of population, prices, and economic activity often showed annual or decadal fluctuations around long-term trends. But fluctuations also occurred on a much longer scale, spanning centuries.

From 1500 to 1600, after more than a century in which population and prices had been stagnant in the wake of the Black Death, all the major countries of western and central Europe, as well as China and the Ottoman Empire, experienced growing population and rising prices. Populations increased by

50% to 100% in the three to four generations after 1500. The rise in prices, though gradual, cumulated in many countries to 500-600% by the mid-1600s, a change that has become known as the "Price Revolution." Then, between 1600 and 1680, depending on the precise region where one looked, such growth slowed and stopped. In many areas, population and prices declined, and remained at low levels or recovered only slowly. For about a century, population all across temperate Eurasia showed little or no net growth, and prices stagnated. Then, between 1700 and 1750, this stagnant trend began to reverse; by 1750, a renewed increase in population and prices was everywhere in evidence.

François Simiand (1932), in his study of these long waves, labelled periods of expanding population and rising prices as "A" phases, and periods of declining population and stagnant prices as "B" phases. Nikolai Kondratieff (1950), examining cycles in prices and economic growth in the nineteenth and early twentieth centuries, identified shorter, roughly 60-year, phases of recession and growth, since known as "Kondratieff cycles." This paper deals with the longest of the long waves—the general trend of increase or decline in population and prices over periods of a century or longer. These very long waves have been labelled as "trends seculaires" by the *Annales* historians (Le Roy Ladurie, 1974, 1981). Whether they also comprise shorter Kondratieff cycles, or even shorter decadal-length cycles, is a question I do not address. My goal is to distinguish the reasons for the very long waves, and the relationships among the variables whose movements constitute the cyclic pattern.

These grand movements in population and prices in the early modern period have attracted attention from historians and sociologists as well as economists. Medieval historians (e.g., see Postan and Hatcher, 1978) have pointed to the long period of high medieval population expansion and rising prices from 1150 to 1300, followed by a slowdown in growth, and then contraction and stagnation from 1300 to 1450 following the Black Death, as forming another, earlier, wave in this same cycle. Modern scholars, in examining the business cycles of the nineteenth and early twentieth century, have asked whether these modern business cycles—including panics and depressions—were due to the same causal framework as lay behind these early modern fluctuations. No less a scholar than Schumpeter (1939), as well as modern comparativists such as Wallerstein (1984a), have answered in the affirmative. Kondratieff suggested in his original paper on long waves that major wars and revolutions have occurred mainly toward the end of "A" periods of rising prices and demographic expansion.

However, there is still considerable confusion over the causes of these cycles. Did rising population and prices indicate prosperity, as Edmund Burke (1955) believed, or, as Malthus (1951) suggested, did rising population bring increasing difficulties? Did the movement of prices and incomes bring changes in population, or did causation operate in the opposite direction? Did factors internal to the economic system—changes in the money supply, or in the rate of exploitation of peasants and workers—cause the long-term fluctuations, or were other factors responsible?

Answers to these questions make an enormous difference for one's view of modern history. The question of what price and population movements imply about prosperity colors most evaluations of France's *ancien régime*, from Toqueville (1955) to Mathiez (1928). The belief that monetary factors were responsible for the Price Revolution is a major prop in arguments about the validity of modern monetarism. The extent to which these cycles were rooted in the exploitation of workers, or in capital flows and investment patterns, affects Marxist economic theory and the conventional theory of business cycles.

This paper presents no new original research; rather it is an attempt to synthesize recent work in a variety of fields to answer the questions I have posed regarding the long economic cycles. The answers that emerge are simply stated: the long cycles were driven primarily by fluctuations in mortality that had non-economic causes. These mortality fluctuations then had their effects on prices through a combination of a "sticky" agrarian economy which responded only slowly to changes in demand with a highly elastic system of purchase and exchange, which showed rapid change in the velocity of circulation of coin and in the availability of credit and non-specie purchasing instruments. "Loose" monetary systems, in combination with a "sticky" real economy, meant that population-induced demand shifts created periods of excess or slack market demand, hence waves of inflation and deflation.

As in Hughes's analysis of the late nineteenth century, early modern long waves were produced by "stickiness" in one component of the system that balanced the supply of goods against the supply of money. However, the exact mechanism was *precisely the opposite* of what Hughes found. In the nineteenth century, rapid shifts in output occurred, while tightly centralized banking kept money and credit "sticky" in response. In the period from 1500 to 1800, *output* was sticky, while the population-linked demand for basic goods fluctuated greatly, and in the absence of central banking, private means for expanding the velocity of money and credit readily followed the expansion of population and demand. In these earlier centuries it appears that periods of rising population and prices were times of impoverishment for the majority of the population, not prosperity; periods of stagnant population and prices were preferable for the average peasant or worker. In addition, monetary factors, if by this is meant changes in bullion flows and the "hard specie" money supply, had little or no impact on prices; changes in the volume of economic activity driven by population movements, and changes in monetary velocity driven by changes in the organization of economic activity, overwhelmed the effect of bullion movements in determining price levels. To simply state these conclusions, however, overlooks the fact that much of the desired data is still incomplete. In the following sections, I first present the trends in the key variables, including population, prices, urbanization, real wages, trade, money supply, and production of bullion. I then examine in more detail three widely current explanations for the long cycles—the Marxist theory, the Malthusian/Ricardian theory, and the monetary theory—and examine the evidence that undermines them. In conclusion, I present what I believe, in the light of current evidence, to be the most acceptable explanation for the long waves, and the relationships among them.

III. A and B PHASES

Figures 1 and 2 show, very roughly, the movements of population and prices for England, France, and China. The synchronization is clear and remarkably consistent across both data series. A period of rapid expansion to 1600, then slower increase to 1650, is followed by a marked fall from 1650 to 1700 (the B phase); growth then resumes, and becomes rapid after 1750. The Chinese population curve differs slightly in dipping from 1600 to 1650, but this reflects the turmoil and rebellions accompanying the fall of the Ming dynasty in 1644. If we state the period of expansion as "late fifteenth century to early seventeenth century," instead of 1500 to 1650, the Chinese data would more closely follow the European pattern. Thus we can speak of an A phase ending sometime between 1600 and 1650, followed by a B phase to 1750, then renewed advance.

Although the data from the Ottoman Empire are more limited, there is considerable evidence for population growth in Anatolia at least from 1500 to 1580, and of decline from 1650 to 1700 (Barkan, 1975; Cook, 1972; Naff, 1977; Dols, 1979). Thus, it appears that the heartland of the Ottoman Empire also followed a parallel demographic path.

Similar patterns are evident in the growth rates of the major metropolises. The rates for London and Paris are shown in Figure 3; however, similar patterns apply to most of the major cities of Europe and to Istanbul (de Vries, 1984; Mantran, 1962).

Real wages follow almost exactly an inverse curve. In fact, as nominal wages tended to adjust only slowly to changing prices, the real wage curve is largely a reflection of the price changes. Figure 4 graphs real wage movements for England and France. While long data series on real wages are not available for China and the Ottoman empire, monographic studies of particular regions also report a marked fall in real wages in both empires in the sixteenth and early seventeenth centuries, again parallel to trends in Europe (Geiss, 1979, p. 175; Faroqhi, 1984, pp. 295-298).

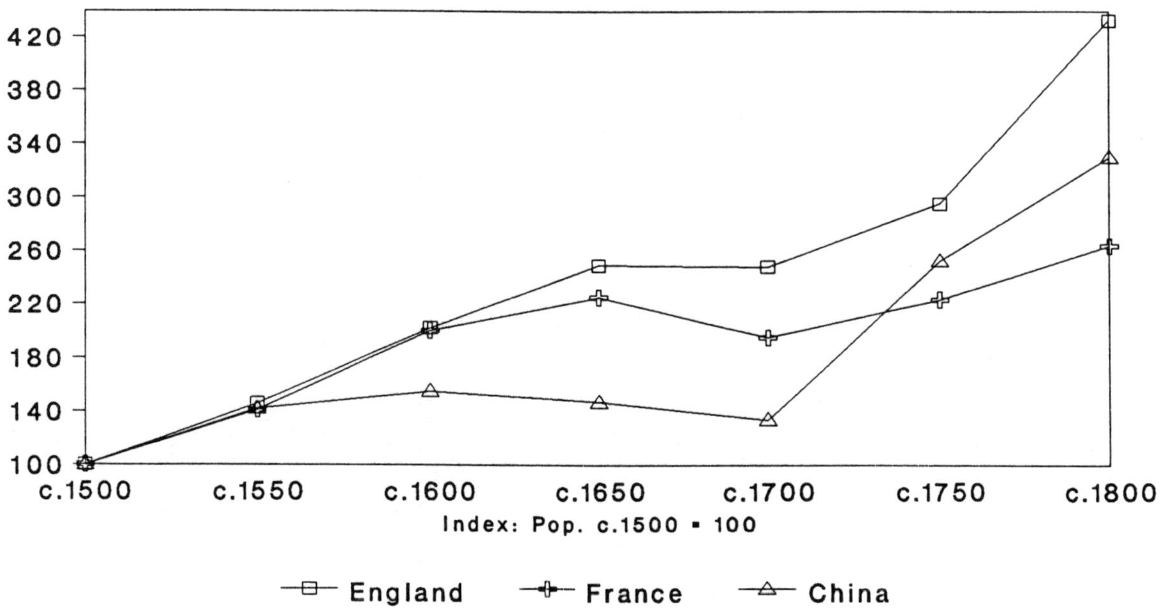

Sources: England: Wrigley and Schofield (1981); France: Le Roy Ladurie (1981, 1987) and Dupaquier (1979); China: Liu and Huang (1977).

Figure 1. Population 1500-1800: England, France, and China

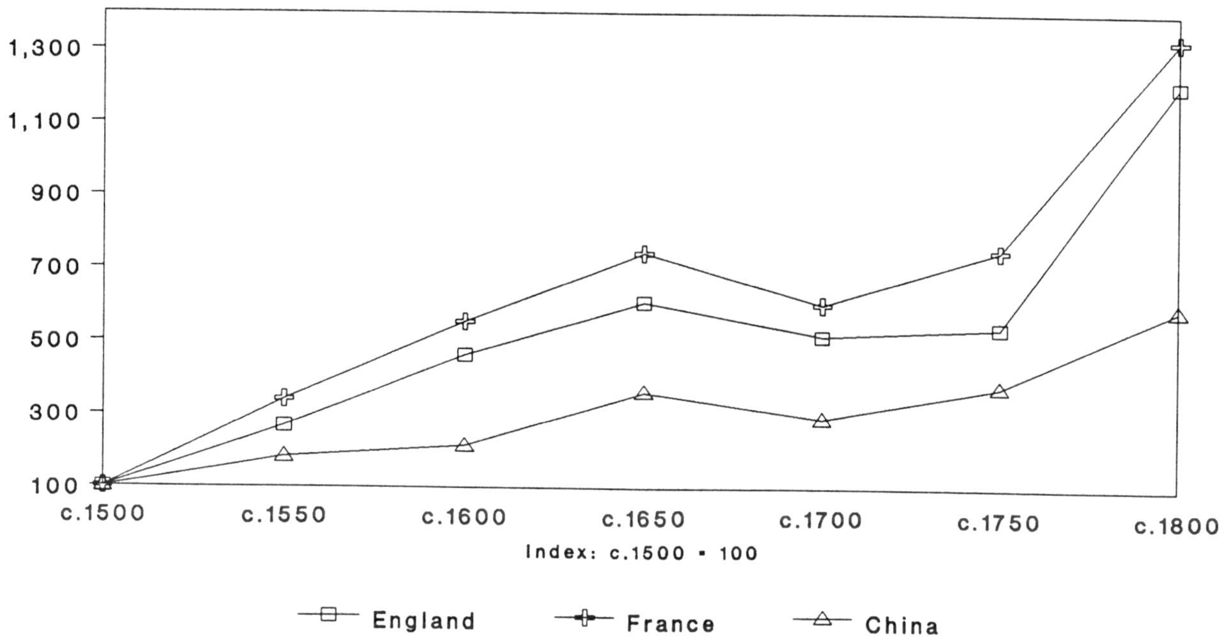

Sources: England: Hoskins (1964, 1968); France: Phelps Brown and Hopkins (1957) for 1500, Baulant (1972) for 1550 to 1700, Labrousse (1970) for 1750 and 1800 (1780-89); China: Cartier (1981).

Figure 2. Grain Prices 1500-1800: England, France, and China

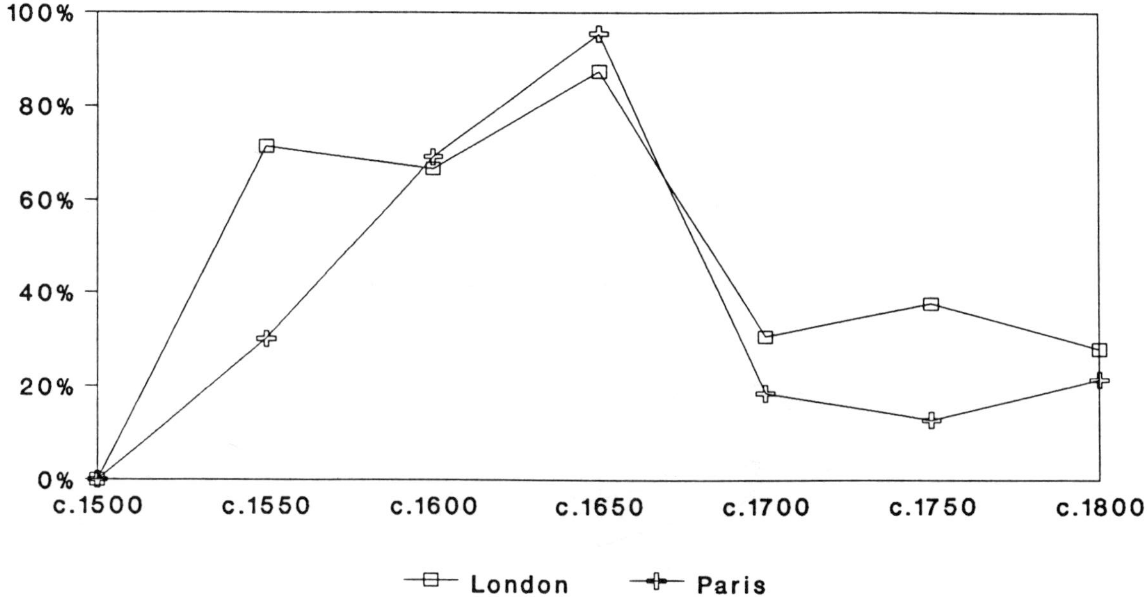

Sources: London to 1700, Beier and Finlay (1986); London after 1700 and Paris, de Vries (1984).

Figure 3. London and Paris 1550-1800
(Percentage Growth, Previous 50 Years)

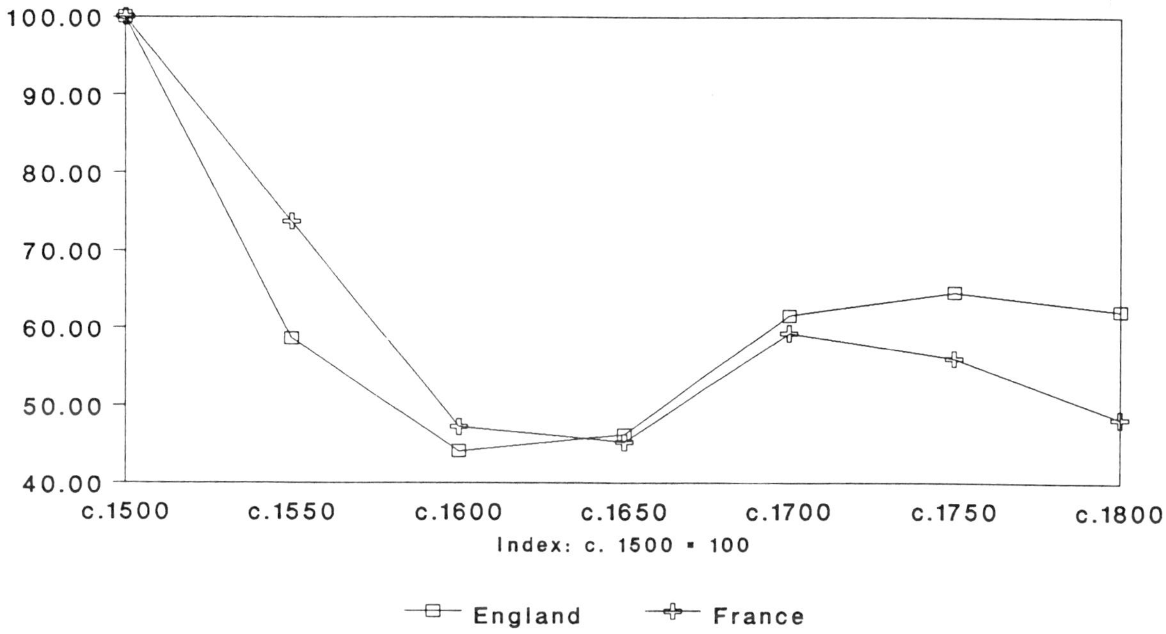

Sources: England: Phelps Brown and Hopkins (1962b) and Hoskins (1964, 1968); France: Phelps Brown and Hopkins (1957) for 1500 to 1600, Durand (1966) and Baulant (1972) for 1650 and 1700; Labrousse (1984) for 1750 and 1800 (1780-89).

Figure 4. Real Wages 1500-1800: England and France

Trade figures, shown in Figure 5, are rather more complex. In the early seventeenth century, the Thirty Years War disrupted trade in Europe, particularly that of France, Germany, and Spain. Thus the indices for Baltic and Atlantic trade, taken from the Sound toll registers and from the tonnage of ships calling at Seville, show a marked downturn between 1600 and 1650. However, the trade of England and Holland flourished. Despite the Japanese civil wars, and the decline and fall of the Ming dynasty, the Dutch steadily increased their carrying trade in Asia, as indicated by the number of ships used by the Dutch East India Company in Asia. This series shows a strong growth all through the seventeenth century. For England, the fall of Antwerp, England's main cloth export center, meant a decline of exports of cloth (index England 1 in Figure 5) from 1550 to 1650. But after 1650, England's growing naval power and colonial markets produced a boom in trade; expansion, as shown in the value in pounds sterling of total exports (index England 2 in Figure 5), was strong and steady for the next century. Thus trade statistics indicate the changing maritime balance of power and do not show the same marked synchronous waves as the population and price data. Indeed, for England, the periods of expanding trade, and of rising prices and population, are completely reversed. A phases in trade corresponded to B phases in population and prices, and vice versa.

Bullion and money supply figures, though questionable due to the difficulty of assessing smuggling, also fail to show a simple pattern. The dominant bullion series for many years was Hamilton's (1934) work on silver imports to Spain in the sixteenth century and early seventeenth century. His data showed a sharply rising level of annual imports in the sixteenth century, then a slightly lower, but stable, level of annual imports after 1600. This cessation of the rise in annual import levels was long thought to be evidence for a sustained seventeenth century decline, and responsible for phase B. Yet Morineau (1968, 1985) has returned to the archives, and continued the series through the seventeenth and eighteenth centuries. Relying on foreign estimates of total bullion imported by Spain, he included estimates of private and smuggled bullion, which give a fuller picture than Hamilton, who relied only on the officially registered bullion imported for the Crown. Morineau finds that bullion shipments to Spain after 1650 returned to their high levels of the late sixteenth century, and even exceeded them. Confirming Morineau, Cross found that the total volume of bullion mined, though it corresponded to the officially registered totals before 1630, sharply diverged thereafter. In the 1630s and 1640s, total bullion output as estimated from mercury imports was 50% higher than the official totals (Cross, 1983, p. 408). When one adds to unregistered silver the Portuguese gold coming from Brazil, the value of bullion annually shipped to Europe from 1650 to 1750, when prices were stagnant, considerably exceeded the value of that acquired during the Price Revolution.

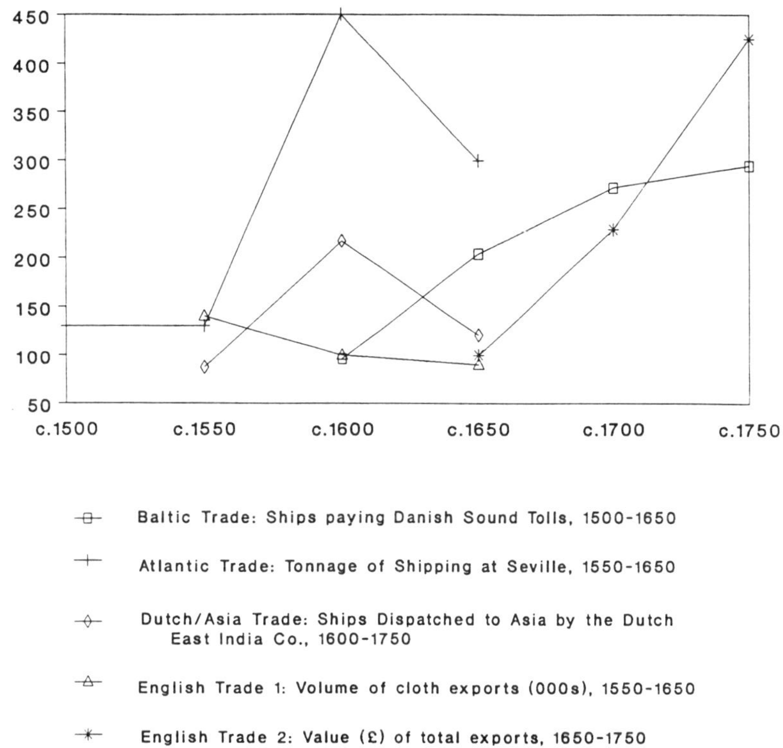

Sources: Baltic and Atlantic series: Romano (1978); Dutch/Asia series: Bruijn, Gaashra, and Schoffler (1979); English series: Coleman (1977).

Figure 5. Trade Volumes 1500-1800:
Baltic, Atlantic, Dutch/Asia, and England

While Hamilton believed that Spanish silver imports slowed after 1600, and declined after 1650, in fact the *reverse* appears to be the case. Morineau (1985, p. 578) presents extensive data, drawn largely from Dutch sources closely concerned with Spain's bullion trade, that show total Spanish silver imports in the seventeenth century comprised more than three times the volume, in tonnes of silver, of that imported in the sixteenth century. He estimates that from 1551 to 1600 the American bullion equivalent to 8,305 tonnes of silver arrived in Europe; from 1601 to 1650 11,413 tonnes; from 1651 to 1700, 16,586 tonnes; and from 1701 to 1750, 25,189 tonnes. Thus, there was no falling off in the volume of bullion exported to Europe; on the contrary, there was a steady increase.

In addition, in calculating the impact of silver imports on Europe's bullion supplies, what is crucial is the not the annual increment, but its ratio to the total stock of bullion. Working from his revised figures, Morineau offers estimates of the increase in Europe's total bullion stocks (from European and African mines, Spanish American silver, and Brazilian gold) after allowing for reexport and loss of metal through wear, equated in terms of millions of tonnes of silver. These estimates, though crude, show a steady rise in Europe's bullion stocks throughout the early modern period, of 30 to 40 percent in every half-century from 1500 to 1800. Unlike the level of population and prices, there is no phase B evident in the levels of Europe's bullion supply.

Morineau's estimates of the European bullion stock, in tonnes of silver equivalent, is shown in Figure 6. For comparison, that figure also shows the latest estimates of French money stock, based on analyses of French mint output by Glassman and Redish (1985) and Riley (1984), and the French grain price series from Figure 2.

There is hardly any relationship at all between the three curves. French money supplies increased far more rapidly than Europe's bullion stocks, suggesting little dependence of the former on the latter. French mint output depended more on the monarchy's need to meet a rising military and bureaucratic payroll than on the availability of bullion produced in the world economy. Moreover, prices did not respond to total money supplies or bullion levels; indeed prices rose most rapidly when money supplies rose slowly, from 1550 to 1650, and rose not at all, in net terms, when money supplies were skyrocketing from 1650 to 1750. Part of the reason is that much money was spent abroad, on military and colonial ventures and purchases in the Orient and Levant. Another factor is that much money was hoarded during the time of lower prices and higher real incomes from 1650 to 1750. We shall return to this problem below. But for the moment, the point to note is that, at least for France, when viewed over several centuries the suspected relationship between Europe's bullion stocks, growth of the money supply, and prices, completely fails to hold. Moreover, the extension of Hamilton's data into the

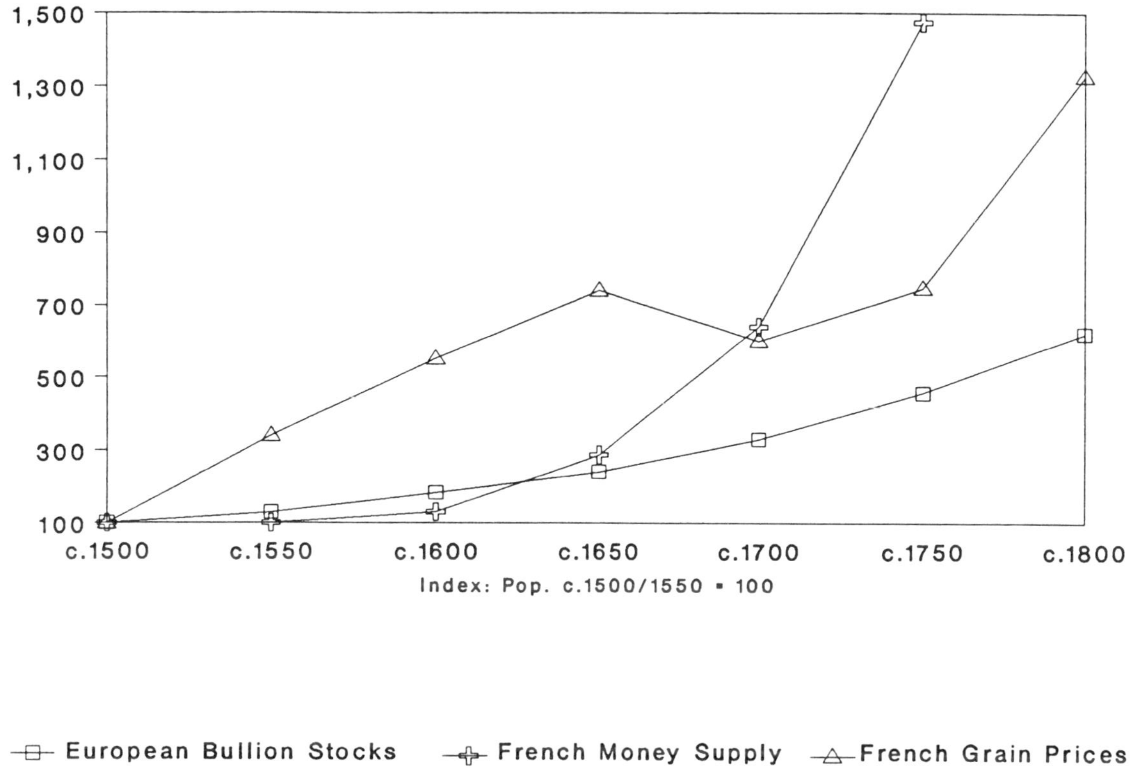

Sources: Europe's bullion stock: Morineau (1985); French Money Supply: Glassman and Redish (1984) and Riley (1985); French Prices, as in Figure 2.

Figure 6. Bullion, Money, Prices

seventeenth and eighteenth centuries, and attention to total silver volumes imported, rather than changes in the annual level of imports, shows that several times more silver arrived in Europe during the B phase of 1650-1750 than during the A phase of 1550-1650.

This rough data compilation makes three points evident:

1. Movements in population, prices, urban growth, and real wages show a strong and consistent correlation.
2. Indices of trade volume show considerable regional variation; there is no consistent pattern. Moreover, trends are not consistent with the other demographic and economic indices.
3. Indices of precious metals production and money supply show only a tenuous, or for some periods even a reverse, relation to the demographic, price and wage indices.

In short, this introductory glimpse suggests that changes in money supply and trade, over the period as a whole, were not as closely correlated with movements in domestic prices, wages, population, and urbanization, as might be concluded from looking only at the sixteenth century, or only at some trade indices. Much additional data is available that bears on these issues, but not always in the form of 300-year series. So let us turn to a closer examination of theories of the population and price cycles, and examine particular countries and time periods in more detail.

IV. WHY DID POPULATION GROWTH FLUCTUATE?

The major demographic event in the pre-industrial world familiar to all westerners is the advent of the Black Death, which reduced the population of many parts of Western Europe by a third at one blow. What is less well known is that the Black Death was equally devastating in the Middle East, and that simultaneously, epidemics, famine, and rebellion accompanied the fall of the Yuan dynasty in China in 1368 (Dols, 1979; Dunstan, 1975). Also, although the Black Death was devastating in the rapidity of its spread, it did not produce merely a short drop in population. It was part of a longer downturn that actually began around 1300 and continued until the mid-fifteenth century. The broad depression in population growth from 1350 to 1500 was not merely the result of the sudden shock of the plague; it was due to a long-term heightening of background mortality, in which disease returned to decimate every generation for over a century (Gottfried, 1978; Hatcher, 1977).

What was true of the Black Death was also true of later mortality incursions: long-term changes in mortality levels, not quick blows, were responsible for halting population growth. Although the "mortality" peaks and "famine crises" of the early modern period have attracted much attention, and were thought to be responsible for long-term fluctuations in population growth, recent research on famines has changed our view (Watkins and Mencken, 1985; Lebrun, 1980). It is now evident that, due to a relatively late age of marriage and considerable adult celibacy, early modern European populations had significant "reservoirs" of unused reproductive capacity. A famine would kill chiefly the oldest and youngest members of the population, who were likely to die in the next few years in any event. Following a famine, mothers who had lost a child would have another, widows and widowers might remarry and bear children, and individuals waiting to inherit land in order to marry would more rapidly do so. Thus, in a few years of slightly elevated nuptiality and fertility, the losses would be made good. Famines, thus, did not greatly affect the long-term trend of mortality or population (Wrigley and Schofield, 1981).

Although family structure was somewhat different in East Asia, the same fact of "reserve" fertility applies. In Asia, although age of marriage was low and children joined the patrilineal household rather than waiting to inherit, celibacy was still widespread, for poor men generally could not afford wives, and wealthier families monopolized women through secondary wives and concubinage. In addition, female infanticide to favor male children skewed the male/female ratio. After a famine, inheritance might provide opportunities for poor men to pay a brideprice and marry, while prosperous families with secondary wives could exploit their "reserves" of women to produce additional progeny. Following widespread child deaths, infanticide would likely be reduced. Thus, in Asia as well, the potential existed for rapid recovery from famine losses.

What determined long-term fluctuations in mortality, therefore, was not sharp, short, crises, but long, sustained increases in background mortality levels, usually associated with the introduction of a new disease into the population. In the fourteenth century, the Black Death spread through the Middle East and Europe, and then returned in the seventeenth century, accompanied by smallpox and typhus. In the nineteenth century, cholera spread to Europe, and in the late twentieth century, the AIDS virus threatens to have a similar impact in Africa and in certain sub-populations of advanced nations.

The expansion of trade, which unified the disease pools of the world, played a role in the spread of diseases (Le Roy Ladurie, 1981; McNeill, 1977). The usual pattern of epidemic spread was for a new microbe to move from the tropical regions of Africa or southern Asia to the Middle East. From there, by international trade routes, it would be conveyed throughout temperate Europe and Asia with devastating effect. Yet trade was more continuous than epidemics. It may thus be that microbial mutation cycles produce more virulent strains at random, several century intervals.

This is not sufficient, however, to explain why microbes, once introduced into the population, have devastating impact, fade, and return, as did the bubonic plague in the sixth, fourteenth, and seventeenth centuries. Here, world climate patterns appear to play a major role. The long-term movement of population in China and Western Europe is closely linked with meteorological series, that in turn reflect solar activity. Figure 7, from Patrick Galloway's (1986) work on climate and population, illustrates these relationships. The very long population and weather series for the Old and New World show that three falls in solar activity—the troughs of the sixth, fourteenth, and seventeenth centuries—appear in a number of climatic indices, and are closely correlated with periods of population decline in both the East and the West. The right-hand graph examines the medieval and early modern period more closely, and demonstrates that in a wide variety of countries, population growth trends rose and fell with solar activity.

The exact mechanisms by which these climate fluctuations affected disease are far from clear. It has been suggested that in colder times, people spent more time indoors, in closer proximity, to keep warm—this would facilitate the spread of infectious diseases. Animals carrying infectious diseases— such as rats—would also seek to spend more time indoors, where they could transmit microbes to human hosts. It is also now known that times of lower temperatures were also times of greater climatic variability—greater extremes of seasonal heat and cold. Thus it was perhaps the extreme and variable weather that weakened constitutions and provided an entry for disease. It seems unlikely that poor weather, by reducing harvests, created chronic hunger and weakened resistance to disease. There is simply no evidence, from studies of real wages and of mortality among different sectors of the population, that access to food was related to long-term mortality trends. As shown in Figure 4, the prosperity of urban workers runs counter to the disease cycles. That is, in both France and England, real wages were far higher in periods of demographic depression, lower during periods of demographic growth. No clear link between movements in the economy and mortality is evident.

It might be argued that this emphasis on mortality is misplaced, and that fertility movements dominated population shifts. This was true, for example, in the population growth in England after 1750 (Wrigley, 1983). But this movement, spurred by industrialization, was exceptional. In England before 1750, and elsewhere in Europe until a century later, the available data show that whether population grew or stagnated was dictated by mortality shifts, while only the *magnitude* of population changes was attenuated by compensating fertility changes. I have shown elsewhere (Goldstone, 1986) that this pattern of mortality leading population movements, and fertility adjustment exerting a lagging, but countervailing, effect, is clearly visible in Wrigley and Schofield's (1981) English population data. Jacques Dupâquier (1979) further shows that in eighteenth-century France, at a time of population

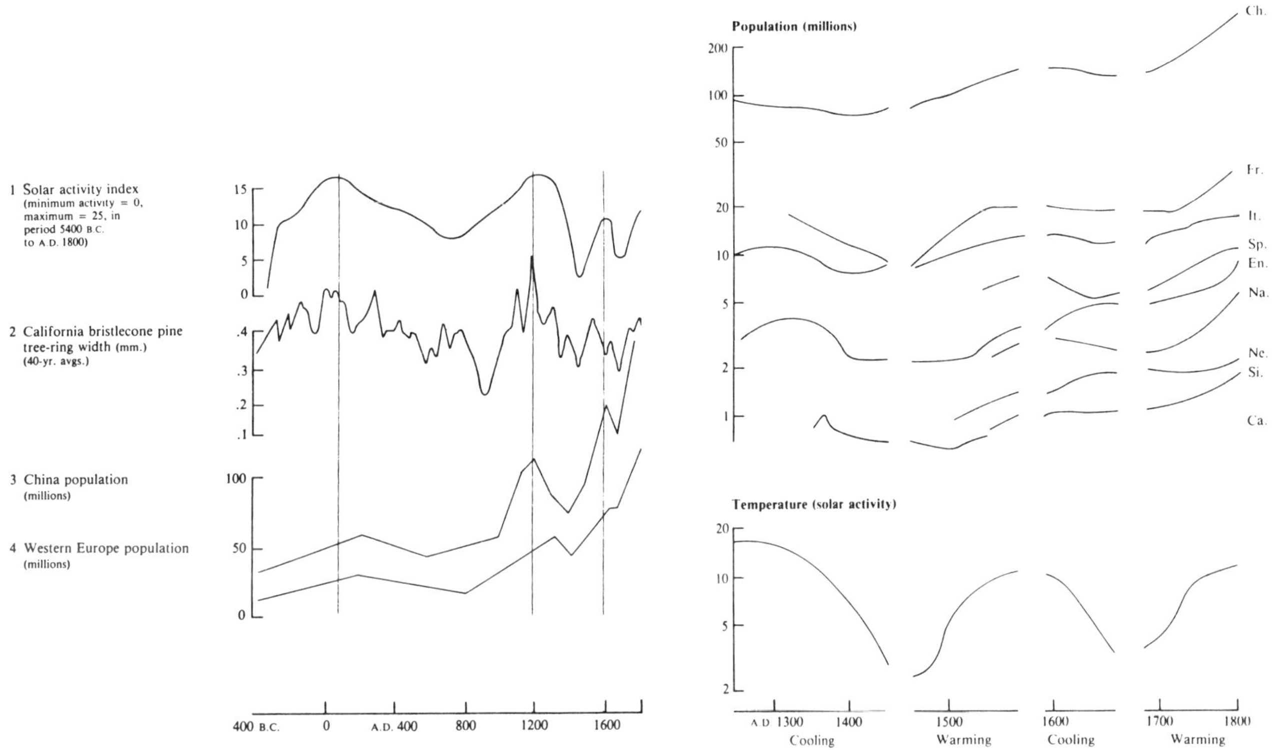

Source: Reprinted with the permission of the Population Council, from Patrick R. Galloway, "Long-term Fluctuations in Climate and Population in the Preindustrial Era," *Population and Development Review*, 12,1 (March 1986): 16-17, Figures 5 and 6.

Figure 7. Population and Climate

expansion, there is no evidence for rising fertility; instead the cause of the expansion is falling mortality, chiefly child mortality. Lee (1979) similarly shows that the expansion of the German population in the 19th century was almost entirely due to falling mortality. Until the onset of industrialization, the pattern in the West seemed to be: mortality shifts led population growth (or decline), slowly compensating fertility shifts then followed. This slow homeostatic system meant that population tended to move in cyclic fashion about its long-term growth path, with each mortality shift triggering a new upward or downward "long wave." In sum, the evidence seems to lead us squarely to the conclusion that long cycles in population, at least until 1750 in England, and 1800 in France, were governed chiefly by exogenous changes in mortality. These were not due to famines, or falling living standards. Instead, mortality patterns followed their own rhythms, set by the climate, and transmitted by disease. In the following section, I take a closer look at causal explanations for the long waves shown by prices, and consider three explanations that have been put forth—the Marxist/exploitation model, the Malthusian/Ricardian model, and the monetarist model. As usually set forth, all are flawed in some manner, which has accounted for their continued contestation. However, by starting from the realization that population movements were exogenous, we can sort out some of the flaws in each model, and construct a better, synthetic, view.

V. MARXIST MODELS OF EARLY MODERN ECONOMIC CYCLES

Marxist economic theorists have for some time suggested that the long waves of both population and prices were produced by cycles of over and underproduction, as capitalists exploited markets to the point where output exceeded demand. Contraction inevitably followed. Kondratieff (1950, p. 42), in his seminal article, thus claimed that "long waves arise out of causes which are inherent in the essence of the capitalistic economy." More recently, E. Mandel (1980) and I. Wallerstein (1984a) have argued in favor of this proposition. Wallerstein (1984a,b) has argued with particular cogency that this model applies to the logistics of the early modern period, as well as to the shorter business cycles after 1800.

Much of the evidence regarding the early modern long waves is consistent with the Marxist view. In this model, the period 1500 to 1650 was a time of expanding markets and production. However, the profits of growth were unevenly distributed, with wealth becoming increasingly concentrated. Prices rose as a result of economic expansion, benefitting capitalists, but reducing the real wages of labor. Eventually, the distribution of income became so skewed that peasants could not afford manufactured goods, and workers' wages barely sufficed to buy their daily bread. Markets for manufacturing production then collapsed, leading to the contraction of economic activity and output. As workers' income fell and jobs were lost, population growth slowed and then stopped. In this model, the high mortality and stagnation of population from 1650 to 1750 are viewed as the result of great popular misery. Moreover, the economic contraction increased conflicts throughout the world economy, leading to civil and international wars that reduced population and further damaged economies. During these struggles, stronger states and economies replaced weaker ones as dominant actors in the world economy, and captured its markets. Thus the B phase from 1650 to 1700 was not merely a period of economic contraction, but a period of the transfer of hegemony in the world economy from Spain to Holland and then England. After 1700, England's commercial ascendancy set the stage for a new cycle of growth (Wallerstein, 1984b).

How does this account square with the historical data? First, as shown in Figures 1 and 2, China's waves of population and price movements are closely in phase with those of England and France. Yet China at this time was only on the periphery of the capitalist world system. To the extent that China did participate in the capitalist world economy, it was through the import of silver in exchange for its manufactures. Yet here is a problem, for the transit of silver to China from the west greatly increased from 1650 to 1750 with the expansion of the British and Dutch East India Companies' trade (Chaudhuri, 1968; Brujin et al., 1979, p. 174). Thus for China's silver trade, the A phase continues from 1600 to 1750; this is totally out of step with the population and price movements of the century. Thus one problem—how is it that China's long waves of population and prices were in phase with those of western capitalist economies, when China internally was not capitalist, and when its trade with the capitalist economies was "out of phase" with the population and price movements? This suggests the motive force behind the logistic waves lay outside the internal dynamics of world capitalism.

Second, we may ask how the Marxist model accounts for the movement of population. The answer offered by Wallerstein, among others, is that an expanding economy, by offering employment, provides the basis for an expanding population, at least until the level of real wages fell so low that mortality rose and marriage and fertility declined, ushering in a stagnant B phase in population. This is the familiar notion that capitalist expansion—in the early modern period assisted by the mechanism of enclosure—created its own "reserve army" for its labor force.

Yet this method for making population movements endogenous to the working of the capitalist economy will not suffice. First, as we have noted, there is no evidence that population growth was primarily determined by living standards. Table 1 shows levels of real wages, crude birth rates, and crude death rates, for several periods in early modern English history, from Goldstone

(1986, p. 32) and Wrigley and Schofield (1981, pp. 532-533). In the first period, at the beginning of the "A" phase, real wages were high, as was fertility. Mortality too was relatively high, though not enough to prevent population growth. Toward the end of the A phase, real wages have indeed dropped and fertility adjusted downward. But mortality fell as well, so that population growth continued, despite the fall in wages. In the next period, well into the B phase, we find that real incomes rose by a half. Yet fertility was unchanged, and, despite higher wages, mortality rose; thus population growth halted. Finally, in the last two periods the next A phase began with higher real wages, and sharply higher fertility. However, mortality also rose, blunting overall growth. Only toward the end of the A phase, when wages again started to decline, do we find both high fertility and lower mortality, creating very strong overall growth. In short, these figures support our earlier assertions that mortality was largely independent of wage levels.

It has, however, been suggested that this wage data is misleading (Woodward 1981). In the seventeenth and eighteenth centuries, "reported" real wages formed only a part of actual incomes, which were supplemented by small-scale husbandry and other family employments. These other income sources might have offset movements in wage-earnings. It is also sometimes suggested that levels of unemployment might not have been correlated with wage levels. In either event, the reported wages would not truly measure the income or welfare of the bulk of the population. Yet this assertion too is confounded by a closer look at reproductive behavior. When one examines not the crude birth rate, which is affected by changes in the age structure and hence by mortality, but the Gross Reproduction Rate, which is corrected for such effects, a strong relationship between wage levels and fertility is apparent. Table 2 (compiled from Goldstone, 1986) shows that the birth cohorts centered on 1591, 1616, and 1641, for whom real wage levels were low for most of their earning years, had relatively low reproduction rates; thereafter, as real wages improved, fertility rose. It is difficult to maintain, in the face of this broad response of fertility, that real wage data did not relate to widely-experienced levels of prosperity. Only mortality shifts were independent of real wage levels. The data shown in Table 1 also confirm that low mortality prior to 1650 was critical to maintaining population expansion, while higher mortality in the later seventeenth century was critical to halting that expansion. As we noted above, population movements, stretching back over centuries, appear to be driven by climate and disease.

Why did food prices increase relative to wages and manufactures? The answer is provided by a simple model, that does not depend on the exploitation of manufacturing workers. In agrarian societies, the main complementary input to labor is land. Where land is fixed in supply, an increase in the labor force, such as is produced by population growth, will reduce land per laborer. Unless capital is applied to increase productivity, the fixed supply of land means that

Table 1. Real Wages, Crude Birth Rates, and Crude Death Rates In England 1540-1750 (Real Wage Index: 1541-60 = 100)

Real Wages	*Avg. CBR*	*Avg. CDR*	*Implied Net*	*Growth Rate*
1541-60	100	35.82	30.98	4.84
1631-50	67	30.97	26.06	4.91
1671-90	92	30.78	30.56	0.22
1721-40	117	34.11	31.12	2.99
1771-90	107	36.58	27.02	9.56

Table 2. Real Wages and Cohort Fertility in England, 1566-1791 (25-year Birth Cohorts Centered on Year Indicated)

		Average Real Wage	
Reproductive Birth Cohort	*Gross Earning Years*	*Approximate Prime Earning Years*	*Level During Prime Rate*
1566	1561-1600	58	2.29
1591	1591-1630	41.2	2.13
1616	1611-1650	38.4	1.92
1641	1641-1680	44.6	1.88
1666	1661-1700	49.5	2.17
1691	1691-1730	56.3	2.21
1716	1711-1750	64.1	2.23
1741	1741-1780	67	2.35
1766	1761-1800	65.8	2.55
1791	1791-1830	69.3	2.63

the output of the land will increase less than the increase in the supply of labor, foodstuffs will become more expensive relative to labor, and returns to the scarce factor (land) will grow fastest. This line of reasoning suggests that regardless of the precise labor system—whether capitalist tenant farmer and hired laborer, or small independent peasant farmer, or share-cropping tenant—periods of population growth in agrarian societies that have already developed their available arable land will be periods in which real wages decline. Thus wealth will be concentrated among the owners of land, and real incomes among labor-suppliers will fall, reducing the per capita demand for manufactures. The implications of this neoclassical model are the same as the Marxist model—they predict that, toward the end of an A phase of population expansion, real wages will fall, demand for manufactures per capita (and if wages fall enough, total demand for manufactures) will decline, and wealth will be concentrated. Yet this will happen in societies that are not capitalist in organization, as well as those that are, as long as land is unequally distributed. Thus this neoclassical model explains why England, France, and China show the same pattern, even though their degree of capitalist organization was greatly different.

In short, the Marxist model reverses the causal order. It claims that economic activity and wage levels determined population growth. Yet as we have seen, this is mistaken; low wages generally occurred during periods of population increase, and higher wages after 1650 did not produce population growth. Independent mortality, not income or exploitation, thus seems a better explanation of population swings. In addition, in assuming that it is an inherent characteristic of capitalism that gives rise to long waves, the Marxist model cannot explain why China follows the same pattern at the same time, and we need to frame a different explanation for the long waves.

VI. THE MALTHUSIAN/RICARDIAN MODEL

Malthus offered a number of speculations regarding the relations between population and prices. First, Malthus suggested that as population increased faster than agricultural output, prices would increase. Indeed Malthus (1951, p. 256) was one of the earliest writers to argue that it was "redundancy of population . . . at the end of the 16th [century,] and not the discovery of American mines" that had raised prices. Adding Ricardo's insights into relative factor prices, the Malthusian/Ricardian model has considerable merit. This view correctly predicts that in the early modern period, when population levels are high, the returns to labor (i.e., real wages) will be low, while the price of products of the land will be high. Conversely, when population levels are low, real wages will be firmer and the prices of agricultural products will fall. The prices of manufactures, as long as they depend chiefly on labor, will move as the price of labor moves. This is in fact the pattern found throughout the period under examination. Thus population models of the price revolution have been defended by many scholars, including Phelps Brown and Hopkins (1957), Chambers (1972), and van Bath (1963).

Yet there is a major flaw in the simple notion that population growth led to rising prices: the Ricardian model only projects the *relative* price of land and foodstuffs to increase. But the long waves, though showing these relative price movements, are chiefly characterized by movements in the *overall* price level. Thus a simple population pressure model will not explain price movements; other elements must be added to explain the source of the increased purchasing power that moves the general price level.

In addition, Malthus suggested that population movements responded to changing prices, so that higher prices would lead to prudential checks, or at worst, to famine, bringing population and output back into balance. Yet as we have seen, long-term mortality levels seem to be independent of real wages. Malthus appears to have been correct in noting that fertility control through delayed and non-marriage helped European populations adjust to imbalances between population growth and food supply. But with mortality an independent feature of the demographic system, Malthus' view of population movements is incomplete.

In short, Malthus and Ricardo were partly correct—fertility did respond to real wage movements, and relative price movements did produce higher prices for foodstuffs during periods of population growth, and lower prices in periods of population stagnation or decline. But these insights are insufficient to explain two key aspects of the early modern long waves. First, population growth or decline occurred in parallel waves in widely separate countries, on a world-wide scale, and largely independent of income. Second, the long waves of prices show not only relative price movements, but large movements in the *general* price level.

We have already noted that the world-wide scale of population movements can be explained by focusing on periodic waves of epidemic disease. The need to explain shifts in the *general* price level leads us to next consider monetary explanations of price movements.

VII. THE MONETARY THEORY OF EARLY MODERN INFLATION

For centuries the great inflation of the sixteenth century, which was quite apparent to contemporaries, has been an object of debate. In the 1600s, Malestroit argued that debasement of the official coinage was its cause; Bodin countered with a more sophisticated quantity argument that blamed the increase in silver imports (Miskimin, 1977, pp. 36-43).

Yet both of these arguments are beset with difficulties. First, debasement unquestionably had marked local and short-term effects on nominal prices. The debasement of English currency by Henry VIII and Edward VI in the mid-sixteenth century, the debasement of Spanish currency in the seventeenth century, and the debasement of the French livre in the eighteenth century, all created a sharp rise in nominal prices. Debasement of silver coinage was general throughout Europe. The Netherlands guilder, the French livre tournois, the Hungarian Florin, all lost 50 percent of their silver content from 1500 to 1650; the English pound sterling lost roughly one-third (Challis, 1978, p. 235; Kiss, 1980, p. 462; Morineau, 1968, p. 194). In Spain, where the silver rial could not be kept in circulation, presumably due to its value as an export commodity in the eastern trade, the currency was debased to a predominantly copper currency, the vellon *maravédi*. Yet what the debasement theory cannot explain is why, even when sound currencies with stable silver content were established (in England under Elizabeth, in France from 1726) prices continued to rise. Prices rose faster and more regularly than the debasement of the coinage. From

1500 to 1600, grain prices in England, France, and the Netherlands more than doubled even in terms of pure silver (Baulant, 1972, pp. 40-41; Houtte and Buyten, 1977, pp. 104-105). In Nuremberg, in Vienna, and in Hungary as well, "prices . . . generally rose more rapidly than could be justified through the decline in the fine weight of the moneys of account" (Verlinden et al., 1972, p. 72).

If we turn to the quantity of silver argument—prices rose because of the increased abundance of silver from imports—we encounter further difficulties. The most obvious, raised by the fact of widespread debasement, is that if prices were rising due to increased supplies of silver, why did monarchs debase their currency, that is, *reduce* the silver content of their coinage? Why not simply mint more coins, or heavier or finer coins, thus absorbing the increased silver, and maintaining nominal currencies? While short-term profits were made from debasement, monarchs could also, if silver was increasingly abundant, have made profits by charging a fee (or lowering the mint price) for converting silver to coin, or for converting old coins to greater fineness. Yet in the period of the price revolution we find that states throughout Europe steadily debased their coinage, and raised their mint prices for silver. In short, they acted as though silver was scarce relative to their demand for currency, and needed to be "amplified" by debasement to go farther. Not merely states, but merchants and tradesmen too complained of a shortage of hard coin. Flynn (1978, p. 395) notes that "there seems to be evidence of an extreme scarcity of bullion in Spain throughout the 16th century . . . at the conclusion of the . . . century, there was practically no specie left in Spain." Even though this might be explained by noting that the ultimate destination of much Spanish silver was the Netherlands, Flynn adds that "the Netherlands sometimes lacked treasure," and noted "a marked scarcity" in the 1550s. Did the Spanish silver then spread elsewhere in Europe? Cipolla (1972, p. 46) notes that the Mediterranean and Italy were "invaded by precious metals from America after 1570"; but it is precisely in this period that Italian inflation ends and prices begin to level off, and then fall! In France, Meuvret (1972, p. 89) tells us the King's ministers in the mid-seventeenth century faced a shortage of coin, and Mousnier (1970, p. 134) remarks that peasants had difficulty paying their taxes due to shortage of money. In England, Challis (1978, pp. 7, 101, 210) notes that "by late 1548 . . . bullion was increasingly hard to come by," and "in 1549 . . . bullion was very scarce, Canterbury and York being compelled to coin groats for lack of bullion." Shortages continued, for, as Chaudhuri (1963, p. 35) points out, "by 1620 the total efflux of silver from England had reached such proportion that the government was seriously alarmed." Plans were being made in the government to again debase English silver to prevent its exportation. English merchants, on their part, complained of a "scarcity of money" (Supple, 1959, p. 14). Even in Hungary, despite continued devaluation of the thaler, "the production of silver coin always remained behind demand" (Kiss, 1980, p. 467).

Where did the bullion go, if, despite the output of the Americas, a scarcity of specie afflicted Europe? There seem to be two chief answers: (1) to the Orient, as a commodity exchange item for trade with India and the Baltic, and (2) into hoarding as private holdings of ornaments and plate.

Parker (1974, p. 529) estimates that the Levant and Far East trade absorbed about one-third of total European and American silver production during the price revolution, and this estimate does not include the considerable volume of specie sent northeast to the Baltic. Bogucka (1980), Van der Wee (1977), and Jeannin (1982) note that vast quantities of silver were used to purchase Baltic grain, timber, furs, and naval stores. Jeannin (1982, p. 19) estimates that 1-2 million thalers a year went to Riga alone. Százdi (1981) suggests that 15 percent of American production after 1576 went directly to Asia via Manila, and another 25 percent remained in the New World for its own use.

Thus much silver never reached the European consumer, being quickly reexported to the Orient. Chaudhuri (1963) has found that both English and Dutch merchants of the East India Companies relied on the trade of Spanish rials to make purchases in the East. By the mid-sixteenth century, the Spanish rial was well established in India from the long Portuguese and Spanish trade; English and Dutch silver coins were unfamiliar and hard to trade. The eastern trade thus sucked bullion out of Europe, through purchase of coin for export.

Bullion disappeared not only into the nations of the East, but also into the private hoards of the West. In England, "household plate, church ornament, and decorative work of all kinds existed in profusion" (Challis, 1978, p. 154). By the late sixteenth century, William Harrison noted: "In noblemen's houses it is not rare to see . . . silver vessel, and so much other plate as may furnish sundry cupboards, to the sum oftentimes of £1000 or £2000 at the least. . .. Likewise in the houses of knights, gentlemen, merchantmen, and some other wealthy citizens, it is not uncommon to behold . . . costly cupboards of plate, worth £500 or £600 or £1000 . . . even the inferior artificers and many farmers . . . have for the most part learned also to garnish their cupboards with plate" (cited in Challis, 1978, p. 154). In France, "a sizable amount of these precious metals went to supply the goldsmith's industry." Bishops and abbots, lords and even tradesmen, sought plate, gold chains, belts, rings, and salt cellars. Silver and gold were sent "in enormous quantities [to] churches, [for] the making of sacred vessels or chalices, in candlesticks, crosses, crucifixes, lamps, and above all in shrines and reliquaries" (Meuvret, 1974, p. 32).

The scale of such effects was quite large. Stone (1972, p. 72) estimates that between 1500 and 1640, the number of gentry families in England increased from 5,000 to 15,000. If each of these 10,000 new gentry families sought to dignify their station to their guests by holding an appropriate display of silver plate on their table and in their cupboards, the demand for bullion would be enormous. If each new gentry family increased their plate holding by a value of £100, a very modest amount to dignify a new station, the increment to total bullion stocks held in plate would be £1,000,000, an amount almost equal to the entire increase in the supply of English coinage during this period. This cautious estimate falsely takes as zero the increment in holdings of plate by wealthy yeomen farmers, merchants, and innkeepers. Thus the amount of bullion flowing into private hands must have been equal to, or perhaps greater than, the amounts flowing into coinage.

The failure of bullion to enter the money supply poses severe problems for any theory linking inflation to increased production of precious metals. To the extent that silver entered commerce as a *commodity*, rather than as money, it should have been *deflationary*. That is, if American silver is exported to the Baltic for grain and timber, or to the Levant for silk, or to Asia for spices, it does not act like an increase in the money supply; it acts merely as an increment to resources. The effect is as if western Europe had acquired new territories that produced grain, silk, and spices, and added them to the economy. The mediating role of American silver was just a link in a chain, whose net impact was to add to the stock of goods available to European states and consumers. This increase in physical wealth, if not accompanied by an increase in the domestic money supply, should have led to a *decrease* in nominal prices as a constant domestic money supply now commanded more goods.

The problem of the fate of American silver and purchasing power is particularly acute in the case of grain. For if silver was largely exported to buy naval stores and luxury goods for the rich, or domestically turned into plate to decorate wealthy tables and houses of worship, there is no reason for prices of popular mass consumption goods to rise. A sixfold increase in the price of daily bread could only be accomplished by a vast increase in the purchasing power of the population as a whole. And there is no evidence that increases in domestic money supplies were of a magnitude to provide this.

Let us consider three pieces of evidence that tell directly on this issue. Challis (1978) has concluded that the value of English gold and silver coin in circulation in 1526 was £1.67 million; by 1603 it had risen to £3.49 million, or slightly more than doubled (in percentage terms, it increased 109%). However, the silver content of the pound had been reduced by a third. Thus the volume of silver in circulation had only increased by 39 percent. During this same time-span, the price of a composite basket of foodstuffs and manufactures rose by 266 percent (Phelps Brown and Hopkins, 1962a, pp. 194-195). Thus prices rose more than twice as much as the money supply in the sixteenth century, and more than six times as much as the amount of bullion in circulation.

For France, Glassman and Redish and Riley, working with French mint data, have provided new estimates of the growth of the French money supply, shown in Figure 5. Riley (1984, p. 235) notes that "increases in the money stock . . . do not explain price level movements." Indeed, as Riley and McCusker (1983) note in a companion article, in the late seventeenth and eighteenth century, "the money stock grew most rapidly when prices were stable, and least rapidly when prices were rising." As in England, the data show prices acting largely independently of the money stock.

A further fascinating bit of evidence on the dispersion of American silver has been provided by collaboration between a chemist and a historian, the husband and wife team of Adon and Jean Gordus (1981). Different silver deposits have different and characteristic impurities. One of these "impurities" is gold, whose level in the resulting refined silver can be used to identify the source of the lighter metal. Chemical assays of silver from the Potosí silver mines in Peru, which produced some two-thirds of American silver during the peak decades of exports in the late sixteenth century, show an unusually low level of gold alloyed with the silver. The Gorduses used nuclear spectroscopy to "fingerprint" the silver in coins minted in a variety of European countries in the sixteenth and early seventeenth centuries. As expected, the coinage of Spain and Italy show a considerable number of specimens comprising Potosí silver. Yet the coins of no other European countries, nor of the Ottoman Empire, show any traces of Potosí silver in their coinage. As they conclude: "The implications of this are hard to escape: there seems to be little correlation between the actual American silver and the 'Price Revolution.' . . . We are certain that the actual treasure itself had very little or no influence on the money systems of countries other than Spain" (Gordus and Gordus, 1981, pp. 238-239).

This striking result confirms suspicions that other scholars had voiced for some time. Hammarström (1957) has reported a large and steady price rise in Sweden from the early sixteenth century, yet found no evidence of Spanish silver entering Sweden at that early date. Kiss (1980) remarks that "it has so far been impossible to confirm that the influx of American silver had any effect at all on the Kingdom of Hungary," yet prices in Hungary, as elsewhere in Europe, rose several hundred percent in the sixteenth century. Hoszowski (1972, p. 91) notes that prices in Poland rose rapidly from the 1520s to the 1630s, and that these price rises "took place there before the invasion of American treasure." The finding that no Potosí silver was evident in Ottoman coinage is particularly interesting, since much silver was sent from Europe to the Levant. However, much of this was again reexported eastward to pay for Persian textiles, Chinese silks, and Asian spices, which transited the Empire on the Caravan trade. In the Ottoman Empire, inflation began in the late 15th century, and reached levels similar to those in Europe, increasing by several hundred percent by 1580 (Barkan, 1975; Faroqhi 1984, pp. 217-218). But like the other areas on the eastern periphery of Europe, there is no evidence for an infusion of Spanish silver into its domestic coinage. Sahilloglu (1983, p. 282) notes that "the silver *gurus* [reales and grosschen] did not occupy a major place in the Ottoman currency until 1584." One step further east, on the west coast of India, by the seventeenth century, silver imports were an important commodity in international trade. Yet here too, according to Brennig's (1983) research, the movement of local prices in the seventeenth century did not follow the movement of silver imports.

Let us turn last to the one country that, we can be fairly certain, was the recipient of large quantities of silver from the Americas in the sixteenth and seventeenth centuries—China. As in Europe, grain prices in China rose in the sixteenth and early seventeenth centuries, and fell from 1650 to 1720 (Cartier, 1981, p. 464; Geiss, 1979, pp. 159-160, 164, 198). Despite China's size, the market appears to have been fairly unified, as grain was transported to market over vast distances along the Grand Canal and the Yangtze river. Moreover, data on silver/copper cash exchange ratios shows that "most provinces and macroregions exhibited similar long-term developments" in the structure of the money supply from 1644 to 1850 (Vogel, 1987, p. 7), excepting only the mining center of Yunnan in the far southwest.

Is there evidence here of a correlation between price movements and silver imports? Rice prices in China rose from 1550 to 1650, as did China's imports of silver from America via Manila. And some historians, working from data that indicates a decline in Spanish bullion imports via Manila, have argued that the decline in Chinese silver prices after 1650 resulted from falling silver supplies (Atwell, 1977, 1982). Yet examined in closer detail, the correlation between silver flows and price movements disappears. In fact, silver imports from Manila furnished only a small portion of China's bullion. In the early seventeenth century, Chinese imports of silver from Japan reached the incredible volume of 150,000 kg/yr, some seven times the level of China's imports of American silver via Manila (Yamamura and Kamiki, 1983, pp. 351-352; Cross, 1983, p. 445). And in the late seventeenth century, when rice prices were *falling*, silver continued to pour into China both directly from Japan and through the trade of the British East India company, which purchased rials and bar silver in Spain, Amsterdam, and London, for export to China. According to Innes (1980, pp. 379-380, 405-416), Japan's exports of silver to China were greater from 1660 to 1710 than from 1610 to 1660. Indeed, Yamamura and Kamiki (1983, p. 343) estimate that Japan's silver mines reached their peak output in the years 1683-1706. In addition, from 1680 to 1720, the British East India Company's exports of silver to China totalled over £10.8 million, or almost 28,000 kg/yr, more than had been imported via Manila in the early seventeenth century (Chaudhuri, 1968, p. 482). Yet Chinese grain prices fell and then stagnated in this period, being almost 30% lower in 1720 than they had been in the 1650s (Cartier 1981, p. 464). In China too, then, grain price movements do not follow the level of silver imports.

In short, except for the fairly brief and local coincidence between silver imports, American silver in the coinage, and rising prices that occurred in Spain in the sixteenth century, the evidence is overwhelmingly against the hypothesis that European and Asian price movements in general reflected changes in bullion stocks, or the spread of American silver in particular. For most of the world, for most of the period of the long waves from 1500 to 1800, the relation between bullion production, money stocks, and grain prices was negative or nil. We are then forced back to the key questions—where did the bullion go, if not into money supplies? And where did the purchasing power come from to push prices upward, if not from a bullion-induced surge in money?

If Europe's supplies of bullion were scarce throughout the late sixteenth and early seventeenth centuries, precisely during the Price Revolution, it must seem that the bullion vanished into a "black hole." And that is not far from the truth. The classical equation relating prices and the money supply, the Fisher (1911) equation, is an identity resting on four variables—the price level (P), the money supply (M), the velocity of money—the number of times coins are actually used for purchase in a given accounting period—(V), and the quantity of goods and services marketed (Q). The equation states that in a given unit of time total purchasing power—that is, the supply of money times the velocity of its use (MV)—must equal the total value of goods and services sold—that is, the quantity of goods and services marketed times the price level (PQ). Hence $MV = PQ$. Clearly, increases in M only result in commensurate increases in P if the ratio of V to Q remains stable. Yet in the sixteenth century, these elements were far from stable. Both the velocity of money and the quantity of goods and services marketed expanded dramatically, though not equally, as a consequence of population expansion, urbanization, and commercialization of the world economy.

To take but one example, consider the need for money in London. As population increased, there was great pressure on the money supply. From 1500 to 1650, the population of the metropolis grew by more than a factor of five. In addition, the nominal wages of manual laborers tripled (although in real terms this was a fall in per capita income of almost 50%). On the very conservative assumption that no one's income increased more than that of a manual laborer—that is, a 50 percent fall in per-capita real incomes—the increase in nominal wages and population still mean that the annual money income of London increased by *a factor of fifteen* in this time-span. But since all income in this urban setting was generated by the marketing of goods and services, this means that PQ must also have increased fifteen-fold. Thus, if the velocity of money were stable, M must have increased by a factor of fifteen to sustain the liquidity necessary to fuel economic activity.

If London were the only such center of growth, one might argue that London could gain this money by sucking funds from elsewhere in the country. But the sixteenth century was a period of urban expansion throughout England, indeed throughout Europe and Asia. Paris grew at the same time, almost as rapidly as London. So did Naples and Newcastle, Lyons and Lwow, Norwich and Ningpo, Istanbul and Ypres (de Vries, 1984; Mantran, 1962; Shiba, 1977).

Smaller marketing towns proliferated as well, as commercial agriculture spread (Everitt, 1967; Jennings, 1976; Faroqhi, 1979). Even in the countryside, Kussmaul's (1981) study of English farm labor and Le Roy Ladurie's (1974) analysis of rural Languedoc show an increase in rural wage labor in the sixteenth and early seventeenth centuries, at the expense of farm servants paid in kind and household subsistence farming. Thus increased market activity was not limited to a few major cities, but widespread.

If increases in population simply brought commensurate national increases in the volume of goods marketed, then given that the population of England, France, and China rose 60 to 100 percent during the price revolution, and that prices rose by 300 to 500 percent, *PQ* would have risen by 540 to 1,100 percent! Even if we suggest that production lagged behind population growth, so that *Q* increased only two-thirds as fast as population, the overall increase in population and prices still implies a four- to seven-fold increase in *PQ*, and hence in *MV*.

This figure is certainly an underestimate, however, because it assumes that there was no change in the proportion of total production that was sold at market. Yet in Europe and China, this period saw a vast expansion of manufacturing for sale, urbanization, and commercial agriculture. In a previous paper (Goldstone, 1984), I presented a crude model of changes in market participation that suggested, at least for England, that during the Price Revolution the proportion of agricultural produce marketed, rather than consumed by producers, increased by 50 to 75 percent. Compounded by population increase and the rise in prices, I concluded that the total value of marketed goods and services in England must have increased by 13.5 to 18 times from 1500 to 1650. This enormous increase in market activity explains why even considerable increases in the money supply left merchants and consumers struggling with a shortage of coin. With an increase in market activity of this magnitude, the demands for increased liquidity were enormous. As Geoffrey Parker (1974, p. 530) has asked, "was the net increase in Europe's monetary stock, substantial as it was, equal to the rapidly rising demand for means of payment? There are several indicators that it was not, particularly after 1600."

There is no evidence that the specie money supply in England or France increased by the 13 to 18 times needed to sustain the observed growth in the economy; the estimates of Challis for England show only a doubling from 1500 to 1600, while those of Redish and Glassman and Riley for France show a tripling from 1500 to 1650. Morineau's examination of European bullion stocks show an increase of just over 133 percent. Given the limited growth in *M*, it is evident that large increases in *V* must have occurred during the price revolution in order to sustain economic activity.

It is sometimes suggested that Europe's bullion imports in the sixteenth century not only produced inflation, but were the spur to economic growth, that is, were so large as to produce an increase in *both Q* and *P*. It should now be clear that this claim is completely inconsistent with the size of the observable increase in economic activity. Indeed, the increases in *prices alone* were far in excess of the increase in the supply of bullion, or of increases in the stock of debased coinage. When one adds to the price increase the observed increases in population and the degree of market participation, the amount of purchasing power exercised toward the mid-seventeenth century was well over a dozen times that in the early sixteenth century. Evidently, if the early modern economies had relied on bullion stocks and hard specie to fuel their growth, the Price Revolution and the economic expansion of the sixteenth and early seventeenth centuries could never have occurred.

Conversely, during the B phase of falling prices and population from 1650 to 1700, there was no net economic expansion. Urbanization rates slowed, and many cities lost population (de Vries, 1984). Nominal wages were nearly flat, and with population falling, total purchasing power likely declined. All of this occurred despite the fact that bullion imports from America surpassed their 16th century levels (Morineau, 1968), and even where money supplies, judging from the French evidence, showed a dramatic increase.

It should be pointed out that a "glut" of money and/or bullion during periods of price deflation has also occurred in modern times. Indeed, J.R.T. Hughes's (1968) article pointed to the paradoxical years of 1891-1897, "when gold had flooded into Europe and prices failed to rise," a problem that also vexed Keynes. The answer to the conundrum, in the nineteenth century as well as in earlier periods, lay in changes in monetary velocity. In the late seventeenth century, as well as in the 1890s, large amounts of gold and currency were going unused because investors and consumers chose to hold their money, not spend it. In contrast, in the sixteenth and early seventeenth centuries investors and consumers were spending their available funds at a frantic rate and seeking more, evidenced, as we shall discuss in the next section, by the expansion of markets and credit facilities to support more extensive and more specialized trade. These changes in velocity, accompanying changes in the organization of trade, were a crucial factor in sustaining the Price Revolution, and in its cessation. Recently, Bordo and Jonung (1986) have presented evidence that even since 1900, there have been long swings in the velocity of money accompanying changes in economic organization.

To sum up, the quantity theory of money fails as an explanation for the long waves of prices. Clearly, we must look well beyond simple changes in bullion or money stocks alone to understand the swings in purchasing power, and the source of the price movements, of the early modern period. In particular, we shall return to the issue of what lay behind the evidently large changes in monetary velocity.

VIII. A SYNTHETIC MODEL: THE CAUSES OF LONG WAVES IN EARLY MODERN ECONOMIES

Let us begin with the proposition that mortality is exogenous. Its long fluctuations then drive long swings in population. In a simple, premarket economy, with no specialized producers and no concentration of landholding, the result of falling mortality would be a search for new land, or failing that, a general decline in living standards. In a market economy with limited arable land, population fluctuations have more complex effects. First, as population grows, so does the market for manufactured goods, leading to opportunities for workers unable to obtain land. To the extent that producers of manufactures congregate in towns and cities, and trade between urban and rural producers increases, the demand for media of exchange will also increase. Some of this may be met by increases in the specie money supply, but much will be met by increases in the provision of credit. Note that this only requires commercialization, not capitalist organization—the effect is the same whether independent artisans or small workshops are supplying the manufactures, and whether hired agricultural laborers or share croppers or dues-paying tenants are working the land.

Let us look more closely at the interplay of population and economic movements to see how patterns unfold. Miskimin (1975) has suggested that we consider changes in credit and debasement of the coinage as increases in the velocity of the money supply, for they stretched the purchasing power of a given amount of specie. I have pointed out in an earlier paper (Goldstone, 1984) that enormous potential for increases in velocity were provided by changes in market structure at a time of rapid urbanization and economic specialization. Let us examine how these factors might better account for the data on price trends.

The modern period exhibited a vast expansion of credit, largely through private sources. Paper instruments were widely used by merchants in the sixteenth and seventeenth centuries (Parker, 1974, p. 531; Challis, 1978, p. 188). "Traders . . . could carry on business almost entirely without a floating capital of money, [as] bills of exchange were already in frequent use as a method of settling accounts" (Meuvret, 1972, p. 93). Even local merchants frequently let their customers run tallies at the town shop or alehouse, and settled at long intervals (Van der Wee, 1977, pp. 300-301). This was not unique to Europe, for the Ottoman empire also showed a considerable level of merchant credit use in this period (Jennings, 1973). Government bonds were also traded. Kiernan (1980, p. 28) notes that in Spain, "annuity bonds or *juros* . . . changed hands among people in want of ready money, and came to form a sort of depreciating paper currency." In addition, base metal tokens were issued by innkeepers, bakers, and brewers in many towns for small denomination transactions; these circulated over distances of a few miles (Mathias, 1979, p. 191; Challis, 1978, pp. 207-210).

Another source of purchasing power was the vast increase in the velocity of money that came from the process of greater urbanization and specialization in trade. I have previously shown using network theory (Goldstone, 1984) that in dense, occupationally specialized trading networks, the potential velocity of circulation of coinage goes up as the *square* of the size of the network, even though the quantity of goods and services traded increases only linearly. This is because the *paths of possible exchange* between purchasing parties increase as the square of the number of trading parties. The number of paths of exchange depends on the structure of the market, not on the volume of goods being traded. In denser trading networks, coin circulates more rapidly to purchase a given volume of goods in a given time period, as a larger number of small, specialized transactions take the place of fewer, larger ones. Thus as the number of trading paths increases, the flow of money through the system is speeded up. The development and expansion of specialized dense trading networks, as arose during the expansion of cities and market towns, would therefore have augmented the velocity of the money supply, independently of changes in the volume of goods marketed, underwriting a vast increase in purchasing power.

Changing organization of the economy—urbanization and the growing volume and sophistication of exchange—thus created its own instruments of purchasing power, through increases in velocity and credit. The process would unfold as follows: as population grew, demand for scarce goods, particularly foodstuffs, increased. Populations would draw upon credit to purchase food, and as demand grew faster than supply, prices would begin to rise. At the same time, urbanization and increased trade density meant that the existing coin and credit instruments circulated more rapidly. (Or viewed in terms of desire to hold money, as buyers and sellers made more specialized and more frequent purchases, their need to hold money for long periods and infrequent purchases declined). This greater velocity of circulation, however, was unmatched by an increase in the supply of grain (Q), which was constrained by limited land and agrarian technique. Thus, V tended to increase with the increased size, urbanization, and market participation of the population, while Q lagged. In other words, though we can grant that both V and Q responded to population growth, V was more elastic with respect to population growth than Q because V increased readily with increased urbanization and denser market activity, while Q was sharply resource-constrained.

Let me add that the evidence for a lagging Q is strong and independent. We noted above that during the period of rising prices, the real wages of laborers in England, France, the Ottoman Empire, and China all fell sharply, suggesting a marked fall in per capita food consumption. Moreover, local studies of agrarian output in England, China, and the Ottoman empire show that grain production or the land in cultivation, though increasing in the sixteenth century, lagged considerably behind population growth (Appleby, 1975a; Skipp, 1978; Perkins, 1969; Cook, 1972; Jennings, 1983).

Of course, the production of manufactured goods was not as constrained as that of agricultural commodities, for the major constraint on their production was labor, not land. Thus population growth allowed a greater increase in manufactures. Not surprisingly, therefore, the rate of price increase for manufactured goods was considerably less than for foodstuffs. As noted, Malthusian/Ricardian factors explain these relative price shifts.

But it was the ratio of V/Q, controlled by a "loose" V which responded exponentially to population increases, and a "sticky" Q, rather than a broad increase in M, that was responsible for movements in the overall price level. If we look at the period of stagnant or declining prices after 1650, the velocity model again proves superior. For after 1650, population growth and urbanization slowed; this ended much of the earlier impetus for increases in V which had stemmed from expanding demand for basic foodstuffs fueled by increases in credit, and from changes in market structure due to rapid urbanization. On the other hand, Q increased considerably, due to both increased trade, which raised the supply of commodities available to consumers, and increased output as agrarian productivity improved due to adoption of new crops and rotations. Thus the ratio of V/Q would likely decline. This could offset the increases in M that might have occurred due to the continued influx of bullion into Europe and Asia (although most of this, as we have seen, likely went to ornament and hoards rather than into the money supply). In short, we would expect that after 1650 prices could remain stable despite massive silver imports, due to increases in production and to cessation of some of the forces which had earlier created massive velocity increases. Changes in market structure, demand, and credit, largely driven by population growth or stability, thus appear to account for the long waves of prices.

What happened to the workers in this sequence? It appears from European wage series that nominal wages tended to be "set," whether by guild or custom, and adjust only at long intervals (Phelps Brown and Hopkins, 1962a, 1962b). Thus, as population expands and prices rise, real wages will tend to fall. Employers may then come under pressure to raise the nominal wage. Yet this will simply increase purchasing power; and to the extent that food production still lags, prices will simply further increase. Moreover, as larger and denser trading networks grow, and are dominated by small, frequent, specialized transactions which rapidly circulate money, then the velocity of money will also increase, multiplying the impact of increases in credit or coinage. Prices will thus continue to rise, and workers' nominal wages will fall still further behind. Real wages will thus continue to fall while prices steadily move upward.

Let us now assume an exogenous rise in mortality, so that population growth halts. If land productivity shows any improvement, and if the population is stable and food demand is inelastic, there will now be a gain in supply relative to demand. For workers, this is a boon. For given their "sticky" nominal wages, the fall in food prices creates a gain in real incomes, which in turn stimulates the market for manufactures, thus providing an incentive for production. And as the labor supply is now fixed, the demand for labor will be firm. The relative price movements will thus be up for labor and manufactures, down for land and its products. If population stagnation halts the growth of trade networks, monetary velocity may stabilize. And the general price level, as increases in Q outpace increases in V, is then likely to fall. Moreover, with prices declining, and real incomes rising, it becomes both profitable and possible to hold cash balances; thus much money may be held even by wage earners, who previously, when real incomes were falling and prices rising, would have found it difficult or impossible to do so. This would accelerate the decline in the velocity of money, reinforcing the downward pressure on the general price level. Thus a new pattern—higher real wages, but a declining general price level, would result. A shift in mortality that increases the population would then repeat the earlier pattern and commence a new wave.

The key assumptions of this model are as follows:

1. Agricultural productivity tends to increase slowly, but during times of rising population, this increase is outstripped by the growth of the labor force;
2. a rising population creates a surplus of labor which migrates to cities, fueling urbanization;
3. rising urban populations create denser trading and credit networks that boost the velocity of circulation of the money supply; and
4. nominal wages tend to be "sticky," so that new laborers are hired at the prevailing wage nominal wage rate.

Given these assumptions, exogenous fluctuations in population will produce all the relative and absolute price, wage, and demographic patterns observed during the early modern long waves, *without* dependence on increases in the bullion supply, or on the particular form of labor employment. This model also avoids a simple Malthusian view of mortality increase as chiefly a consequence of population growth, instead taking mortality as exogenous, and variable fertility as the population's means of adjusting to changes in mortality.

IX. CONCLUSION

Monetarist, Marxist, and simple Malthusian explanations of the long waves all fail, because they focus on "one cause" type processes. Explaining the long waves requires a combination of factors, including mortality shifts, urbanization and credit structures. Long waves were produced when the ebb and flow of disease impinged on a particular form of economic organization—an agrarian market economy with limited land, a rapidly developing commercial sector, and a labor market with "sticky" nominal wages. It was the combination of specific demographic forces and structural constraints that produced the long waves. What are the implications of this view for the study of later business cycles? Clearly, the key factors in this model no longer apply after 1800. Scientific disease control and birth control mean that population is no longer at the mercy of climate-driven disease waves. Modern population growth rates have risen in the developing world (and fallen in many parts of the industrialized world) to ranges well outside of those normal in the early modern period. In addition, capital intensive farming and the expansion of the industrial sector mean that labor productivity no longer falls automatically with population growth. Finally, the advent of modern banking means that central government decisions, not merely the density of urban trade networks, can affect the velocity of circulation of money. It thus would seem that the conditions for the long waves of the early modern period no longer apply.

In a strict sense, this is true. The mortality-driven waves of population and prices that characterized the period before 1800 are probably a thing of the past. Yet the general principles behind such models may still be active. That is, dynamic forces, such as the development of new products or markets, may give rise to long waves if the response of the economy is "sticky" in some aspect. As Hughes pointed out in his 1968 paper, such stickiness in the discount rate of the Bank of England likely was responsible for turning long-term shifts in the natural rate of interest—a structural change—into long waves of price inflation and recession. In America, the "stickiness" of fiscal policy—which political factors often constrain to be too loose or too tight—may have the same effect. To the extent that labor markets and money markets prove sticky, and to the extent that the economy is still subject to exogenous, even demographic, shifts—such as posed after World War II by the baby boom—long waves in prices and wages are liable to persist. And, as for earlier long waves, their explanation will depend on identifying how particular patterns of economic organization respond to impinging forces. No single-factor explanation is likely to be satisfying, or helpful, any more for the future than for the past.

APPENDIX

The quantity and quality of the data behind the simple lines in the figures varies enormously. However, the general *shape* of the key population and price curves is robust, being found in a great variety of regional and local studies of population, prices, and real wages. Thus, although the magnitude of the rise and fall in different areas may be considered only approximate, the general pattern of the cycles of population and prices—rise across the sixteenth century, inflection point in early seventeenth century, stability or decline until renewed rise in early eighteenth century—can be considered firm and robust. For a more exhaustive discussion of the local studies and available data, see Goldstone (1991).

The data has been greatly simplified for presentation. Where the source provided annual data, I computed a decadal average for the years 1500-1509, 1550-1559, 1600-1609, 1650-1659, 1700-1709, 1750-1759, and 1800-1809, and used these points. For France, however, the decade 1780-89 was used in lieu of 1800-1809, to capture the "end" of the trend under the Old Regime. Where decadal, or less frequent data was provided, I generally used the figure for the date closest to that shown on the graph. In addition, wherever the decadal data was not "smooth"—that is, if there were major fluctuations so that data for a single decade would fail to represent the long-term trend, I averaged two, or if necessary, three decades around the point shown in the Figures.

REFERENCES

Appleby, A. (1975). "Agrarian Capitalism or Seigneurial Reaction? The Northwest of England." *American Historical Review* 4: 20-23.

Atwell, W.S. (1977). "Notes on Silver, Foreign Trade, and the Late Ming Economy." *Ch'ing shih wen-t'i* 3(1): 1-33.

Atwell, W.S. (1982). "International Bullion Flows and the Chinese Economy *circa* 1530-1650." *Past & Present* 95: 68-90.

Barkan, O.L. (1975). "The Price Revolution of the Sixteenth Century: A Turning Point in the Economic History of the Near East." *International Journal of Middle East Studies* 6(1): 3-28.

Baulant, M. (1972). "Grain Prices in Paris, 1431-1788." Pp. 22-41 in *Social Historians in Contemporary France: Essays from Annales*, edited by M. Ferro. New York: Harper & Row.

Baehrel, R. (1961). *Une Croissance: la Bas-Provence rurale (fin du XIV siecle-1789). Essai d'Economie historique statistique* (*A Case of Expansion: Rural Lower Provence* [*Late 14th Century to 1789*]. *An Esssay in Quantitative Economic History*). Paris: S.E.V.P.E.N.

Beier, L.A., and Finlay, R.A. (Eds.) (1986). *London 1500-1700: The Making of the Metropolis.* London: Longman.

Bogucka, M. (1980), "The Role of the Baltic Trade in European Development from the XVIth to the XVIIIth Centuries." *Journal of European Economic History* 9: 27-35.

Bordo, M. D., and Jonung, L. (1987). *The Long-Run Behavior of the Income Velocity of Money: The International Evidence.* Cambridge: Cambridge University Press.

Braudel, F. (1967). *Capitalism and Material Life 1400-1800.* Translated by M. Kochan. New York: Harper & Row.

Brennig, J. J. (1983), "Silver in Seventeenth Century Surat: Monetary Circulation and the Price Revolution in Mughal India." Pp. 477-496 in *Precious Metals in the Later Medieval and Early Modern World*, edited by J.F. Richards. Durham, NC: Carolinas Academic Press.

Bruijn, J.R., Gaashra, F.S., and Schöffler, I. (Eds.). (1979). *Dutch-Asiatic Shipping in the 17th and 18th Centuries.* The Hague: Martinus Nihoff.

Burke, E. (1955). *Reflections on the Revolution in France.* Edited by Thomas Mahoney. Indianapolis: Bobbs-Merrill.

Cameron, R. (1973). "The Logistics of Economic Growth: A Note on Historical Periodization." *Journal of European Economic History* 2: 145-148.

Cartier, M. (1969). "Notes sur l'histoire des prix en Chine du XIVe au XVIIe siècle" ("Notes on the History of Prices in China from the 14th to 17th Centuries"). *Annales, E.S.C.*, 24(4): 876-879.

Cartier, M. (1981). "Les Importations de Metaux Monetaires en Chine: Essai Sur la Conjoncture Chinoise" ("Imports of Buillion into China: An Essay on the Chinese Crisis"). *Annales E.S.C.*, 36(3): 454-466.

Challis, C. (1978). *The Tudor Coinage*. Manchester: Manchester University Press.

Chambers, J.D. (1972). *Population, Economy, and Society in Pre-Industrial England*. London: Oxford University Press.

Chaudhuri, K. (1963). "The East India Company and the Export of Treasure: the Early Seventeenth Century." *Economic History Review*, 16(2nd ser.): 23-38.

Chaudhuri, K. (1968). "Treasure and Trade Balances: The East India Company's Export Trade 1660-1720." *Economic History Review*, 21: 480-502.

Cipolla, C. (1972). "The So-called 'Price Revolution': Reflections on the Italian Situation." Pp. 43-46 in *Economy and Society in Modern Europe: Essays from Annales*, edited by P. Burke. New York: Harper & Row.

Coleman, D. (1977). *The Economy of England 1450-1750*. Oxford: Oxford University Press.

Cook, M.A. (1972). *Population Pressure in Rural Anatolia 1450-1600*. New York: Oxford University Press.

Cross, H.E. (1983). "South American Bullion Production and Export 1550-1750." Pp. 397-423 in *Precious Metals in the Later Medieval and Early Modern World*, edited by J.F. Richards. Durham, NC: Carolinas Academic Press.

de Vries, J. (1984). *European Urbanization 1500-1800*. Cambridge, MA: Harvard University Press.

Dols, M.W. (1979). "The Second Plague Pandemic and Its Recurrences in the Middle East: 1347-1894." *Journal of the Economic and Social History of the Orient*, 22: 162-189.

Dunstan, H. (1975). "The Late Ming Epidemics: A Preliminary Survey." *Ch'ing-shih wen't'i*, 3: 1-59.

Dupâquier, J. (1979). *La population française aux XVIIe et XVIIIe siècles* (*The French Population in the 17th and 18th Centuries*). Paris: Presses Universitaires de France.

Durand, Y. (1966). "Rechêrches sur les salaires de maçons à Paris au XVIIIe siècle" ("Research on the Salaries of Masons in Paris in the 18th Century"). *Revue d'histoire economique et sociale*, 44: 468-480.

Everitt, A. (1967). "The Marketing of Agricultural Produce." Pp. 446-592 in *The Agrarian History of England and Wales: 1500-1640*, edited by J. Thirsk. Cambridge: Cambridge University Press.

Fisher, I. (1911). *The Purchasing Power of Money*. London: Macmillan.

Flynn, D. (1978). "A New Perspective on the Spanish Price Revolution: The Monetary Approach to the Balance of Payments." *Explorations in Economic History*, 15: 388-406.

Faroqhi, S. (1984). *Towns and Townsmen in Ottoman Anatolia*. New York: Cambridge University Press.

Galloway, P. (1986). "Long Term Fluctuations in Climate and Population." *Population and Development Review*, 12: 1-24.

Geiss, J.P. (1969). *Peking Under the Ming 1368-1644*. Ph.D. Dissertation, Princeton University.

Glassman, D., and Redish, A. (1985). "New Estimates of the Money Stock in France 1493-1680." *Journal of Economic History*, 45: 31-46.

Goldstone, J.A. (1984). "Urbanization and Inflation: Lessons from the English Price Revolution of the Sixteenth and Seventeenth Centuries." *American Journal of Sociology*, 89(5): 1122-1160.

Goldstone, J.A. (1986). "The Demographic Revolution in England: A Reexamination." *Population Studies*, 49: 5-33.

Goldstone, J.A. (1991). *Revolution and Rebellion in the Early Modern World.* Berkeley, CA: University of California Press.

Gordus, A., and Gordus, J.P. (1981). "Potosi Silver and Coinage in Early Modern Europe." Pp. 225-241 in *Precious Metals in the Age of Expansion: Papers of the XIVth International Congress of the Historical Sciences*, edited by H. Kellenbenz. Stuttgart: Klett-Cotta.

Gottfried, R.S. (1978). *Epidemic Disease in Fifteenth Century England: The Medical Response and the Demographic Consequences.* New Brunswick, NJ: Rutgers University Press.

Hamilton, E. (1934). *American Treasure and the Price Revolution in Spain.* Cambridge, MA: Harvard University Press.

Hammarström, I. (1957). "The 'Price Revolution' of the Sixteenth Century: Some Swedish Evidence." *Scandinavian Economic History Review* 5: 118-54.

Hatcher, J. (1977). *Plague, Population and the English Economy 1348-1530.* London: Macmillan.

Hobsbawm, E. (1965). "The Crisis of the Seventeenth Century." Pp. 5-58 in *Crisis in Europe*, edited by T. Aston. London: Routledge.

Hollingsworth, T.H. (1965). *The Demography of the English Peerage.* London: London School of Economics.

Hoskins, W. (1964). "Harvest Fluctuations and English Economic History 1480-1619." *Agricultural History Review*, 12: 28-46.

Hoskins, W. (1968). "Harvest Fluctuations and English Economic History 1620-1759." *Agricultural History Review*, 16: 15-31.

Hoszowski, S. (1972). "Central Europe and the Sixteenth and Seventeenth Century Price Revolution." Pp. 85-103 in *Economy and Society in Modern Europe: Essays from Annales*, edited by P. Burke. New York: Harper & Row.

Hughes, J.R.T. (1968), "Wicksell on the Facts: Prices and Interest Rates, 1844 to 1914." Pp. 215-255 in *Value, Capital, and Growth: Papers in Honour of Sir John Hicks*, edited by J.N. Wolfe. Edinburgh: Edinburgh University Press.

Innes, R.L. (1980). *The Door Ajar: Japan's Foreign Trade in the Seventeenth Century.* Ph.D. Dissertation, University of Michigan.

Jeannin, P. (1982). "The Sea-borne and Overland Trade Routes of Northern Europe in the XVIth and XVIIth Centuries." *Journal of European Economic History*, 11: 5-60.

Jennings, R.C. (1973). "Loan and Credit in Early 17th Century Judicial Records—The Sharia Court of Anatolian Kayseri." *Journal of the Economic and Social History of the Orient*, 16: 168-216.

Jennings, R.C. (1976). "Urban Population in Anatolia in the Sixteenth Century." *International Journal of Middle East Studies*, 7: 21-57.

Jennings, R.C. (1983). "The Population, Society, and Economy of the Region of Erciyes dagi in the 16th Century." Pp. 149-250 in *Contributions a l'histoire economique et sociale de l'empire Ottoman* (*Contributions to the Economic and Social History of the Ottoman Empire*), edited by O.L. Barkan. Leuven: Editions Peeters.

Jones, A.H.M. (1974). *The Roman Economy.* Edited by P.A. Brunt. Oxford: Basil Blackwell.

Kiernan, V. (1980). *State and Society in Europe 1550-1650.* Oxford: Basil Blackwell.

Kiss, I. (1980). "Money, Prices, Values, and Purchasing Power from the XVIth to the XVIIIth Century." *Journal of European Economic History*, 9: 459-490.

Kondratieff, N.C. (1950). "The Long Waves in Economic Life." Pp. 20-42 in *Readings in Business Cycle Theory.* Selected by a Committee of the American Economic Association. London: George Allen & Unwin.

Kussmaul, A. (1981). *Servants in Husbandry in Early Modern England.* Cambridge: Cambridge University Press.

Labrousse, C.E. (1970). *Le Prix du Froment en France au temps de la monnaie stable* (*1726-1913*) (*The Price of Wheat in France in the Era of Stable Money* [*1726-1913*]). Paris: S.E.V.P.E.N.

Labrousse, C.E. (1984). *Equisse du mouvement des prix et des revenus en France au XVIIIe siècle* (*A Sketch of the Movement of Prices and Revenues in France in the 18th Century*), 2 vols. Paris: Editions des archives contemporaines.

Lebrun, F. (1980). "Les crises demographiques en France aux XVIIe et XVIIIe siècles ("Demographic Crises in France in the 17th and 18th Centuries"). *Annales, E.S.C.*, 35: 205-234.

Lee, R. (1985). "Population Homeostasis and English Demographic History." *Journal of Interdisciplinary History*, 15: 35-60.

Lee, W.R. (Ed.). (1979). *European Demography and Economic Growth*. New York: St. Martin's Press.

Le Roy Ladurie, I. (1981). *The Mind and Method of the Historian*. Translated by Sian and Ben Reynolds. Sussex, U.K.: Harvester Press.

Le Roy Ladurie, I. (1974). *The Peasants of Languedoc*. Translated by John Day. Urbana: University of Illinois Press.

Le Roy Ladurie, I. (1987). *The French Peasantry 1450-1660*. Translated by Alan Sheridan. Berkeley, CA: University of California Press.

Levy, C., and Henry, L. (1960). "Ducs et pairs sous l'Ancien Régime" ("Dukes and Peers under the Old Regime"). *Population*, 15: 807-30.

Lindert, P. (1985). "English Population, Wages, and Prices 1541-1913." *Journal of Interdisciplinary History* 15, 609-634.

Liu, P., and Huang, K. (1977). "Population Change and Economic Development in Mainland China since 1400." Pp. 61-81 in *Modern Chinese Economic History*, edited by C. Hou and T. Yu. Taibei: Institute of Economics, Academia Sinica.

McNeill, W. (1977). *Plagues and Peoples*. New York: Doubleday.

Malthus, T. (1951). *Principles of Political Economy*. New York: Augustus M. Kelley.

Mandel, E. (1980). *Long Waves of Capitalist Development: The Marxist Interpretation*. Cambridge: Cambridge University Press.

Mantran, R. (1962). *Istanbul dans la seconde moitié du XVIIe siècle* (*Istanbul in the Second Half of the 17th Century*). Paris: Librarie Adrien Maisonneuve.

Mathias, P. (1979). "The People's Money in the Eighteenth Century: The Royal Mint, Trade Tokens and the Economy." Pp. 190-208 in *The Transformation of England: Essays in the Economic and Social History of England in the Eighteenth Century*, edited by Peter Mathias. New York: Columbia University Press.

Mathiez, A. (1928). *The French Revolution*. Translated by Catherine Phillips. New York: Knopf.

Meuvret, J. (1974). "Monetary Circulation and the Use of Coinage in Sixteenth and Seventeenth Century France." Pp. 89-90 in *Essays in European Economic History 1500-1800*, edited by Peter Earle. Oxford: Clarendon Press.

Miskimin, H. (1975). "Population Growth and the Price Revolution in England." *Journal of European Economic History*, 4: 179-86.

Miskimin, H. (1977). *The Economy of Later Renaissance Europe 1460-1600*. Cambridge: Cambridge University Press.

Morineau, M. (1968). "De quel realite l'histoire de prix est-elle le miroir?" ("Which Reality is Mirrored in the History of Prices?"). *Annales, E.S.C.*, 23: 178-205.

Morineau, M. (1985). *Incroyables Gazettes et Fabuleaux Métaux* (*Incredible Gazettes and Wonderous Metals*). Cambridge: Cambridge University Press.

Mousnier, R. (1970). "The Fronde." Pp. 131-159 in *Preconditions of Revolution in Early Modern Europe*, edited by R. Forster and J. Greene. Baltimore: Johns Hopkins University Press.

Naff, T. (1977). "The Central Administration, the Provinces, and External Relations: Introduction. Pp. 3-14 in *Studies in Eighteenth Century Islamic History*, edited by T. Naff and R. Owen. Carbondale, IL: Southern Illinois University Press.

Parker, G. (1974). "The Emergence of Modern Finance in Europe 1500-1730." Pp. 527-594 in *The Fontana Economic History of Europe 2: The Sixteenth and Seventeenth Centuries*, edited by C. Cipolla. Glasgow: Collins/Fontana.

Perkins, D.D. (1969). *Agricultural Development in China 1368-1968.* Chicago: Aldine.

Phelps Brown, E., and Hopkins, S. (1957). "Wage Rates and Prices: Evidence for Population Pressure in the Sixteenth Century." *Economica*, 24 (new series): 289-306.

Phelps Brown, E., and Hopkins, S. (1962a). "Seven Centuries of Building Wages." Pp. 168-178 in *Essays in Economic History 2*, edited by E. Carus-Wilson. London: Edward Arnold.

Phelps Brown, E., and Hopkins, S. (1962b). "Seven Centuries of the Prices of Consumables, Compared with Builders' Wage-Rates." Pp. 179-196 in *Essays in Economic History 2,* edited by E. Carus-Wilson. London: Edward Arnold.

Postan, M.M., and Hatcher, J. (1978). "Population and Class Relations in Feudal Society." *Past and Present*, 78: 24-37.

Riley, J. (1984). "Monetary Growth and Price Stability: France, 1650-1700." *Journal of Interdisciplinary History*, 15: 235-254.

Riley, J. and McCusker, J. (1983). "Money Supply, Economic Growth, and the Quantity Theory of Money: France, 1650-1788." *Explorations in Economic History*, 20: 274-293.

Romano, R. (1978). "Between the Sixteenth and Seventeenth Centuries." Pp. 165-225 in *The General Crisis of the Seventeenth Century*, edited by G. Parker and L. Smith. London: Routledge & Kegan Paul.

Sahillioglu, H. (1983). "The Role of International Monetary and Metal Movements in Ottoman Monetary History 1300-1750." Pp. 269-304 in *Precious Metals in the Later Medieval and Early Modern World*, edited by J.F. Richards. Durham, NC: Carolinas Academic Press.

Schumpeter, J. (1939). *Business Cycles.* 2 vols. New York: McGraw-Hill.

Shiba, Y. (1977). "Ningpo and its Hinterland." Pp. 391-439 in *The City in Late Imperial China*, edited by G.W. Skinner. Stanford: Stanford University Press.

Simiand, F. (1932). *Les Fluctuations économiques à longue période et la crise mondiale* (*Economic Long Waves and the World Crisis*). Paris: Librarie Félix Alcan.

Skipp, V. (1978). *Crisis and Development: An Ecological Case Study of the Forest of Arden 1570-1674.* Cambridge: Cambridge University Press.

Stone, L. (1972). *The Causes of the English Revolution 1529-1642.* New York: Harper and Row.

Supple, B. (1959). *Commercial Crisis and Change in England 1600-1642.* Cambridge: Cambridge University Press.

Szàzdi, A. (1981). "Preliminary Estimates of Gold and Silver Production in America 1501-1610. Pp. 151-223 in *Precious Metals in the Age of Expansion: Papers of the XIVth International Congress of the Historical Sciences,* edited by H. Kellenbenz. Stuttgart: Klett-Cotta.

Tocqueville, A. (1955). *The Old Regime and the French Revolution.*

van Bath, and Slicher, B.H. (1963). *The Agrarian History of Western Europe 500-1850.* New York: St. Martin's Press.

Van der Wee, H. (1977). "Monetary, Credit and Banking Systems." Pp. 290-393 in *The Cambridge Economic History of Europe V: The Economic Organization of Modern Europe,* edited by E. Rich and C. Wilson. Cambridge: Cambridge University Press.

van Houtte, J. and van Buyten, L. (1977). "The Low Countries." Pp. 81-114 in *An Introduction to the Sources of European Economic History*, edited by C. Wilson and G. Parker. Ithaca, NY: Cornell University Press.

Verlinden, C., Craeybeckx, J., and Scholliers, E. (1972). "Price and Wage Movements in Belgium in the Sixteenth Century." Pp. 55-84 in *Economy and Society in Early Modern Europe: Essays from Annales*, edited by P. Burke. New York: Harper and Row.

Vilar, P. (1976). *A History of Gold and Money 1450-1920.* Translated by J. White. London: NLB.

Vogel, H. U. (1987). "Chinese Central Monetary Policy, 1644-1800." *Late Imperial China*, 8: 1-52.

Watkins, S.C., and Mencken, J. (1985). "Famines in Historical Perspective." *Population and Development Review*, 11: 647-675.

Wallerstein, I. (1984a). "Long Waves as Capitalist Process." *Review*, 7: 559-575.

Wallerstein, I. (1984b). *The Modern World System II.* New York: Academic Press.

Wiens, M. (1980). "Lord and Peasant: The Sixteenth to the Eighteenth Century." *Ming Studies*, 8: 57-64.

Woodward, D. (1981). "Wage Rates and Living Standards in Pre-Industrial England." *Past and Present*, 91: 28-44.

Wrigley, E.A. (1983). "The Growth of Population in Eighteenth Century England: A Conundrum Resolved." *Past and Present*, 98: 121-150.

Wrigley, E.A., and Schofield, R.S. (1981). *The Population History of England 1541-1871: A Reconstruction.* Cambridge, MA: Harvard University Press.

Yamamura, K., and Kamiki, T. (1983). "Silver Mines and Sung Coins—A Monetary History of Medieval and Modern Japan in International Perspective." Pp. 329-362 in *Precious Metals in the Later Medieval and Early Modern World*, edited by J.F. Richards. Durham, NC: Carolinas Academic Press.

PORTFOLIO BEHAVIOR AND ECONOMIC DEVELOPMENT IN LATE NINETEENTH-CENTURY GREAT BRITAIN AND GERMANY:

HYPOTHESES AND CONJECTURES

William P. Kennedy

I. INTRODUCTION

The curious performance of the Victorian economy has perplexed a long succession of economic observers. During the half century before World War I, (1) no major wars disturbed Britain, (2) international trade, which Britain heavily depended on, flourished to an unprecedented extent, (3) British governments, by twentieth-century standards at least, drained off, through taxation, only a small proportion of national income and spent a considerable fraction of that small proportion usefully,[1] (4) British producers and consumers operated for the most part in competitive markets generally free both from state interference and from giant enterprises wielding market power, and

Research in Economic History, Suppl. 6, pages 93-130.

ISBN: 1-55938-150-7.

(5) no obvious barriers thwarted innovation and initiative. In short, the British people, then the wealthiest in Europe, were generally free to dispose of their resources and energy in the ways they thought most fit and were actively encouraged to do so. Yet they did not appear to enjoy the fruits which this martial tranquility and invigorating economic freedom promised. Britain's struggling economy faltered further in the late nineteenth century, at a time when other countries achieved conspicuous technological advances, thereby improving or maintaining a level of economic performance already superior to Britain's (as manifested in trend rates of growth of GNP, which over a period of decades were 50-100% greater than Britain's). R.C.O. Matthews and his collaborators (1982, pp. 497-507) show that the Victorian economy's increasing difficulties culminated in an actual productivity decline in the period 1899-1913, an unprecedented event in an advanced industrial economy not locked in total war. The economic exuberance and confidence that marked Britain in the 1850s (Hughes 1960, pp. 3-33, 285-289) and again in the late 1860s and early 1870s had vanished, to be replaced by a persistent, baffling malaise that had no obvious cause and, worse, no obvious cure.

Such a puzzle could not fail to engage the wide-ranging attention of Jonathan Hughes, whose own graduate work at Oxford concerned the earlier Victorian economy which brimmed with the vitality strangely missing later in the century. In a carefully argued piece, Hughes (1968) noted the curious pattern of British real interest rates in the late nineteenth century and suggested that the legally mandated operations of the Bank of England, promulgated in the interests of stability in the Bank Act of 1844, tended to stifle British growth. Although he did not precisely specify how the Bank of England caused Britain's natural rate of interest (in the Wicksellian sense) to fall to such a low level that it was often actually below a Bank Rate which in the late nineteenth century was itself historically low, he made it clear that the Bank's influence operated through Britain's capital markets. In this manner, already motivated by an abiding interest in the process of long-term economic growth (particularly the puzzles of growth), I was introduced to the Victorian enigma. Moreover, as Stanley Reiter, Hughes' long-time friend, colleague and sometime collaborator stressed, capital markets, where investors take specific actions on the basis of imperfect information in the face of an uncertain future, are a good place to begin the investigation of curious behavior (Reiter, 1977; see also Hughes and Reiter, 1967).

One of the most prominent Victorian curiosities was the unprecedented transfer of investment funds (relative to the scale of domestic savings) from Britain to the rest of the world.[2] This vast foreign investment took place at a time of intense technological expansion, yet an expansion in which Britain conspicuously failed to participate either at home or abroad. Whereas, in the first half of the nineteenth century, Britain led the world in the introduction and diffusion of new technologies, by the late nineteenth century it was seriously lagging (Kennedy, 1987, Chapter 2). Lack of success in advanced technology areas was certainly *not* due to lack of perceived opportunity, as the structure of Britain's rapidly rising imports of manufactured goods readily attests. Moreover, so strong and sustained was the inflow of direct foreign investment that Britain achieved the distinction—usually reserved for relatively backward countries—of becoming a major host to foreign-based multinational manufacturing companies. Nor did Britain compensate for weak performance in high technology areas at home by heavy investment participation in these industries abroad; what limited investment Britain made in these areas was generally made at home, not abroad.

In such circumstances, the size of Britain's foreign investment has persistently created unease in observers from Victorian times to the present, yet this unease has generally failed to find analytical expression and thus has been neither exorcised nor justified. After all, Victorian Britain's public capital markets, the pinnacle of which was the London Stock Exchange, were the largest, deepest, and most sophisticated the world had ever known before 1914. And they were open markets, supported by an active, independent financial press and largely free of the kinds of blatant manipulation and control that blighted the capital markets, particularly the stock exchanges, of Britain's leading industrial competitors. Consequently, those observers from Victorian times to the present who have been impressed by the benefits alleged to flow from informed, competitive markets have absolved capital markets of blame for Britain's economic problems, arguing instead that Britain's performance, no matter how unprepossessing by international standards, was nevertheless as good as immutable circumstances allowed (McCloskey, 1970).

On the other hand, both Victorians and later writers have been struck by the fact that economies served by less sophisticated capital markets nevertheless managed to achieve markedly better long-term economic growth performances. This contrast was particularly stark in Germany's case. Germany was of a size that mattered in the world economy during the late nineteenth century, its dynamism too broadly based to be dismissed or ignored. Moreover, Germany did not possess the vast natural resource wealth that could comfortingly (if misleadingly) account for much of American growth without immediately inviting misgivings about Britain's inability to match it. German expansion in the late nineteenth century was not simply driven by making good a backlog of innovations already fully utilized in Britain but was prominently based on rapidly evolving domestic science-based industries—most notably electrical engineering and organic chemicals—which had never been central to Britain's own previous development but which were seen at the time as of vital importance, a judgment fully vindicated in the twentieth century. Yet this achievement occurred in a country whose stock exchanges were small, where but few domestic companies and even fewer foreign ones were quoted on them, and where the general pattern of firm financing—marked by heavy dependence first on internal sources and second, when necessary, on close bank support—more nearly resembled Britain in the first half of the nineteenth century than in the second. By 1905, nearly as many British firms (4000 of them) were annually added to the register of limited companies as existed in all Germany (Clapham, 1938, p. 222; Tilly, 1982, p. 654); the flow of German new registrations at 200-300 annually was correspondingly smaller.[3] The wide disparity of publicly available domestic financial assets between Britain and Germany was even wider for foreign assets. No center on earth could offer a wider range of cheaply traded, liquid foreign assets than London. Moreover, German nonfinancial firms literally paid for the comparative backwardness of their commercial money markets, to the point where German banks found a profitable arbitrage business in borrowing themselves in London's highly developed money markets in order to lend further to clients at home (Cottrell, 1980, p. 240).

Clearly, the puzzle of how to account for Britain's curious pattern of growth and investment invites further investigation, as Jon Hughes noted twenty years ago.[4] The invitation is enhanced by the realization that Victorian Britain's loss of economic dynamism is in broad terms not unique, although the particular details obviously are. The broad experience may be seen in eighteenth-century Holland and mid-twentieth century America, and, hence, an understanding of it has wider ramifications than may appear at first sight.[5] Most importantly, however, new developments in the economic analysis of risk offer a fresh, promising way of approaching the complex relationship between the operations of financial markets and the performance of the real underlying economy. Edelstein's pioneering work, drawing on these new developments, revealed their potential (1970, 1971, 1976, 1982). To exploit these new possibilities and to build on Edelstein's work, the approach taken in this paper is to examine the end products of capital market operations, that is, the portfolios of assets individuals were able to hold.

Technological advance and the creation and penetration of new markets underpin all sustained economic growth, yet are intrinsically risky. The rational response to risk is diversification, so that when events turn out badly, as they inevitably must from time to time, total ruin will not follow. For any given individual's tolerance of risk, inefficient means of diversification will result in some promising opportunities being lost because they appear, incorrectly, too hazardous. Such lost opportunities impose a real economic cost. Inefficient diversification also results in the costs of failure being needlessly high. Over time, the cumulative losses of promising ventures not taken up and marginally viable ventures that had to be abandoned rather than successfully rescued become great. Moreover, because the obstacles to efficient diversification will cause risky assets to be systematically mispriced relative to their intrinsic contribution to an efficient portfolio, a more favorable allocation of investment is difficult to achieve. Risk-averse wealth-holders will value risky assets with high *ex ante* expected yields too low because they are needlessly exposed to failure, and safer assets with lower *ex ante* yields too high, because they rely for security upon individual assets with low risk rather than on efficient diversification. Such a badly aligned structure of prices, when long maintained, inevitably has a devastating impact on entrepreneurial efforts to foster innovation and change. These efforts are simultaneously devalued and condemned to higher rates of failure. To the extent individuals respond rationally to price signals, entrepreneurship declines, incomes stagnate and structural rigidity becomes embedded deeply within the economy.

In technologically demanding areas of economic activity, poor diversification blunted the demand for competent entrepreneurs and trained workers in Victorian Britain just as the scope for their skills mushroomed in all directions (Locke, 1984, Chapter 1). It was this perversion of incentives, not a strange, broadly based antipathy toward the unfamiliar and complex (Landes, 1969, pp. 341-46; Wiener, 1981, Chapters 1, 2), that stunted the development of new technology in the Victoria economy. The systematic failure of capital markets to place significant resources in the hands of new-comer entrepreneurs made it possible for so many entrenched Victorian managers and former entrepreneurs to work at play and play at work, as David Landes (1969, p. 336) so vividly expressed it.

The study of diversification is a study of the consequences of the operations of an economic system; it does not constitute an explanation for those operations. However, once patterns of diversification become clear, it is possible to raise in an informed and systematic manner those questions concerning information flows, control costs, incentives, and resource allocation patterns that ultimately determine the characteristics of both diversification and economic performance. There is no presumption in the analysis here that entrepreneurs and wealth-holders as a group are stupid or irrational—quite the reverse. But intelligence and rationality are exercised within institutional bounds that entrepreneurs and wealth-holders are not free to alter unilaterally. Hence, there always exists the possibility (and often the probability) that a given institutional environment will generate signals that lead individuals to take actions that are rational and optimizing in the circumstances but are harmful to the long-term performance of the system as a whole. Moreover, because change is inevitably acutely unwelcome by some while the benefits are often diffuse in effect and remote in time, institutional reform is generally slow, expensive, and piecemeal even when the need for change is widely accepted. A debilitating yet long-lasting gridlock may thus exist despite individual rationality (Hughes, 1982).

All institutional arrangements have been, and indeed are now, flawed to some degree, although the nature of the flaws changes over time. Yet it is unlikely that in any given period all arrangements are equally flawed. International comparisons, guided by theory, constitute an essential means of identifying the unique features of a given economic system and assessing their particular contributions to the system's overall performance. In this paper, comparisons of portfolio behavior between Britain and Germany—explicit where possible, implicit where necessary—will highlight the special features of each system and clarify the linkages between capital markets and economic development in the nineteenth century. The evidence needed to realize fully the objectives of this research is not yet available, and further analytical work remains to be done. Nevertheless, sufficient material exists to sketch out a fruitful story and thereby to create a useful basis for future work.

II. SOME EVIDENCE: SCOTTISH PROBATE INVENTORIES

The British portfolios that have been examined consist of the inventories of estates passing through probate in Scotland between 1876 and 1913. The distinctive Scottish administrative system allows probate inventories to be systematically examined there whereas access to such records in England is haphazard. Hence, although it would obviously be advantageous to examine English as well as Scottish inventories, the nature of the available data dictated that the well-ordered Scottish evidence be examined separately first. It must be left to future papers to compare and contrast Scottish and English portfolio behavior.

The Scottish inventories were generally carefully recorded and covered most assets in the possession of wealth-holders at the time of death, including (a) cash on hand, (b) bank deposits, (c) the value of household effects, (d) the estimated market value of patents, insurance policies, leases, and (e) unincorporated business property, as well as the market value of all financial instruments such as the bonds, equities, loans, debentures, mortgages, and Consols that comprised much of the wealth of the time. Even assets in these categories that were worthless at the time of death but had once been valuable were recorded, generally with a note of the original purchase price. However, despite the high quality and rich detail of the data, there are some gaps and omissions in coverage which must be borne in mind while assessing them.

First, real estate holdings (apart from transferrable leaseholds) were not reported in the inventories. Because of this, landowners appear in the probate inventories to be less wealthy than they actually were, although, because wealth in Scotland was highly concentrated, the great landowners are revealed by their inventories to be rich indeed despite only a partial listing of their assets. Hence, the omission of land values is not serious as a first approximation because its consequences can be relatively easily noted.

More intractable difficulties arise from wealth-holders' responses to the gradual increase in estate duties, especially after 1894. The probate inventories were compiled for tax as well as inheritance purposes. Hence, as estate duties rose, wealth-holders almost certainly increased *inter vivos* gift-giving and lodged assets overseas where taxes were lower or non-existent, thereby altering the size and character of the recorded estates they retained until death. It appears, however, that this possibility, for all its scope for large impact, remained of relatively minor importance before 1914. For example, in one recently documented case (Moss, 1983, pp. 69-71), William Todd Lithgow was shown to have dispersed, largely for tax purposes, at least £250,000 to relatives in the five years before his comparatively early death in 1908 at age 54. Despite this effort, Lithgow still left £1,000,237, one of the largest estates recorded in the Scottish inventories before 1914, incurring a tax liability of over £100,000. Clearly tax avoidance, while a genuine factor in estate planning, was not a factor dominating all else.

This conclusion is supported by other evidence. The value of estates passing through probate did not diminish over time as estate duty increased but instead rose sharply after 1880, so that millionaire estates were recorded increasingly frequently in the late Victorian period. The men who possessed estates of this size could avail themselves of the best legal and financial advice obtainable, yet still did not choose to restrict the reported size of their estate in the obvious manner that has become familiar in Britain since 1914 (and particularly since 1945) (Rubinstein, 1981, pp. 227-246). On the other hand, while evidence of systematic tax avoidance—a legal activity and thus not likely to be disguised at considerable cost—is sparse, those known to be wealthy from other sources are in fact duly shown by the probate inventories to possess large estates. This suggests that the inconvenience of tax avoidance was widely considered more onerous than paying the comparatively light duties that ruled before 1914 (Rubinstein, 1981, p. 101). Accordingly, in most instances the inventories are a reliable indication of wealth-holding patterns at the time of death.[6] The type of asset most likely to be recorded without detail, or omitted altogether, was direct foreign investment, although assets in this category were frequently listed in detail in the inventories.

In summary, while there are difficulties with incomplete coverage in several respects which must be noted, these do not seem to be sufficiently pervasive or severe to vitiate the insights into portfolio behavior offered by the Scottish inventories in large numbers. However, whatever the reliability of the probate records themselves, there are two inherent limitations placed upon the generalizations that may be made from this information.

The first limitation arises from what may be described as life cycle considerations. Most (but not all) probate inventories belonged to elderly persons. The average age at death of the owners of the largest portfolios examined was well over sixty. Many of these people may have retired from the active management of their assets long before dying and, while retired, may have changed significantly the composition of their portfolios. Lesser wealth-holders, for whom the scope for an obvious 'retirement' was more restricted, were more likely to maintain until death some semblance of the wealth-holding patterns of their earlier years. Thus it is not straightforward to infer the portfolio behavior of the population at large from the portfolio characteristics revealed by the probate process. The limitations that arise from this consideration, however, are themselves reduced in two significant ways. First, the same life-cycle considerations that created the problem in the first place ensure that the largest portfolios will be concentrated among the elderly and that the manner in which the elderly construct their portfolios does in fact determine the allocation of a preponderant fraction of available investment resources. Moreover, a large portion—30 percent of the largest estates, falling to 16 percent for some categories of lesser ones—of the total assets of estates of all sizes was held in the wealth-holder's own firm. The inheritors of family firms, especially large ones, generally continued to hold much of their wealth in the family firm, and this tendency created a strong element of continuity in portfolio construction over time and across generations. Thus, to the extent that great wealth in particular was obtained through inheritance, as has been found to be the case for between 60 percent and 80 percent of all top British wealth-leavers for the last two centuries (Rubinstein, 1981, pp. 122-131; Harbury and Hitchens, 1979, pp. 43-52, 129-131), the composition of large estates at the time of probate is a useful guide to their structure for a long time before and afterwards. What is true of very large estates is likely to be true in merely large estates as well. It is not until the smallest estate sizes are reached that the relationship between the composition of the estate of the deceased wealth-holder and that of his heir(s) becomes problematical.

The second way life-cycle complications are reduced stems from the fact that, to the extent there was any systematic difference in portfolio behavior between wealth-leavers and inheritors, inheritors were generally more risk averse. The heirs to large fortunes tended to distance themselves from the entrepreneurial activities that created the fortunes. Thus taking both these opposing tendencies into account—on the one hand some entrepreneurs sharply reducing their venturesome investments after retirement and on the other inheritors often forsaking the demanding investments of their predecessors—it seems that an analysis of portfolios at probate is unlikely to bias downward estimates of the extent of industrial commitment in the society at large. If there is a bias at all, it tends to overstate the degree of entrepreneurial commitment of the living. Only in the unlikely situation future research shows that on average inheritors, particularly large inheritors, managed their portfolios at least as aggressively as their predecessors' would the impression conveyed by probate inventories significantly underestimate the entrepreneurial commitment of the living.

The second limitation to the inferences warranted by the probate inventories arises because the inventories do not represent intentions but outcomes recorded at a specific, possibly arbitrary, moment in time. Aside from the predictable influences of life-cycle factors, the composition of a portfolio at the time of probate may differ considerably from its composition a short while earlier, either because the wealth-holder was in the process of actively transforming his portfolio himself by trading or because he had the composition of his portfolio transformed radically for him by sudden, large price movements. Of these two possibilities, the impact of differential price movements appears more worrisome because the price of assets was surely more volatile than the rate of turnover of assets. A data base of asset prices is now being constructed. Upon completion, it will be possible to calculate the value of a given inventory for some time prior to probate and, with share turnover data, to estimate the extent of portfolio transformation through time, thereby relating the probate observations to a longer timespan.

The problems reviewed so far arise in any study that relies upon probate data to reveal portfolio behavior. Use of Scottish data to draw inferences concerning British behavior introduces a further complication: to the extent that Scotland systematically differed from the rest of Britain, Scottish-based inferences will be misleading. Nevertheless, Scottish inventories provide important clues to British wealth-holding behavior. First, Scotland as a whole made up a significant proportion of the aggregate British economy. The great staple industries that were the basis of the Victorian economy were well represented in Scotland as were chemicals, general engineering, and, briefly, even automobile manufacture. In terms of both size and economic composition Scotland offers an important and revealing insight into the Victorian economy. Second, comparatively little of the Scottish wealth listed in the probate inventories was invested in England. Investments were made either close to home or overseas. It is likely that English wealth-holding patterns will reveal, for similar reasons of monitoring and control, the same attachment to local industry and well-known foreign ventures found in the Scottish inventories. The general strengths and weaknesses of Scottish portfolio behavior will thus be those of English portfolio behavior as well. Finally, many of the assets listed in the probate inventories—about 22 percent by value in the larger estates, somewhat less in the smaller ones—were closely held, representing the ownership of enterprises by the immediate families of those who created and ran them. The concentration of wealth in family enterprises, however, was not a uniquely Scottish trait but was also a well-known English one. It is, therefore, plausible that the same tendencies toward concentration of local assets in entrepreneurial portfolios will be found in both England and Scotland. Thus, Scottish portfolios are unlikely to be systematically misleading in guiding inferences to British behavior.

The evidence on British portfolio behavior comes from a subset of a sample of 1140 Scottish inventories confirmed in the years 1876-1913. The overall sample frame consists of the following: (1) the ten largest estates (generally valued at more than £100,000) confirmed in Scotland in each year between 1876 and 1913, or 380 in all; plus (2) five randomly chosen observations for each year on estates confirmed at more than £20,000 but not including the ten largest, or 190 in all; plus (3) five randomly chosen observations for each year on estates confirmed at between £5,000 and £20,000, or 190 in all; plus (4) five randomly chosen observations for each year on estates confirmed at between £1,000 and £5,000, or 190 in all; plus (5) five randomly chosen observations for each year on estates confirmed at values under £1,000, or 190 in all. The sample frame was constructed to give disproportionate coverage to the wealthy while ensuring that for each year for each lower wealth level there were sufficient observations to permit simple kinds of statistical analysis.

Because the full sample frame is still being completed, the results presented below relate only to a subset of the designated inventories and the results set out below must be considered provisional.[7] Some precautions were taken, however, in the collection of data after 1890, when the sample targets were least met, to reduce the chance that increased sample error would underestimate the extent of technologically progressive investment in Scotland. The inventories belonging to those who were both extremely wealthy and who were most likely to have invested heavily in the most technologically important activities of the period were given priority in selection. For example, the portfolios of the very wealthy Glasgow engineers in the post-1890 sample were collected while those of most rural rentiers were not.

III. PORTFOLIO BEHAVIOR IN VICTORIAN BRITAIN: SOME PRELIMINARY RESULTS

We begin by examining the structure of portfolios that contained investments in technically advanced activities. Such investments were chosen because the growth performance of any industrial economy, not least Victorian Britain's, depends on the realized rate of technological progress. Therefore, investments in technologically advanced areas during the late nineteenth century (broadly but not exclusively encompassing the automobile, chemical, and electrical and mechanical engineering industries) played a strategic role in the process of economic growth. Because investment in these areas may reasonably be considered risky *ex ante*, the efficient holding of such assets by even mildly risk-averse wealth-holders required a wide ranging effort to achieve adequate diversification. This is not, however, the behavior that is revealed in the Scottish probate inventories. Although a small minority (less than 5%) of wealth-holders had portfolios that generally combined on a broad basis assets in technologically progressive activities with safer assets, the great majority did not. Rather, the portfolios of those who did invest in technologically progressive ventures generally exhibited very substantial risk-taking, manifested by the concentration of the bulk of their assets in a narrow range of activities. This suggests that much of the difficulty encountered in attempting to diversify the turn-of-the-century Scottish economy was due not to an unwillingness of entrepreneurs to take risks, but to the fact that the risks that were taken were unnecessarily exposed to failure.

However, the paucity of technologically progressive investments should also be noted. In the aggregate, there was a marked absence of assets, even among the zero-valued ones that represented failed investment attempts, related to the most important technological opportunities of the period. (See Table 1 for additional information). Despite a very broad definition of the strategic areas of technology—including well-established activities such as ship-building, steel production and Le Blanc soda manufacture, which either did support or potentially could have supported logical attempts to diversify into new activities such as automobile manufacture or profitable chemical production—only 11.44 percent of the total recorded value of the assets of the largest estates and much lower proportions of smaller ones were committed to them. Had a stricter definition of strategic technologies been adopted, the proportions would have been markedly lower still, perhaps no more than 2-3 percent overall. Moreover, this low proportion of the value of assets in technologically progressive areas was not due to disproportionately higher rates of observed failures in them, but to lack of attempts. Among the estates of the largest wealth-holders, once valuable investments found worthless comprised only 8 of 76 (10.5%) separately listed assets in engineering and 10 of 63 (16.0%) assets in electricity supply, but 57 of 202 (28.2%) separately listed assets in gold mining and 75 of 329 (22.8%) assets in other mining ventures. And while one can find evidence of huge losses in mining and exploration ventures—such as the investment made by Archibald Coats (who died in 1912, at age 72, leaving an estate valued at £1,365,132) of £203,405 in the Glasgow and Western Exploration Company Ltd. and valued at precisely zero at the time of probate—the comparable losses in mechanical and electrical engineering run to only hundreds or thousands of pounds, not to tens or hundreds of thousands.

More damning of capital markets than evidence of excessive risk taking by the few is the virtual absence of risk taking, especially in technologically advanced areas, by the many. The capital markets' ability to channel the wealth of country landlords, merchants, textile magnates and virtually everyone else into technologically important activities was conspicuously lacking. Outside small identifiable groups, such as Glaswegian metallurgists and chemists, there was little commitment to these activities at all, and what there was more often than not was overseas rather than in Britain. Among the largest estates, the total holding of English assets was only 83.3 percent (by value) of the aggregate foreign holding. As an example, Table 2 presents a subsample (198 cases) of the 380 largest estates recorded between 1876 and 1913, restricted to 10 observations per year.

Table 1. Sectoral Breakdown of Investments and Failures

	Failures[a]	*All Others*[b]	*Total Attempts*
Unknown	0	3	3
Iron and steel	40	212	252
Engineering	8	68	76
Shipbuilding	0	18	18
Electricity	10	53	63
Telecommunications	2	88	90
Paper	10	21	31
Construction	6	71	77
Chemicals	8	93	101
Ships	11	307	318
Railways	37	2,554	2,591
Harbors, docks, and so on	3	58	61
Roads	2	22	24
Trains	5	59	64
Alcohol	2	68	70
Oil	4	75	79
Commerce	20	258	278
Consols	0	29	29
Government stock	5	303	308
Municipal	2	143	145
Local services	49	373	422
Banks, Royal, commercial	0	100	100
British Linen Bank	0	20	20
Anglo-foreign banks	4	71	75
Other banks	2	116	118
Insurance companies	6	185	191
Other financial companies	64	823	887
Coal	22	116	138
Sulphur	7	66	73
Gold	57	145	202
Other mining	46	72	118
Loans to individuals	54	653	707
Book debts	5	111	116
Undistributed estates	0	62	62
Rent due	0	234	234
Insurance policies	1	182	183
Investment companies	53	743	796
Cash	0	286	286
Deposit account	1	341	342
Current account	0	323	323
Personal effects	0	424	424
Business effects	0	155	155
Textiles	2	168	170
Total	548	10,272	10,820

Notes: [a] Failures are defined as an outcome at time of death in which the investment was worth less than 10 percent of the price paid for it. Failures are understated because an asset was not counted as a failure unless the price paid was given or the asset was considered completely worthless.

[b] Attempts are defined as separately listed assets. Thus, the holding of a bond and an equity share in a given company is counted as two attempts. Two types of bond for the same company are counted as two separate attempts. The same asset in two separate portfolios is counted as two attempts. Because successful firms tended to be more widely held than failures, this procedure understates failures relative to a procedure that counted identical assets in two or more portfolios as only one attempt.

The limited holdings of assets in technologically advanced activities may be illustrated by consideration of Sir James King's portfolio, which might reasonably have been expected, given his business contacts, occupation and location, to have been biased toward these activities in Scotland. Sir James died on October 10, 1911 at the advanced age of 81, leaving an estate in the United Kingdom of £608,436, with a further £71,600 of enumerated assets held abroad. His portfolio had 222 separately listed assets, more than any other examined. In his probate inventory he was identified as a director of the Clydesdale Bank, the Irrawaddy Flotilla Company, the British and Burmese Steam Navigation Company, Burmah Oil, and J & P Coats, among others. In each of these companies he had a substantial personal stake; for example, he held £44,245 in the equity of Burmah Oil (thus giving him an indirect but important link to two of the most important strategic industries of the period, automobiles and chemicals) and £54,386 in the equity of J & P Coats.

Sir James was also a manufacturing chemist himself although his stake in his own Huslet and Campsee Alum Company was a modest £26,017. On a much less grand scale he held assets directly in the most rapidly expanding industries of the period, but very little of it in Scotland. In the United States, he held £205 in the equity of General Motors, with a further £2,413 in General Motors first lien 6 percent gold bonds (valued at 97¾ percent of par); £3,010 in American Telephone and Telegraph Company 4 percent convertible bonds (107½ percent of par); and £3,097 in the first general mortgage 4½ percent gold bonds (103¼ percent of par) of the New York Telephone Company. In England, he held £200 in the equity (valued at par) of the Tyneside Electrical Development Company Ltd. This was significant despite its small size for Tyneside was the center of some of the most promising developments in the pre-war British electrical engineering industry. In Scotland, however, the only comparable asset was a holding worth £1,190 of the 4¼ percent mortgage debenture stock (valued at 60½ percent of par) of Argyll Ltd., presumably the floundering automobile manufacturing firm. Sir James's commitment to the most advanced industries of his time was thus highly indirect, concentrated on activities located outside Scotland, and almost entirely a product of holdings in natural resources, in his case oil.

A further prominent feature of Scottish probate behavior revealing institutional obstacles to efficient diversification was the extreme segmentation of asset choice along lines of wealth, occupation and regional location. Some safe (low variance) assets, such as first-class railway bonds, Consols, and colonial debt, which might be expected to have been important elements in the small portfolios of the cautious less wealthy, for whom transactions costs would tend to limit opportunities for diversification, turn out to be almost exclusively the property of the wealthy and very wealthy. Another notable feature of the impact of wealth level on portfolio structure was the decreased importance of both the issues and the liabilities of formal intermediaries as

Table 2. Top Ten Estates
(198 Cases)

Average estate: £347,586 of which 30.23% was in own firm and 19.29% was abroad[a]					
*Average Holdings In**	*Total* (£)	*Scotland* (£)	*England* (£)	*U. S.* (£)	*Other* (£)
(1) Manufacturing Industry					
(a) Strategic[b]	39,759 (96,383) 11.44%	33,210 (93,641) 15.00%	1,920 (5,451) 3.28%	1,063 (6,769) 5.63%	3,564 (13,881) 7.40%
(of which Metal fabrication and processing)[c]	28,998 (90,775) 8.34%	27,016 (89,982) 12.20%	798 (4,614) 1.36%	451 (5,021) 2.39%	731 (6,738) 1.52%
(b) Textiles[d]	47,292 (199,230) 13.61%	44,663 (196,861) 20.17%	162 (790) 0.28%	267 (2,313) 1.42%	2,190 (18,900) 4.55%
(c) Food, drink and household[e]	17,289 (58,391) 4.97%	11,446 (39,835) 5.17%	2,913 (20,610) 4.97%	53 (587) 0.29%	2,875 (19,579) 5.97%
(2) Commerce and Shipping	36,866 (79,584) 10.61%	29,660 (75,997) 13.39%	3,399 (16,665) 5.80%	174 (1,576) 0.93%	3,628 (13,274) 7.53%
(3) Book Debts and Business Effects	3,697 (11,780) 1.06%	2,958 (8,885) 1.34%	554 (4,616) 0.95%	51 (597) 0.27%	75 (629) 0.16%
(4) Passive Investment (public goods)					
(a) Current and deposit account	16,793 (32,471) 4.83%	11,330 (28,437) 5.12%	2,169 (11,280) 3.70%	22 (251) 0.12%	3,271 (11,900) 6.79%
(b) Railways	75,605 (141,571) 21.75%	35,376 (82,470) 15.98%	22,464 (51,102) 38.33%	10,530 (32,644) 55.76%	7,205 (19,422) 14.96%
(c) Central government bonds	18,767 (52,698) 5.40%	— — —	9,999 (45,027) 17.06%	1,184 (5,776) 6.27%	7,583 (21,731) 15.74%
(d) Bank and insurance stock	13,276 (33,083) 3.82%	8,179 (25,620) 3.69%	3,316 (15,040) 5.66%	10 (106) 0.06%	1,768 (7,214) 3.67%

(*continued*)

Table 2. (Continued)

*Average Holdings In**	*Total* (£)	*Scotland* (£)	*England* (£)	*U. S.* (£)	*Other* (£)
(5) Local Assets[f]	8,960 (20,363) 2.58%	4,856 (15,108) 2.19%	1,026 (4,802) 1.75%	562 (2,286) 2.98%	2,467 (10,190) 5.12%
(6) Investment Companies[g]	10,960 (22,618) 3.16%	1,576 (5,600) 0.71%	459 (2,084) 0.78%	4,413 (13,456) 23.37%	4,460 (12,031) 9.26%
(7) Loans to Individuals	16,190 (27,573) 4.66%	13,745 (25,507) 6.21%	866 (35,701) 1.48%	363 (3,876) 1.92%	1,023 (8,744) 2.12%
(8) Cash and Personal Effects	22,612 (68,924) 6.51%	16,099 (30,068) 7.27%	6,460 (61,889) 11.02%	5 (54) 0.03%	47 (358) 0.10%
(9) Other	19,497 (74,774) 5.61%	8,337 (30,941) 3.77%	2,893 (8,732) 4.94%	180 (936) 0.96%	8,004 (66,351) 16.62%
Total	347,586 (333,869) 100.00%	221,441 (263,530) 100.00%	58,605 (115,271) 100.00%	18,884 (43,375) 100.00%	48,168 (86,990) 100.00%

Notes:

* Standard deviations are in parentheses.

[a] Own firm" means *either* family firms where the individual had a controlling (or substantial) interest or a firm where the individual served as a director or manager, or otherwise had a close executive connection, but did not necessarily possess a controlling or even substantial interest. For most individuals, the family firm comprised the great bulk of the wealth given in this category. The geographical location of the holding was determined by the location of the physical asset involved (e.g., a railroad or manufacturing plant), or, where a physical asset was not necessarily involved, as in a government bond or loan to an individual, where the financial instrument originated. Where the location of the physical asset or originator of the financial instrument was unknown, the allocation was made to Scotland if the asset claim were located in Scotland at the time of probate or to England if the asset claim were located there at the time of probate. If the asset claim 5 were known to relate to foreign assets, individuals or institutions, but the precise location were unknown or were distributed among several countries, the allocation was made to the "other" category. In the event of inaccuracies, this procedure would bias upwards the Scottish and English share of assets and bias downward the foreign share.

[b] This category is comprised of iron and steel manufacture; mechanical and electrical engineering (including shipbuilding); paper manufacture, printing and publishing; construction; electricity supply; telecommunications; scientific instrument manufacture; brick, cement, and glass manufacture; and chemical manufacture. Where iron and steel manfacturers and chemical manufacturers maintained mining operations as an integral part of their production process, these mining operations are *included* in this category because they could not be accurately separated out. Otherwise they are excluded. This heterogeneous group of industries is designated "strategic" because of the conspicuous role the industries played in late nineteenth century technological change and, hence, economic growth. For an extended discussion of the significance of the "strategic" industries in the economic growth of the period, see Kennedy (1987, Chapter 3). The industries designated "strategic" in the tables are a larger group of industries than those closely associated with the technological change of the period. This larger grouping is employed in order to bring together industries connected by obvious linkages to the most technologically advanced industries in addition to those industries themselves. Thus shipbuilding is included in the "strategic" group not because of its technological sophistication but because shipbuilders had the potential (which several tried to realize unsuccessfully) to manufacture automobiles, a key strategic industry of the time.

(continued)

Table 2. (Continued)

Notes: (*continued*)

[c] This category includes iron and steel making and engineering (including shipbuilding). Coal mining is excluded *except* in those cases where an iron or steel-making firm maintained coal mines to supply its own operations.

[d] This category includes all textiles, carpets, and clothing.

[e] This category includes drink, biscuits, and such items as linoleum, furniture, and boots and shoes.

[f] "Local assets" comprise municipal bonds and holdings in public utilities such as docks, harbors, gas and waterworks, cemeteries, local halls, and clubs. Electricity supply, electric trams, urban or suburban train services, and telephone companies are excluded. (See "strategic" sector definition. Local train services are included in "railway" category.)

[g] The geographical allocation of the assets of investment companies was based on available information of the disposition of the companies' portfolios. Such information is found, for example, in Burton and Corner (1968). Where the disposition of the assets of a company was unknown, the assets were allocated to the country where the head offices of the company were located. Generally this was Scotland but in some instances England. Where the assets were known to be located outside the United Kingdom but their exact foreign location was unknown or the known foreign assets were distributed across several countries, the allocation was made to the "other" category.

estate size rose. The very wealthy, in particular, were inclined to do their investing themselves rather than to entrust the task to an intermediary, even when they were directors of banks or insurance companies. Similarly, occupation was a strong determinant of portfolio choice, with little tendency for wealth-holders, especially entrepreneurs, to hold assets outside their own area of business experience and knowledge. Thus steel manufacturers tended to hold the assets of their own steel mills and of industries linked to steel, either as suppliers (such as coal or iron ore) or as customers (forges, engineering works), but comparatively little in chemical manufacture, say, or textile manufacture or in the equity of banks and insurance companies. When evidence of asset choices made across occupational lines was found, almost invariably it represented investment by engineers and chemists in traditional activities such as textile manufacture rather than the other way around, a pattern which intensified rather than reduced the commitment of resources to the established staple industries.

Reinforcing the impact of occupation on portfolio choice was the pronounced tendency for the residential location of entrepreneurs to influence portfolio behavior. Thus Glaswegian wealth-holders owned a much smaller share of the equity and fixed interest debt issue of banks and insurance companies than did Edinburgh wealth-holders. The industrial assets held by large Edinburgh wealth-holders differed sharply from those of their Glaswegian counterparts. Edinburghers held substantial amounts of assets in the light industrial sector (food, drink, and household goods), but little in heavy industry and engineering, a pattern which was the reverse of the Glaswegian wealthy. Because most industries were regionally concentrated, distinctive regional influences generally served to compound occupational segmentation of asset choice.

Such extreme segmentation in portfolio choice is itself strong evidence of formidable institutional barriers to efficient portfolio construction. Only if the risk-return characteristics of industries differing widely in technology and markets were similar would the segmentation observed in Scottish probate inventories represent only a small cost in terms of unnecessary exposure to diversifiable risk. That this was not the case might best be demonstrated more formally, utilizing financial data collected by Michael Edelstein (1970, pp. 248-300). Edelstein's data refer to a wide range of first and second class financial assets—those that paid dividends and interest with few interruptions and for which a ready market existed—and consist of the price and pay-out experience in real terms of both equity and fixed interest instruments issued by firms and governments at home and abroad. These were the assets most readily available to wealth-holders in the period 1870-1914 and also the ones with the most consistent histories of long-term appreciation and cash pay-out. While Edelstein's data is not an ideal basis for an examination of efficient portfolio behavior in the Victorian period, it nevertheless is by far the best data for this purpose currently available.[8]

In processing the data, the risk associated with each asset was calculated by the proportional variance of the actual annual outcome around the log-linear time trend of total asset value (including dividends or other payments). The latter measure, trend total asset value, was used to estimate the return earned by holding the asset. A safe asset would thus be one whose total value grew by virtually the same percentage rate each year. A risky asset would exhibit wide swings of value about the long-term trend. This procedure assumes that asset yields were exogenously determined and wealth-holders formed their expectations, and hence their investment choices, on the basis of a restricted form of foresight.[9] It is assumed that the relative structure of asset yields actually realized, as reported in Edelstein's data, as well as the variance-covariance relationship with other assets, was foreseen. Thus if the realized yield on U.S. railway debentures was twice that on domestic British railway debentures, it is assumed that wealth-holders anticipated this differential when making their portfolio choices. The procedure does *not* assume that decision makers knew, for example, when a peak or trough in the business cycle was approaching or whether at any given time the covariance of asset yields observed in the past would hold, since no asset yields were perfectly correlated. The procedure is, in this manner, capable of accommodating considerable *ex ante* uncertainty while still reflecting the historical structure of the opportunities for expansion in different sectors of the economy. The half century before 1914 was one of fairly smooth and continuous adjustments, in sharp contrast to much of the twentieth century. Therefore, the procedure of attributing expectations to accurate forecasts of relative (but not actual) yields and volatility may serve as a useful first approximation.

Given the characterizations described above of mean and variance for each asset, the following equation was minimized with respect to X_i, the portfolio shares chosen by the wealth holder:[10]

$$Z = -\alpha \sum_{i=1}^{N} X_i E_i + \sum_{i=1}^{N} \sum_{j=1}^{N} X_i X_j C_{ij} + \lambda \left(1 - \sum_{i=1}^{N} X_i\right); \tag{1}$$

where: $E\rho = \sum_{i=1}^{N} X_i E_i$ represents the expected annual portfolio yield;

$V\rho = \sum_{i=1}^{N} \sum_{j=1}^{N} X_i X_j C_{ij}$ represents the expected portfolio variance (annual basis);

$\sum_{i=1}^{N} X_i = 1$, is the "full investment" budget constraint;

X_i, $i=1, \ldots, N$ represents the average share of the portfolio comprised by the ith asset; $0 \leq X_i \leq 1$ characterizes all X_i in this paper; this assumption rules out the possibility of short sales; E_i, $i=1, \ldots, N$ represents the expected mean yield on the ith asset in the period $t=1, \ldots, T$, calculated as the product of each possible yield the asset could obtain over the entire period times the probability that a given possible yield would be realized; hence

$$\sum_{m=1}^{M} {}_iY_m \cdot P_m = E_i$$

where: ${}_iY_m$ is the mth possible yield asset i could assume for the period, $m = 1, \ldots, M$, and P_m is the probability that ${}_iY_m$ may be realized; hence

$$\sum_{m=1}^{M} P_m = 1\ ;$$

${}_iY_m$ may be defined over an interval (say $.03 \leq {}_iY_3 \leq .04$); operationally, E_i is estimated by r in the OLS regression equation, $\ln Y_t = \ln Y_0 + rt + u_t$, where $\ln Y_t$ is the natural logarithm of realized total yield (current price plus cumulated dividend), $\ln Y_0$ is the natural logarithm of initial price, t is time, and u_t is the error term associated with the tth observation;

$$C_{ij} = \frac{1}{T} \sum_{t=1}^{T} (R_{jt} - E_{jt})(R_{it} - E_{it})\ ;\ i, j = 1, \ldots, N$$

R_{jt} = actual payout yield of asset j in year t;
R_{it} = actual payout yield of asset i in year t;
E_{jt} = expected yield of asset j in year t;
E_{it} = expected yield of asset i in year t;

$0 \leq \alpha \leq L$ where α represents a parameter denoting the relative importance attached by the wealth-holder to yield compared with risk; L may be set arbitrarily large; the lower bound on α is zero, indicating a situation in which a wealth holder is indifferent to yield and seeks in his portfolio behavior only to minimize risk (indicated by the variance of portfolio yield); wealth-holders for whom larger values of α are appropriate attach greater and greater importance to expected yield; α reaches a maximum when a wealth-holder (now regarded as a plunger) places all his resources in the highest yielding asset available, eschewing all opportunities for diversification in the search for high yield; all risk averse wealth-holders will choose for themselves according to their taste for risk an α less than the maximum; hence as α increases from zero it sketches out the locus of optimal portfolio choices in mean-variance space for wealth-holders ranging from the most risk averse (who choose $\alpha=o$) to the most risk loving (who choose $\alpha=L$); λ is the Lagrangian multiplier associated with the full investment budget constraint and may be interpreted as the value of relaxing the budget constraint by a small amount.

Finding the minimum of Z will generate the $N+1$ equations necessary to solve for N values of X_i and the value of λ. N of the equations will have the form:

$$2C_{i1}X_1 + \ldots + 2C_{ii}X_i + \ldots + 2C_{iN}X_N - \lambda = \alpha E_i, \; i=1, \ldots N. \qquad (2)$$

The $N+1^{th}$ equation will be of the form of the constraint:

$$\sum_{i=1}^{N} X_i = 1.$$

Using Edelstein's data, with each activity given a mean-variance characterization as described above, Table 3 sets out the composition of four illustrative efficient portfolios, denoted by gradually rising values of α.[11] Four features are noteworthy. The most risk averse portfolio reported here, α = 0.1, which would be the most appropriate value for rentiers seeking security, had substantial holdings (about 33 percent) of domestic industrial assets, the bulk of which were in technologically progressive activities. Second, in the most risk averse portfolios, high levels of foreign investment were used to off-set domestic industrial risks, not least in technologically progressive areas, corroborating the argument that access to high-yielding foreign assets with relatively low levels of covariance with domestic British yields opened up new and valuable portfolio opportunities.

In general these opportunities were badly exploited, however. Most often high levels of foreign investment, even conservative foreign investment, were combined with safe, well-known domestic securities, thus vitiating the inherent diversification possibilities offered by foreign investment. Conversely, where industrial risk-taking was greatest, foreign investment tended to be low, again vitiating the diversification possibilities offered by access to foreign assets. The efficient combinations were almost never found in the Scottish probate inventories.

This claim may be demonstrated in two ways. First an examination of Table 2 reveals that the variance of holdings across asset categories was considerably greater than the variance of total wealth across large estates, indicating wide differences in portfolio behavior among wealthy individuals. These high coefficients of variation confirm the impression of segmentation of asset choice across wealth-holders conveyed by inspection of individual inventories.

Table 3. Composition of Efficient Portfolios (Financial Assets)

	$\alpha = 0.1$	$\alpha = 0.3$
Domestic textile equity	.0027	.0000
Domestic iron, steel, coal, and heavy fabrication equity	.1442	.2057
Domestic chemical equity	.0867	.1381
Telephone and telegraph equity	.0782	.0670
Domestic tram and bus equity	.0263	.0213
U.S. railway equity	.0000	.0239
Australian and Asian banking equity	.2606	.3443
Latin American banking equity	.0182	.1978
Foreign tramways equity	.0237	.0019
U.S. railway debentures	.3593	.0000
Total	1.0000	1.0000
Portfolio yield	.0648	.0821
Standard deviation of yield	.0410	.0667
	$\alpha = 0.7$	$\alpha = 3.7$
Domestic iron, steel, and heavy fabrication equity	.2319	.1215
Domestic chemical equity	.0911	.0000
U.S. railway equity	.1851	.0659
Latin American banking equity	.4919	.8125
Total	1.0000	1.0000
Portfolio yield	.0944	.1014
Standard deviation of yield	.1031	.1557

Note: All values of X_i are in the range of $0 \leq X_i \leq 1$; that is, no short sales are permitted.
Source: See text.

An alternative way of illustrating the deficiencies of British portfolio behavior is by examining a few large estates, the ones most likely to be professionally advised and to contain holdings of assets in technologically advanced activities. Here two are presented. First is that of Sir William Arrol, a Glasgow industrialist whose interests included automobile manufacture and who died on February 20, 1913, age 74, leaving a gross estate of 45 separately listed assets valued at £316,589. All of Sir William's assets were Scottish, with £91,035 in his own firm, Sir William Arrol and Company Ltd.(in the form of ordinary and preference shares and a loan); £10,300 in Clyde Shipbuilding and Engineering Company Ltd. £10,000 of which was in the form of 4 percent debentures); £22,053 in Stewarts and Lloyds Ltd., the steel maker and engineering concern (in the form of various classes of shares, of which ordinaries predominated); and £122,053 in J & P Coats Ltd. (in the form of various classes of shares, of which ordinaries redominated). Other large holdings consisted of £18,672 in personal effects (including cash on hand) and £14,250 of insurance policies, "mostly with Scottish Union and National Insurance Co." Most of the remainder of his assets were in 12 personal loans to named individuals resident in Scotland, presumably friends, relations and business associates; the largest was £2,453 to James McLardie, a dyer and finisher of Paisley who also served as one of the executors of Sir William's will. The great bulk of Sir William's diversification out of Glasgow engineering was thus into Scottish textiles and thread (J & P Coats). Sir William held not a single railway share of any sort.

Another useful illustration is offered by the estate of the Rt. Hon. William Wallace Hozier, Baron Newlands, who died on January 30, 1906, leaving a gross estate of 161 separately listed assets valued at £932,407. Although obviously a wealthy man, Hozier was not an active industrialist. In contrast to Sir William, Baron Newlands had large holdings of foreign assets, with no less than 51 separately listed holdings valued at £211,000 in foreign railways (in Brazil, Canada, and England but none in the United States) and a further £30,000 in colonial government fixed interest issues. He also had large holdings of Scottish railways, valued at £225,000 in 30 different listings, as well as many holdings of Scottish municipal securities valued together at more than £135,000 (none were electricity supply undertakings). Other holdings included over £60,000 in loans to named individuals, £36,000 in British government Consols, £12,000 in Bank of England stock, and £22,000 in leasehold property in England. His holdings of assets in any activity even remotely resembling 'high technology' were small to vanishing: £1,250 in the Class B debenture stock of Linotype Machinery Ltd., an English company whose debentures were valued at a deep discount to par (62½ percent of par): £466 in the 6 percent cumulative preference shares of the same company, valued at 9s.4d. per £1 par; £4,020 in National Telephone Co. Ltd., 3½ percent debenture stock at £100½ (a small premium over £100 par); £2,025 in the reference shares of Summerlee and Mossend Iron & Steel Company Ltd.. This was a markedly different pattern of wealth-holding to Sir William's, one much less exposed to industrial risks (especially those arising from new technologies), but for all that, no closer to the efficient frontier (see Table 3). Sir William's and Baron Newland's inventories were not in any way atypical in their composition, and their cases illustrate the capital market segmentation marring the British economy.

Returning now to the efficient portfolio frontier, two other interesting features emerge. As the willingness to accept risks increased (indicated by a rising value of α), up to $\alpha = 0.3$, the proportion of the total portfolio committed to domestic investment also rose, with telecommunications and chemicals being the main beneficiaries. Interestingly, as α increased, American railway debentures, a favorite choice of Scottish wealth-holders, fell out of the efficient portfolio frontier completely, in fact they appear in the efficient portfolio set *only* at $\alpha = 0.1$, suggesting that such debentures were over-priced for all but the very most (rational) conservative investors. This finding corroborates Michael Edelstein's results (1982, pp. 130-140), which showed the risk premium demanded for debentures in general to be greater than their contribution to portfolio stability.[12] Finally, even under the assumption of perfect foresight, for high values of α, domestic iron and steel fabrication appear in the efficient portfolio set, suggesting that at least some domestic industrial assets, even in circumstances of relatively low rates of domestic expansion and restricted demand, exhibited yields high enough to bear comparison with the best found abroad. It might also be noted that for values of α greater than 0.03, portfolio yield rises only slightly whereas portfolio risk (measured by the standard deviation of yield) rises sharply, suggesting that almost all wealth-holders would optimally have chosen widely diversified portfolios containing large holdings of assets in technologically progressive industries.

The evidence of portfolio compartmentalization along lines of wealth, location and occupation is far too marked and too pervasive to be attributed to data deficiencies alone. Given the characterizations of the economic opportunities of the period, very few actual portfolios were found even remotely to approximate optimality. In particular, there was no evidence of systematic use of Britain's excellent international connections to reduce risk exposure. This failure was especially marked in technologically advanced areas. The relatively few assets invested in these activities were heavily concentrated in only a small number of portfolios, which typically included few foreign assets, whereas the optimal portfolio structure (using financial data) showed risky domestic investments in areas of high technology being combined with a wide range of overseas investments, generally in well established activities. Inefficient diversification clearly did not stop wealth-holders from taking risks, but it did reduce their chances of eventual success. The explanation of this phenomenon surely lies in information and control weaknesses embedded deeply in the organization, structure and operation of British capital markets. As Adam Smith ([1776] 1976, Vol. 1, pp. 15-20, 476-478) recognized more than two centuries ago, it is always a reasonable presumption that people are rational and will make the best choices they can in the circumstances they face. Markedly undiversified portfolios such as those so readily found in Victorian Scotland thus indicate institutional shortcomings, not stupidity. These shortcomings go a long way in explaining the disappointing performance of British industry during the second Industrial Revolution.

IV. PORTFOLIO BEHAVIOR IN GERMANY: THE OUTLINES OF THE ARGUMENT

Lack of space and, at present, access only to secondary German sources permit no more than a skeletal treatment of portfolio behavior in Wilhelmine Germany. Germany shared with Britain a reliance by domestic firms on internal and personal sources of long-term finance, primarily the cash flow of existing enterprises and the wealth of friends and relatives (Cottrell, 1980, pp. 179-190, 248-262; Tilly, 1983, pp. 12, 20). But German financial intermediaries, particularly the credit banks which grew most rapidly in the period 1890-1914 (Tilly, 1983, Table 7), were much more consciously involved in industrial risk taking than were their British counterparts. This greater involvement inevitably affected the portfolio choices open to German wealth-holders. Whereas individual Britons in the early years of the twentieth century acquired the publicly issued securities of nonfinancial companies, including many of foreign origin, at a rate of approximately 6 percent to 7 percent of national product, their German counterparts acquired comparable issues, predominantly of domestic origin, at the slower rate of 4 percent. Concerning assets of financial institutions, the positions of the two countries were reversed. The British rate of acquisition of the assets of financial intermediaries in the early twentieth century was approximately 3 percent of national product whereas that of their German counterparts, at nearly 9 percent of national product, was nearly three times larger (Goldsmith, 1969, pp. 112-120). It is not surprising then that, in 1913, 14 of Germany's largest 25 incorporated enterprises were banks, including the three largest. The dominance of banking in the next 25 largest firms was nearly as great, 12 out of 25, including many of the largest in this group (Weder, 1968).[13] In contrast, the largest British bank of the period, the Midland, enters the comparable British list of 1905 at number 27, with the other British banks trailing far behind. Although the patterns in which the financial instruments of banks and other intermediaries were combined with alternative forms of wealth in private German portfolios cannot be established at this time, it is clear that the possibilities for diversification open to private wealth-holders in Germany depended, more than in Britain, on the diversification strategies pursued by banks. Accordingly, at least the institutional basis existed in Germany for more systematic diversification of wealth than was possible in Britain (Tilly, 1986, pp. 114, 140-143).

The historical process of German economic development acted to ensure that this institutional structure was used to further industrial objectives. Although the German states in 1830 lagged well behind Britain in economic development, they were nevertheless sufficiently advanced to create, and to finance, a strong demand for transport improvements. Indeed, precisely because Germany's transport system on the eve of the railroad's advent was less well developed than Britain's, railroad construction in Germany was potentially more profitable than in Britain, where nonrail transport competition was stronger. Yet Germany did not then have the extensive coal mines, iron mills and foundries which Britain had accumulated earlier as a result of long decades of relatively rapid growth and which were essential for railroad construction. To seize the opportunity for rapid development that railroads offered, Germany had to invest (proportionately) more and more quickly, than Britain had done (Fremdling, 1977). The means devised for these two tasks, the simultaneous construction of an extensive rail network and the rapid expansion of the manufacturing base, was to adapt to German conditions the French type "crédit mobilier" bank, in which a highly capitalized bank consciously and purposefully took long term, illiquid, but highly profitable positions in commercial and industrial enterprises. Thus, in the 1850s, numerous banks, such as the Schaafhausen'scher Bankverein, the Darmstadter Bank, the Disconto-Gesellschaft and the Berliner Handelsgesellschaft, involved themselves enthusiastically in the promotion of mines, foundries, iron mills, railroads and a host of other ventures.

These banks and others like them directly linked railroad and industrial financing. Operating through contacts with bank officers, railroads frequently purchased their capital equipment from suppliers who were also clients of the same bank as the railroads (Tilly, 1966, pp. 90-91). The ability to meet the financial requirements of important clients in this manner was obviously valuable to banks, for it meant that individual banks could forecast more accurately than otherwise the ebb and flow of deposits (Tilly, 1986, pp. 122-123). Not only did a bank earn a fee for handling the transactions among its clients but it would also be able to operate, for any given structure of depositors, with a lower ratio of deposits to liabilities than would be prudent in a situation where clients' investment purchases would automatically result in their banker's loss of deposits and reserves. Capital equipment suppliers benefitted from the business directed their way by their bankers and presumably railroads also benefitted through the attractive prices for equipment that they were able to obtain. So clear were the long-term benefits of these arrangements that all parties had incentives to act responsibly. Railroads would be weakened if they paid too much for inputs and similarly suppliers would be weakened if they sold their products for too little. It was in the long-term interests of banks to prevent either of these situations arising to a dangerous degree and to ensure that their clients perceived this reality as well. More generally, the banks' position at the centre of a widespread network of transactions afforded them sufficiently reliable information to guide a wide array of investment decisions consistently and knowledgeably. While banks themselves were undoubtedly the main beneficiaries of this situation, on balance their clients also gained, sometimes handsomely, from improved information and reduced uncertainty.

This institutional foundation had two key aspects, both of which directly affected the portfolio choices of German wealth-holders. First, the great German joint-stock banks were large relative to the private German banks of the time and were also large relative to their British counterparts. From their creation, German joint-stock banks had the advantages of scale on their side and, as we have seen, this meant that the financial issues of German banks constituted the largest and most obvious class of assets available to German wealth-holders. Second, the earnings that accrued to holders of bank securities were generated by a broad and diversified group of activities. The German 'Great Banks' were dedicated to using their resources not only to support the most worthy and lucrative ventures available in any given period, but also, simultaneously, to maintaining prudent diversification, avoiding, as Riesser ([1911] 1977, p. 231) expressed it, "giving too much credit to one industry, or one branch of industry, or even a single establishment." The stability this allowed, combined with a proven record of earnings growth, secured a handsome market premium for German bank shares (Tilly, 1986, pp. 140-144).

As a matter of policy the banks maintained close links with the firms whose debt issues they sold to the public. The banks saw their reputations, and hence their future ability to sell profitably further debt emissions, as dependent on the successes of the enterprises they supported (Riesser, [1911] 1977, pp. 343-347, 370). The close operating links were of two main types. The first type of link was that forged by the provision of current account credit, whereby credit balances held by a client with his bank earned interest at a rate 1 percent below the Reichsbank's rate while debit balances were charged at a rate 1 percent above the Reichbank's discount rate (Riesser, [1911] 1977, pp. 266-270). Through the flexible current account provision banks obtained an accurate picture of the state of a client's business. The current account also provided the preliminary information necessary to determine whether closer ties were desirable as well as constituting an important source of revenue (Riesser, [1911] 1977, pp. 259-275). The second type of operating link consisted of the placement by banks of their own personnel on the supervisory boards of client firms, thus assuring themselves both an "insider's" access to important business information and a means of conveying the banks' own views—which often included new information on relevant matters, gathered from other sources—directly to the top management of client firms. Gradually, the networks of interlocking directorates became even tighter and more effective as an information channel as the directors of large and successful firms secured positions of power and influence on the supervisory boards of banks.

The close operating links to industrial enterprise formed in this manner provided banks at any given moment with a wide range of useful investment possibilities as their loanable resources expanded and as their private clients pressed them for attractive assets for their own personal portfolios. On the other hand, the great banks sought to widen their deposit base in order to achieve diversification in their sources of funds as well as in their current account loan portfolios. A deposit base well diversified across geographical regions, occupations, markets and technologies had inherently greater stability than one that was more heavily concentrated in any of these categories. Moreover, as investment projects grew larger over time, banks acted to protect themselves by acting together in consortia or syndicates in order to reduce their individual risk exposures and to assure themselves, through reciprocal consideration by other banks, of access to promising new business (Riesser,

[1911] 1977, pp. 396-401). The syndication of loans and debt flotations reduced the possibility of a given bank reaping extraordinary gains as a result of fortunate contact with particularly well-placed enterprises, but it substantially reduced risks. Diversification was also aided by firms' independent attempts to establish links with a number of different banks in order to lessen their dependence on any one of them. Such maneuvering by firms also served to reduce the opportunities for individual banks to extract monopoly rents solely on the basis of their early ties to firms, when client firms were often in a much weaker bargaining position than they were to be later.

These distinctive aspects of German banking practice permitted more efficient risk-taking than was possible in Britain and created a superior range of investment alternatives. The most dramatic example of German banks' ability to force technological changes, is to be found in the history of the electrical engineering industry, where the German Great Banks played a conspicuous role in bringing about expansion (Kennedy, 1987, pp. 118-119). The bank-induced rivalry between the giants of the German electrical industry, Siemens and Halske (later Siemens-Schuckert) and AEG, benefited not only the banks themselves, as demand for current account credits and security emissions by these firms expanded, but the principal protagonists as well. Both firms were able to sustain well-above-average rates of profitable expansion down to the outbreak of the World War I and beyond. Indeed, the rapid expansion of the German electrical engineering industry gave an important boost to the entire German economy as sector after sector electrified.

Although electrical engineering affords perhaps the best example of the German banking system's ability to force the pace of technological advance, further evidence can be found in other industries. Steel fabrication is the next most obvious example. The price stability permitted by bank-inspired cartels and tariffs systematically encouraged the construction of larger steel mills in Germany than were built in Britain (Webb, 1980). These larger mills had higher fixed costs and hence generated larger losses for their owners if they were forced to shut down during a recession but were able, when operating near their optimum rate, to produce steel at substantially lower average cost than could smaller plants. The tariff-protected cartels could not shield German steel producers as a group from fluctuations in demand, but they could serve as a kind of limited term insurance scheme to spread the impact of business fluctuations among all producers according to the cartel agreement and thus relieve individual firms of the fear that their particular group of customers would reduce orders disproportionately. German economic institutions thus reduced costs and risks along a broad range of metal-using industries.

German banks also contributed to technological development on a modest scale in other industries. One obvious way in which this occurred was through the well-established practice of banks seeking to link their clients together on a supplier-customer basis whenever possible. Such practice, if appropriately pursued, would allow unusually rapid growth for a firm—especially a smaller firm without its own elaborate marketing channels—that had acquired some competitive advantage in supplying a particular input extensively used by bank clients. It would also operate to secure on favorable terms for such a firm the external resources to permit rapid expansion. With a sufficiently long planning horizon and a sufficiently well-diversified group of clients that included many users of the particular input, it would always pay a bank to support the expansion of the most efficient producers, even if others were adversely affected. Such practice would thus expose lagging firms to competitive pressure earlier than would otherwise have been the case, and would either stimulate them toward improved performance or hasten their exit from the market, in either case improving productivity.[14] In this manner, the more capable smaller firms, especially in metal working, which tended to be either neglected or disadvantaged by the Great Banks, benefitted from their activities. Even for firms not able to exploit significant economies of scale in the manner of steel producers and electrical manufacturers, the German banking system may have methodically encouraged more sustained and rational risk-taking than was forthcoming in Britain. If some of the greater risks German entrepreneurs were encouraged to take as a result of access to superior diversification opportunities resulted in technological advance, perhaps as a result of learning-by-doing, over a long period the cumulative impact would have been significant, even if each individual advance were slight.

The logic of German banking, with its relentless pursuit of both turnover and diversification, imparted a momentum which carried German banking activity from the 1870s onwards increasingly into foreign operations. The earliest moves were to provide financial services abroad to German exporters and importers. This can be seen as a logical step to encourage market diversification both for the banks themselves and for their clients. Extensive foreign trade connections represented an important means of keeping expensive plant and skilled employees profitably employed during the inevitable periods of relatively slack activity at home. Strengthening trade relations soon began to offer further investment opportunities which the great German banks, by virtue of their own patterns of development and evolution were well placed to serve. Thus, German banks, through experience and technological expertise gained at home, were in a unique position to finance a broad range of investment abroad. As long as German industry could maintain its relative position of technological leadership, foreign markets for its capital goods were virtually unlimited. As import substitution spread in those markets, German firms could offer more advanced ranges of goods for which there had been no significant demand at a previous, less developed stage. The ability to find lucrative export markets in the late nineteenth century for Germany's most advanced industries represented an important new means of diversification which significantly reduced the risks inherent in complex, large-scale investments in new technologies at home. The Great Banks with their vast resources, their trade connections, and their close ties with most domestic industries played a key role in making the most of the opportunities offered by the global spread of industrialization in the decades before 1914.

By operating both at home and abroad, in old industries and in new ones, in both routine work and in new ventures, and in projects with quick payoffs and in those slow to yield, the German banking system appears to have been instrumental in helping overcome the segmentation which was such a conspicuous feature of Scottish investment patterns. In Britain, information about and investment opportunities in promising new industries were concentrated in small groups, whereas in Germany both were widely if not equally shared and open to some degree to the investment resources of the entire nation, as the long lists of the banks supporting the great Wilhelmine electrical concerns demonstrate (Riesser, [1911] 1977, pp. 716-717). Information regarding opportunities spread only slowly from isolated group to isolated group in Britain, with some groups never being affected at all. In contrast, they tended to spread rapidly in Germany as resourceful and well-informed groups sought to ensure that they benefitted fully from new developments in activities such as electrical engineering and steel. In important instances, such vigorous arbitrage taking place in technologically fertile areas did not cause the yield on further investment to fall, but rather sustained it as new opportunities were uncovered. Whereas, in Britain, foreign investment and domestic industry were remote from and only indirectly influenced by each other, these two activities in Germany as a rule were closely and directly linked. Moreover, British management and ownership were separated by a wide gulf that encouraged abuse and often defeated beneficial collaboration; in Germany interlocking networks of active directors supported by large blocs of voting shares forged an important channel of communication and control. Thus, despite the inherent risks of the more rapid pace of technological change in Germany, investment there was better informed, better diversified and more rationally directed than in Britain, and for these reasons was actually safer as well.

The banking system of Imperial Germany performed crucial tasks of financial intermediation more efficiently and purposefully than its Victorian counterpart, but the German system was not flawless. Although on balance German capital markets nourished economic progress, it is important not to lose sight of their weaknesses. The most serious weaknesses of the German capital markets were surely the powerful conflicts of interests they generated and the absence of any reliable method for efficiently resolving them. The banks, after all, were pursuing their own interests. In some notable instances, these interests clashed with those of client firms. Such clashes occurred from the very start of investment banking, in the 1850s, as private banking interests, adopting the joint-stock corporate form, greatly expanded the scope of their operations while taking care to see that newly created or enlarged enterprises would continue to favor, or at least not interfere with, their established interests (Tilly, 1966, pp. 95-96). While in some cases this concern for existing interests created no problem, in other instances it meant that yields on new ventures were lower than they should have been, and the earnings of established enterprises were higher than they deserved to be. A flagrant example of such a conflict occurred in 1904. A dispute arose between the managers of the Phoenix Iron Works and their bankers over the terms of membership in the great steel cartel proposed in that year. The Phoenix managers clearly saw that their interests as important downstream steel finishers lay outside the cartel. Their bankers, who were in a much better position to benefit from the cartel's creation, did not wish to see such a powerful integrated firm producing and selling independently of their interests. In a bitter extraordinary meeting of share-holders, the banks and their industrial allies in the Stahlwerksverband successfully imposed their will on Phoenix to enforce participation on the cartel's terms, thereby providing a powerful and public reminder of the latent costs of bank support.

The strong support German banks provided to cartels introduced a significant anti-competitive bias into the German economy, which may have imposed a real cost offsetting to some degree the gains implied by the superior diversification possibilities. To be sure, cartels were usually of finite duration (Webb, 1980, pp. 310-11) and not all sectors were equally cartelized. Nonetheless, cartels blunted the competitive pressures that assure that technological progress diffuses rapidly among firms and that improvements in productivity are converted into lower consumer prices.

A more subtle but potentially more pervasive and more serious cost of German bank operations arose through the possibility that the banks 'creamed off' too large a share of the entrepreneurial profits of their clients, especially the profits of smaller firms that were at a particular disadvantage in negotiating terms with banks because they were less able than larger firms to make credible the threat to find alternative financial agents. Banks could exploit their position by the systematic imposition of opportunistically large charges for routine services and through the monopolistic provision of credit. Moreover, banks were frequently able to manipulate the victim firm's share price. For example a concerted move to sell a firm's shares just as the firm embarked on an expansion programme would weaken the firm's bargaining position with its bank and perhaps force it to accept otherwise objectionable loan terms. Similarly, "inside" information on a firm's improving prospects (such as the eminent receipt of a large and lucrative contract) would allow a bank to begin advantageous purchase of the firm's shares ahead of the wider market.

Because banks generally had long planning horizons there were clear limits to the extent to which they would press their advantage, since too energetic exploitation would permanently diminish, if not destroy, firms and markets that in the long run were more valuable intact than plundered. On the other hand, it is too much to believe that the future was so little discounted that no manipulation or exploitation ever took place (Tilly, 1966, p. 108). To the extent that it did occur, banks received undeserved capital gains for the risks client firms undertook. In general, however, large and prosperous firms were able to take care of themselves, either avoiding, as the great chemical firms did (Riesser, [1911] 1977, pp. 712-713, 721-725) close relations with banks, or, alternatively, devising means of exerting countervailing influence. It was comparatively small firms that were at the greatest disadvantage. Part of the disadvantage stemmed from neglect, for the Great Banks were slow to seek smaller clients likely to generate in the foreseeable future only marginally profitable business. But part stemmed from fear of active bank exploitation of a superior bargaining position, which the banks carefully sought to preserve by collusive arrangements among themselves. The consequences for the economy as a whole of the disadvantages suffered by smaller firms were limited to the extent that the majority of small firms were not in a position to expand rapidly anyway, but the penalty for neglecting or exploiting the vital few small firms that were capable of rapid growth was a serious loss of "grass roots" dynamism that caused the German economy to be more ponderous and to grow less rapidly than circumstances permitted. This is especially evident in the hesitant growth of the early German automobile industry, despite a favorable technological position and the rapid growth of markets, particularly abroad.[15]

Before 1914 it was clear that the advantages of German banks' comprehensive knowledge of German industry and commerce, coupled with an ability to achieve systematic diversification and exert widespread influence and control, outweighed the disadvantages. Although the rapid development of German industry—not least those branches with the closest bank connections—suggests that whatever abuses occurred at least took place within tolerable bounds, it is reasonable to believe that German expansion would have been even more rapid, and would have beneficially affected more industries and more firms, had there existed greater safeguards against the exploitive use of bank information and influence. Moreover, there is no reason to believe, given the grave imperfections in German capital markets, that the balance between strengths and weaknesses would forever favor expansion, even by a small margin. For Germany, just as for Victorian Britain, the possibility must always exist that flaws that cause no serious problems in one period may become more dangerous as circumstances change.

V. CONCLUSION

This paper has attempted to demonstrate that in the late nineteenth century Germany had managed to create a more effective capital market than Britain had done. While the German capital market suffered from numerous flaws, it was nevertheless on balance able to accomplish a larger concentration of resources in key sectors—especially those related to advanced technology—and to manage those resources more effectively than occurred in Britain. The most obvious manifestation of the superior German arrangements lay in the accurate and timely information they provided to key groups of investors and the opportunities for systematic diversification they offered to all wealth-holders. By these means Germany avoided the worst effects of the capital market segmentation that severely handicapped British risk-taking, leaving some Britons exposed to formidable risks, while many others, even if they too were willing to accept considerable risks, had no reliable access to investment opportunities in crucial sectors of the economy.

This argument immediately raises an obvious question. If German capital market arrangements were as superior as has been suggested here, why were they not adopted in Britain? The brief answer is that large-scale institutional change is inherently difficult. Institutional arrangements build up a momentum of their own, buttressed by those who have a deeply vested interest in the established order and who are generally better organized to defend their interests than are those who can see benefit in radical change. Often only a great crisis resulting in the utter repudiation of existing institutions creates an environment where rapid, profound change is possible. Victorian Britain was spared such trauma and consequently no radical changes took place, although efforts were made to alter or reform crucial aspects of British capital market operations in the years after 1860.

These efforts at alteration and reform generally took one of two directions. The first, involved changes in banking practice to permit the kinds of industrial involvement that were so attractive in the German states and elsewhere on the Continent. This initiative, however, was short-lived. In the early 1860s, a number of discount houses, some with considerable financial backing, enthusiastically took up long-term industrial finance (King, 1936, pp. 232-259). With the Gurney crisis of 1866, and the unyielding stance subsequently taken by the Bank of England towards illiquid finance houses, this line of development abruptly ended, to be followed, especially after 1878, by ever more cautious behavior by all financial institutions except the most fraudulent or incompetent (Clapham, 1932, pp. 375-377; Kennedy, 1987, pp. 120-134). Increasingly, the Bank of England set the tone, and, as Hughes (1968) noted, that tone bespoke caution and liquidity. While this stance did indeed promote the stability it was intended to, it did so only at the cost of inhibiting beneficial (and occasionally disruptive) change. Here surely was one vital channel by which the Bank of England systematically dampened expansion in the late nineteenth century.

Again, the German comparison is illuminating. In order to undertake extensive investment with a reasonable chance of success, not only did the great German universal banks require a stronger capital base than did the great

British clearing banks, which focussed on prudent short-term lending (Riesser, [1911] 1977, pp. 460-472; Tilly, 1986, pp. 140-142), they also increasingly required the consistent, reliable support of the central bank, a role filled from 1876 by the Reichsbank. Unlike the Bank of England, the Reichsbank kept the specification of the financial instruments eligible for discount invariant over the business cycle, despite heavy demands at times of crisis by large banks deeply committed to industrial clients (McGouldrick, 1984, pp. 334-339). Reichsbank support may have been expensive, but it was available on known, secure terms. Solid, but temporarily embarrassed, German houses did not fear being spurned by their lender of last resort like their British counterparts did. Moreover, the gulf between German and British institutional arrangements before 1914 was too great to be bridged by incremental changes. Despite growing British unease about economic performance, no major institutional reforms in banking practice occurred before World War I. Changes only began to come in the later 1920s when the Bank of England under Montague Norman began to orchestrate financial support for troubled firms.

The second main direction of Victorian alteration and reform by-passed the banking system altogether and focussed instead on changes in company law that were generally intended to improve the quality of publicly available information, thereby making company managers more accountable to their shareholders (Cottrell, 1980, pp. 53-75). Although some reforms in this direction occurred before 1914, usually only after fierce legislative battles, company outsiders (often including a majority of shareholders) had no reliable access to the information needed to make informed, timely judgments of a firm's management. While current debates on corporate disclosure, take-over bidding, leveraged buy-outs and insider trading reveal no consensus today on how these activities are best regulated, they are at least recognized as being of fundamental importance and thus are considered with an intensity completely absent in the Victorian period. Although Victorian disquiet over relative economic performance was growing as the nineteenth century drew to a close—witness the flood of books such as E.E. Williams' *Made in Germany* (1896) and articles such as *The Times'* "Crisis of British Industry" (1902)—it never reached a pitch and focus that made radical reform of either banking practices or company law likely. What reforms were enacted—whether in Bank of England practice to make protection of its reserves less disruptive to industry or in company law better to inform outsiders—took place gradually and their impact was only felt gradually as well. Thus, while in retrospect Victorian capital markets appear seriously defective, the Victorians themselves had to make the best choices they could within the possibilities those markets offered. In this manner, in a complex process played out on a vast scale, Britain's sophisticated but limited capital markets trapped individually rational Victorians into collective behavior ultimately no more rewarding than that practiced in the Alaskan fish cannery so vividly described by Jonathan Hughes (1982).

ACKNOWLEDGMENTS

Parts of the research reported in this paper were supported by the Social Science Research Council of Britain, Grant HR4963 and the LSE Staff Research Fund. I gratefully acknowledge the very able research assistance of Rachel Britton, who assembled much of the data from archival sources and undertook its initial computer processing. This paper and, it is hoped, future work growing out of it, have also benefited greatly from the thorough and constructively critical comments of Joel Mokyr and two anonymous referees. Responsibility for any remaining errors are mine alone.

NOTES

1. For a recent comprehensive discussion of Victorian patterns of taxation and government spending, see Davis and Huttenback (1986: Chapter 5). These authors argue that while overall British government spending before 1914 was low by the standards of the later twentieth century, as a fraction of national income it was high by contemporary standards and much of this high expenditure, perhaps a full quarter of all British central government expenditure in the period 1860-1912, was directed towards maintaining a costly empire of dubious benefit. However, Davis and Huttenback's calculation of the relative burden of Victorian taxation hinges on their treatment of the implicit costs imposed on military conscripts in France and Germany. By valuing each conscript's annual labour at an amount equal to annual per capita rural savings, they find French and German military costs low. More plausibly, had those two nations satisfied their military manpower requirements in the open labour market as Britain did, their recorded military costs would have been far higher, at least comparable to Britain's and probably greater. Note, however, that this observation does not contradict Davis and Huttenback's argument that Britain would have been economically better off without its Empire.

2. A.K. Cairncross (1953, p. 3) conveyed well the size of the tranfer when he observed that, adjusted for the smaller size of the Victorian economy, between 1870 and 1913 Britain transferred resources overseas every six months at an average rate equivalent to all American Marshall aid extended in the years 1948-1951.

3. These figures refer to firms with full corporate status (Aktiengesellschaft), without legal restrictions on the transfer of shares. There also had existed in Germany since 1892 a more restricted form of incorporation, Gesellschaft mit beschrankter Haftung (G.m.b.H.), or private limited liability company with restriction on share transfers. Not until 1907 was a comparable form of company organization officially recognized in Britain (although in practice the form was well established long before then.) In both Germany and Britain growth of the number of private limited liability companies was rapid once legal recognition was granted (Clapham, 1938, p. 290-291; Tilly, 1982, p. 653). The importance in both countries of private limited liability companies reflects the large extent to which investment depended on personal knowledge and contacts rather than upon widely available public knowledge.

4. For a more detailed discussion of the weaknesses in Britain's economic performance in the late nineteenth century and the relationship of these weaknesses to high levels of foreign investment, see Kennedy (1987, esp. Chapters 2, 6).

5. David Landes (1969, p. 339) has noted that a link may have existed between wealthy Holland's failure to industrialize in the eighteenth century and its high level of investment overseas. Joel Mokyr (1976) has sharply contrasted Dutch economic stagnation with Belgian growth in the early nineteenth century and has explicitly drawn parallels between the Dutch experience at that time and the experiences of both late Victorian Britain and mid-twentieth century America (Mokyr, 1981, pp. 770-772).

While this paper does not afford the opportunity to draw full parallels between Victorian Britain and late twentieth century America, two observations may help establish the point. The first is that for long periods of time since 1945 American rates of overall growth and, perhaps more importantly, of productivity have lagged behind that of other advanced countries to the point where now (late 1990), on a wide range of plausible exchange rates, American income and output per capita are lower than in those countries. The second observation is that these foreign gains do not represent merely slight refinements of American practices or fleeting advantages, but in many instances, such as the production of computer memory chips (*The Economist*, March 9, 1985, pp. 66-67), constitute more radical advances that U.S. manufacturers will probably not be able to match for many years.

6. It should be noted that many of the inventories record gross wealth without a full listing of debts. After the tax law changes of 1894, which marked the start of a process that saw rates of estate duty rise from near-negligible levels to a maximum of 11 percent before 1914, the total value of debts are reported, but without further detail. Recorded indebtedness was rarely great, usually no more than a few thousand pounds for even the largest estates, but exceptions did occur. For example, George Coats, who died in 1901 at the age of 55 with recorded assets valued at £571,973 also had unenumerated debts of £100,000; his net estate was still so large that it would easily have been counted among the largest estates even if the debts were deducted. This would not have been the case with George MacLachlan, a wine and spirit merchant of Glasgow who died in 1909 at the age of 59 with an inventory listing assets of personal worth £262,362 but with debts of £230,083, sufficient to change the estimate of his net wealth by an entire order of magnitude. In the analysis that follows, only gross values are considered unless there is evidence that debt was incurred to purchase a specific asset. In these rare cases, the encumbered asset is valued net.

7. Collection of Scottish probate inventories has been hampered by the obstructive record-keeping practices of the Register-General at Somerset House. In August 1980, without consultation, the Registrar-General's office ordered destroyed the copies of the Scottish probate inventories kept at Somerset House. Consequently the Scottish probate inventories can now only be examined in Edinburgh. Since many (probably the majority) of the largest Scottish wealth-holders had filed a duplicate copy of their inventory in London, the destruction of these records seriously slowed research, causing part of the sample to remain incomplete when the research grant supporting the work expired. The costing for this grant (SSRC Grant HR 4963) was calculated on the basis that the records available in London at the start of the work would remain available.

8. Lewchuk (1986) has recently shown that Edelstein's data excluded too readily securities with high but erratic yields. Recent work promises to enrich substantially the pioneering data base provided by Edelstein. In addition to Lewchuk's research, Davis and Huttenback (1986), for their work on the economics of Britain's Empire, 1860-1912, have compiled extensive financial data. At present, however, neither Lewchuk's nor Davis and Huttenback's data are available for processing in a manner comparable to Edelstein's, but it is hoped that it will become so in the near future. Preliminary examination of the risk-return characteristics of important categories of domestic British assets excluded or only partially covered in Edelstein's sample suggests that use of his data will lead to optimal portfolio choices biased away from technologically advanced domestic activities (that is, Edelstein's evidence is probably inherently biased *against* the argument of this paper).

9. The calculations made here make no allowance for speculation, defined as the attempt to reap arbitrage gains through the correct anticipation of the short-term movement of asset prices. The choices of wealth-holders modelled here are assumed to be determined by long run factors. Wealth-holders are assumed to take a view of these factors and construct their portfolios accordingly, altering their choices more than marginally only as their perception of long term factors change. To the extent that measures of portfolio performance are intended to assess how

well wealth-holders as a group bore the risks to which the economy as a whole was exposed, this treatment should be adequate, for as long as attempted arbitrage trading can be treated as a zero-sum game, the arbitrage gains of one trader will be exactly offset by the losses of another (or of others).

Evidence to support the zero-sum treatment of arbitrage trading can be found in Sharpe (1981, pp. 587-607). In fact, Sharpe's evidence suggests that speculators as a group cannot even recoup the transactions costs speculation entails. Widespread speculation would, however, tend to increase the variance of observed portfolio choice among individuals because a larger proportion of portfolios would be consciously in disequilibrium relative to long term factors. At present, on available evidence of portfolio turnover, speculative trading does not appear a major element in most of the portfolios observed. If subsequent research does not support this tentative conclusion, it will be necessary to obtain a larger sample than that proposed for this study.

10. For a more detailed discussion of the procedures used to obtain optimal portfolio shares, see Sharpe (1970, pp. 244-256).

11. These are only four of an infinite number of possible portfolios that form the efficient portfolio frontier. Each rational wealth-holder is assumed to choose for himself one point on this frontier, corresponding to his choice of α. The four portfolios reported were selected, after much experimentation, as most indicative of optimal portfolio choice. In particular, $\alpha = 0.1$ generated the largest number of assets to enter an efficient portfolio.

12. Edelstein's analysis assumes that all assets are priced according to their value in an efficient portfolio. The present study makes no such assumption, but instead searches through the asset data to determine, given the realized pattern of risk and return across assets, what the structure of efficient portfolios would have been had optimality been achieved. Edelstein's own evidence and his interpretation of the negative coefficient he finds on the dummy variable D (1982, pp. 131-135) indicates that Victorian wealth-holders did not behave optimally—they persisted in paying too much for debentures generally.

13. The rankings used here are determined by nominal capitalization which corresponded closely to the size of the firm at the time of its initial flotation [Grundkapital]. Since almost all German firms were well established before obtaining a public quotation and any subsequent issues were included in nominal capital (as was any market premium over nominal price at time of issue) nominal capitalization is not a totally misleading guide to firm size, although annual rankings on the basis of market valuations would be more reliable.

14. These arrangements may constitute another example of 'super-fast' technological diffusion which Gary Saxonhouse (1974) has identified as operating with conspicuous success in the cotton spinning industry of Meiji Japan.

15. The German domestic market for automobiles grew more slowly than might have been expected. It appears that wealthy Germans, taking their cue from the Kaiser himself remained attached to horses and carriages long after the wealth elites in other countries had become avid motorists. The more humble orders of German society accepted this elite stance as their own. Even had they wished to do so, the inability of most Germans to borrow in order to buy a car would have limited effective demand in the German automobile market.

REFERENCES

Burton, H. and Corner, D.C. (1968). *Investment and Unit Trusts in Britain and America.* London: Elek.

Bordo, M. D. and Schwartz, A. J. (Eds.). (1984). *A Retrospective on the Classical Gold Standard, 1821-1931.* Chicago: University of Chicago Press.

Cairncross, A.K. (1953). *Home and Foreign Investment, 1870-1913: Studies in Capital Accumulation.* Cambridge: Cambridge University Press.

Clapham, J.H. (1932). *An Economic History of Modern Britain, Vol. II: Free Trade and Steel, 1850-1886*. Cambridge: Cambridge University Press.

Clapham, J.H. (1938). *An Economic History of Modern Britain, Vol. III: Machines and National Rivalries*. Cambridge: Cambridge University Press.

Copeland, T.E., and Weston, J.F. (1983). *Financial Theory and Corporate Policy*. 2nd ed. Reading, MA: Addison-Wesley.

Cottrell, P.L. (1980). *Industrial Finance, 1830-1914: The Finance and Organization of English Manufacturing Industry*. London: Methuen.

Davis, L. E., and Huttenback, R. A. (1986). *Mammon and the Pursuit of Empire: The Political Economy of British Imperialism, 1860-1912*. Cambridge: Cambridge University Press.

Edelstein, M. (1970). *The Rate of Return on U.K. Home and Foreign Investment, 1870-1913*. Ph.D. dissertation, University of Pennsylvania.

Edelstein, M. (1971). "Rigidity and Bias in the British Capital Market, 1870-1913." Pp. 83-105 in *Essays on a Mature Economy: Britain After 1840*, edited by D.N. McCloskey. London: Methuen.

Edelstein, M. (1976). "Realized Rates of Return on U.K. Home and Overseas Portfolio Investment in the Age of High Imperialism." *Explorations in Economic History*, 13(July):283-329.

Edelstein, M. (1982). *Overseas Investment in the Age of High Imperialism: The United Kingdom, 1850-1914*. London: Metheun.

Feinstein, C.H. (1968). "Changes in the Distribution of National Income in the United Kingdom Since 1860." Pp. 115-148, in *The Distribution of National Income*, edited by J. Marchal and B. Ducros. London: Macmillan.

Feinstein, C.H. (1972). *National Income, Expenditure, and Output in the United Kingdom, 1855-1965*. Cambridge: Cambridge University Press.

Fremdling, R. (1977). "Railroads and German Economic Growth: A Leading Sector Analysis With a Comparison to the United States and Great Britain." *Journal of Economic History*, 37(September): 583-604.

Goldsmith, R. (1969). *Financial Structure and Development*. New Haven, CT: Yale University Press.

Hannah, L. (1974). "Takeover Bids in Britain Before 1950: An Exercise in Business 'Pre-history.'" *Business History*, 16 (January): 65-77.

Harbury, C.D. and Hitchins, D.M.W.M. (1979). *Inheritance and Wealth Inequality in Britain*. London: Allen & Unwin.

Hoffman, W. G., Grumbach, F. and Hesse, H. (1965). *Das Wachstum der Deutschen Wirtschaft seit der Mitte des 19. Jahrhunderts*. Berlin: Springer Verlag.

Hughes, J.R.T. (1960). *Fluctuations in Trade, Industry, and Finance: A Study of British Economic Development*. Oxford: Clarendon Press.

Hughes, J.R.T. (1968). "Wicksell On the Facts: Prices and Interest Rates, 1844 to 1914." Pp. 215-256 in *Value, Capital, and Growth: Papers in Honor of Sir John Hicks*, edited by J.N. Wolfe. Edinburgh: Edinburgh University Press.

Hughes, J.R.T. (1982). "The Great Strike at Nushagak Station, 1951: Institutional Gridlock." *Journal of Economic History*, 42 (March): 1-22.

Hughes, J.R.T. and Reiter, S. (1967). "The First 1945 British Steamships." *Purdue Faculty Papers in Economic History, 1955-1966*. West Lafayette, IN: Purdue University Press.

Kennedy, W. P. (1987). *Industrial Structure, Capital Markets, and the Origins of British Economic Decline*. Cambridge: Cambridge University Press.

King, W.T.C. (1936). *History of the London Discount Market*. London: G. Routledge & Sons, Ltd.

Kocka, J. (1978). "Entrepreneurs and Managers in German Industrialization." Pp. 492-589 in *Cambridge Economic History of Europe, Vol. III, Part I–The Industrial Economies: Capital, Labour, and Enterprise*, edited by P. Mathias and M.M. Postan. Cambridge: Cambridge University Press.

Landes, D. S. (1969). *The Unbound Prometheus*. Cambridge: Cambridge University Press.

Lewchuk, W. (1986). "The Return to Capital in the British Motor Vehicle Industry, 1896-1939." *Business History*, 28(March): 3-25.

Locke, R.R. (1984). *The End of Practical Man: Entrepreneurship and Higher Education in Germany, France and Great Britain, 1880-1940*. Greenwich, CT: JAI Press.

McCloskey, D.N. (1970). "Did Victorian Britain Fail?" *Economic History Review*, 23(December): 446-459.

McCloskey, D.N. (Ed.). (1971). *Essays on a Mature Economy: Britain after 1840*. London: Methuen.

McGouldrick, P. (1984). "Operations of the German Central Bank and the Rules of the Game, 1879-1913." Pp. 311-349 in *A Retrospective on the Classical Gold Standard, 1821-1931*, edited by M.D. Bordo and A.J. Schwartz. Chicago: University of Chicago Press.

Marchal, J. and Ducros, B. (Eds.). (1968). *The Distribution of National Income*. London: Macmillan.

Mathias, P. and Postan, M.M. (Eds.). (1978). *Cambridge Economic History of Europe, Vol. VII, Part I–The Industrial Economies: Capital, Labour, and Enterprise*. Cambridge: Cambridge University Press.

Matthews, R.C.O., Feinstein, C.H., and Odling-Smee, J.C. (1982). *British Economic Growth, 1856-1973*. Oxford: Clarendon Press.

Michie, R.C. (1981). *Money, Mania and Markets: Investment, Company Formation and the Stock Exchange in Nineteenth Century Scotland*. Edinburgh: John Donald.

Mokyr, J. (1976). *Industrialization in the Low Countries, 1795-1850*. Cambridge: Cambridge University Press.

Mokyr, J. (1981). "Review of J.C. Riley, 'International Government Finance and the Amsterdam Capital Market, 1740-1815.'" *Journal of European Economic History*, 10(Winter): 770-72.

Moss, M. S. (1983). "William Todd Lithgow—Founder of a Fortune." *Scottish Historical Review*, 63: 47-72.

Mottek, H., Becker, W. and Schröter, A. (1974). *Wirtschaftsgeschichte Deutschlands, Bd. III*. Berlin: Springer Verlag.

Reiter, S. (1977). "Information and Performance in the $(\text{New})^2$ Welfare Economics." *American Economic Review* (*Papers and Proceedings*), 67(February): 226-234.

Riesser, J. ([1911]1977). *The German Great Banks and Their Concentration in connection with the Economic Development of Germany*. Senate Document No. 593 (National Monetary Commission), 61st Congress, 2nd Session. Reprinted. New York: Arno Press.

Rubinstein, W.D. (1977). "Victorian Middle Classes: Wealth, Occupation, and Geography." *Economic History Review*, 30(November): 602-623.

Rubinstein, W.D. (1981). *Men of Property: The Very Wealthy in Britain Since the Industrial Revolution*. London: Croom Helm.

Saxonhouse, G. (1974). "A Tale of Japanese Technological Diffusion in the Meigi Period." *Journal of Economic History*, 34 (March): 149-165.

Sharpe, W. F. (1970). *Portfolio Theory and Capital Markets*. New York: McGraw-Hill.

Sharpe, W. F. (1981). *Investments* (2nd ed.). Englewood Cliffs, NJ: Prentice-Hall.

Shiller, R. J. (1981). "Do Stock Prices Move Too Much to be Justified by Subsequent Changes in Dividends?" *American Economic Review*, 71(June): 421-436.

Smith, A. ([1776] 1976). *An Inquiry into the Nature and Causes of the Wealth of Nations*. Chicago: University of Chicago Press.

Tilly, R. (1966). *Financial Institutions and Industrialization in the Rhineland, 1815-1870*. Madison: University of Wisconsin Press.

Tilly, R. (1982). "Mergers, External Growth, and Finance in the Development of Large-scale Enterprise in Germany, 1880-1913." *Journal of Economic History*, 42(September): 629-658.

Tilly, R. (1983). "Financing Industrial Enterprise in Great Britain and Germany in the Nineteenth Century: Testing Grounds for Marxist and Schumpeterian Theories." Mimeo.

Tilly, R. (1986). "German Banking, 1850-1914: Development Assistance for the Strong." *Journal of European Economic History*, 15(Spring): 113-152.

Trebilcock, C. (1981). *The Industrialization of the Continental Powers, 1780-1914*. London: Longman.

Webb, S. B. (1980). "Tariffs, Cartels, Technology and Growth in the German Steel Industry, 1879-1914." *Journal of Economic History*, 40(June): 309-330.

Weder, D. (1968). *Die 200 Grossten Deutschen Aktiengesellschaften, 1913-1962*. Inaugural-Dissertation, Johann Wolfgang Goethe-Universitat, Frankfurt am Main.

Wiener, M.J. (1981). *English Culture and the Decline of the Industrial Spirit, 1850-1980*. Cambridge: Cambridge University Press.

Wolfe, J.N. (Ed.). (1968). *Value, Capital, and Growth: Papers in Honor of Sir John Hicks*. Edinburgh: Edinburgh University Press.

LUCKY FOOLS AND CAUTIOUS BUSINESSMEN:

ON ENTREPRENEURSHIP AND THE MEASUREMENT OF ENTREPRENEURIAL FAILURE

John Vincent Nye

> *. . . the man who changes the stream of allocation of resources over time by introducing new departures into the flow of economic life is not necessarily an inventor of anything. He is an innovator, and plays a vital role in the economy. Andrew Carnegie, . . . is credited with the remark, "Pioneering don't pay." Yet he was a mighty pioneer in the steel industry and his pioneering paid off in astronomical figures. What he meant by "pioneering" was activity in which the probability of failure seemed to him to be high. He was an innovator* par excellence, *and American history has many like him.*
>
> — Hughes (1986, p. 5).

Research in Economic History, Suppl. 6, pages 131-152.

ISBN: 1-55938-150-7.

As a student of Jonathan Hughes, I was impressed by the finely-honed skepticism he brought to the use of economic theory and by his preference for explanatory realism and messy historical details over formal, aesthetic satisfactions. He had great respect for theory and never objected to formalism per se. Rather, he was keenly aware of the fact that theory more often tells us when we are wrong than when we are right. John used to say that, "Economic theory is not very good at telling us what we will observe in the real world but, in telling us what we ought to observe, it calls our attention to what is odd and worthy of thought."[1]

Economists and economic historians have been somewhat deficient in dealing with the study of entrepreneurship.[2] John was dissatisfied with this general lack of interest in entrepreneurship and set out to remedy the problem in his magnum opus, *The Vital Few*. In that work the more analytic, quantitative economic history he had helped pioneer was abandoned for a traditional biographical approach designed to illuminate the lives of specific people whom he felt were pivotal individuals in American economic development. And so much the worse for formal theory if it had no easy way of characterizing or taking account of these people.

But entrepreneurship, like a great many things in this world, is often more fascinating when one feels it to be lacking than when it is present. Thus, economic historians have often backed into the problem of entrepreneurship, by arguing about entrepreneurial failure.

By the late 1960s, it had become fashionable to attribute a country's poor economic performance to the failure of her entrepreneurs and commercial managers. Prominent examples seemed to abound. Victorian Britain—by far the most popular target—was said to have grown fat and lazy, unable to summon that youthful vigor that produced its early triumphs. Britain's relative decline over the last quarter century was said to have been anticipated by its poor performance a hundred years ago. Another popular example was nineteenth-century France—a nation reputedly composed of conservative businessmen and small landowners that was so restrained in its willingness to innovate, that the nation industrialized, if at all, only grudgingly. And the examples continue, including the United States during the 1970s and 1980s when it was threatened by a wave of superior technological toys and mechanical marvels sent there by Japan and her Pacific neighbors.

These explanations were so much taken for granted, and their formulation so vaguely stated in the economic historical literature, that the thesis of entrepreneurial failure became an easy target for the first generation of theory-laden, statistic-wielding cliometricians.

The most prominent frontal attacks on the literature of entrepreneurial failure were delivered by McCloskey and Sandberg (collectively and individually)[3] in their reassessment of English industrial performance during the Victorian era. Taking aim at the lack of quantifiable evidence in favor of the failure thesis, and working from the motto—"If you're so smart, why aren't you rich?"—the cliometricians demonstrated that on the whole British businessmen were sound investors, making careful calculations in their decisions to adopt or to reject a new product or process, that they were shrewd in their financial dealings, and on the whole did not pass up any hugely profitable investment opportunities. That is, they were good approximations to that marvelous inhabitant of our most prized economic models, the rational economic man.

However, dissatisfaction with this line of research has persisted, despite the care and scholarship with which McCloskey, Sandberg, and several others made the case against entrepreneurial failure.[4] The general feeling being that somehow, entrepreneurship could not be measured with simple statistics nor examined in the profit-maximizing framework of standard theory. The assertion remained that the quality of entrepreneurship required something beyond the rational calculations of homo economicus (cf. Lazonick 1981). However, the problem remained: How to put entrepreneurship on an operational footing that would allow it to be measured against the rationalist hypothesis?

Part of the problem may be one of definition: that is, of an inability as a profession to sort out the conflicting claims of formal theory and our understanding of historical processes. What I propose is to explore the concept of entrepreneurship and to set out some conditions that make the study of entrepreneurial failure feasible and logically consistent, even in a world where neoclassical economic theory holds. In the future, it might then be possible to work out a more detailed framework in which one could test for the presence of entrepreneurial failure in a way that is distinct from simply making ex post attacks on the judgment of an entire nation or a nation's businessmen. Recent attempts to revive the issue of entrepreneurial failure in Victorian Britain will be discussed to show why these accounts have been inadequate to deal with a world that permits both competitive adjustment and individual entrepreneurship. I conclude by suggesting a future research agenda that encompasses the visions of both Hughes and McCloskey.

I. WHAT IS AN ENTREPRENEUR?

Defenders of Schumpeterian entrepreneurship have chosen to see the innovators as super-rational beings, able to perceive investment opportunities in an uncertain world where more limited, risk-calculating creatures failed. Sometimes this emerges as a simple assertion regarding relative risk preferences, in which some groups or classes are said to be more risk-loving than others.[5] Often, there is something more. There is the view that the rational, profit-maximizing businessman is not enough, that making do with the best available technologies and gambling on future innovations in accord with the dictates of expected utility theory is suboptimal from society's point of view. The entrepreneur sees more, so he does more.

This is a mistake, misperceiving the role of entrepreneurship. It suffers from the problem that well-informed businessmen are always on the lookout for a good investment, and it only takes the marginal entrepreneur to undermine established laggards. Moreover, the characterization of the entrepreneur as enlightened but unfairly neglected leaves out the extent to which most would-be entrepreneurs, and would-be innovations, end up as failures, even when advanced by previously successful innovators. It is in the nature of a broad understanding of the incentives provided by a market economy that truly rational businessmen consider not just short-run profit maximizing opportunities for investment but take into account the difference between long- and short-run benefits, properly discounting future returns.

The appropriate framework would reverse the view of the entrepreneur as a prescient visionary, and instead make of him a heroic failure. The point is that we are better off viewing the true entrepreneur not as a superman, nor a risk-loving madman, but rather a benign, somewhat overoptimistic fellow, who has systematically *overestimated* the returns to a given innovation or research project (or underestimated the risks). He only learns through hard work and repeated failure that few things in life are free, and the reason that nobody else was working on his great idea is that the idea probably was not so hot in the first place. Only every now and then do one of these ill-informed entrepreneurs happen to luck out and win the bad gamble, just as the odd player may win the big prize in the lottery or at the slot machine.[6]

However, the entrepreneur is *not* a risk-lover. Outside the realm of his peculiar delusion, he is no more nor less risk averse than the run of humanity. Entrepreneurship is something other than his willingness to undertake risks, because market-determined risk premia correctly identify the expected benefits and costs of any undertaking.

The entrepreneur need not be the same as the general population. Aptitudes may differ with respect to invention or innovation. The entrepreneur may well be more productive on the average than other businessmen. But, his "ordinary" successes are fully discounted in the marketplace and it is only at the margin that he can be mistaken. His optimism is specific to a particular venture.

Where are the economic forces? What of the rational economic men that the new economic historians have shown to inhabit the world? Will they not drive these fools away? They will. But, along with the old adage that asks, "If you're so smart, why aren't you rich?" is another that says, "A sucker is born every minute." Over time, either the fool will become a wise investor, learning to calculate risks and profits with care, or he will be driven from the market. Having lost his shirt countless times, he will become repentant, and learn the error of his ways. This will be the case for the overwhelming majority of the entrepreneurial fools. But, a few—a very few—will become successful, and a number of these fabulously successful.

There is one more problem. If these are truly bad gambles then the total sums lost by all the eager entrepreneurs will exceed the gains to the lucky few. We may never be quite certain when the losses add up to more than the gains (although these losses might not be apparent to the scholar, distracted by the observable successes of the few).[7]

However, if there is a large public goods component to some of these innovations, and if the nature of the measurement or property right is so vague as to make it impossible for an individual to capture all the rents to the innovation, then it may be that a gamble would be individually foolish from the standpoint of the private investor, though socially beneficial for the world at large. The possibility is consistent with the view of the gains from innovation espoused by Schumpeter and his intellectual progeny. To the extent that positive externalities are present and inappropriable, then the usual public goods/free rider problems apply. Where they do not, society does not gain on the average from these "leaps in the dark." Moreover, this perspective is consistent with the view of entrepreneurship and innovation that one gleans from the accounts in the popular press and from case studies of history's success stories.

The appeal to the presence of positive externalities is not made casually. It is the *necessary* starting point to any serious discussion of entrepreneurship and entrepreneurial failure. Appeals to the special benefits conferred on society by the entrepreneurs are really assertions regarding the spillovers from entrepreneurial activity and the difficulty with which a society—through the market or otherwise—appropriates these benefits. Alternative conceptions strike me as ex-post searches to blame the loser.

Retrospective condemnation of decisions made by the business community of another time or place does not constitute a scholarly contribution to the entrepreneurial debate. It consists of nothing more than a conviction that the actors in the market made the wrong decisions, and that moreover, a different system would have produced a systematic basis for making the right decision. Demonstrating the latter is difficult and insufficient to make a case for widespread entrepreneurial failure. Otherwise we will always be judging the overall soundness of the group by a few mistakes.[8]

Therefore, if we accept the general soundness of neoclassical theory in describing the normal functioning of the market, we must talk about entrepreneurship in the context of the need to capture positive externalities. This leads to my emphasis on the entrepreneur as the valiant, but overoptimistic investor rather than the heroic seer. In a competitive market, the heroic investor, no matter how unique, will simply find his rents bid up to the point where his skills and willingness to take risks earn no supernormal returns.

II. ENTREPRENEURSHIP AND COMPETITION: AN EXAMPLE

Consider the situation in which there is a continuum of players $h \in [0,1]$. Each player has to decide whether or not to invest some amount x in a project in the first period. All players are assumed to be risk neutral. But, the players are not fully informed as to the probability of success of the project, and have to infer that information from a private signal $t(h)$. A fraction $1/k$ of the people receive a favorable signal 1, and the remaining $(k\text{-}1)/k$ receive the unfavorable signal 0. Thus,

$$t(h) = \begin{matrix} 0 & (k-1)/k \text{ players} \\ 1 & 1/k \text{ players} \end{matrix}$$

The signal $t(h)$ tells them something about the probabilities regarding the outcomes of the investment if they spend x dollars. But, the distribution of the states of the world $a_t\ (h)$ is known with certainty only for $t(h) = 0$. Thus the signals result in the following states of the world and their probability distributions:

$$\text{If } t(h) = 0 \qquad a_0(h) = \begin{matrix} 0 & (\mathrm{m}-1)/\mathrm{m} \\ 1 & 1/\mathrm{m} \end{matrix}$$

where m is known to the player and $1/m < x$.

$$\text{But if } t(h) = 1 \text{ then} \qquad a_1(h) = \begin{matrix} 0 & (\mathrm{n}-1)/\mathrm{n} \\ 1 & 1/\mathrm{n} \end{matrix}$$

where n is unknown.

The states of the world at (h) indicate the success or failure of the investment ($1 =$ good investment/success, $0 =$ failure).

Each player has to decide whether to invest or not, and cannot see what information everyone else has. Therefore, when players observe $t(h)$, the following are the possible courses of action.

a. If $t(h) = 0$ then $1/m - x < 0$ and no investment is made.

b. if $t(h) = 1$ then he assigns priors of $1/2$ to each of the states of the world $a_0(h) = 0$, $a_1(h) = 1$. This is because the player has no information about the distribution of $1/n$. It is assumed that his priors assign a uniform distribution to $1/n$ drawn from [0,1] and thus the priors of $1/2$ each for $1/n$ and $1 - 1/n$. If $1/2 - x > 0$, the investment will be made.

Since $P(a(h) = 1) = 1/n$, for the case where $1/n - x < 0$,

$$(1/k)(1/n - x) < 0.$$

This represents the net private cost to society of the investment. Only $1/n$ of the $1/k$ entrepreneurs are successful. The outcomes from the first round of investments are observed and all the players update their priors. This process repeats itself until we reach an equilibrium. Even in the specific case of the uniform distribution, calculating the updated priors is a complicated task. Fortunately, McKelvey and Page (1986) and Geanakoplos and Polemarchakis (1982) have demonstrated conditions under which a process of announcement with different private information converges to a common knowledge equilibrium in a finite number of periods.

If there is no positive externality, the misperception of the investment opportunities leads to a net loss to society. Only if there is some nonappropriable public good large enough to compensate for the loss will society benefit from the unfortunate players.

If the public good is great enough to offset private losses, society may benefit but no one will have an incentive to be individually foolish in equilibrium. This corresponds to the notion that private gains may be less than social gains, but it traces the decision to invest to limited, incorrect information at the start of each process.[9] In this simple example, the entrepreneur—even if successful—looks back and realizes that he would never repeat the experience once he understands how unfavorable the odds were.

Thus, $1/k$ can be said to represent the fraction of society imbued with "entrepreneurial spirit." That agents can learn from each other's mistakes (i.e., their posteriors are equal in some finite iterative process) does not remove the missteps resulting from investments made out of equilibrium. The size of $1/k$ is determined exogenously by history, culture, institutions, and so forth. Each generation loses the incentive to innovate, and the process is set into motion only with the coming of each new generation. The knowledge that others systematically err is no comfort to any new generation, since for any given individual, the signals are private. There is no credible way to reveal the signal and convince others of its validity except by acting on that signal. Thus, the belief that a particular signal is correct can only be confirmed after the fact.

Obviously, the relative size of the externalities determines whether or not society can benefit from the process. To the extent that areas of large positive externalities can be correctly identified (and therein lies the rub), we have the standard arguments for governmental subsidies of research and development or education. But we also have a nonstandard argument for allowing the optimistic fools of capitalism to provide their own subsidies.

III. DISCUSSION AND COMPARISON WITH OTHER FORMULATIONS

There have been a number of important studies in the last few years that attempt to get at the problem of entrepreneurial failure in Victorian Britain while grappling with the cliometric demonstrations that British businessmen were on the whole rational, sensible individuals, that the market in Britain worked as well as it did anywhere else, and that no great opportunities were missed by failing to adopt some of the technological and organizational innovations developed by Britain's competitors, the United States and Germany. In dealing with the issue the post-revisionists have not only enriched our store of historical tales, but have also brought to the fore the problems of conceptualizing entrepreneurship in a world where several market models seem to fit very well.

What sets the modern neoclassical economic perspective apart from all other social science perspectives is its attention to the primacy of marginal over average considerations in the determination of market outcomes. Although few attempts have been made to formalize the intuition, our arguments regarding the market's operation rely more on evolutionary rather than perfect rationality arguments.[10]

No one seriously believes that all or even most firms in an industry are run by rational calculators maximizing perfectly on all margins, although our simplest models assume this. This has no effect on our theoretical deliberations because (1) we are interested in equilibria more than the shape of adjustment processes, and (2) because in a "competitive" market, we only require that the marginal firm, investor or consumer behave correctly to force the average to follow suit. (This marginal convergence intuition has been generally, but not always, confirmed in laboratory situations. Experiments have been performed under conditions far more "imperfect" than those assumed in standard theory, suggesting the robustness of the argument to deviations between abstract description and observed reality.)

For these and other reasons, Robert Allen's (1981) descriptions of entrepreneurial failure and his test for it in Victorian Britain do not meet our needs. Allen claimed that one could reconcile the neoclassical—or as he calls it, the profitability—hypothesis and the entrepreneurial one by arguing that both "are concerned with different aspects of economic behavior. The profitability hypothesis is concerned with cost minimization in a comparative static framework; the entrepreneurial hypothesis is concerned with the speed of adjustment with which an industry adjusts to disequilibrium" (p. 38). In his examinations of the diffusion of the tall blast furnace between 1850 and 1875, Allen shows that considerations of profit played an important role. However, Allen argues that the slow diffusion was an inadequate adjustment to the demands of the new technology.

This is not fair to the rational actor thesis. To state that the industry adjusted "too slowly" is to state that the owners and managers of British firms calculated profits incorrectly by looking at short-run over long-run considerations. The value of the firm is the correct neoclassical maximand, and this is long run. Accusations of short-sightedness are common enough when describing cases of managerial failure and may have occurred. But it is simply not right to ascribe such a process to the theory of profit-maximization that forms the core of the cliometric case against entrepreneurial failure. While it is quite true that neoclassical theory has been weak on dynamic specifications, the most basic versions would maintain that—to the limit of the capital market's ability to function correctly, given transaction and information costs—there is no difference between the long run and the short run. Future benefits and costs are appropriately discounted and considered in the decision to adopt new technology or to make adjustments in the firm's institutional arrangements. The assertion that British managers moved too slowly to adopt new technology is virtually identical to insisting that they were not economically rational, and profit-maximizing entrepreneurs.

Leaving aside the problems of definition, Allen's test for the plausibility of entrepreneurial failure is inadequate in principle to the task of demonstrating such failure. His reasoning is based on evidence that the average age of the owners of the furnace firms was greater at the end of the century than in the 1850s and 1860s and that older men or second-generation owners were "less likely to innovate than other firms" (Allen, 1981, p. 52). The reference to a change in managers' conservatism (or taste for security) that Allen attributes to age has much in common with the original sociological arguments that McCloskey was attacking. But it is not sufficient to show that the average businessman was older and had a preference for caution. One has to ask why or how they were able to indulge these nonmaximizing preferences in the face of competition from the younger and/or more vigorous members of the industry. As previously mentioned, what matters is the marginal not the average firm. Firms that stumbled, even if accidentally, onto the optimal changes would benefit greatly at the laggards' expense.

Moreover, even if my characterization of theory is dismissed, it still must be demonstrated and not simply assumed that Britain and British firms stood to gain (properly discounting future benefits) from having introduced such innovations earlier and had ignored the ex ante reasons for doing so. No externality is argued in the problem of choosing to adopt the new technology and therefore one must show that the individuals and the industry as a whole behaved foolishly and irrationally.[11]

Similar problems of characterizing the neoclassical benchmark against which to measure the extent of entrepreneurial failure mar the extensive and otherwise excellent researches of William Lazonick (1981) on this subject. Also, in Elbaum and Lazonick (1986), the British entrepreneurs' failure is traced to their overreliance on "market mechanisms to coordinate economic activity" (p. 3) and their inability to adopt the new corporate structures that seemed to characterize American and German business. The accusation relies, however, on the presumption that failure to adopt corporate structures to the same extent as American firms was necessarily a failing. There is no demonstration of this. Moreover, the articles seem to suggest that a noncompetitive or nonmarket (planning? cartels?) mechanism enforcing the shift to American-style corporations would have been socially beneficial. Despite the impressive work of Chandler on the subject of corporate control and the benefits to be derived from modern management, it is clear that various types of organizations coexisted and continue to coexist to the present day. It is unclear whether vertical integration was the universal road to growth and prosperity. Elbaum and Lazonick merely assert it. It is not evident for any given economic situation that the stereotypical American corporation or conglomerate was superior to a raft of small firms that may have satisfied different market segments or responded to different relative prices. It has to be demonstrated that Britain and British industry, as a whole, suffered from their non-adoption of these forms and that there existed a means of doing so that was cost-effective.

Lazonick (1981) has been critical of neoclassical theory's handling of vertical integration and in particular of the work of Ronald Coase. Citing Coase's (1937) reference to vertical integration as "substitution at the margin" Lazonick states that,

> Coase's approach has little empirical relevance and is also highly misleading for three basic reasons.
>
> First, the modern enterprise, if it is to reap the benefits of mass production, cannot shift its mode of operation with every change in relative factor prices, but rather must engage in long-term planning . . . Indeed, in the post-World War II Lancashire cotton industry we find that . . . firms combined and then separated for the sake of short-term supply and demand advantages without in the least altering their organizational or technical methods of production. Such actions constitute precisely Coasian managerial decision making but, ironically, exemplify the failure to develop the modern corporate enterprise. The manager who integrates and disintegrates his firm according to the ebb and flow of the market situation does so in lieu of the long-term planning of the organizationally interconnected and technically interrelated production and distribution processes that characterize the modern corporation.
>
> Second, the Coasian approach ignores the role of concentrated market power in the development of the corporate enterprise.
>
> Third, Coase's approach ignores the problem of managerial structure in the development of the enterprise (p. 35).

To characterize neoclassical theory in general and Coase's work in particular in this fashion is to miss its point. I have already addressed the issue of short-run versus long-term maximization in general and, in any case, such a distinction is not a central issue in Coase's writings. More important,

Lazonick's version of Coase ignores the extent to which many of Coase's concerns mirror his own. The work of Coase and others has done much to address the very issues of vertical integration and managerial structure that Elbaum and Lazonick feel are absent in standard economics.

It has long been Coase's contention that in assuming away transactions costs, standard neoclassical models were simplistic in their description of economic behavior and inadequate in describing the true nature of organization at the level of the firm. He criticized the tendency to treat the textbook model of "perfect" competition with its many small firms and atomistic consumers as the appropriate benchmark. Obvious real-world deviations from this model—large firms, hierarchical ordering, "fixed" pricing contracts, special retail arrangements—were traditionally blamed on some form of monopoly power, whether resulting from collusive behavior or imperfect markets.

It was Coase's achievement to point out that such views were wrong and that corporate structure, large-scale enterprise, vertical integration, and so forth could all be natural efficiency-enhancing responses to competitive pressures in a world of positive, often asymmetric transactions costs. It is not an accident that the new institutional economics of Williamson, Alchian, Goldberg, and many others draws inspiration from the writings of Coase. It has focused attention on such areas as intrafirm contracting, principal-agent problems, and pricing mechanisms under uncertainty, thus putting flesh on the powerful but skeletal framework we think of as neoclassical theory.

The point is not that neoclassical theory is incorrect, but that it is incomplete. It describes accurately the environment in which firms compete and provides us with analysis of the more important forces that characterize market allocation of resources. But it does not tell us enough about the nature of the firm, because we do not have enough detail about transactions costs and specific institutional arrangements.

Any attempt to come to grips with entrepreneurship and entrepreneurial failure must demonstrate some externality that makes individually rational actions socially sub-optimal. Dynamic questions must be tied to demonstrable failures on the part of the nation in question. Any mechanism that directly challenges the neoclassical adjustment mechanisms should be stated explicitly in terms of different behavioral hypotheses with observable dynamic deviations from the standard optimizing story.[12]

IV. THE VITAL FOOLS

The aspects of entrepreneurship emphasized in this paper can be seen clearly in the biographies that come under the headings of invention and innovation in Hughes's *The Vital Few*. The quotation that begins the section on Thomas Edison is: "Results? Why, man, I've gotten a lot of results. I know several thousand things that won't work" (Hughes, 1986, p. 149). Hughes then goes on to inform us that "Edison spent nearly a decade in the search for a dependable storage battery which could make electric automobiles competitive with those driven by internal-combustion engines" (p. 149). We now know, of course, that neither Edison nor anyone else was successful in accomplishing this.

It is a commonplace for economists to cite the zero economic profit theorem. In equilibrium it is not possible to make positive economic profits in a competitive market. And in the event of monopoly power, the rents to the monopoly factor will be bid up to drive economic profits to zero. With entrepreneurship the same should be the case. We often notice the ex post successful inventor without paying attention to the ex ante chances of success.

What is especially bracing about the Edison that Hughes portrays is that he was both persistent in his work and consistently wrong on so many occasions. His successes were many, but the truly profitable ideas were few and almost fortuitous in their occurrence, while the failures were so commonplace as to be almost uncountable. In addition to the electric car battery, Edison championed direct current electricity over commercial a.c. voltage. "He was convinced that, transformers or not, the high voltage of the a.c. system made it extraordinarily dangerous" (Hughes, 1986, p. 194) and that Westinghouse's developments of the a.c. system were a danger to the public at large. Believing that the backers of a.c. systems were "common thieves" he "openly charged that 'patent pirates' were trying to put a lethal force into the American home indiscriminately."

Even when Edison did develop something of lasting value, he was often blind to its potential. This was especially important given Edison's dual role as inventor and entrepreneur. Edison had abandoned the phonograph shortly after he had worked out an early version of it, and continued to misunderstand the nature of its market even when he returned to exploit a product that others were showing to be profitable. He refused to consider the entertainment value of the phonograph and insisted that it be sold for business purposes only (Hughes, 1986, p. 201). To add insult to injury the company he founded to exploit the phonograph potential did poorly and soon was bankrupt. The man who had said, "'I'm an inventor . . . I measure everything I do by the size of the silver dollar. If it don't come up to that standard, then I know it's no good'" (Hughes, 1986, p. 190) found himself unable to profit from his own creation while others sold cheap machines that made flat-disc records commonplace. In addition to misunderstanding the nature of the market, Edison could not change with the changing demand for phonographs. He resisted changes and improvements, and "he hated radio." As Charles Edison (his son) remarked, "'My father's past experience had simply got in his way'" (Hughes, 1986, p. 202).

Even the story of Edison's greatest invention, the incandescent light bulb, is a story of the adaptability of the market and an object lesson in the problems of judging the ex ante soundness of an investment decision by its ex post success. Edison was certainly not the first person to work on the problem of incandescent lighting. Inventors in England and France had experimented with the process as far back as 1820, although with little success. Sir Joseph Swan received a patent for the incandescent lamp in the 1860s but did not have a "commercially practicable" device (Hughes, 1986, p. 180). Other men in Russia and America had experimented with incandescent lighting before Edison's success in 1878, but none had been successful. Edison's problems were further compounded by the need to divide electric current so as to make it available to thousands of individual households and businesses. Hughes quotes several eminent authorities of the time who announced that such subdivision was impossible. Any incandescent system was doomed to failure. As Hughes triumphantly notes,

> It could not be said that Edison was embarking upon a promising quest so far as received doctrine was concerned. The main problems, the production of a continuous glow, its possible distribution and its effective supply of current, had never been solved. Edison solved them all (p. 180).

It is tempting to read a deterministic inevitability into the account of Edison's tribulations and triumphs, but the converse is the case. We have benefited from Edison's eventual success, but it is not unreasonable to argue that he was wrong-headed, and as such, we would be looking back in hindsight to conclude he was simply wasting his time. But Edison liked to tinker, and he liked to work out such challenges. It is fortunate for us that his inventions produced so much gold along with the dross, but we should be careful to note how individually foolish much of Edison's research was, viewed from the standpoint of cost-benefit analysis. Moreover, it is important to point out how responsive the market was to successful inventions. Although most people were wary of Edison's bulb even after reports of his success had appeared, there were many ready imitators at hand by the time of his successful introduction of an inexpensive light bulb. The skepticism was certainly reasonable, given this technology's history of failure.

Does this mean that cost-benefit analysis is wrong? No. If everyone working in the areas Edison chose to explore had been as stubborn and obsessed as Edison was, and if there were no positive spillovers to the research, we would all be worse off for their work.

In his analysis of Edison's life as the creation of an American myth, Wyn Wachhorst (1981) argues that there are three discernible periods. The first and most productive period starts from the invention of the phonograph in 1877 to 1888 when it was developed. This is the period of the incandescent lamp and electric power distribution. The second period, stretching from 1888 to the first decade of the twentieth century saw an Edison who, "growing ever older, less energetic, and more disillusioned, . . . increasingly talked more and invented less" (Wachhorst, 1981, p. 89). The third period—continuing until his death—saw Edison as the public figure, pretending to be inventive and innovative rather than actually producing.

Edison was both inventor and business tycoon, but succeeded in the latter capacity only on the basis of his earliest triumphs. Later attempts to recapture former glories, such as the large scale project in the 1890s to develop steam shovels for heavy-duty mining, were embarrassing and only served to fritter away a substantial portion of the monies earned in the previous decade. In the twentieth century Edison became preoccupied with developing an electric automobile, only to have his dream killed by Henry Ford (Wachhorst, 1981, p. 99).

Hughes rightly stressed that Edison was more an inventor rather than an innovator. Ford was less creative. But this pattern of intense, self-deluding persistence coupled with hard work, foresight, and plenty of luck emerges from Ford's history as from Edison's. It is a commonplace today to note that the spectacular early successes of the Ford corporation were followed by a period in the late twenties and in the thirties characterized by poor business judgment, foolish attempts to ignore the dictates of the marketplace, and consequent loss of market share. The story is important as a fable of the life cycle of many a large business founded on a handful of brilliant and successful innovations. Nonetheless, it is important to remember how precarious even those early successes were (that seemed to be the product of good judgment and a creative vision) and how fortunate Ford was that his guesses proved to be correct. The precariousness was evident from his earliest work on automobiles. Ford's decision to build his own motor car in 1896 was daring but neither original nor unusual. Certainly the construction of any motor vehicles in those days was a difficult and demanding task, but it was possible and had been done with some regularity by others. The real question was, How good a business investment was the automobile? Hughes (1986) notes that,

> It was one thing to make an automobile in one's spare time out in the woodshed, it was quite another thing to get together enough money and men to make cars, in 1896, and then attempt to displace the horse. It was not at all certain that an automobile factory would be a good business investment. How much of a market would there be for such a contraption? Ford was not overrun with encouragement, financial or otherwise (p. 281).

The very business of automobile manufacture was a source of dramatic successes and fairly routine failures. Allan Nevins and Frank Hill (1954) note in their massive biography of Ford:

> according to a careful historical table compiled in 1909 for Motor by C.E. Duryea, who gave it months of work, the total number of companies formed to manufacture automobiles 1900-1908 inclusive was 502; and the total number which retired from business altogether

> was 273, while 29 more entered some other area. Three-fifths of the whole roster were failures.
>
> If a man stood three chances in five of losing what he put into the Malcomson-Ford enterprise (and on its small capitalization the risk looked greater) what wonder that investors turned away (p. 234).

As the story is told today, emphasis is placed on Ford's fortunate start and succeeding miscalculations in an industry that was already characterized by uncertainty and frequent failures. If truth be told, the young Henry Ford was just as prone to business miscalculations as the old. By the time the Ford Motor Company was formed, he had already managed to bankrupt two other companies. While working as a superintendent and mechanical engineer for the Edison Company, Ford carried out home experiments in creating gasoline-powered engines at a time when the official policy of the Edison Company funneled research in the direction of the electric carriage. Ford produced a working car in 1899 with the financial support of William Maybury, the mayor of Detroit. This led to the founding of the Detroit Automobile Company on August 5, 1899 with Ford as a stockholder, but having paid in no money (Nevins and Hill, 1954, p. 175). Faced with the need to choose between the two firms, Ford left Edison and went to work as a superintendent for Detroit Automobile—the first firm in the city of Detroit to manufacture motor cars. A little over a year later, in November 1900, the company ceased trading and notice of its dissolution was filed in January of 1901 (Lacey, 1986, p. 48). Apparently Ford, whether out of perfectionism, insecurity or fear, could not fully commit himself to the business. He submitted no automobile design, seemed to hold back what he did have, and continually stalled for time. His work habits were spotty and indicate that he changed his mind about the company which had been formed solely to produce his motor cars barely months after its capitalization (Lacey, 1986, p. 50).[13] Ford claimed that "machine it could make was not good enough, and was too expensive" (Nevins and Hill, 1954, p. 191). Ford argued for a better machine but was vetoed by the stockholders.

Robert Lacey (1986) comments in his popular history of the Ford Company that:

> Over the debris of the Detroit Automobile Company lingers the unmistakable impression that Henry Ford got out of his depth, for producing cars to sell in quantity required very different skills from designing and producing a single prototype.
>
> Compared to America's other automotive pioneers like Duryea, Haynes, or even Charles B. King, Henry Ford had come quite late to the business of car making. The Detroit Automobile Company had offered him a chance to catch up, or even to get ahead of the game—and Henry had muffed it (p. 50).

Next, Ford moved on to building a racing car, with which he proceeded to win an important race at Grosse Pointe in October 1901, setting a new

American record (Nevins and Hill, 1954, p. 218). Almost solely on the basis of this victory, several of the men who had lost out on the Detroit Automobile Company chose to renew their support for Ford by putting up some $50,000 to help start the new Henry Ford Company. Rather than work on a production car from his designs, however, Ford chose to work on another racer. This led to Ford's dismissal from the company and its dissolution, to be reformed by the old partners as the Cadillac Automobile Company (Lacey, 1986, p. 61).

Although Henry Ford had by now acquired quite a reputation as race car designer, he was also well-known for having closed two corporations in two years. It should not be surprising therefore that investors came to view Ford as a risky investment in an already volatile industry.

When Ford did found the automobile company that was to make his name, his was neither the first nor, initially, the most successful of the pioneering car manufacturers. Furthermore, the innovation for which he became famous, the mass-production assembly line, was not original to him either. What he managed to do was to produce a car at a low enough price that huge numbers would come to buy it. This required the development of a chassis made up of an alloy that was light enough and strong enough to be built cheaply, and the decision to insist on a design that was spartan, uniform and easily mass-produced. Above all, he had to believe that there would be people to drive the thing. One way of viewing the story of the Model T is that (leaving aside the various technical accomplishments that made its construction possible) it represented the successful gamble on Ford's part that the lower end of the demand curve for automobiles was farther out than any of his competitors in Europe or America were willing to bet on. Had this not been the case, and had the Model T not overcome the one large problem hindering general acceptance of automobiles—the difficulty of driving without good roads and highways—it is unclear that Ford would have been more than the reasonably successful business figure that many of his rivals are remembered as.

The importance of this conjecture is demonstrated by the conflicts that emerged between Ford and his friend and financial partner, Alexander T. Malcomson.[14]

> Malcomson could argue that the country wanted cars costing from $2275 to $4775. In 1906 nearly half of the automobiles distributed fell within this upper price range; and nobody could foresee that ten years later they would enjoy less than two per cent of the market.
>
> Malcomson's position was given seeming strength by the fact that the movement of the market toward heavy, expensive touring cars. . .was unmistakably accentuated as the spring of 1905 wore on. Automobile journals expended considerable pains upon an analysis of the demand for high-priced automobiles, coming to the conclusion that too many manufacturers had rushed into the small-car business, with a resulting shortage of expensive models, that the country was "full of money," and that many buyers who had started with cheap runabouts had been educated to the larger, more costly types.

> Ford, however, had from the beginning wished to make just one type of car by quantity production of a simple standardized design, at prices enabling the great body of Americans to substitute a family automobile for the family horse (Nevins and Hill, 1954, pp. 275-276).

The decision to produce a one-model, one-color, all-purpose automobile greatly simplified the engineering and technical problems of producing a sturdy, cheap automobile whose price would start out low and be pushed down further over time. It paid off partly because Ford guessed rightly that the demand for a cheap automobile was there to be exploited. But, this self-same simplicity of concept became a hindrance to Ford's success in a later world in which roads were better, automobiles were ubiquitous, and people chose to pay for the privilege of greater comfort, better styling, and more individualized designs. Although it is always difficult to fathom the motivations of any one individual, especially one so eccentric as Henry Ford, Hughes notes for instance that "Ford . . . believed that he could always reach a larger stratum of buyers with a lower price" (p. 334). This was fine at the start, but by the late twenties the competition from the used car market and the increasing demand for improved design gave the edge to General Motors over Ford. The great entrepreneur, whose odd ideas were to be heralded (by among others, himself) as visionary and far-reaching was to see his success undermined by this vision. In the end, it seems, Malcomson's ideas prevailed.

Perhaps too much is made of the more eccentric qualities of Ford's personality and the foolish decisions of his later years. It is more important to note that, however astounding his success, General Motors was the greater beneficiary of his innovative largess. There have been many situations in which firms have grown to great size in fledgling industries, driven by the hard work, vision and technical inventiveness of their founders only to see themselves floundering when these same entrepreneurs could not adapt to the harsh demands of a mature, competitive market. We would probably be much the poorer had Ford acted differently, but it is likely that a budding, reflective entrepreneur, seeing Ford's example might choose to shrink back from following his peculiar path to success.[15]

The life stories of Edison and Ford have common features. By definition, the phenomenal successes that catapulted men like Edison and Ford into the limelight were extra-ordinary achievements—unrepresentative triumphs deviating from average successes even the most talented of men could expect to obtain. In both Edison and Ford inventive genius was wedded to entrepreneurial vigor and a touch of folly. In the latter half of his life Edison managed to throw away the bulk of the profits earned from the incandescent lamp on his failed steam-drilling project. Ford found himself completely overtaken in the automobile industry he had virtually created, by dogmatically clinging to the principles of production that had made his success possible in the first place. In the long run, people did want fancier cars, clever features, attractive design, a wide selection of body colors. Without Ford there might have been no mass auto market, but that selfsame mass market, changing as the nation changed, left Ford's vision behind.

In both cases, these great men misled themselves into thinking that their past triumphs could be replicated simply with hard work and the same faith in their ideas. But times were different, and both Ford and Edison paid a price to find out that they had been luckier than they might have cared to admit earlier on in their lives. And luck, unlike hard work or faith, is not reproducible on demand.

Hughes did not attempt to cover a representative sample of the multitude of entrepreneurs that made up the landscape of American business in the last century and a half, and there is no easy way to demonstrate that the characteristics I have cited are truly typical of many great breakthroughs.

In the Economic History Society's volume on business history, T.C. Barker (1977) examined the success of the Pilkington Brothers in the twenty years following World War II in developing and marketing the revolutionary Float process of glass-making despite competition from established giants with larger, wealthier research and development laboratories in the United States and France. In this case, a more efficient and cost-effective method of producing flat glass was developed that was to fully displace plate glassworks within a decade after the first Float glass license was granted in 1962. Nonetheless, the success came only after years of continuing failure and sustained financial loss. A small profit was first made in 1960-1961 with larger ones to follow. But by the time the process was well-established, it was quickly taken up by competitors under license who often made better use of technology than Pilkington did (Barker, p. 202).[16]

Relevant to this discussion are the observations regarding the technical team that created the Float glass process:

> The engineers, all enthusiastic young men—age may have been important—pressed on in ignorance. 'If we had known all these horrors at the beginning,' sir Alastair later commented, 'we would certainly not have gone ahead.' The scientists, all too aware of the theoretical difficulties of what was being attempted, would not have set off in the first place and were generally discouraging when difficulties began to reveal themselves (Barker, 1977, p. 203).

V. SEARCHING FOR ENTREPRENEURSHIP AND ENTREPRENEURIAL FAILURE

Where do we go from here? There is probably no difficulty with demonstrating that the phenomenon, as already described, exists. But, it still remains to devise a means of testing its importance for a given economy. I admit that the problem of how to go about doing this has not yet been solved, although I have some ideas of what such tests would involve. For one thing, unless one is dealing with assertions that a given nation's entrepreneurs were uniformly stupid, or constrained to behave nonrationally, it will not do us much good to go any further in devising tests that the market performed satisfactorily or that businessmen from Britain (or France, the United States, the Third World, Medieval Europe, and so on) were not sufficiently careful in their cost-benefit analysis. Such an exercise—although still instructive—should be left for debates about the usefulness of economics in general, or else should be used as devices to help us discover the sources of institutional or legal inefficiencies.[17] This would give rise to a methodology that is almost the opposite of what is typically used to demonstrate entrepreneurial failure. The real problem is in identifying innovations with large positive spillovers that made for an ex post nationally beneficial outcome but which were ex ante bad investments. Moreover, we have to establish that some of the benefits were locally confined to the "entrepreneurial" nation and not easily transferable or easily imitated by rival nations. After having done all this, it then becomes necessary to link these innovations to some observed "entrepreneurial" behavior on the part of the innovating nation's citizens. It would only then be appropriate to speculate on how culture or history or tradition produced the environment that produced the entrepreneurs.[18]

This difficult task should not discourage us in our efforts to deal with the questions of entrepreneurship and individual initiative. It is presented as a positive framework within which very different conceptions of the debate can still be fitted in and in which different sorts of studies can be used to help clarify historical events. We should all be grateful for a profession and for scholars such as J.R.T. Hughes that make both cliometric research and *The Vital Few* possible and complementary.

ACKNOWLEDGMENTS

The author is grateful to Lee Benham, Philip Keefer, Kevin McCabe, Donald McCloskey, Douglass North and Lisa Nunn for helpful comments and discussion. The comments of Joel Mokyr and two anonymous referees helped to clarify the arguments presented here.

NOTES

1. This is a rough paraphrase of some remarks he made in classes at Northwestern.
2. This complaint has been with us for some time. In a celebrated article, Arthur Cole (1946), argued that the study of the high degree of free competition "on the part of 'self-centered, active' individuals . . . has attracted less scholarly attention than it has deserved" (p. 2). Though he blamed this at first on the "evolving socialized economy" he then went on to show how famous scholars from Ricardo on chose to overlook the focus on entrepreneurship suggested by Say and Cantillon.

3. For a selection of essays on the problem of entrepreneurial failure in Victorian England, see McCloskey, (1971).

4. I was sufficiently impressed by the general sensibleness of the rational, neoclassical viewpoint that I applied it to a study of nineteenth-century French industry (Nye, 1987) which affirmed the evidence that Frenchmen were as rational as anyone else. Nonetheless, I was aware that I had not dealt fully with the problem of entrepreneurship, and that a segment of scholars would continue to remain unimpressed by this or any other cliometric demonstrations.

5. R. Allen's (1981) attempt to distinguish between the hypotheses of rational versus entrepreneurial behavior by arguing that entrepreneurial failure is concerned with the speed with which innovation occurred can be classified as being in this vein. See below.

6. The use of the term "foolish" is not meant to imply that the behavior of the entrepreneur is deplorable. I use it to stress the fact that there must be an underlying element of limited rationality or imperfect information in the entrepreneurial decision, else it becomes like any other economic decision and we are back to the pure neoclassical world. Although Schumpeter may not have viewed it as such, this work is intended to provide a framework within which we can deal with entrepreneurship as a creative rather than an adaptive response (e.g., Schumpeter, 1947).

7. As an aside I might add that this calls into question some of the traditional measurements that value the worth of an innovation or invention. To the extent that we only measure the explicit costs of an investment and ignore the costs borne by those working on related ventures that ultimately failed we may incorrectly estimate which are the beneficial and which the costly inventions from society's standpoint. We recognize this when discussing public works such as a bridge or railroad that benefits society once it has been built but that we judge should never have been built given the initial expenditures lavished on the project.

8. The difficulty of even establishing the ex-post mistakes of historical actors motivated the early cliometric work. That a few studies in McCloskey, 1971 and afterwards were able to demonstrate that some decisions were unsound ex post is hardly sufficient evidence to claim massive, growth-hindering entrepreneurial failure.

9. I am using the term "information" in the broadest possible sense to include both hunches and non-verifiable convictions that one has the "right" answer or the correct perception of market realities.

10. See, for instance Alchian (1950).

11. My criticism of Allen's work is confined to the logic of his argument about entrepreneurial failure. I do not call into question the usefulness of the empirical research he has pursued on the British iron and steel industry which has immeasurably enlivened the traditional debate. For example, "International Competition in Iron and Steel, 1850-1913" (Allen, 1979) makes a useful contribution to the debate on Victorian failure by indicating that British productivity had fallen behind that of the United States and Germany around the turn of the century. However, where Britain could not match German prices, Allen himself notes that such a "failure" may have stemmed from an inability to "overcome the cost disadvantages under which it labored in the early twentieth century" (Allen, 1979, p. 935) primarily high labor costs and expensive ore. The observed failure rests upon the presumption that Britain could have produced steel more efficiently by switching to the basic open hearth technology and making use of Cleveland ironstone, but did not due to entrepreneurial inertia. However, Allen notes that the non-switch may have been motivated by rational reasons having to do with the overall unprofitability of the British industry and the costs of constructing new plants. This sounds very much like a vintage capital argument with marginal firms making the switch and older plants falling behind in productivity.

12. One example can be found in Nelson and Winter, 1983.

13. It should also be mentioned that although the company was capitalized at $150,000, only $15,000 in shares was paid in, mostly by a group of prominent individuals headed by Mayor Maybury (Nevins and Hill, 1954, p. 175).

14. It is worth mentioning Nevins and Hill's comments that Malcomson, who came through for Ford when financing was most difficult to obtain, "was essentially a plunger, impetuous and excessively sanguine. Having expanded his coal operations too rapidly, he was being given heavy credits by Detroit banks and possessed little ready cash. He stipulated that nothing was to be said to the bankers about this new undertaking. The bills were to be paid from an account opened in a new bank in the name of James Couzens, Malcomson's clerk, office manager, and business adviser" (Nevins and Hill, 1954, p. 226).

15. Of course, that too is uncertain. Perhaps the timing might have been different and the particulars of the early motor industry would have changed had Ford not worked on the Model T but, given the conditions under which Ford worked it is hard to imagine that others would not have succeeded in laying the foundations for the modern automobile industry. The choice of cars today might not have been significantly altered by different success in Ford's early years.

16. From Barker (1977, p. 202): "The minutes of the General Board on 25 July 1963 capture his mood: 'Sir Harry stated that the Group Executive had been disappointed that the last few months had not seen a solution to the main troubles, such as bloom, undercleaning, and the production of some of the thin substances. Our position as the only manufacturer of Float in the world, and the resultant freedom from competition in sales of Float, was fast drawing to a close, and we really had not grasped our opportunity.'"

17. This is consistent with the research agenda that identifies market failures and then traces it back to the institutional or transactions cost features that account for the problem.

18. This daunting sequence is not meant to suggest that such a situation is impossible. For instance, I think that Germany's successes in chemicals and electrical engineering were related to the educational system that had been developed and the technical mentality instilled in the graduates of this system. These graduates, in turn, may have put more into the system than they could have gotten out of it. Still, it is not easy to show that this was the case, and that Germany was substantially better off than they would have been otherwise. My comments are meant to indicate how difficult it is to show that entrepreneurial success or failure at the aggregate national level (even if it does exist) was remarkable enough to account for significant differences in national economic development.

REFERENCES

Alchian, A.A. (1950). "Uncertainty, Evolution and Economic Theory." *The Journal of Political Economy*, 58(3): 211-21.

Allen, R.C. (1979). "International Competition in Iron and Steel, 1850-1913." *Journal of Economic History*, 39(December): 911-937.

Allen, R.C. (1981). "Entrepreneurship and Technical Progress in the Northeast Coast Pig Iron Industry: 1850-1913." Pp. 35-71 in *Research in Economic History*, Vol. 6, edited by P. Uselding. Greenwich, CT: JAI Press.

Barker, T.C. (1977). "Business Implications of Technical Developments in the Glass Industry, 1945-1965: A Case Study." Pp. 187-206 in *Essays in British Business History*, edited by B. Supple. Oxford: Oxford University Press.

Coase, R.H. 1937. "The Nature of the Firm." *Economica*, IV: 386-405.

Cole, A. ([1946] 1953). "An Approach to the Study of Entrepreneurship." Pp. 181-198 in *Enterprise and Secular Change*, edited by F.C. Lane and J.C. Riemersma. Homewood, IL: Richard Irwin, Inc.

Elbaum, B. and Lazonick, W. (1986). *The Decline of the British Economy*. Oxford: Oxford University Press.

Geanakoplos, J.D. and Polemarchakis, H.M. (1982). "We Can't Disagree Forever." *Journal of Economic Theory*, 28, (1): 192-200.

Hughes, J.R.T. (1986). *The Vital Few*. New York: Oxford University Press.

Lacey, R. (1986). *Ford: The Men and the Machine*. New York: Little, Brown.

Lazonick, W. (1981). "Competition, Specialization and Industrial Decline." *Journal of Economic History*, 41(1): 31-38.

McCloskey, D.N. (ed.). (1971). *Essays on a Mature Economy: Britain After 1840*. Princeton, NJ: Princeton University Press.

McClosey, D.N. (1981). "Did Victorian Britain Fail?" Pp. 94-110 in *Enterprise and Trade in Victorian Britain,* edited by D.N. McCloskey. Boston: George Allen and Unwin.

McCloskey, D.N. and Sandberg, L.G. (1981). "From Damnation to Redemption: Judgments on the Late Victorian Entrepreneur." Pp. 55-72 in *Enterprise and Trade in Victorian Britain*. Boston: George Allen and Unwin.

McKelvey, R.D. and Page, T. (1986). "Common Knowledge, Consensus and Aggregate Information." *Econometrica*, 54(1): 109-127.

Nelson, R.R. and Winter, S.G. (1983). *An Evolutionary Theory of Economic Change*. Cambridge, MA: Harvard University Press.

Nevins, A. and Hill, F. E. (1954). *Ford: The Times, The Man, The Company*. New York: Little, Brown.

Nye, J.V.C. (1987). "Firm Size and Economic Backwardness: A New Look at the French Industrialization Debate." *Journal of Economic History*, 47(3): 649-670.

Schumpeter, J.A. (1947). "The Creative Response in Economic History." *Journal of Economic History* (November): 149-159.

Supple, B. (1977). *Essays in British Business History*. Oxford: Oxford University Press.

Wachhorst, W. (1981). *Thomas Alva Edison: An American Myth*. Cambridge, MA: MIT Press.

CARVING THE NORTHWEST TERRITORY INTO STATES

Louis P. Cain

Q: Why does Michigan have an Upper Peninsula?
A: Because it doesn't have Toledo.

This apparent *non sequitur* happens to be the truth. The drawing of state boundaries has not been as simple a task as one might suppose. This was particularly true in the Northwest Territory, the present states of Ohio, Indiana, Illinois, Michigan, Wisconsin, and a piece of Minnesota. There were no clear divisions inherited from colonial times; often more than one colony laid claim to the same piece of land. Chicago, for example, was claimed by Virginia, Connecticut, Massachusetts, and even Quebec. Clear lines were drawn in the Northwest Ordinance of 1787, but these were not the boundary lines of the resulting states. This essay examines the consequences of the difference between what was ordained and what was admitted.

In spite of obvious differences in such variables as tax structures, welfare benevolence, and tuition at state universities, state boundaries have not entered the choice set of most Americans. Tiebout (1956) effects involving state-to-state comparisons prove relatively unimportant today because the reduction

Research in Economic History, Suppl. 6, pages 153-168.

ISBN: 1-55938-150-7.

in location-specific costs are often cancelled by increased commuting costs. They were likely to have been less significant 150 years ago. Why then was there any controversy over where state boundaries were drawn?

There are both political and economic reasons for expecting disputes to arise. The political reasons stem from the fact that the disputed boundaries usually were between a state and a territory, not between two states. The rules for becoming a state codified in the land ordinances of the 1780s were such that there was a considerable benefit in becoming a state. These benefits took the form of differences in legislative representation at the federal level and greater control of the executive and judicial functions at the state level. A territory's claim on land included within the boundaries of a previously-settled state was simultaneously a claim on population that would allow the territory to apply for statehood at an earlier date.

The economic reasons stem from the expected benefits of canals. The Northwest Territory was settled during an era of waterborne transport. Cities such as Toledo and Chicago were located at the mouth of rivers that reached far into the interior. If a canal was necessary to develop the inland waterway, the primary responsibility for developing such an internal improvement lay with the states. Economic location theory predicts that the greatest effect of such canals will be at the end-points, the trans-shipment points (see Heilbrun, 1981, Chap. 4). Although such entrepots involved a greater than proportionate share of the costs, the private development of the commercial (and possibly manufacturing) function at the site was expected to produce a net benefit for the state. Thus, whether a state decided to become involved directly, or whether it contracted for construction and operation, it was considered desirable to have such canals under the control of a single state, wherever possible. The alteration of a boundary line in what was then a relatively uninhabited area was thought to be of little consequence.

The bicentennial of the Northwest Ordinance attracted the attention of many scholars, Jonathan Hughes among them. Tying the Ordinance to his existing research, Hughes (1987) identified the important role the "great" land ordinances of the 1780s played in defining U.S. property rights. Concomitant with the specification of rights was the need to measure the property, and Hughes discussed the development of the 36 square mile township. This was the basic unit of measure for all U.S. land adopted in the companion piece of legislation, the Ordinance of 1785. The U.S. then sold off the land, township by township, once the land was secure from the British and their native allies. Hughes does not consider the surveying errors that contributed to the first boundary dispute in the Northwest Territory, that between Ohio and Michigan. To Hughes the importance of the Northwest Ordinance was that it efficiently transferred public land to the private sector:

> What was important in the long run was that the land be distributed into private hands in the standard American land tenure, and that the titles be perfectly secure, and that the American political democracy be expanded in its pure form from east to west as the continental nation was formed piece by piece, township by township (Hughes, 1987, p. 13).

A second scholar attracted by the bicentennial was Douglass North, one of Hughes' teachers. North examined the Ordinance as part of his continuing effort to understand institutions and the way they evolve (North and Rutten, 1987). As it did to Hughes, North saw the Ordinance as representing a change in land policy from the pre-Revolutionary war policy, a change in response to new incentives that emerged with American independence. In particular, North pointed to the need to finance the war, the commitment to representative government, and the antislavery sentiment of the northern states. The decisions to raise federal revenues through land sales and to admit additional states to the union on an equal basis gave rise to disagreements as to how the benefits of this policy were to be distributed. These disagreements, in turn, contributed to the evolution of land policy, such as the political development of the territories, the distribution of benefits from the public lands, and the terms of sales (see North and Rutten, 1987, pp. 27-30). Disagreements with respect to boundary lines, how they were drawn in the Ordinance versus when the land was divided into states, lie largely outside the scope of North's analysis.

Neither Hughes nor North addressed the issue of how the Northwest Territory was formed state by state, although North did note that Jefferson's initial draft called for the creation of more states than emerged. The process of carving the five states from the Northwest Territory proved quite different than the efficient long-run mechanism envisioned in the underlying land policy. To Hughes and North, it has mattered little in the long run whether Toledo is in Ohio or Michigan, whether Chicago is in Illinois or Wisconsin. In the short run, however, the east-west boundary dividing the two northern states (Wisconsin and Michigan) from the three southern states (Illinois, Indiana, and Ohio) provoked an extreme form of the "disagreements" to which North alluded. In two cases violence was threatened, and in one case fighting did erupt. Michigan and Ohio fought over the right to Toledo, while Wisconsin's territorial legislature passed and forwarded to Washington a petition that reads like a potential declaration of war. Did the potential benefits justify the actual costs incurred in these disputes?

Economic historians are familiar with most, but not all, of the details underlying the two land ordinances of the 1780s.[1] Following the Revolutionary War, the land west of the Appalachians came under control of the new nation. The founding fathers had to confront multiple state claims for this land and resolved them by creating a public domain, the nation instead of the king (Jensen, 1936). In turn, the federal government pledged to grant land to

Revolutionary War veterans and to return the public land to private ownership as expeditiously as possible. In 1784, a five-man Congressional committee chaired by Thomas Jefferson prepared an ordinance for ascertaining and disposing the public domain, particularly the Northwest Territory (see Hibbard, 1939, Chap. 3).

Jefferson's committee proposed that the Northwest Territory be divided into ten parts. When the population reached 20,000 in any one of them, it could form a territorial government. Prior to that, it would be ruled by a temporary government based upon any one of the original thirteen states' constitutions of its choosing. Once the area qualified for territorial status, it could write its own constitution. When the territory reached a population equal to the least populous original state (then somewhere between 40,000 and 50,000), it would be admitted as an equal partner in the union, subject to a two-thirds vote of the existing states.

The ten states Jefferson proposed all had classical names and reasonably complete boundaries. The present city of Chicago, for example, was to be included in the state of Assenisipia, the area "thro' which the Assenisipi or Rock river runs" (see Map 1). Directly to the east, and with the same northern and southern boundaries, was the state of Metropotamia, "in which are the fountains of the Muskingum, the Miamis of Ohio, the Wabash, the Illinois, the Miami of the lake and Sandusky rivers" (Old South Leaflets No. 127, n.d.).[2]

The following year, while Jefferson served as Ambassador to France, a second committee considered his proposed ordinance. This committee limited its recommendations to the question of land survey and disposal. With few changes, Congress passed them as the Land Ordinance of 1785 (see Carter, 1934, pp. 12-19). The fate of the Northwest Territory was postponed. James Monroe's letters to Jefferson in Paris reveal a change in strategy.

Following a western trip, Monroe wrote, in January 1786, that he feared their measures with respect to the territory were impolitic. He was most concerned about the creation of *ten* new states. He felt the new states might have different interests than the newly emerging constitutional, federal government. The addition of ten new states would increase the likelihood of sectional division. Monroe suggested the number of new states be reduced in order to increase the new government's probability of success.

Monroe also proffered a second reason for reducing the number of new states:

> A great part of the territory is miserably poor, especially that near lakes Michigan and Erie and that upon the Mississippi and the Illinois consists of extensive plains which have not had from appearance and will not have a single bush on them, for ages. The districts therefore within which these fall will perhaps never contain a sufficient number of inhabitants to entitle them to membership in the confederacy (Hamilton, 1904, p. 117).[3]

Map 1. The Northwest Territory under the 1784 Ordinance

Consequently, Monroe submitted a motion to Congress later that year which, when adopted, limited the number of new states in the Northwest Territory to between three and five (see, U. S. Library of Congress, 1904, p. 390-394, for Friday, 7 July 1786). This motion was then incorporated into the Land Ordinance of 1787 (Carter, 1934, pp. 39-50). The Northwest Territory was to be organized as a district; a district governor and judges would be appointed by Congress.[4] When one of the three-to-five districts contained 5,000 male residents of voting age (rather than 20,000 population), an elected territorial legislature would be established and a non-voting delegate sent to

Congress. The executive and judicial functions were still to be filled by federal government appointees. When the territorial population reached 60,000 free inhabitants (rather than a population equal to the least populous original state), the territory would become a state "on an equal footing with the original states, in all respects whatever."

While a territory had considerable control over its internal affairs, it did not have a vote at the federal level; a state was guaranteed of two Senators and one Representative. Furthermore, territories were still subject to executive and judicial appointments which were dependent on federal, not local, concerns; a state was not. There was, therefore, a benefit to achieving statehood. The test was based on population, and the 1787 ordinance involved a more stringent test than the 1784 draft.[5]

Of particular interest are the "fixed" boundaries established for the three to five states included in the fifth article of the ordinance:

> There shall be formed in the said territory, no less than three nor more than five states; and the boundaries of the States . . . shall become fixed and established as follows, to wit: The *Western State* in the said territory, shall be bounded by the Mississippi, the Ohio and Wabash Rivers; a direct line drawn from the Wabash and post Vincents due North to the territorial line between the United States and Canada, and by the said territorial line to the lake of the Woods and Mississippi. The *middle State* shall be bounded by the said direct line, the Wabash from post Vincents to Ohio, by the Ohio, by a direct line drawn due North from the mouth of the great Miami to the said territorial line, and by the said territorial line. . . . The *eastern State* shall be bounded by the last mentioned direct line, the Ohio, Pennsylvania, and the said territorial line; provided however, that the boundaries of these three States, shall be subject so far to be altered, that if Congress shall hereafter find it expedient, they shall have authority to form one or two States in that part of the said territory which lies north of an east and west line drawn through the southerly bend or extreme of lake Michigan (Carter, 1934, pp. 48-49).

As is clear from Map 2, where the five states described in the ordinance are superimposed on the five states that were admitted to the union, the ordinance did not establish fixed boundaries. In several cases, the redefinition of these boundaries created intractable problems. Two of these are "the Toledo War" of 1835 and the Wisconsin proclamation of 1843.

The phrase—an east and west line drawn through the southerly bend or extreme of lake Michigan—reappears in the 1802 act enabling Ohio to become a state and the 1805 act creating the Michigan Territory. The dispute over Toledo arose because the detailed map used to draw that boundary in the Northwest Ordinance placed the "southerly bend" to the north of its actual position (see, Millis, 1934; Wittke, 1936). This was discovered by the time of the Ohio Constitution Convention which accepted the boundaries in the enabling act with the proviso that, if the southern tip of Lake Michigan was so far south that the east-west line would not intersect Lake Erie, or would hit Lake Erie south of the mouth of the Maumee River, then the line should

Map 2. The Northwest Territory under the 1787 Ordinance

be drawn to the most northerly cape of Maumee Bay.[6] In short, Ohio claimed Toledo regardless.

Ohio's interest in Toledo was never related to the need for a sufficient population to apply for statehood. There were few residents of the Toledo area when Ohio achieved statehood in 1803. A more plausible explanation is related to the fact that this was a period of waterborne transportation. The Maumee was expected to be an avenue of commerce. Toledo, at the mouth of the Maumee, would become the entrepot for commerce rising in what unambiguously was Ohio. Whether the potential for canal construction was considered prior to statehood is unclear. After the opening of the Erie Canal in 1825, canal construction was considered in a great many states, but it has not been one of the themes discussed in the literature on the Toledo War. During the 1840s the Maumee River became part of the Miami and Erie Canal system built in Ohio and the Wabash and Erie Canal system built in Indiana (Scheiber, 1988). The commercial potential of the Maumee and the expected economic growth of the entrepot at its mouth provides an obvious, albeit conjectural, explanation why Ohio would want to retain the Toledo area.[7]

Congress took no action on the boundary proviso when Ohio was admitted as a state, waiting until the facts were established. The fact was (and is) that the mouth of the Maumee River lies to the north of the southern tip of Lake Michigan, and the Territory of Michigan claimed the disputed area on that basis. Ohio claimed Congress intended that it should have the area.

Just before the outbreak of the War of 1812, Congress ordered a survey of the disputed boundary. The war delayed the work until 1815, at which time President Madison ordered the Ohio surveyor-general to do the job. He in turn instructed his surveyor, William Harris, to follow the line defined by the proviso to the Ohio Constitution. Michigan promptly protested, and Madison ordered a second line drawn in accord with the original wording. This line, surveyed by John Fulton, intersected Lake Erie approximately seven miles south of the Harris line, moving the mouth of the Maumee to the Michigan side of the border. Ohio protested that Fulton failed to establish the latitude of the southern tip of Lake Michigan or that of the point where the line intersected Lake Erie. Congress ultimately ordered a third survey to be completed by the end of 1835. This job, performed by U.S. Army Captain Andrew Talcott and his assistant Lieutenant Robert E. Lee, traced Fulton's line almost exactly.

Between the last two surveys, Indiana was admitted as a state in 1816 with a northern boundary 10 miles north of the southern tip of Lake Michigan.[8] The Territory of Michigan promptly filed a protest, but it apparently became part of the ongoing dispute. Michigan exercised jurisdiction in the area under dispute with Ohio, but not in Indiana. Residents in the Port Lawrence (Toledo) area paid taxes to Michigan and in return received improvements such as roads as well as police protection. Ohio was content to press its claim on paper. This changed dramatically in the early 1830s when the settlement at the mouth of the Maumee began to grow, and the Michigan Territory, particularly with the inclusion of Toledo, reached a sufficient population to become a state. Michigan wanted its statehood first, and then the boundary could be resolved in court. Ohio preferred that the boundary be resolved first; Ohio believed it was in a stronger position politically if it dealt with Michigan as a territory rather than as an equal state.

On February 23, 1835 the Ohio legislature passed an act extending the state's jurisdiction to the boundary line drawn by Harris, requiring the remarking of the boundary line, and, for the first time, exercising jurisdiction in the disputed area. Michigan parried by passing an act that would punish any Ohio citizen for attempting to exercise jurisdiction in that area and sent a sheriff with deputies to prevent the remarking of the boundary. Governor Lucas of Ohio then mobilized his state's militia and sent 600 men to Perrysburg. Governor Mason of Michigan responded by sending 1000 men to Port Lawrence, twenty miles away. It was merely a show of force; after a few days the militias were withdrawn. Nonetheless, people were arrested in the Port Lawrence area. There were documented stories of fisticuffs and wild rumors of much worse. The most serious casualty apparently was a fellow who had some difficulty sitting after being hit with buckshot.

This whole affair was a political embarrassment for President Andrew Jackson, inasmuch as both governors were fellow Democrats. Jackson requested the U.S. Attorney General to issue an opinion, and he found in Michigan's favor. Jackson personally favored Ohio, if for no other reason than it had more electoral votes, and was not inclined to accept the report. Instead, he sent two commissioners to act as conciliators. They quickly returned to Washington reporting that neither side welcomed their mission. At this juncture, Jackson removed Mason from his position as territorial governor, and replaced him with a man more likely to accede to Ohio's claim. This set Michigan into motion once again.

The Legislative Council of the Michigan Territory, armed with an 1834 census indicating sufficient population, called a constitutional convention without any enabling legislation from Washington. This convention drafted and received approval for a state constitution, and, by November 1835, had duly elected a governor (the ousted Mason) and other state officers. They had also established courts and the other apparatus of government under the provisions of its new constitution. Two senators and a representative were sent to Washington, but Congress refused to seat them. Undaunted, Michigan continued to operate in this fashion until it was finally admitted as a state.

By 1836, an election year, Jackson sought to bring the controversy to an end. With strong presidential urging, Congress passed an act on July 15 to admit Michigan as a state on the condition that it resign claim to the disputed area and accept what became known as the Upper Peninsula, a much larger area. A convention of delegates selected by the people of Michigan rejected this compromise on September 4, 1836; they did not want "the sterile region on the shores of Lake Superior, destined by soil and climate to remain forever a wilderness" (Wittke, 1936, p. 318).

This was the last hurrah; Jackson's supporters in the forthcoming election and those desirous of statehood increasingly came to favor the compromise. It also appeared that a distribution of public lands (or the proceeds from their sale) was to take place, and Michigan would not receive a share without statehood. In the end, Michigan's Jacksonians assumed the mantle of all

Michiganders and called a second convention. On December 6, 1836, with almost no legal authority, they accepted the Congressional compromise. The meeting of the "Frost Bitten Convention" was widely ridiculed, but the Jacksonians who dominated Congress found it advantageous to assume it had legal authority. Consequently, on January 26, 1837, replete with two peninsulas but *sine* Toledo, Michigan became a state.

The Illinois Territory, including present-day Wisconsin and a piece of Minnesota, was split from the Indiana Territory in 1809. Following the War of 1812, there was a significant inflow of migrants from Virginia, North Carolina, and Kentucky to the southernmost portion of the territory, but there were a large number of others who preceded them.[9] These people created a problem. The Northwest Ordinance provided that only landowners could vote, and these people were squatters whose claims to the land were contested. When Illinois became a second-grade territory, Congress enfranchised all free white males who lived in Illinois for a year and paid any amount of county or territorial tax.

In January 1818 the territory petitioned Congress for statehood. The legal claims of many squatters remained unresolved, so Congress approved an amendment that permitted Illinois to become a state with two-thirds the specified population. Even then, it was doubtful Illinois had 40,000 population.[10] Judge Nathaniel Pope, Illinois' territorial delegate, was placed on the committee to which the petition was referred. Judge Pope offered an amendment to change Illinois' northern boundary, moving it approximately 60 miles north of the boundary in the ordinance. Congress adopted Pope's amendment without exception and without recorded debate.

Judge Pope evidently offered this amendment on his own. His principal objective was to gain a Lake Michigan coastline and an outlet for the proposed Illinois and Michigan Canal to connect the lake and the Illinois River. If the only commercial avenues available to the new state were the Mississippi River and its tributaries, then Judge Pope noted, "There is a possibility that her (Illinois') commercial relations with the South may become so closely connected that in the event of an attempted dismemberment of the Union, Illinois will cast her lot with the Southern States" (quoted in Mather, 1913, p. 143).[11] A Lake Michigan coastline, an east-west commercial avenue, afforded some security to the union's perpetuity. The potential for such a canal had been acknowledged by every visitor from the time of Marquette and Joliet. By extending the boundary, the canal would be contained within a single state. Since Toledo was in the same geographical relation to a river system as Chicago, it is surprising the rationale for the change in Illinois' boundary does not play a greater role in the debate over Toledo in the 1830s.

Illinois was granted statehood on December 3, 1818, and the Wisconsin Territory was established from the balance of the old Illinois Territory. The rate of settlement in northern Illinois accelerated almost immediately centering on the Galena lead mining district. Most of this district was to the north of the 1787 boundary line. Yet the political power in Illinois remained in the more populous south. Consequently, in October 1828 residents of the Galena district petitioned Congress for the creation of a new territory. Basing their claim on the 1787 ordinance, they argued that people in the district had a "right to expect" that the entire district north of the 1787 boundary line "would remain together" (Radebaugh, 1904, p. 123). They argued that, as unrepresented people, their sovereignty had been transferred without their knowledge or consent. These issues were not resolved until Wisconsin became a state.

Michigan's receipt of the Upper Peninsula convinced Wisconsin politicians, notably Governors Henry Dodge and James Doty, that Michigan's assertion of the north-south boundary line in the 1787 ordinance was correct. Given that Illinoisans residing north of "the southerly bend or extreme of lake Michigan" seemed anxious to sever their connection to Illinois, the addition of that area would give Wisconsin a sufficient population to petition for statehood.

Residents of the disputed Illinois region supported this quest. Townsmen from Galena and Rockford assumed the leadership. In most of the fourteen northern Illinois counties involved, elections were held during 1842 which overwhelmingly favored union with Wisconsin. Votes such as 570 for union, 1 against in Stephenson County; 495 to 11 in Boone County; and 971 to 6 in Winnebago County were typical (Radebaugh, 1904, p. 136). Only Cook County, through which the canal was to pass, was disinterested. Northern Illinoisans, largely migrants from New York and New England, supported union with Wisconsin because they found they had much more in common with their neighbors to the north than those to the south. Southern Illinoisans had a three-to-one advantage in the state government, and there was a heavy state debt from an overly ambitious program of internal improvement that would have benefitted these northerners little, if at all. Most of these projects were abandoned when the Panic of 1837 bankrupted the state.

Many promises were made in the attempt to lure northern Illinoisans to cast their lot with Wisconsin. John Wentworth noted in his reminiscences:

> The disputed tract had two Congressmen, the Hon. Joseph P Hoge, of Galena, . . . and myself. And Wisconsin offered to make us the first two Senators, and also offered to give the disputed tract the first Governor. It was proposed to enact a law submitting the binding force of the ordinance of 1787 to the Supreme Court of the United States. Our Chicago people were much divided upon the question, and I really believe serious consequences would have grown out of it but for the embarrassments that would be caused by having the Illinois and Michigan Canal owned by two states. As an original question, all the five states being out of the Union, there is no doubt but Congress would have enforced the provisions of the ordinance, and Illinois been saved from the annoyance of Chicago lobbyists. But might made right. Wisconsin being out of the Union she could only come into it with boundaries prescribed by a majority of the states in it, and I lost the honor of being a Wisconsin United States Senator (quoted in Andreas, 1884, p. 171).

Residents of the Wisconsin Territory were not as zealous for statehood as their political leaders; they defeated it four times between 1841 and 1845 (Gara, 1962, pp. 71-73). The turnout was invariably light, while the vote was typically two-to-one against. The ready explanation for this is indifference; statehood was the lonesome quest of "politicians and newspaper editors." James Willard Hurst argued that by 1840 "the challenge of the continent" was of greater interest than constitution making, but all that was to change quickly (quoted in Nesbit, 1973, p. 212). The Wisconsin territory was growing rapidly. A census taken at the time Wisconsin reached territorial status in 1836 found only 11,000 whites. Four years later, the federal census reported just under 31,000 residents.

Some insight as to why the residents of Wisconsin initially lacked their leaders' enthusiasm for statehood can be found in an 1842 report issued by the territorial House of Representatives. They considered the existing government well-suited to their needs. A merger would shift the political balance in Wisconsin southward. Further, the Wisconsin house believed it should have some say about accepting the fourteen Illinois counties, and, should such a merger be approved, the fourteen counties should be free of any debt. Nonetheless, the governor pursued the goal of statehood and the boundary question. After almost a year of political quarreling, a committee of the territorial council produced a memorial to Congress in December 1843 that is strongly reminiscent of states' rights proclamations issued seventeen years later:

> it is the opinion of many that we ought, without further delay, form a constitution and State government, adopting that (1787) line as our southern boundary. . . . The People of Wisconsin, regret the necessity which has been imposed on them by the unauthorized action of the general government. In consideration of these repeated assaults upon our right of boundary by that government which should have been our guardian, and the protector of our rights while in our infancy . . . , we have entertained a most serious doubt as to what course to pursue. . . . Should Congress, however, turn a deaf ear to our claims upon their justice, or refuse to atone for the wrongs they have done us, we ask them . . . to reflect upon what they may reasonably imagine will be the consequences and to know . . . that Wisconsin will never peaceably submit to so gross a violation of her rights, and that after she has done all to obtain a peaceable redress . . . , and shall have failed, she will resort to every measure in her power to protect and to preserve her rights. . . . The people of Wisconsin . . . now call upon the Congress of the United States to take this subject under their candid and deliberate consideration, and to do justice while it is not too late to a people who have hitherto been weak and unprotected, but who are rapidly rising to giant greatness, and who at no distant day will show to the world that they lack neither the disposition nor the ability to protect themselves (quoted in Radebaugh, 1904, pp. 139-140).

Curiously, by this time the Wisconsin Territory, without the fourteen Illinois counties, had a population sufficient to achieve statehood. By the Spring of 1846, approximately 15,000 residents voted five-to-one in favor of statehood.[12]

A special census showed the territory's population to be in excess of 155,000, two-and-a-half times the required minimum. Statehood had always been of greater concern than the contested territory, which was more important to Wisconsin's leaders for its population than its land. Congress required that Wisconsin forswear any claim to Illinois land before statehood could be granted, and this was accomplished easily. Wisconsin became a state on May 29, 1848 without its intended northern part which became Michigan's Upper Peninsula, its intended southern part which became part of Illinois, and its intended northwestern corner which became part of .Minnesota (see Wells, 1978).[13]

The northwestern boundary of the Northwest Territory ran along the Rum River to Lake of the Woods. As Wisconsin approached statehood, lumbermen in the St. Croix valley concluded it would be easier to control their destiny under the less stringent, less distant territorial form of government than under a state government in Madison. Let by Caleb Cushing, these lumbermen went to Washington and successfully lobbied friends in Congress to draw Wisconsin's northwest boundary along the St. Croix River and move the remainder to the Minnesota Territory. Thus, Wisconsin lost the Twin Cities as well as Chicago. It could have become the predominant state of the Northwest Territory.

As interesting as these various boundary disputes are, the consequences of the Illinois-Wisconsin dispute present even more interesting speculations. By 1850 the disputed territory was the most populous in Illinois. In the elections of 1854 and 1860, Illinois elected Lyman Trumbull a U.S. Senator. Trumbull was a staunch advocate of the union position in a state with considerable sympathy for the confederacy. Trumbull's influence made the nomination of Abraham Lincoln possible. Lincoln was a southern Illinoisan with northern views. Had the fourteen northern counties become part of Wisconsin, Lincoln would have been a man with few supporters in his home state. He could well have remained a Springfield lawyer in a state sorely tempted to join the confederacy.

It made relatively little difference after the fact where state boundaries were drawn. There have been few attempts to have them altered.[14] Tiebout effects arise in the choice between place of work and place of residence, if a state line falls within the tolerable commuting range, but such effects are the exception. Most of us are indifferent about such issues.

Before the fact, however, emotions were much stronger. Statehood appeared to present two major political benefits to territorial residents. First, it gave them voting representatives at the federal level. Second, it gave them control of the executive and judicial branches at the state level. Territorial status only conferred control of the legislative branch. Statehood required 60,000 residents. A strict interpretation of the borders in the Northwest Ordinance was seen by those anxious for statehood in Michigan and Wisconsin as a way of accelerating the process. Both territories more or less dropped that interpretation when their territorial population reached the level sufficient for statehood.

A second motive was economic, the expected benefits of what in hindsight is known as the canal era. The fact that the Chicago River and its branches were placed in Illinois was a result of the belief that the state would find it advantageous to include the Chicago River in a canal system connecting the Illinois River and Lake Michigan. Fifteen years later, geographical similarity must have played a role in Ohio's claim to Toledo. While the Illinois and Michigan Canal would not be completed until 1848, evidence from eastern canals must have suggested that the potential net tax revenues that would be derived from Toledo justified Ohio's strong posture with respect to its claim. It should also be noted that the railroad reached Toledo in 1836. In the end, Ohio received Toledo. Michigan was "compensated" for the loss of Toledo with reputedly valuable land to the north and statehood, for which it then qualified without the Toledo area. Why the federal government took so long to resolve this dispute remains an outstanding question.

After the fact, these disputes amount to little more than a tempest in a teacup. It seems doubtful the Wisconsin territorial legislature wanted someone to call its bluff. On the other hand, a majority voted in favor of bluffing. Such passion is hard to arouse over a trifle. The decision to mobilize 1,600 militia is seldom made without at least an implicit calculation of costs and benefits. The actual costs incurred in these disputes were not trivial. Before the fact, the political and economic benefits must have been perceived as large enough to justify the effort.

ACKNOWLEDGMENTS

The author is grateful for the comments of the editor, the referees, and the honoree. An earlier version of this essay was presented to workshops at the Universities of Alberta, British Columbia, Michigan and Chicago, and the North Carolina Research Triangle. In each case, the discussion helped shape my thinking about this subject.

NOTES

1. See any competent textbook in American economic history; Hughes (1990) will suffice.

2. A small map found in the papers of David Hartley, a diplomatic agent who represented the English in negotiating the peace treaty in 1782 (and represented the Americans the following year) indicates a total of fourteen potential states in the area west of the original thirteen. It has been suggested that Hartley received this map from Jefferson, but the map was not drawn by Jefferson. The ten classical names for the northern states were included, but none for the four southern states. Both Polypotamia and Pelisipia were drawn in the same rectangular fashion as those to the north; the Ohio River passed through those states. Disposition of the lands to the

south of the Ohio River was not addressed at this time ("Liberty's Legacy," 1987 p. 29). The original is contained in the David Hartley Papers at the Clements Library in Ann Arbor, Michigan.

3. Letter to Thomas Jefferson from New York, January 19, 1786 (Hamilton, 1898, pp. 117-118). See also his letters of August 25, 1785 (p. 107) and July 16, 1786 (p. 140). The lack of equality between the number of northern and southern states may be a third reason.

4. The 1787 Ordinance prohibited slavery in the Northwest Territory. An ordinance was passed in 1790, without the prohibition of slavery, that extended these rules to other areas that might one day aspire to statehood, Hughes (1987, p. 6).

5. Gara (1962, pp. 69-70) argues that, at least for Wisconsin in the 1840s, residents believed statehood had economic significance as well. In the aftermath of the Panic of 1837 eastern capitalists were wary of western investments. The ability to make laws with respect to internal improvements and banking would attract needed funds to the area.

6. This is a diagonal line from the southern tip of Lake Michigan to the northern cape of Maumee Bay.

7. The historiography of this episode simply reflects a debate over the legitimacy of the two states' claims.

8. Also added were some small areas east of the Wabash River between Vincennes and Terre Haute. See Esarey (1918, p. 216).

9. A census of 1800 reported there were 2,458 residents in the Illinois country, many of them French. Howard (1972, p. 70).

10. See Ford (1945-46). Ford was Governor of Illinois from 1842-46. See also Howard (1972, pp. 101-102). Following Indiana's admission into the union in 1816, Mississippi, Illinois, Alabama, and Missouri were admitted in little more than four years. A second reason why Illinois was admitted with less than the stipulated population is to maintain the balance between free and slave states.

11. See also Boggess (1908, pp. 115-118) and Ford (1945-46).

12. Florida and Texas had been admitted in 1845, and Iowa and Wisconsin were the logical candidates to restore the balance now required by the Missouri Compromise.

13. Wisconsin also lost Duluth.

14. There are those who have advocated creating a new state from northern Wisconsin and the upper peninsula of Michigan to avoid what they perceive as the redistribution of income toward Milwaukee and Detroit. They have had little influence beyond producing a popular bumper sticker.

REFERENCES

Andreas, A. T. (1884), *History of Chicago from the Earliest Period to the Present Time*, Vol. 1, Chicago: A.T. Andreas.

Boggess, A. C. (1908). *The Settlement of Chicago, 1778-1830*. Chicago: Chicago Historical Society.

Carter, C. E. (Ed.). (1934). *The Territorial Papers of the U.S.*, Vol. 2, *The Territory Northwest of the River Ohio, 1787-1803*. Washington, D.C.: U.S. Government Printing Office.

Esarey, L. (1918). *A History of Indiana*. Indianapolis, IN: Bowen.

Ford, T. (1945-46). *Ford's History of Illinois from its Commencement as a State in 1818 to 1847*, 2 Vols. Chicago: The Lakeside Press.

Gara, L. (1962). *A Short History of Wisconsin*. Madison, WI: The State Historical Society of Wisconsin.

Hamilton, S. M. (Ed.). (1898). *The Writings of James Monroe*, vol. 1. New York: G. P. Putnam's Sons.

Heilbrun, J. (1981). *Urban Economics and Public Policy*, 2nd ed. New York: St. Martin's Press.

Hibbard, B. H. (1939). *A History of the Public Land Policies*. New York: Peter Smith.

Howard, R. P. (1972). *Illinois: A History of the Prairie State*. Grand Rapids, MI: William B. Eerdmans.

Hughes, J. R. T. (1987). "The Great Land Ordinances: Colonial America's Thumbprint on History." Pp. 1-18 in *Essays on the Economy of the Old Northwest*, edited by D. C. Klingaman and R. K. Vedder. Athens, OH: Ohio University Press.

Hughes, J. R. T. (1990). *American Economic History*, 3rd ed., Glenview, IL: Scott, Foresman.

Jensen, M. (1936). "The Cession of the Old Northwest," *Mississippi Valley Historical Review*, 23(June): 27-48.

"Liberty's Legacy: Our Celebration of the Northwest Ordinance and the United States Constitution." (1987). An illustrated catalogue from a traveling exhibition of historical documents sponsored by nine alumni associations of Big Ten universities celebrating the bicentennial of the Northwest Ordinance.

Mather, I. F. (1913). *The Making of Illinois*. Chicago: A. Flanagan Company.

Millis, W. (1936). "When Michigan was Born," *Michigan History*, 18: 208-224.

Nesbit, R. C. (1973). *Wisconsin: A History*. Madison: University of Wisconsin Press.

North, D. C. and Rutten, A. R. (1987). "The Northwest Ordinance in Historical Perspective." Pp. 19-36 in *Essays on the Economy of the Old Northwest*, edited by D.C. Klingaman and R.K. Vedder. Athens, OH: Ohio University Press.

Old South Leaflets No. 127. (n.d.), "The Ordinance of 1784 and Jefferson's Services for the Northwest Territory." Boston, MA: The Directors of the Old South Work.

Onuf, P.S. (1987). *Statehood and Union*. Bloomington, IN: Indiana University Press.

Radebaugh, W. (1904). "The Boundary Dispute between Illinois and Wisconsin." An address read before The Chicago Historical Society at a Special Meeting held May 19, 1904. Chicago: Chicago Historical Society.

Scheiber, H. N. (1988). *Ohio Canal Era: A Case Study of Government and the Economy, 1820-1861*. Athens, OH: Ohio University Press.

Tiebout, C. M. (1956). "A Pure Theory of Local Expenditures." *Journal of Political Economy*, 64: 416-424.

U. S. Library of Congress. (1904). *Journals of the Continental Congress, 1774-1789*. Washington, D.C.: U. S. Government Printing Office.

Wells, R. W. (1978). "Wisconsin Loses the Twin Cities." Pp. 59-70 in *Daylight in the Swamp*. New York: Doubleday.

Wittke, C. (1936). "The Ohio-Michigan Boundary Dispute Reexamined." *Ohio Archaeological and Historical Society*: 299-319.

SOCIAL SECURITY AND THE AMERICAN WELFARE STATE

Edward Berkowitz and Kim McQuaid

Jonathan Hughes recently noted, with characteristic flair, that the American welfare state has grown "unimaginably in cost," and now automatically consumes a large proportion of the federal government's resources (Hughes, 1986, pp. vii, ix). Explaining the government's appetite for money forms a major theme of Hughes's work, as his *Governmental Habit* and his portraits of two government "entrepreneurs" in the second edition of the *Vital Few* demonstrate. In *Governmental Habit*, for example, Hughes tackles the Social Security Act and what he calls the American "social insurance system." He notes our debts to the poor laws of Tudor England which have produced an "administratively cumbersome and expensive" system. He realizes that such historical inheritances exercise as much influence over our present social welfare system as do the rational precepts of economists. "From an economist's viewpoint, what our social insurance methods have done to labor mobility, factor use and prices, and managerial practices is beyond imagination" (Hughes, 1977, p. 193).

Research in Economic History, Suppl. 6, pages 169-190.

ISBN: 1-55938-150-7.

According to Hughes, political tradition and historical circumstance exercise their own form of logic, which we will probe in this paper. We examine the creation, contents, and implementation of the Social Security Act, America's single most important piece of social welfare legislation.

Conventional wisdom holds that we lagged far behind pioneering nations until 1935, when we passed the Social Security Act and initiated our own nationwide social welfare state. This wisdom overstates both the distance by which America trailed Europe, and more importantly for our present purposes, the immediate effects and importance of the Social Security Act.

As we will demonstrate, social security provided no panacea for America's social welfare problems during or after the great depression. Old age insurance, ultimately the largest and most respectable of our nonmarket social controls, put nothing in any elderly person's pocket until 1937 and did not pay any pensions until 1940. Those pensions that it did pay were modest; more of the elderly depended on welfare than on social insurance until 1951.

This slow development of social insurance derived from political pressures, turf battles and debates among technocrats, and the dominant fact of federalism in America's social and political order. Social insurance, by its very nature, produced political tensions and required political protection and nurturing. It was a long-range reform that had little or nothing to do with short-run problems. Furthermore, the creators of the Social Security Act understood this fact. They wanted to create a program that bypassed normal political channels, a program that was self-contained and self-financing. America's conservative and often contradictory social welfare system resulted from the need of politicians to respond to the immediate political and economic pressures of the depression and from the very different desire of technocrats to implement a future-oriented and non-political social insurance program.

In time, the social insurance program became popular and politicians learned to appreciate it. It brought them votes at little cost. The reformers and their allies in the government, meanwhile, realized the futility of administering a program that was somehow beyond politics. Program administrators also learned how to compromise with state officials, professional groups like the AMA, and other interested groups in order to expand the program.

President Roosevelt signed the Social Security Act into law on August 14, 1935. A complex and varied statute, it nevertheless created four types of programs: federal grants for traditional "welfare" programs, federal grants for state public health programs, an old age insurance program, and unemployment compensation. Without becoming bogged down in the fine points of social welfare policy, we define welfare as government grants that go only to people who can demonstrate they are poor and who are out of the labor force. The public health programs mentioned in the Social Security Act owed their existence to scattered federal laws, passed in the twenties for highly restricted clientele, such as the vocational rehabilitation (injured workers), crippled children's, and infant and maternal health programs. Much broader in its impact, old age insurance represented the first federally administered social insurance program, with universal coverage among industrial and commercial workers. Unemployment compensation, the last of the four elements of social security, was a state-run program that paid temporary benefits to workers who had been laid off.

With the exception of old age insurance, none of the programs mentioned in the Social Security Act was new. The novelty of the Act lay both in the old age insurance program and in the way in which it brought federal funds to activities previously funded on the state and local levels.

To illustrate, old age pensions for civilians had tended, in the American manner, to be state and local responsibilities, and coverage was very spotty before the Social Security Act. All of the state old age "pension" laws were noncontributory in nature. Many of those that were passed before 1929 even allowed individual counties the option of participating in a state program for the relief of the aged.

The terms of these state and non-contributory old age programs were stringent. The 1926 Kentucky law, for example, proposed a maximum pension of $250 a *year* to be paid by the counties only to indigent people over age 70 who had lived in the state for ten years or more. Fourteen other states had an age 70 requirement. None of the states paid pensions to a person who had more than $3,000 worth of property. The most any of the states paid was a dollar a day (Witte, in Committee on Ways and Means, 1935, p. 83). Even a liberal and wealthy state like New York could do no better than providing an average monthly pension of $23.80 in 1931.[1] When the Social Security Act was being considered in 1935, old age pensions existed in 28 states, but only about 180,000 people received old age pensions.

The Social Security Act continued this hesitant tradition of non-contributory state pensions to the elderly, many of whom were already retired and hence would never be eligible for the federal old age insurance program. The Act provided for federal financial assistance directly to the states: The federal government matched state contributions, up to a limit of $15 in federal money per elderly person (Patterson, 1981, p. 67; Achenbaum, 1986, p. 22). In this manner, the Social Security Act bailed out the financially strapped states and provided a financial inducement for all states to adopt aid to the elderly. The other welfare programs, such as aid to the blind or dependent children, also preserved the tradition of the state as the primary purveyor of relief.

Even when the Social Security Act crossed the line into relatively new territory, as was the case in unemployment compensation, it did so on politically cautious terms that continued the pattern of state control. Instead of allowing the federal government to run the unemployment insurance program, the Social Security Act created an incentive for the establishment of state programs (Nelson, 1969, p. 128; Lubove, 1968).[2] In fact, politicians, advisors, and other interested parties considered three options and chose the one that left the most discretion to the states. Under option one, exclusive federal control, the central government would have collected contributions and dispersed benefits. The law would have been uniform from place to place and protected employees' rights when they moved from state to state. The second option, the "subsidy plan," represented a half-way point between federal and state control in which the federal government would collect money for unemployment compensation and then give it back to the states in the form of grants. The third proposal, the one ultimately adopted, left administrative matters completely to the states.[3]

One reason for this muting of federal authority was that years of debate had polarized expert opinion on the many questions related to unemployment insurance. Even political allies differed among themselves over the best way to plan for the future. Many an expert, weaned in the Progressive Era, continued to believe that the states, not Washington, D.C., provided the best "laboratories for reform." A lingering distrust of the federal government figured in this thinking, motivated by a feeling that the federal government would keep taxes too low to make programs effective or that Congress, responsive to rural and southern interests, would cripple social welfare programs with exemptions for farmers, blacks, and others.

In one example of the internecine battles over unemployment compensation, Paul U. Kellogg, the progressive editor of the *Survey Magazine*, engaged in a long debate with Labor Secretary Frances Perkins, his friend and fellow liberal, over the need to write explicit federal standards. He wanted to write minimum benefit levels, applicable to all states, into the unemployment program. Perkins disagreed. She saw political advantages to state autonomy. From her Washington perspective, Perkins feared that states righters (Southern Democrats) in Congress would become entangled in extensive debate over the specifications of an unemployment insurance bill that would indefinitely delay the passage of the Social Security Act. Perkins also worried about the constitutionality of a federal law and about how future administrations would implement it. Perkins shared Roosevelt's fears. "We've got to keep a lot of responsibility and a lot of functions in the states," Roosevelt had told her. "Just think what it would be like to have all the power in the federal government if Huey Long should become President" (Roosevelt, quoted by Thomas Eliot in Nash, 1988, p. 36). Perkins viewed state laws as a "safer" course to follow.[4]

In the unsettled legal atmosphere of 1935, Perkins wanted to dress federal programs in as much state clothing as possible. Federal funds would complement state funds and state control. "I am more than ever convinced that any law which intimately affects the daily lives of people must have a considerable proportion of state and local opinion back of it," Perkins told Kellogg.[5]

Perkins correctly anticipated the controversy that federal standards raised. Businessmen and reformers differed, for example, over the proper level of the payroll taxes that should be used to support unemployment compensation.[6] Sam Lewisohn, a business executive from Miami Copper, wanted to keep the payroll taxes below 3 percent for fear of discouraging businessmen "from expanding or embarking on new ventures." Lewisohn, like many of his fellow businessmen, also wanted but did not get a federal requirement that employees be forced to contribute, "to induce a stronger sense of responsibility among employees in preventing the unemployment insurance system from being exploited by a minority."[7] Labor leaders like William Green strongly disagreed with Lewisohn. Nor did business and labor see eye to eye on the proper design of the program. Businessmen favored plant or industry unemployment insurance funds. Green objected to individual company reserves, fearing that the funds would be used as a weapon against labor (Green, in Committee on Ways and Means, 1935 p. 394).

In the end, Congress simply refused to come to grips with these and other economic and political issues and left them to the individual states. The result was that in unemployment compensation, as in most other areas of social policy, the Social Security Act conserved what had come before. The state system of welfare operation preceded the Social Security Act and remained in place after its enactment.

Why, then, did the Social Security Act initiate a completely new and distinctively federal program of old age retirement insurance that grew to be so large that it usurped the very name of social security? Part of the answer was that Congress had no way of knowing that old age insurance would become so large. The program, as passed in 1935, would provide modest pensions to industrial and commercial workers, financed by a 2 percent payroll tax on the first $3,000 of an employee's wages that would begin to be collected in 1937. (Employers and employees split the tax evenly then, as now.[8]) Another part of the answer was that old age insurance failed to encounter organized opposition precisely because it was a new venture, on which political positions had not yet hardened as they had on unemployment compensation. The policy discussion among experts, conducted in the middle of America's most severe depression, centered on unemployment, not old age. Still another part of the answer lay in the fact that, given the political situation in 1935, the old age insurance program appeared to be only a moderate extension of the federal government's economic and political power. Radical alternatives to a social insurance approach existed in abundance and one of them, the Townsend Plan, received serious consideration from Congress. It marked an ambitious attempt to raise new federal revenues through a national sales tax and simply to give the money to the elderly. Subject to constant change, the Plan, in its most representative form, called for everyone over age 60 to receive an automatic pension of $200 a month, provided the person spent all of his money each month. The plan's very existence made a federal old age insurance proposal look less radical than it would otherwise have been.

Compared with the Roosevelt administration advisors who worked on unemployment compensation, then, the staff members who concentrated on old age insurance worked with far fewer political and administrative constraints. As J. Douglas Brown, a Princeton labor economics professor, noted, "we were left largely alone to work out a national system of old age insurance" (Brown, 1969, p. 4).

Despite the relative freedom that Brown and the other staff members assigned to old age security enjoyed, it proved difficult to create a feasible old age insurance plan. The first recorded proposal, put together by Barbara Armstrong, a lawyer from the University of California, contained eight variations. In recognition of America's social welfare realities, six of these eight variations involved state or private administration. In one of them, employers and employees each contributed 1 percent of the employees' wages into a federal fund. States then established old age insurance plans, and if these plans met the minimum standards mandated by the federal government, the states received money from the federal government in order to pay old age benefits. In other variations, private companies or entire industries, rather than the state governments, established the old age plans and received the federal subsidy. This proposal marked a return to the welfare capitalism of the 1920s. Compulsory coverage of industrial employees also remained an issue in the fall of 1934. As these proposals made clear, federal bureaucrats were not rushing in to take the social welfare system over.

The staff, which was not as wedded to state, local, or private precedents as the politicians who needed to sell social security to Congress, decided on a federally administered old age insurance plan with compulsory coverage in November 1934.[9] Freed from the orthodoxy that inhibited discussion of unemployment compensation, the staff simply followed the administrative logic to its limits. "How, would a single state be able to estimate its pension liability years in advance, given the mobility of the American wage earner and the constant shift in age distribution?" (Brown, 1972, pp. 10-12). People were pressing the committee to come up with something on old age security, one staff member later noted, and Brown and Armstrong were able to say, "We've got it for you. Here it is."[10]

Brown later admitted that he deliberately exaggerated the problems of establishing separate state old age insurance systems, writing memos to the other staff members with "awesome descriptions of the complexities" (Brown, 1969, p. 8). As Brown and Armstrong realized, however, the same logic could be applied to unemployment compensation. The real difference between unemployment and old age was that existing state laws and state-oriented expert opinion blocked a national approach to unemployment compensation; fewer roadblocks stood in the way of a recommendation for a national system of old age insurance. It was not an issue of program "complexity," but of politics.

Although the roadblocks to a federal old age insurance program were fewer, they still existed. One was legal. The Supreme Court had approved few New Deal initiatives up to 1935, and thus the constitutionality of an old age insurance plan, like most of the rest of the New Deal, remained in doubt (Brown, 1969, p. 8).

Another was political. Politicians needed to do something for the elderly and do it immediately. The elderly, after all, were "God's beloved old people, who have read newspapers, who have studied the Bible, who have read books, who are intelligent, but who are pitifully helpless in their old age" (McGroarty, in *Congressional Record*, 1935, p. 5794). Social insurance programs, according to Senator Byrd, "are not relief provisions and they are not going to be any relief to the destitute or needy now or for years to come" (Senate Committee on Finance, 1935, p. 303). "This will not buy bread for anybody now" (Congressman Jenkins, in *Congressional Record*, 1935, p. 5993).

Congressional rhetoric of this sort strengthened the policy experts' desires to insulate old age security from politics. In contrast to non-contributory plans, such as the Townsend Plan, the old age insurance that these experts designed was a conservative piece of legislation that was tied to the private labor market and had many of the same features as a private pension plan. Furthermore, by delaying the start of benefit payments and relating benefits to contributions, the plan contained a built-in fiscal safeguard, even if it also strengthened the notion that the elderly were entitled to a pension from the public sector. At the time, experts placed great importance on this fiscal safeguard, in the hope of preventing raids on the public treasury such as they feared from the Townsend plan.[11]

Even with the safeguards, the old age insurance portions of the bill still encountered serious opposition from people who did not think them conservative enough. In essence, the administration muted this opposition by offering Congress an omnibus measure that combined state administered programs covering children and the unemployed with a fully federal program covering the elderly. Because of these features, even conservatives had difficulty voting against the bill. As Carolyn Weaver has noted, Roosevelt presented Congress with a tie-in deal, which bundled together popular measures, like state-administered and federal-state financed welfare for the elderly, with less popular measures, like federal old age insurance. Congress, aware that the administration had just won an impressive victory in the 1934 mid-term elections, accepted the package.[12]

Few Congressmen understood the details of the varied bits of the legislative package; one inside observer stated after the bill's passage that the "Congressmen have a very confused idea of what this whole program is about. . . . They mix up old-age insurance with unemployment insurance."[13] Almost no one read the technical reports that the staff had prepared (Witte, 1962. p. 40). This ignorance about social insurance, however, was based on concrete political calculations about what paid short-term political dividends and what did not. "Let me say frankly at the outset that the only part of the President's economic security bill I am very greatly interested in for the moment or that many Members are very greatly interested in, is Section I of that bill [the welfare section of concern to the poor elderly flocking into the Townsend movement]," noted Congressman Mott (in *Congressional Record*, 1935, p. 5457).

The most significant legislative fight over social security, as things turned out, erupted in the Senate and concerned the right of employees who already had old age pensions from private companies to opt out of the federal law. Presented as an amendment to the bill by Senator Bennett Champ Clark, this proposal would have permitted an employee to choose between the federal plan and his employer's private plan, provided that his employer's plan was "not less favorable" than the federal plan. Because it would have produced competition between private and public systems, many employers welcomed it.[14]

Almost alone among the social insurance provisions of the Social Security Act, the Clark Amendment caused considerable controversy. It passed the Senate and remained in the bill until a conference committee deleted it. Nearly all large companies, for example, were nominally in favor of it, and they did what they could to secure its passage.[15]

The federal planners strenuously disagreed. They argued that the Clark Amendment would leave the federal plan with more of the worst risks to insure: relatively old workers who would not have many years in which to make social security contributions and fewer younger workers. The private sector could simply refuse to insure such "bad risk" workers and leave the load to the public sector. The public sector would therefore face prohibitive costs. Social security taxes would have to rise to cover the costs, driving more workers away from the system. Support for social security would be undermined by the fact that many "good risk" workers would have chosen not to participate by holding on to their private pension plans to the exclusion of a federal plan that had to insure everyone (Douglas, 1936, pp. 271-291).

In the end, FDR insisted on the withdrawal of the Clark Amendment for "further discussion." As he did on other aspects of the legislation, the President got his way.

The Clark Amendment soon became a non-issue. Supporters tried to pass the measure in 1936 and met with little success. Marion Folsom of Eastman Kodak, regarded as *the* business authority on social security, captured the mood within the cooperatively inclined segments of the business community. "In the future the employee will accumulate part of his annuity with the insurance company and part with the government. The total cost to us will be approximately the same as it has been in the past."[16]

Early in 1936, officials in the Chamber of Commerce expressed a general sense of the futility of opposing the federal old age insurance program. In a confidential note, a Chamber staff memo said that no effort should be made to amend the Act. If amendments were attempted, the universal dole Townsendites might prove just as successful with Congress as would the Chamber. From that perspective, a joint-contributory social insurance approach looked good.[17]

For all of the comparative conservatism in the old age insurance law, however, the funding provisions were not without their problems. The resolution of these problems paved the way for amendments to the program that, although they appeared conservative in their short-run political contexts, laid the groundwork for a major expansion of the program. These amendments came in 1939 and 1950.

Even in 1934 experts realized that, as time passed, the costs of the federal old age retirement program would increase, without an extension of coverage or an increase in the generosity of the benefits. The reason was that the percentage of the retired population eligible to receive joint contributory pensions would rise over time. For a person who retired in 1936 or before social security, old age insurance meant nothing. Such a person had not contributed to the program and could expect zero in return. In 1960, by way of contrast, nearly all of the retired people who had worked in covered industrial and commercial occupations would expect a pension. Social security would, therefore, cost far more in 1960 than in 1936.

One response to this problem was to collect only enough money each year to pay for current expenses. This approach, called pay-as-you-go, meant that social security taxes would be low at first and then gradually rise. Ultimately, it was assumed by Douglas Brown and other administration advisors, the government would have to step in and put general revenues into the fund. After all, depression era planners predicted a low birth rate and therefore relatively few young people to relieve the burden on the old when the workers of the 1930s retired.

Another approach, favored by Roosevelt, was to collect enough so that general revenues never became necessary. This approach, called fully funded, depended on collecting enough money in the early, cheap part of the program in order to build up reserves that would later be used to pay benefits in the later, expensive part of the program.

Other than the President, few people had wanted to take the fully funded approach. From the left economists feared its deflationary aspects and from the right politicians worried about the government's ability to hold large funds in reserve. As the technical committee of bureaucrats advising the Roosevelt administration put it, "reserves such as become necessary under a full reserves plan are unthinkable."[18]

Instead, Perkins and the other cabinet members entrusted with designing a social security program had accepted a plan that allowed state-administered welfare to be paid immediately and that contained an old age insurance program with gradually rising tax rates and an eventual subsidy from general revenues. This plan was stopped only by Roosevelt himself, who realized, at the very last minute, that his old age insurance plan would develop a deficit in the 1960s. The President ordered Treasury Secretary Henry Morgenthau to make the plan fully funded without the need for general revenues.

Tempers flared among staff members as the President undid their work. Barbara Armstrong, the Berkeley law professor, refused to believe that Treasury Secretary Morgenthau could contemplate a huge reserve plan "without a qualm," since the Treasury Department's previous attitude had been "clearly in the other direction." Armstrong believed that the President's provisions would doom the bill since Democrats as well as Republicans would oppose the accumulation of large reserves.[19] Democrats as well as Republicans would entertain suspicions about the federal government's ability to avoid using the unanticipated surpluses that would now reside in the federal treasury for vote buying and other nefarious purposes.

Armstrong correctly forecast the objections that were made in Congress. To cite just one example, the Business Advisory Council, an influential group of industrial leaders, testified against both the high tax rates and the large reserves that the President's plan entailed.[20] Despite these and similar objections, the funding provisions of the old age insurance law formed part of the President's take-it-or-leave-it offer, and the Congressmen took it.

The dilemmas of social security financing, however, continued after the bill's passage. In the first place, the plan would not pay regular pensions to anybody until 1942. That meant people would pay into the system for five years without any real assurance they would ever get anything back. In the second place, the reserves required to fund the program still caused considerable stir.

The reserve plan rested on complicated and intimidating computations. In 1937, for example, $511 million went into the social security account, only $5 million of which was required for current expenses. In 1937, therefore, most of the social security money rested in what government officials called the "reserve account." In 1967, with the system much further along the road to maturity, the collection of social security taxes would amount to more than $2 billion. For the first time, however, benefits would cost more than the amount taken in, and money from the interest on the more than $38 billion that had accumulated in the reserve account would make up the difference. By 1980 the amount of money held in reserve for social security would reach over $46 billion.

Marion Folsom noted that the reserve features of the Act constituted its "greatest defect," because they presented two sorts of temptations. One was for the government to spend the money for anything Congress or the President wanted, and the other was to increase the benefits. If benefits were increased, future generations would find themselves with a staggering burden.[22] In a rare show of unanimity, The Brookings Institution, the American Federation of Labor, the Chamber of Commerce, the heads of most insurance companies, and the editorial board of the *New York Times* all agreed with Folsom on this issue.[23]

Republican presidential candidate Alfred Landon expressed the fears of many when he said: "We have some good spenders in Washington. With this social security money alone running into billions of dollars, all restraint on Congress will be off."[24] Other Republican politicians hastened to add their voices to the growing chorus of those who wanted to change the old age insurance program so that the huge reserves did not form.[25] Michigan's Senator Arthur Vandenberg, for example, noted that not only were the reserves a "positive menace to free institutions and sound finance," they were financed through a regressive payroll tax that penalized the poor. If the reserves were abandoned, sound finance and more liberal benefits could be achieved simultaneously. Vandenberg recommended that the payments of benefits should begin sooner than 1942, that the initial benefits be more generous, and that payroll tax increase scheduled for 1940 be postponed (Vandenberg, in *Congressional Record*, 1937, p. 548).

An advisory council of businessmen, labor leaders, and academics, which met in 1937 and 1938, reached a compromise on old age insurance that formed the basis for the 1939 Social Security Amendments. Explaining the differences between public and private insurance to the council, R.A. Hohaus, an actuary of the Metropolitan Life Insurance Company, established a philosophical basis for the compromise. In voluntary private insurance, he noted, the principle of "actuarial equity" was crucial. The notion of an earned return on a worker's investment or premium predominated. In compulsory public insurance, the federal government, with its power to tax, should emphasize what Hohaus called "adequacy." The principle of paying benefits large enough to protect an individual against economic insecurity should predominate, regardless of the amount of the worker's contributions into the system. "Just as private insurance would collapse if it stressed considerations of adequacy above those of equity, social insurance will not remain intact if considerations of equity are emphasized more than those of adequacy."[26] In other words, the private insurance industry could not afford to give away a free lunch and the government often had to do so.

Using this justification, the advisory council accepted recommendations that, when adopted by Congress, radically changed old age insurance. During the April 1938 meeting of the advisory council, Douglas Brown, who chaired the council, unveiled a plan with benefit provisions for the young children of workers who died before retirement age. Furthermore, these benefits were to be based on a worker's "average" wages, a statistic that approximated a worker's earnings at the time he died, rather than "credited wages," a concept related to the amount of money a worker had paid into the social security trust fund. The penalty on younger workers was therefore considerably lessened.

In the end, the advisory council recommended the payment of benefits to dependent children, retired workers' wives, and workers' widows. These moves reduced the similarity in treatment between two workers with the same wage records. The worker who died and left behind dependent children would get back more on his social security investment than would the worker who lived until old age, never married, and never had children.

Just as Hohaus had recommended, the 1939 amendments, featured a shift from equity, the notion of getting back what you paid into the system, to a system that recognized certain social problems as more pressing than others and took steps to solve those problems. Radical in retrospect, the law appeared conservative at the time. By liberalizing benefits and beginning payments earlier (1940), Congress reduced the size of the hypothetical social security reserve account. Conservatives and the Republicans were relieved of their fears regarding the reserve problem and rested more content that America's social welfare system would be based on a social insurance model which did not over-expand benefits rather than on non-contributory welfare models which would. Liberals and the Roosevelt administration gained an end to the political embarrassments caused by the reserve and credit for liberalizing the system. It was a nice bit of quid pro quo bargaining, typical of the deals that would be struck in the years that followed.

In the 1940s, the amount in the social security trust grew steadily, increasing from $2 billion to well over $13 billion, but the system still encountered problems that were not resolved until 1950 (*Social Security Bulletin*, 1981, p. 79). In particular, Congress refused to make retirement benefits more liberal and to extend coverage to new groups. Welfare, which proved to be at least as popular as social insurance during the entire decade, took up the slack. As no less an authority than Robert Ball, who ran the social security program from 1961 to 1973, has noted, "social security just was not very important" for the first 15 years of the old age retirement program's existence.[27] In 1940, for example, total government spending for social welfare amounted to 9.2 percent of the country's gross national product. Yet in that year the nation spent more than six times as much on state workers' compensation payments as on federal social security. Veterans programs cost fifteen times as much as social security in 1940 and remained more costly until the middle of the 1950s.[28]

Throughout the 1940s, more than twice as many people were on the state welfare rolls, receiving old age assistance, than were receiving retirement benefits from the federal government under social security. By the end of the 1940s, just over a fifth of the elderly received old age assistance payments; in a few states it was over half. The average monthly state-federal welfare payment was $42 in 1949, compared to an average federal social insurance retirement benefit of $25 (Altmeyer, 1968, pp. 169-170; Mark H. Leff, in Berkowitz, 1987a, p. 42).

The reasons for these differences in costs and benefits had to do with differences between welfare and social insurance programs. State administered welfare covered any needy elderly person; federally administered old age insurance limited coverage to industrial and commercial workers who had contributed into the system. Congress refused to raise federal social security benefits significantly; many of the state legislatures did not hesitate to serve their elderly constituents by raising the level of state old-age assistance.

Responding to this situation, Congress substantially modified the federally run old age retirement program in 1950, choosing to raise the level of benefits and extend coverage. For the first time, Congress raised the tax rate so that it reached 3 percent (2.25 percent for the self-employed), and increased the level of wages on which taxes were payable ($3,600 in 1951).[29] Administrator Arthur Altmeyer noted with some relief that eight million workers, most of whom were self-employed, were brought into the system and that average benefits were increased by about 80 percent. The social security system picked up almost immediately. The state old age assistance rolls declined as soon as the new social security law went into effect and, for the first time, the number of federal social security beneficiaries exceeded the number receiving state old age assistance in February 1951 (Altmeyer, 1968, p. 185; Achenbaum, 1986, p. 45).

Congress extended federal social security coverage to the self-employed, such as farmers and other proprietors of small businesses, for two reasons. One was ideological, and the other was a pragmatic concern related to public finance. Social security officials portrayed a federal program of social insurance as a moderate program when compared with state welfare, which was painted as demeaning, capricious, and uncontrollable. Further, welfare cost the states more money than would social insurance, since welfare required a state contribution. Once again, a major expansion of the welfare state had been rationalized in conservative terms. Social insurance was better than "dole-like" pensions, which all too often became mini-veterans or Townsend plans.

Economic growth also assisted the growth of federal social welfare activity. Because social security collected a share of so many people's paychecks and because wages were rising, social security harnessed the growth of the American labor force and grew considerably in the fifties. The amount of money paid into the social security trust fund more than doubled between 1950 and 1955; the amount paid out in benefits more than quintupled during those years, and still the trust fund managed to grow by $8 billion. A program that had involved $767 million in 1937 had grown to over $21.6 billion in 1955.[30]

Social security owed its success to the performance of the economy. When the social security old age insurance program began in 1937, experts, trying to predict future events from their depression vantage point, failed to foresee the prosperity of the war and postwar eras and the accompanying baby boom. These unforeseen events brought far more money into the system than had been predicted. Any lingering fears about the system's future were eased by the realization that, beginning in the middle of the sixties, the members of the baby boom would enter the labor force and pay social security. No wonder, then, that Congress decided to increase social security benefits and hold down social security taxes, as benefit increases in 1952, 1954, and 1958 illustrated.

After the early 1950s, few members of Congress wanted to change the system. Because of the extension in coverage, social insurance conferred its benefits on people who lived in every Congressional district in the nation. Congressmen quibbled over details, but accepted the general principles of the program. It appeared to buy them political advantages at relatively little cost. For the first time, a federal, civilian social welfare program had become a source of local political advantage. The locus of control in the U.S. social welfare system was beginning to shift, yet not decisively enough to usher in an era of federally administered health and disability programs.

Despite the enormous success of social security, it proved difficult to extend social insurance to cover new risks. The critical issue of the 1960s and 1970s proved to be health care, in which the popularity of social security and the political muscle of the elderly were directly matched against the popularity of medical doctors. The advocates of national health insurance cast the issue in terms of a logical extension of social insurance to cover the expensive risk of ill health; medical associations portrayed the fundamental issue as whether or not the provision of medical care should be regulated by the government.

In the progressive era and the twenties, health care first became perceived as a desirable good that could be budgeted for in advance. Economist Irving Fisher linked the promotion of health, which he called national vitality, to the productive efficiency of the country. Premature death and preventable illness cost the country money. Using European rates of sickness incidence, I. M. Rubinow, a social insurance expert, computed that America annually lost 200 million man-days of productive work on account of illness and that health insurance, which would finance the costs of medical care, would pay "handsome dividends" (Rimlinger, 1971, pp. 67-68). In part because these arguments lacked the more direct bottom line appeal of workers' compensation, a progressive era campaign to pass state health insurance laws went nowhere. In the twenties, however, reformers continued to concentrate on spreading the costs of individual illnesses across a large group, as means of bringing medical care within the financial reach of the common man.[31]

By the end of the 1930s, the American Medical Association (AMA) had settled into a pattern of opposition to the notion of government sponsored health insurance, and the issue was joined. At first, the AMA got the better of the political argument, even as it was losing in the struggle against health insurance. By 1949, when President Harry Truman attempted to press a national health insurance program, the issue had been transformed from budgeting health care costs to socializing medicine. The Association could seriously argue that "the taking over of medicine is but the first step toward nationalization of every interest and activity of the nation" (Rimlinger, 1971, p. 241). By this time, however, people already budgeted for the cost of medical care by purchasing private health insurance and substituting regular premiums for catastrophic costs, often with the assistance of their employer or union. Hospitals assisted in this effort by organizing non-profit Blue Cross plans, in which they agreed to deliver a specified number of days of hospital care for a fixed monthly fee.

The federal social insurance approach symbolized by social security remained irrelevant to this discussion, because it was only a relatively small and unimportant program in the decades during which the private health insurance movement gained strength. Consequently, ambitious proposals for national health insurance in the 1940s received little serious discussion.

In 1951, federal officials, happy about the recent growth of the old age retirement program but frustrated in their fight to extend social insurance principles to cover health and disability, hit upon the notion of hitching less-popular programs to more-popular ones and asking Congress to begin a program of national health insurance, but limited to people receiving old age insurance. In this manner, the federal officials allowed the market for private health insurance, which concentrated on the working population, to develop at the same time that federal old age insurance underwent what could be portrayed as a modest and logical expansion. They avoided competing with private insurance companies in the 1950s, just as they had avoided competing with the states regarding unemployment insurance in the 1930s. In effect, social security would take the place of the employer and pay elderly people's health insurance premiums. The medicare proposal, packaged as an amendment to the newly popular and expanded old age insurance program, was born. This health insurance proposal's trip from idea to law would, however, take 14 years.

Passage of the first disability insurance law in 1956 further indicated the political ability of the social security officials to tailor their proposals to the political process, the popularity of old age insurance, and state-oriented social welfare traditions. Limited to people fifty or over, disability insurance was first sold as a modest and relatively inexpensive addition to the federal retirement system. Further, the delicate administrative tasks of the program would be handled through state employees, acting on behalf of the Social Security Administration (Derthick, 1979, p. 319; Berkowitz, 1987b).

Passage of disability insurance for the elderly only accelerated efforts to join together national health insurance and old age insurance. Even as the way was being cleared for Medicare, however, social security officials approached the issue gingerly. In the late fifties, for example, trade union and social security officials collaborated on a bill in which they considered excluding doctors fees and limiting coverage to hospitalization.[32]

But as the 1960 election approached, social security officials and their political allies got their chance. Care for the aged suddenly became a major national issue, one that figured prominently in the presidential campaign. Pat McNamara, a Michigan Senator, conducted colorful hearings in which he demonstrated a need for subsidized health insurance among the elderly. John F. Kennedy endorsed Medicare and made it an important priority of his administration. The AMA reacted, to use Martha Derthick's words, by seeking delay and preemption. The Association joined the Republicans in looking for an alternative means to finance health insurance for the elderly. Social insurance principles, by now, had become a golden mean of American political discourse.

Not everyone, however, was equally convinced and Wilbur Mills, the chairman of the House Committee on Ways and Means, became a stumbling block to Medicare. Here two problems presented themselves. One was that Mills took a proprietary interest in a 1960 welfare law, bearing his name, that provided federal grants to assist states in financing medical care for the elderly who were "medically indigent." The bill was the beginnings of the modern medicaid program. Before Mills agreed to Medicare, he wanted to give this welfare approach a chance to work. Another problem was Mills' concerns that a social insurance approach to health care for the elderly would bankrupt the social security system. He saw health insurance costs as difficult to predict and as acting contrary to the self-financing tendencies in the old age insurance part of the program. Aging did not require much bureaucratic foresight. Clocks ticked the same for everyone. Illness, with its individual variations, was more of a "crap shoot" in terms of policy and financing. Medical costs were also far more prone to inflation. Rising medical costs would mean rising Medicare costs, draining money from the social security system.

In response, federal social security officials argued that the bill was modest in scope and hence relatively inexpensive and that a state administered welfare program was neither an adequate nor correct response to the problem of health insurance for the elderly. It was the same dole versus social insurance argument of the 1930s and 1950s all over again. Years of compromise had turned the administration's social insurance bill into one limited to hospitalization, skilled nursing-home care for recuperation, home health services after hospitalization, and outpatient diagnostic services. Its virtues, administration officials believed, lay precisely in its use of social insurance rather than public assistance or welfare. "Any assistance program is unsatisfactory," one social security official told Congressman John E. Fogarty of Rhode Island. "Public assistance," the official said, "helps older people meet their healthcare costs only after their resources are depleted to the point that they cannot afford these costs." Social insurance, by way of contrast, prevented dependency by allowing people to make contributions during their working lifetimes and have hospital protection beginning at age 65.[33] It was familiar rhetoric applied to a new field.

Conservatives tried to compete with the social security officials by offering alternative proposals with more liberal benefits but more conservative means of financing. Congressman John Byrnes of Wisconsin, the ranking minority member on the Ways and Means Committee, produced a bill that would have paid for 80 percent of the elderly's medical expenses, including doctors' fees, but would have made participation voluntary and required the elderly to pay part of the costs out of their own pockets (with two-thirds being paid from general revenues). The amount an elderly person would pay would vary by his income.

In 1965, after the death of President Kennedy and the Democratic landslide, Wilbur Mills skillfully picked and chose from among the alternatives and came up with an omnibus bill that combined three different approaches to health insurance. Part A of Medicare covered hospital insurance, financed through payroll deductions in a manner similar to old age insurance, as the administration had proposed; Part B of Medicare applied to doctor's bills, on much the same terms as Brynes had proposed. In particular, Supplementary Medical Insurance, as it was called, would be voluntary and funded in part from general revenues and in part from money that the elderly paid themselves. Medicaid, the third part of the plan, extended state-run health insurance plans to welfare recipients of all ages, rather than just the elderly welfare recipients who had been covered by previous legislation. Mills got exactly what he wanted. He preserved the spirit of the previously passed Kerr-Mills welfare bill and limited social security's (the federal old-age, survivors, and disability social insurance system) financial risks to hospital insurance (and not doctors' bills). Disappointed with Part B but happy to secure passage of Part A, the administration went along with the bill. It was a typical solution to social welfare problems in America's federal system: in which conflict was avoided by adopting conflicting solutions simultaneously. Everyone got something: feds, states, and private groups.

Within a very few years, the issues in health care shifted. The issue had traditionally been access, but after the federal government entered the system, using the politically popular cover of the old age retirement section of the social security program, it quickly became cost. Cost acquired a new meaning; it had previously referred to the high cost that kept medical care out of people's reach. Now it meant the high cost of the medical care itself. We had come full circle, from underinvestment in health care to overinvestment.

After the passage of Medicare, the pattern of health care financing shifted. Prior to the enactment of Medicare and Medicaid, 70 percent of health care expenditures for the aged were privately funded. By 1978, public programs underwrote 88 percent of the elderly's hospital expenditures, 59 percent of their physicians' bills, and 46 percent of their nursing costs. The federal government paid approximately 40% of *all* health care costs.

Part of the reason for this increase in costs lay in Medicare's distinctive features in which Washington financed and others controlled. With the Medicare program, the government simply bought into the health care system on permissive terms that allowed private health care providers to pass their costs along to the government. Even before the passage of Medicare, social security officials realized, in Robert Ball's words, that, "any bill that gets enacted will likely involve Blue Cross administration."[34] In planning for Blue Cross participation, government officials noted, in a paper prepared for Wilbur Mills, that Blue Cross "would not wish to run the risk of incurring losses," and that hospitals would be reimbursed on the basis of their costs; rather than on their charges. In this spirit, hospitals got to include a substantial portion of their overhead costs and of other costs, such as "bad debts," in their Medicare rates.[35] In most states, Blue Cross acted as a "fiscal intermediary" between Social Security and the hospitals. Social security, in other words, did little to control hospital costs and much to raise them.[36] It was "cost-plus contracting," removed from its usual military setting and applied to an important domestic concern. In the process, Medicare guaranteed profits to doctors and hospitals and saddled the federal government with a costly social welfare program.

That was the American version of national health insurance: federal money and private control. In some ways, it mirrored the American versions of unemployment insurance, disability insurance, welfare, and medical insurance for the poor, all of which featured federal money and state administrative control. Even as American social insurance and welfare programs have grown large, therefore, they have retained the participation of states and of private "vendors," such as hospitals and insurance companies as a matter of sheer and expensive political necessity.

This introduction to the Social Security Act points out the historical complexities that surround the creation of an American social welfare system. Certain themes unify the discussion. Our federal system has a built-in bias toward self-financing social insurance and solutions administered by the states. Social insurance has become America's governmental habit, yet it did not start out that way—the distinctively federal old age insurance program did not acquire its present popularity until 1951—nor has it taken a consistent administrative form: Unemployment compensation continues to be run by the states, rather than the federal government; private physicians largely run Medicare; old-age insurance, although often rumored to be on the edge of bankruptcy, remains a securely federal program.

Yet social insurance endures. At its base it reflects a mistrust of governmental—and especially federal—power that is shared by experts who distrust the politicians, by politicians who distrust the experts, and by the people who distrust both. The system also carries a great deal of historical baggage, such as the welfare programs begun in the great depression. Economic logic, as Mae West might have said, had nothing to do with it. As one perceptive economist realizes, however, the resulting system is complicated, awkward, and expensive. We, therefore, conclude our account of the Social Security Act in the same way as that economist did his. American "nonmarket social control, inevitably has such consequences, for good or ill" (Hughes, 1977, p. 193).

NOTES

1. For a good overview of the early laws on behalf of the elderly see Epstein (1968, pp. 534-535).
2. The law used a federal "tax offset" scheme to encourage the passage of state unemployment compensation laws.
3. Edwin Witte to Members of the Technical Board, November 9, 1934 (Murray Latimer Papers, George Washington University Library Special Collections, Washington, D.C.). The Wisconsin proposal was introduced in Congress in 1934 as the Wagner-Lewis bill.
4. Frances Perkins to Paul Kellogg, February 28, 1935 (Kellogg Papers, Social Welfare History Archives, University of Minnesota).
5. Frances Perkins to Paul U. Kellogg, February 19, 1935 (Kellogg Papers).
6. Paul Kellogg to Sam Lewisohn, January 16, 1935 (Kellogg Papers).
7. Sam Lewisohn to Paul Kellogg, December 29, 1934 (Kellogg Papers).
8. We leave aside here the problems related to the true incidence of the tax. We are unable to locate evidence on how contemporaries thought of this matter.
9. See Brown (1969); "Contributory Old Age Pension Plan: Receipts and Payments" (Altmeyer Papers, CES File 1, Box 1, Wisconsin State Historical Society). "The Dead Sea Scrolls of Social Security," in personal possession of Robert J. Myers (Silver Spring, Maryland), contains a detailed list of the various plans that were considered.
10. Eveline Burns Interview, p. 52. (Columbia Oral History Collection, Columbia University, New York).
11. Draft statement by Frank P. Graham (circa 1936, n.d., Kellogg Papers). Graham, the President of the University of North Carolina at Chapel Hill, chaired the advisory council on social security that preceded the enactment of social security.
12. See Weaver (1982). In 1933-1935, the Congressional margins in the House were: Democrats, 310; Republicans, 117; in the Senate; Democrats, 60; Republicans, 35. In 1935-1937, after the 1934 election, the margins shifted—in the House: Democrats, 319; Republicans, 103; in the Senate; Democrats, 69; Republicans, 25.
13. Wilbur Cohen to Joseph P. Harris, August 19, 1935. (RG 47, National Archives, Washington, D.C.).
14. Rainard B. Robbins, "Supplementary Report on the Proposed Substitute for the Clark Amendment to the Committee on Social Security of the SSRC," May 27, 1936. (Murray Latimer Papers, George Washington University, Washington, D.C.).
15. A list of companies known to favor the amendment on July 11, 1935 numbered more than one hundred and included, among many others, American Cyanamid, the Borden Company, Eastman Kodak, Gulf Oil, Kimberly Clark, and Standard Oil of Ohio. See "Companies Known to Favor Clark Amendment to Social Security Act," in Dr Rainard B. Robbins, "Confidential Material Collected on Social Security Act and Clark Amendment," July 11, 1935 (Murray Latimer Papers).
16. Marion Folsom to Rainard B. Robbins, December 18, 1935 (Murray Latimer Papers).
17. T. F. Cuneen, Manager, Insurance Department, Chamber of Commerce, to Rainard B. Robbins, January 4, 1936 (Murray Latimer Papers).

18. Technical Board on Economic Security, "Minutes of the Executive and Old Age Security Committee," November 22, 1934. (Murray Latimer Papers).

19. Barbara N. Armstrong to Murray Latimer, January 22, 1935. (Murray Latimer Papers).

20. Altmeyer to Secretary Perkins, May 9, 1935. (RG 47, Chairman's Files, Box 11, National Archives). For more on the Business Advisory Council, see McQuaid (1982, pp. 53-61).

21. "Cumulative Tax Collections, Benefit Payments, Net Excess of Tax Collections" (n.d.) and "Annual Appropriations, Benefit Payments and Reserves" (n.d.), (File 025, RG 47, National Archives, Washington, D.C.).

22. M.B. Folsom, address before Round Table on Industrial Relations, Chamber of Commerce, April 29, 1937 (Murray Latimer Papers).

23. Mark Sullivan, "Security or Income Taxes," *Washington Star* (November 1937), (File 705, Old Age Reserve 1937, Chairman's Files, RG 47 National Archives); Paul Mellon, "News Behind the News," *Cleveland Plain Dealer* (February 28, 1938); "The Reserve Fund," *New York Times* (September 5, 1938), p. 14; Jay Iglauer to Douglas Brown, March 7, 1938 (File 025, RG 47, National Archives).

24. "Text of Governor Landon's Milwaukee Address on Economic Security," *New York Times* (September 26, 1936), p. 31.

25. The following account of the 1939 amendments is drawn from Berkowitz (1987a, pp. 55-79).

26. R.A. Hohaus, "Memorandum for Meeting with Social Security Advisory Council," December 10, 1937 (RG 47, Box 13, National Archives).

27. Robert Ball, "The Original Understanding of Social Security: Implications for Later Developments," unpublished paper prepared for the Yale Conference on Social Security, April, 1985.

28. *Social Security Bulletin, Annual Statistical Supplement* (1981, pp. 53- 54). By federal social security, we mean old-age and survivors insurance.

29. Congress raised the tax level in 1950 to where it was originally supposed to have been in 1940. See "Annual Maximum Taxable Earnings and Actual Contribution Rates, 1937-1986 and "Scheduled Contribution Rates, 1935-2000," in *Social Security Bulletin, Annual Statistical Supplement* (1984-85, pp. 23- 25).

30. See "Old Age and Survivors Insurance, 1937-1984," in *Social Security Bulletin, Annual Statistical Supplement* (1984-85, p. 77). The figures refer to the total amount in the social security trust fund that had accumulated over the years.

31. The most famous vehicle to advance this view was the Committee on the Costs of Medical Care, which functioned at the end of the 1920s and the early 1930s. See Fox (1986).

32. In typical social security style, these benefits for the elderly were to be financed by the usual small tax increase (0.5% of covered payroll). See Derthick (1979, pp. 322-324) and Sundquist, (1968, pp. 296-297).

33. Robert Ball, "Report for Representative John E. Fogarty about the American Medical Association's Eldercare Program" (n.d.) (RG 235, Accession A-1793, Box 53, Washington National Records Center Suitland, Maryland).

34. See Robert M. Ball, Commissioner of Social Security, to the Secretary, July 23, 1964 (RG 235, Office of the Secretary, Department of Health, Education), and Welfare, Accession A 1793, (Box 43, Washington National Records Center, Suitland, Maryland).

35. Blue Cross Participation in Social Security Hospital Insurance, Staff Paper, 4/28/64 in Wilbur Cohen to Secretary, May 5, 1964, (RG 235, Accession 69A-1793, Box 41, Washington National Records Center).

36. The basic Medicare benefit is 90 days of inpatient care for each spell of illness or benefit period. A person is covered for the first 60 days of hospitalization after a considerable deductible, which was $520 in 1987; then between day 61 and 90, a person "copays" at the considerable rate of $130 per day. Part B generally pays 80 percent of approved charges for most covered services,

but it is acute, emergency oriented care that does not include routine physical examinations and tests and other routine care, such as dentists' visits. See Kingson (1987). Beginning in 1983, Medicare moved toward a prospective payment system, in which hospitals received a fixed amount for treating a patient whose diagnosis fell into one of more than four hundred diagnosis related groups. Even with this new "competitive" system, however, vestiges of the old system remained.

REFERENCES

Achenbaum, W. A. (1986). *Social Security: Vision and Revisions.* New York: Cambridge University Press.

Altmeyer, A. (1968). *The Formative Years of Social Security.* Madison: University of Wisconsin Press.

Berkowitz, E. (Ed). (1987a). *Social Security After Fifty: Successes and Failures.* Westport, CT: Greenwood Press.

Berkowitz, E. (1987b). *Disabled Policy: America's Programs for the Handicapped.* New York: Cambridge University Press.

Brown, D. (1969). *The Genesis of Social Security in America.* Princeton, NJ: Industrial Relations Section.

Brown, D. (1972). *An American Philosophy of Social Security: Evolution and Issues.* Princeton, NJ: Princeton University Press.

Committee on Finance, U.S. Senate (1935). Economic Security Act: Hearings Before the Committee on Finance, United States Senate, Seventy-Fourth Congress, First Session on S. 1130, A bill to alleviate the hazards of old age, unemployment, illness, and dependency, to establish a social insurance board in the department of labor and to raise revenue, and for other purposes, January 22 to February 20, 1935, revised. Washington, D.C.: U.S. Government Printing Office.

Committee on Ways and Means, U.S. House of Representatives (1935). Economic Security Act, Hearings Before the Committee on Ways and Means, House of Representatives, Seventy-Fourth Congress, First Session on HR 4120, A bill to alleviate the hazards of old age, unemployment, illness, and dependency, to establish a social insurance board in the department of labor, to raise revenue and for other purposes. January 21,22, 23,24, 23, 26, 28, 29, 30, 31, February 1,2,4,5,6, 7,8,9, and 12, 1935. Washington, D.C.: U.S. Government Printing Office.

Congressional Record. (1935). Washington, D.C.: U.S. Government Printing Office.

Congressional Record. (1937). Washington, D.C.: U.S. Government Printing Office.

Derthick, M., (1979). *Policymaking for Social Security.* Washington, D.C.: The Brookings Institution.

Douglas, P. H. (1936). *Social Security in the United States: An Analysis and Appraisal of the Social Security Act.* New York: McGraw-Hill.

Epstein, A. ([1938] 1968). *Insecurity: A Challenge to America–A Study of Social Insurance in the United States and Abroad.* 2nd rev. ed. New York: Agathon Press.

Fox, D. M. (1986). *Health Policies, Health Politics: The British and American Experience, 1911-1965.* Princeton, NJ: Princeton University Press.

Hughes, J. (1977). *The Governmental Habit.* New York: Basic Books.

Hughes, J. (1986). *The Vital Few: The Entrepreneur and American Economic Progress.* Expanded Edition. New York: Oxford University Press.

Kingson, E. R. (1987). *What You Must Know about Social Security and Medicare.* New York: Pharos Books.

Lubove, R. (1968). *The Struggle for Social Security.* Cambridge, MA: Harvard University Press.

McQuaid, K. (1982). *Big Business and Presidential Power.* New York: Morrow.

Nash, G. et al. (Eds.). (1988). *Social Security: The First Half Century*. Albuquerque, NM: University of New Mexico Press.

Nelson, D. (1969). *Unemployment Insurance: The American Experience, 1915-1935*. Madison, WI: University of Wisconsin Press.

Patterson, J. T. (1981). *America's Struggle Against Poverty*. Cambridge, MA: Harvard University Press.

Rimlinger, G. V. (1971). *Welfare Policy and Industrialization in Europe, America, and Russia*. New York: Wiley.

Social Security Bulletin. (1981). Washington, D.C.: Social Security Administration.

Sundquist, J. L. (1968). *Politics and Policy: The Eisenhower, Kennedy, and Johnson Years*. Washington, D.C.: The Brookings Institution.

Weaver, C. L. (1982). *The Crisis in Social Security*. Durham, NC: Duke University Press.

Witte, E. (1962). *The Development of the Social Security Act*. Madison, WI: University of Wisconsin Press.

CALL ME ISHMAEL—NOT DOMINGO FLORESTA: THE RISE AND FALL OF THE AMERICAN WHALING INDUSTRY

Lance E. Davis, Robert E. Gallman,

and Teresa D. Hutchins

I. INTRODUCTION

Jonathan Robert Tyson Hughes grew up in Twin Falls, Idaho. His parents, western populists, had drummed into him a concern for the environment, and the need for conservation. They had also imbued in him a belief that, if citizens ever dropped their guard—even for a moment—robber barons were prepared to rape and pillage the region's natural resources. Finally they had taught him that only the union stood between the worker and the robber barons. For Jonathan, the three lessons came together in Nushagak, Alaska in the summer of 1951—a story told in his Presidential address to the Economic History Association (Hughes, 1982).

Research in Economic History, Suppl. 6, pages 191-233.

ISBN: 1-55938-150-7.

While this paper is not about the salmon fishing industry, nor is it strictly about the relationship between fishermen, workers, and the firm that bought the catch, it is about the problems of business decisionmaking in a competitive maritime "fishing industry." Thus it parallels, in some important ways, the developments Hughes treated in his address. The subject of this paper is whales not salmon, and the time frame is the nineteenth not the twentieth century. American whaling, however, like the salmon fishery industry served by Nushagak, was competitive, depended for its existence on the exploitation of a natural resource with common property rights, and passed through an entire life-cycle within a span of less than a century.

Hughes concludes his address with the argument that, had the economic environment only been different—had management and workers not been forced by the constraints imposed by institutions and the history of their past relations to continue their strategic game of chicken—it might have been possible to save, or at least to extend, the economic life of the Nushagak cannery in particular, and the Alaskan salmon canning industry in general. The early chapters of the history of American whaling were very different from those of the salmon fishery of Hughes's story. In whaling both management and workers proved very flexible, and most innovations, both technical and institutional, were enthusiastically adopted. The concluding chapter in both histories was, however, the same: the patient died.

In an attempt to explore the questions raised by Hughes, this paper analyzes the economics of the American whaling industry from its beginnings at the end of the War of 1812 to its demise in the first decade of the next century. The study begins with an introduction to nineteenth-century whaling, the story of the triumph of the American industry over its British competitors, and a brief outline of its decline over the ensuing three-quarters of a century. The focus then shifts to the resources that went into the capture of whales: capital, labor, technology, the stock of whales, and management. Finally, the paper tracks changes in the productivity of those inputs; it concludes with a brief comparison of the industry and Hughes' Alaskan counterpart.

II. OF WHALES AND MEN

The subject of this work is American—more precisely New Bedford—whaling. (Davis, Gallman, and Hutchins, 1987a).[1] New Bedford whalers hunted five varieties of whales: one type of toothed whale—the sperm or cachelot—and four kinds of baleens—rights, bowheads, grays, and humpbacks. The humpback is representative of an entire class of whales, rorquals. It is the only one of that class that could be successfully hunted by whalers employing nineteenth-century techniques. The rest, the blues, the seis, the minkes, and the fins—whales that made up most of the catch in the present century—were too fast for nineteenth-century whalers.

Salmon are hunted for food (the dispute at the heart of Hughes's analysis was between the workers and the owners of the packing plant, with the native fishermen caught in the middle), as whales have been in the present century. One hundred and fifty years ago, however, sperm whales were valuable because they yielded sperm oil and spermaceti; baleens, because they were the source of whale oil and whale bone. Spermaceti was used in candle-making, and sperm oil—the product of rendering the sperm whale's blubber—was sold as a very high-quality illuminant and as a lubricant for light, high-speed machinery. Whale oil—rendered like sperm oil—was a low quality, but inexpensive, illuminant; later, as the composition of demand changed, it was increasingly used to lubricate heavy machinery. Whale bone (the sieve that the baleen whale employs to extract its food from sea water) was used to make corset stays, buggy whips, umbrellas, and a variety of other products that required both strength and flexibility.

Today, whalers go forth in large mother ships that serve as packing plants for the whales, which are hunted down by fast, motor-driven killer boats. Four centuries ago most whaling was done in small shore-based whaleboats—boats that were used to search out and kill the whales and to tow the carcasses back to shore for rendering. This study is focused on the nineteenth century when a technology intermediate between mechanized mother ships and shore-based whaleboats prevailed. It was a technology (both institutional and technical) that had evolved over the previous two centuries. Over the history of American deep sea whaling there was little change in the basic organization of the industry or in the process of catching whales, but there were important changes in detail.

A vessel's owners (often including the captain) hired an agent (also often a part-owner) who was responsible for choosing the grounds to be hunted, signing the crew, provisioning the vessel, and otherwise preparing it for sea. Because the agents, the captain, and even the owners frequently changed from one voyage to the next, the vessel-voyage approximates the notion of a "firm" in economic theory, and is a particularly useful unit of analysis.

The captain ran the vessel while it was at sea. Like any merchant captain, his responsibilities included, in addition to navigation and general management, any refitting, reprovisioning, or recruiting that was required. In view of the peculiar nature of whaling—particularly the long periods spent away from home—he was usually called on to do more along these lines than the typical commander of a merchantman. Despite the weight of these labors, the captain was valued chiefly for his ability to locate whales and for his skill in attacking and killing them.

The attack was not conducted from the whaling vessel, but from small six man whaleboats. Typical whaling vessels carried from four to six boats, although some small vessels had as few as two. The specialists in the boats were the steersmen and the harpooners. The latter speared the whale and made it fast by a line attached to the harpoon. If the harpoon held, the whale would gradually wear itself out attempting to get free of the boat. When the animal tired, the oarsmen again maneuvered the boat close to the whale, and the steersman, having changed places with the harpooner, attempted to kill it with an implement called a lance.

When the whale had been killed, the whaling vessel hove to, the whaleboats were hoisted aboard, and a work stage was rigged. The crewmen, while standing on the stage using cutting instruments called spades, removed the blubber from the carcass. Ambergris (on the rare occasion there was any), spermaceti (if the whale was a sperm whale) and baleen (if it was not) were removed. The blubber was then loaded aboard the whaling vessel and there on the deck it was tried out—the blubber reduced to oil by boiling it over a fire built in a brick try works—and barreled.

III. HISTORICAL BACKGROUND

Britain and the United States

In 1607, Henry Hudson, while exploring a northern route to Russia, saw hundreds of bowhead whales in the waters off Spitzbergen (Conway, 1967). Seamen from the European maritime nations responded to Hudson's reports, and soon were engaged in open warfare over access to the Greenland fishery. Nine years later in an attempt to reduce the costs associated with these disputes, and perhaps to save a few lives as well, the principal whaling nations agreed to divide the fishery amongst themselves.

The British and the Dutch received the largest allocations, but it was the Dutch who proved best able to exploit their prize. Their initial allocation, coupled with their low cost structure and the willingness of their captains to search out new hunting grounds, made it possible for the Dutch to dominate world whaling for almost one hundred and fifty years.

By 1750, however, conditions in Britain had begun to change. As the country began to industrialize and, concomitantly, as cities grew, the demand for both lubricants and illuminants increased. The nation also faced the renewal of what had been and was to be a long series of military struggles with the French. The government, concerned with the supply of trained seamen, doubled the bounty offered to whaling vessels heading north to the Greenland fishery. Even the increased subsidy might not have been sufficient, had other conditions, more political than economic, not changed as well. Sensing a threat to its maritime dominance, Whitehall moved to protect the home market. Continuing problems with the French led to a period of continental blockade, and the Dutch, perhaps in part because of the extra costs imposed by the Royal Navy, found competing maritime pursuits more attractive. As a result, on the average for each year between 1785 and 1818, more than one hundred and twenty-five British vessels returned from the Northern ground (a ground that included the Greenland fishery). From the 1760s until the second decade of the nineteenth century, the British whaling industry stood unchallenged. Year after year the catch increased, and shipowners banked healthy profits.

Across the Atlantic, however, New England-based seamen remained a potential competitive threat. Modern whaling in America dates from 1712 when Christopher Hussey discovered sperm whales too far out in the Atlantic to be hunted from shore. Within a very few years, vessels had ventured north, to challenge the Dutch and British fleets off Greenland, and south as far as the Falkland Islands. Finally, in 1789, Captain James Swain pushed the hunting margin around Cape Horn and into the Pacific.

Until 1776, the New England colonies were a part of the British empire, and their whalers part of the British fleet. The fact is that they supplied three-quarters of the oil sold in the British market and were, therefore, a very important part. With the outbreak of the Revolutionary War and the imposition of a naval blockade off the Atlantic coast, the New England whalers could no longer operate. The end of the war meant the removal of the blockade. American whalers arrived in the Thames soon thereafter "with full cargoes of oil of excellent quality, which was offered below the prevailing London price" (Fairburn, 1945-55; see also, Jackson, 1978). Political manipulation, however, has more than a single dimension. Given the industry's past history, American captains should not have been surprised to find themselves facing a prohibitive protective tariff. Moreover, the embargo of the early nineteenth century coupled with the British blockade of 1812-1814 made it very difficult for the Americans to operate anywhere in the world. As a result the Americans provided no effective competition for the British during the prosperous decades of the late eighteenth and early nineteenth century.

In 1814 almost 200 British whalers hunted in the northern and southern fisheries; across the Atlantic, two American vessels were active. Three decades later the American fleet numbered more than 1000, but there were only 27 vessels in the British fleet. Since both fleets had access to the same whales and the same technology, they should have stood on near equal footing. What factors, then, account for the shift in the industry's leadership from the old to the new world? The evidence indicates that the American fleet was more productive, that it faced a more attractive set of input prices, and that the British demise was hastened by a constellation of changes in the political environment. A contemporary, Charles Enderby, a knowledgeable observer, said that the British suffered from bad vessel design, poor seamen, and the high cost of vessels (Fairburn, 1945-1955). In addition, shifts in government policies proved damaging.

A comparison of productivities of the British northern fleet and the American Atlantic fleet indicates that, although there was substantial year-to-year variation, on average, between 1817 and 1842 the British fleet was about two-thirds as productive as the American (Davis, Gallman, and Hutchins, 1987b).[2] The difference can be traced in large measure to differences in the productivity of labor in the two countries and to differences in the way British owners chose to employ their vessels.

In terms of technology as traditionally defined, the British used larger vessels and a production configuration that was characterized by a much lower capital-labor ratio. The typical British whaler was often more than 500 tons, was rigged as a ship, carried six whaleboats, and employed just fewer than fifty men. The American fleet included, in addition to the numerically dominant ships, a substantial number of barks, and even a few brigs, sloops, and schooners. During the two decades of serious British-American rivalry (1820-1840), its vessels were usually smaller (a 400 ton vessel was considered very large), carried only four whaleboats, and the crew seldom totaled more than 25. Thus, on average during the period of active hunting, an American vessel used only .08 men per vessel ton as compared with the .14 employed by its British competitor.

Although there appears to be no completely compelling way to explain the difference, the evidence suggests that it may, at least in part, reflect the poorer quality of British crews. Both twentieth-century historians and contemporary observers commented unfavorably on British whalemen. Charles Enderby's views have been noted; the industry's historian, Gordon Jackson, has come to much the same conclusion. Writing about the Northern fishery in the period of British preeminence he wrote:

> . . . to recruit 'Greenmen,' a term which had nothing to do with Greenland, but indicated that they were new to the job—and therefore cheaper. Such moves are perhaps best illustrated by the *Robert* of Peterhead . . . which in 1795 had only two 'sailors' among its crew of twenty-three. The final stage . . . came when the cheapest native crews were swelled by half-starved wretches picked up for a song in the Shetlands (Jackson, 1978).

Neither does it appear that the relative quality improved over time. In 1844, the owner of a British whaler testified before a Parliamentary Select Committee that British seamen, who had been the "best sailors in the world" in 1801, were now of "the worst description" (Jackson, 1978). The turn of the century crews he praises were, of course, those that Jackson says were swelled by "half starved wretches." The same committee reported that British ship owners believed that American "crews, bred to the trade and enthusiastic in their pursuit of it," were better whalemen than the British (Jackson, 1978).

Anglo-American differences were not, however, limited to those rooted in traditional technology and labor quality; there were major differences in the choice of institutional technology as well. Given the weather—vicious storms and a threatening icepack—no captain, British or American, attempted to hunt off Greenland or in the Davis Strait for more than a few months in the late spring and summer. British vessels returned to their home port after each hunting season; most American vessels remained at sea for at least two. While British ships set out from their home ports each spring, the Americans went north at the beginning of one season, moved to the South Atlantic in the early fall, and then returned to the northern ground in the following spring. Between 1816 and 1843, a British vessel spent, on average, five and a one-half months at sea on each voyage; its American counterpart was out more than two and one-half times as long. In order to be able to stay out so long Americans had to be able to try out the blubber of the whales captured. The British, however, because they were at sea so short a time, could bring back raw blubber for refining at home. British vessels remained in port for more than six months between voyages, while the inter-voyage refitting period for the Americans was less than two-fifths as long.

The low quality of British crews may not only have affected productivity directly but also indirectly through its effect on the length of voyage. Although there is a clear question of causality, there is no doubt that the skill composition of the two nations' crews was very different. British vessels usually carried a carpenter and his mate but few other artisans (Jenkins, 1921). In contrast American vessels almost always included coopers, carpenters, and blacksmiths among their crews, and, at times, second coopers, carpenters, and blacksmiths, as well as sailmakers, boat builders, painters, mechanics, machinists, caulkers, and coopersmiths. As a result, British vessels depended on domestic shipyards for most of their refitting and repair, but American crews carried out a surprisingly large fraction of those tasks during the voyage itself. The ships' logs indicate that, while the capture of whales remained the captains' major concerns, maintenance and repair were almost equally important activities during the winter months.

While American whalers were about one-half as productive as their British rivals, they were almost twice as profitable. The profitability comparisons, like the productivity estimates, are sensitive to the assumptions chosen; but, the data indicate that, even under the most favorable assumptions, British profits would have been less than 60 percent of those earned by ship owners in the United States. The difference between the productivity and profit comparisons reflects the relative input and output prices prevailing in the two countries. Although interest rates were substantially lower in the United Kingdom, both the cost of vessels and the cost of labor were higher. The United States had a significant cost advantage in the manufacture of wooden sailing vessels, and the whaling fleets at the time were made up of nothing but wooden sailing vessels. While there is some dispute about the size of the advantage, it was clearly substantial (the estimates range from one-third to three-fourths). Such cost differences would not have been important had the British been able to buy American vessels, but His Majesty's government required that only British-built vessels be used (Hutchins, 1941).[3]

In the case of labor, despite the greater proportion of skilled workers in an American crew, an average crewman in Britain cost 1.2 times as much per year as his North American counterpart. Although the evidence is not directly applicable to the North Atlantic competition, the conclusion also is supported by the experience of the British vessels in the Southern Fishery. British owners testified that they were unable to attract seamen despite agreeing to pay 44 percent of the value of the catch. The Americans appear to have had no trouble attracting men with percentage payments that were only three-quarters that high (Jackson, 1978; Davis, Gallman, Hutchins, 1989).

Finally, profits in Britain were affected by both direct and indirect government subsidies. Until 1824, a direct bounty of twenty shillings a ton was paid to every whaler returning from the Northern ground (because the payment accounted for between one-fourth and one-fifth of the profits of a typical voyage, it may partially explain the British owners' attachment to short voyages), and the tariff on imported whale oil effectively eliminated all foreign competition. In 1843, for example, when American whale oil sold for one shilling and eight pence a gallon, the British *tariff* was three shillings. Moreover, substantial tariffs were also levied on whale oil substitutes (rape seed, for example).

It appears that British preeminence, was not, and had never been, the product of a natural comparative advantage, but of an advantage born of war and government policy. There are no examples of industries operating in markets completely free of laws and regulations, whether political or social, restrictive or supportive. If, however, British owners had been forced to confront the same economic environment in terms of regulations, tariffs, and the absence of subsidies faced by their American competitors, profits in the United Kingdom would have been less than one-third of those earned on the other side of the Atlantic, even when the benefits accruing from an ability to buy cheaper American vessels are factored into the calculation. Government policy was no more immutable under George IV and George Canning than it was under Ronald Reagan and Jim Wright. With Napoleon long since defeated and Britain the world's unchallenged superpower, defense was a much less pressing issue. As Britain industrialized, ship owners and oil merchants found their political power diluted. The subsidy was not renewed in 1824; between 1822 and 1827 the tariff on rape seed was reduced from one pound to one shilling a quarter (imports rose by 650 percent); and, finally, in 1843, the tariff on whale oil was all but removed. By that date, however, the competitive struggle was long over—for at least the previous decade and a half the United States had controlled the world's largest and most efficient whaling fleet.

The Rise and Fall of the American Industry

By 1825, Yankee whalers dominated the industry. From the early 1820s until the late 1880s, the American fleet accounted for about 80 percent of all

Table1. United States Whaling Fleet: Average Yearly Catch, 1816-1905

	Catch			*Real Price: 1880 = 100*			
Years	*Sperm Oil*	*Whale Oil*	*Whale Bone*	*Sperm Oil*	*Whale Oil*	*Whale Bone*	*Real Value*
1816-1825	1428	1213	76	0.62	0.34	0.11	1292
1826-1835	3049	3147	370	0.77	0.31	0.20	3397
1836-1845	4562	6904	2034	0.93	0.37	0.28	7309
1846-1855	2995	7651	2973	1.34	0.54	0.39	9289
1856-1865	1984	4368	1316	1.30	0.66	0.89	6610
1866-1875	1367	1907	586	1.22	0.54	0.78	3145
1876-1885	1055	937	305	1.01	0.50	2.41	2262
1886-1895	522	502	306	0.83	0.48	4.58	2071
1896-1905	483	115	165	0.65	0.46	4.61	1124
Average	1938	2971	903	0.96	0.46	1.58	4668

Note: Catch of Sperm Oil and Whale Oil in thousands of gallons, of Whale Bone in thousands of pounds, Real Value in thousands of Dollars of 1880. Prices are for gallons of oil and pounds of bone.

Source: Davis, Gallman, and Hutchins (1987a, p. 340, Table 10.1).

whaling activity. Table 1 outlines the history of the American industry. The annual production of sperm oil increased more than six-fold between 1820 and 1837 and remained at about 1.8 million gallons until the mid 1840s. From then until the end of the century, it declined at a rate of about 1.7 percent a year. It was the domestic market that underwrote the initial increase, but from 1840 to 1860 it was exports—particularly exports to the United Kingdom—that ameliorated the decline. The overseas market, however, faced with rising supplies of first coal gas, then camphene, and finally kerosene and increasingly cut off by continental tariffs, never recovered from the interruption of the Civil War. If there had not been a domestic demand for lubricants, there would have been almost no market for sperm oil after Appomattox.

In the case of whale oil, the years from the early 1820s to the early 1850s saw an eight-fold increase in output. The rise in annual production from less than one-half to almost four million gallons can be traced to increases in both domestic and foreign demand. The latter market absorbed about one-half of American production during those years of rapid expansion. From the 1850s onward, however, all, but particularly foreign, sales declined rapidly. By the turn of the century, the American whalers were returning with only 10,000 gallons a year.

Given what would appear to be a biological complementarity between whale oil and whale bone, a comparison of the time trends of the two commodities is puzzling. The trend of bone output is similar to that for whale oil, but the timing is different. The output of bone actually declined in the early 1830s, but it increased rapidly (a more than twenty-fold increase) over the next two decades. While the harvest of bone does track its complement downward after the 1860s, the decline is less rapid. Between 1870 and 1890 whale oil output declined by more than 90 percent, but the output of bone fell less than 75 percent. Clearly, despite the biological complementarity, the ratio of bone to oil was not a stable one. If the catch actually reflected biological reality, late nineteenth century whales would have looked like characters in a Disney cartoon—all mouth and no body. In the earliest decades a typical whale yielded 16 barrels of oil for each pound of bone, by 1840 the ratio was down to three, and by 1880 it had fallen below unity.

Although shifts in the composition of the baleen catch (particularly the displacement of rights and humpbacks by the Arctic bowhead) can explain a portion of this change, they can not account for it fully. It is necessary to take into account the whalemen's response to the trends in the real prices of the two commodities. As demand (particularly export demand) for bone increased, the real price of baleen rose from $.08 in 1816 to $5.07 in 1906. The ratio of the price of a barrel of oil to a pound of bone fell from 4.5 to less than .1. Although whalers regarded the taking of a whale just for its baleen or just for its oil as sinfully wasteful, the two products competed for space on the whaling vessel. As between two sins—the killing of a whale for only bone or oil and the deliberate decision to forgo a potential profit—many whalers were obviously prepared to choose the former.

The five varieties of whales that were commercially hunted lived in different parts of the oceans. Sperms were most often found in tropical and subtropical regions; rights in the Atlantic from Bermuda north to Greenland and from Brazil south to the Antarctic, and in the Pacific from Japan and the Washington coast as far north as the Arctic Ocean and from Chile to the Antarctic; grays from the Baja peninsula to the Northwest coast and in the Sea of Japan. Bowheads lived in the Arctic Ocean, the Bering Strait, the Pacific north of the 54th parallel, and, in smaller numbers, in Davis Strait and Hudson's Bay. Humpbacks were in the waters populated by both sperms and rights.

American whalers hunted in all these places. While the vessels from some ports tended to specialize in particular species or particular grounds, the New Bedford agents and captains viewed all of the world's oceans and all of the world's whales (at least those they could catch) as their particular preserve. The logs of the city's vessels list no fewer than 51 different grounds, including such exotic places as Patagonia, Delago Bay, the Okhotsk Sea, Desolation Island and Altaho. In this analysis the 51 have been grouped into just four: The Atlantic, the Indian, the Pacific, and the Western Arctic. The first three had been systematically hunted before the Embargo and the War of 1812 disrupted the American efforts, but the Western Arctic was not reached until 1848 when Captain Roys, in the bark *Superior*, worked his vessel through the Bering Strait and into the Arctic Ocean. There he found, "whales innumerable, some of which yielded two hundred and eighty barrels of oil" (Scammon, 1874).

Table 2. Voyages by Ground: 3,372 Returning New Bedford Voyages, 1816-1905

Years	*Total Voyages*	*Atlantic*	*Percent of Total*		
			Indian	*Pacific*	*Arctic*
1816-1825	136	58.9	0.7	40.4	0.0
1826-1835	380	54.8	2.6	42.6	0.0
1836-1845	583	27.4	21.4	51.2	0.0
1846-1855	697	6.2	23.8	61.7	8.3
1856-1865	665	14.2	14.0	55.7	16.1
1866-1875	373	34.9	18.2	33.5	13.4
1876-1885	377	52.7	6.1	28.5	12.7
1886-1895	109	56.9	5.5	37.6	0.0
1896-1905	52	100.0	0.0	0.0	0.0
Average	3372	30.5	14.6	47.1	7.8

Source: Davis, Gallman, and Hutchins (1987a, p. 364, Table 10.9).

All grounds were not hunted with equal intensity in any given year nor, for that matter, over the entire ninety years. Table 2 provides a composite picture of the changing geographic distribution of the New Bedford fleet. When the British Navy lifted its blockade and American whalers again put to sea, activity was concentrated in the closest ground. Between 1816 and 1835 the Atlantic was the primary destination of more than one-half of the fleet, but over the following two decades the ground was largely abandoned. It accounted for less than four percent of the total during the heady decade 1846-1855, and, to underscore its decline, in 1847 not a single New Bedford vessel sailed for the Atlantic. After the Civil War, however, the ground regained its original relative, and, in the decade 1876-1885, at least, its absolute position as well. The Atlantic was closest to New Bedford, and, thus, voyages were relatively short; but even there, a typical voyage lasted twenty-one months.

Although the Atlantic was the most frequent destination in the first and last decades, it was the Pacific (the setting for *Moby Dick*) that was *the* most important. The Pacific was the destination of almost half of all the vessels and more than half of all the tonnage that set out from the city between 1816 and 1905. This dominant position was achieved despite the very long voyages. The mean length increased from two years in 1816-25 to 50 months in 1866-75, and overall it averaged three years and two months.

The Indian Ocean attracted more than a fifth of the city's whaling vessels at the industry's peak. Over the entire ninety years, it drew about one ship in seven. As whalebone became more valuable and after the western Arctic grounds were discovered, those northern waters became a major source of oil and bone. From 1850 until the San Francisco whalers' competitive advantage prevailed, the Arctic was the destination of 15 percent of the returning New

Bedford vessels. Given the very high loss rates (more than 5 percent of the vessels were lost each year), it was the initial destination of an even larger number. Like a voyage to the Pacific, a typical Arctic voyage took 38 months, while a voyage to the Indian Ocean took 34 months.

IV. CAPITAL

The capital used in whaling can be divided into three quite distinct categories: the vessels used to carry the men and equipment to the hunting ground, to serve the crew during the hunt, and to transport the oil and bone; the "whalecraft'"—the tools employed in actually catching and killing whales; and the provisions and other stores taken board. The first two call for further description.

The vessels employed by the New Bedford agents were almost all sailing craft—sloops, schooners, brigs, barks, and ships (see Table 3). The names refer to the way the vessels were rigged, but the differences were more pervasive. Sloops and schooners were small fore-and-aft rigged vessels; the former had one mast, the latter two. Brigs were small, two-masted, square rigged vessels. These three classes played no significant role, except in the Atlantic. Although their importance increased somewhat after the Civil War, the three together accounted for less than one-fourth of the voyages to the Atlantic ground and only nine of the 2354 completed voyages to the other three. Here the three classes have been grouped together in a single category: "other."

The fourth class—barks—accounted for about 35 percent of the New Bedford fleet, and the fifth—ships—more than 60 percent. Barks and ships were large three-masted vessels. The latter were square rigged; the former, square rigged on the fore and the main masts, but fore-and-aft rigged on the mizzen. Ships were usually, but not always, larger than barks.

Ships represented almost 90 percent of the fleet's tonnage in the years before 1836; thereafter, the importance of barks gradually increased in both absolute and relative terms. In 1840, they accounted for less than 15 percent of the total. Their share more than quadrupled over the next three decades, and they made up two-thirds of the fleet in the last 30 years. By the end of the century, the shift to the new, now dominant technology was complete; so complete, in fact, that no ship sailed from New Bedford after 1895.

Not only were there changes in rigging, but the average size of the vessels in each class changed as well. For ships, tonnage increased from less than 300 in the first decade to almost 380 by the early 1890s (the average was 340). Although the increase was a fairly stable 5 percent a decade from 1816 to 1860, there was little increase thereafter. The average size of a bark (285 tons) was just more than four-fifths that of a ship, but it increased by 30 percent between 1816 and 1845 and by another 30 percent between then and 1880.

Table 3. Annual Averages: Number and Tonnage-The New Bedford Fleet, 1816-1905

	Number of Vessels			*Tonnage of Vessels*			*Percent*		
Years	*Ships*	*Barks*	*Other and Unknown*	*Ships*	*Barks*	*Other and Unknown*	*Ships*	*Barks*	*Other and Unknown*
1816-1825	28	2	5	8619	518	769	87.0	5.2	0.1
1826-1835	93	14	7	30868	3451	972	87.5	9.8	0.0
1836-1845	158	37	8	54071	9699	1027	83.4	15.0	
1846-1855	199	81	4	71187	22518	515	75.6	23.9	0.0
1856-1865	143	132	3	53021	40156	202	56.8	43.0	0.0
1866-1875	49	110	7	18190	33954	790	34.4	64.1	0.1
1876-1885	24	34	17	8699	22929	2307	25.6	67.6	0.2
1886-1895	47	17	7	1810	5097	932	23.1	65.0	0.8
1896-1905	0	9	6	0	2307	837	0.0	73.4	2.3
Total	741	436	63	246462	140626	8349	—	—	—
Average	82	49	7	27385	15625	928	62.3	35.6	2.1

Source: Davis, Galllman, and Hutchins (1987a, p. 348, Table 10.4).

Independent of rig class, larger vessels hunted the more distant grounds and smaller ones remained closer to home. The Arctic drew the largest vessels: ships in that ground were 10 and barks 20 percent larger than the average of all grounds. In the Pacific ships were 2 and barks 8 percent above the mean. The vessels, whether ships or barks, that operated in the Indian Ocean were about 10 percent smaller than the fleet average; but in the Atlantic ships lay 15 and barks 20 percent below the all-ground benchmark.

Despite high loss rates, the transfer of younger vessels in and older vessels out, and the addition of a substantial number of new vessels that were built explicitly for whaling, the average age of the New Bedford fleet rose over time. If the first and last decades are excluded (there were very few barks in the first and no ships in the last), both the average ship and the average bark aged at a rate of just under five years per decade. Between 1816 and 1905, age tripled—by 1890 it was more than 38 years for ships and, by 1900, 47 years for barks.

Some vessels were "born" into the fleet—that is, constructed to order—some transferred in from other maritime activities or from another whaling port, and some were "reborn"—that is, rerigged. Of the 592 ships and barks whose genealogy can be traced, 71 ships and 49 barks were "born into the fleet," 239 ships and 175 barks transferred from mercantile pursuits or other ports, and one ship and 57 barks were the result of the rerigging of vessels of another class.

Transfers were by far the most important source of new entrants, but it was births and rebirths that, from the point of view of the industry's development, were the most significant. Rerigging—and in whaling rerigging almost always meant changing ships into barks—was important only in the decade-and-a-half after 1850, but in that period it accounted for one of every four entering barks. The burst of activity can be traced to the market's response to the rapid expansion of the Arctic grounds, where the more maneuverable barks were more efficient. The decision to rerig was the product of an increased demand for barks to exploit the newly discovered whale stocks (it took less time to rerig an old vessel than to build a new one), coupled with a temporary decline in the profitability of the ships hunting in their favored Pacific and Indian grounds.

The destinations of the vessels that left the fleet can also be traced. One hundred eight ships and 125 barks transferred to other ports or to other maritime activities (including at least 15 that joined the Stone Fleet during the Civil War,—a fleet purchased by the federal government, filled with stone, and sunk in an attempt to block the ports of Charleston and Savannah). Forty-eight ships were rerigged and reborn as barks. Paralleling "birth," "death" came by condemnation (41 ships and 45 barks) or, more frequently, by loss at sea (125 ships and 101 barks).

Two further characteristics of the New Bedford vessels are important. First, in an era when a typical merchant vessel had a life of about a dozen years, whalers were very long-lived. The average age of a condemned vessel was 37 years, and there are examples of ships and barks that operated for 75 years and more. The whaler's relative longevity can be traced to the wood preserving qualities of whale and sperm oil in an age when rot was a vessel's worst enemy.

Second, from the viewpoint of a safe return, whaling was a risky business. Of the 733 New Bedford vessels, 226 (30 percent) were lost at sea. Especially heavy losses were experienced during the Civil War and in two years in which the Arctic fleet was trapped in the ice, but there were few years with no losses. While there was no apparent trend, there were marked differences among the losses experienced by the three classes of vessel, and, for a given class, marked differences among the grounds hunted. The loss rate per year at sea for all classes of vessel averaged 3.2 percent, but it was 2.6 for ships, 3.5 for barks, and 8.7 for the others. The Indian Ocean was the safest ground for ships, but the second most dangerous for barks. The Atlantic displays the same loss rate for ships and barks, but the figure is relatively high for the former and moderately low for the latter. For both classes, however, the Arctic was by far the most treacherous: each year on the average, 4 percent of the ships and 7 percent of the barks were lost.

V. TECHNICAL CHANGE AND THE CAPITAL STOCK

Wind remained the source of power. Sailing ships, barks, brigs, schooners, and sloops still dominated the technological menu in 1906 almost as completely as they had in 1816, but the whaling industry had undergone a major technical transformation. The advances can best be divided into three groups: those that came from the improvement of sailing ships in general, those that were rooted in the design of whaling vessels in particular, and those that related to whalecraft—the tools used to kill whales.

Maritime historians long believed that there was little improvement in the design of sailing vessels in the nineteenth century in general, and in the years before 1850 in particular. More recent work, however, has shown that there were significant improvements before that date and major ones thereafter. In the 1820s and 1830s, iron rod rigging and turnbuckles were introduced, and it became much easier and less demanding to work aloft (Chapelle, 1967). In addition, between 1820 and 1845, a wide range of new equipment—capstans and windlasses, iron strapped blocks, geared steering, hold ventilators, and geared winches—came on the market and were widely adopted (Chapelle, 1967). The innovations in rigging and the new equipment reduced the need for labor in general and skilled seamen in particular. For whaling, because the size of the crew was established chiefly by hunting demands and always included many more men than those required to sail the vessel, this change had little effect on overall labor demand, but it had a substantial impact on the skill composition of the crew. Finally, in the 1840s, a technique for salt pickling designed to protect the keelson from rot was introduced and a vessel's life expectancy was increased substantially (McKay, 1928).

If the years from 1820 to 1850 saw substantial improvement in equipment, the period after 1850 was one of near revolution in the design and construction of sailing vessels. Donald McKay introduced machinery into his shipyard, and boat building became much less costly than it otherwise would have been (Hutchins, 1941). Sails and rigging were almost totally redesigned, and the results were greater speed and reduced labor costs—the new sails needed both fewer and less skilled seamen to operate. Builders recognized that increasing the number of sails made handling easier, and, conventional wisdom aside, they concluded that flat sails were more efficient than baggy ones. "In response they subdivided the larger sails, abolished the studding sails and other expensive 'kites', and radically altered the design of the sail—baggy sails were replaced by much flatter ones" (Chatterton, 1909). In addition, building on the rigging improvements of the 1820s and 1830s, there was a nearly total technical transformation aloft. Iron fittings were widely adopted, chains replaced rope, and the design of the mast was greatly simplified (McKay, 1928; Chapelle, 1935). Once again, the consequences of these changes for whaling productivity are not likely to have been as great as for the merchant marine. Speed was no great advantage for a whaler; and, since the vessels always carried more men then those necessary to sail them, the effect on crew size was minimal. The changes did, however, significantly reduce the demand for skilled seamen.

The 1850s also saw a fundamental change in naval architects' approach to ship design, and a significant change in their vision of the vessel to be designed. The traditional half-scale model was replaced by blueprints based on mathematical analysis (Chapelle, 1935). Supported by the new analytical approach to vessel design, but tracing their lineage directly to the successful China clippers, a series of structural changes were incorporated in many of the vessels that were launched from the nation's shipyards. Among those most widely adopted were alterations in the shape of the bow and stern. The new bows were sharper and more concave, and the sterns were redesigned to let the ship run smoothly and with less water resistance (Chatterton, 1909). Finally, although less radical than the clippers, "merchantmen gradually attained a more elongated configuration, with flat floors and hard bilges to give them both increased carrying capacity and shallow draft" (Chatterton, 1909).

The vessels newly built for whaling were affected by all these generalized changes, but they were most directly affected by the medium or California clipper—a vessel that was the product of Donald McKay's designs. Those vessels, and the whalers that followed, "combined two elements—buoyancy and stability—to a degree never before seen. They had very little deadrise, but a very wide floor; between the curves of their bilges each ship was 35 or more feet wide; and, although all their soars were aloft and their boats stowed on gallow frames on top of their houses, a typical vessel drew only ten and a half feet of water" (McKay, 1928). A number of these modified clippers were built specifically for whaling, and more than a few joined the New Bedford fleet. They were designed with raking stems and even sharper lines than traditional whalers, and many of them were bark rigged. Because they were, "sharp floored and easy bilged to make them roll down when 'cutting-out' a whale," they differed substantially from vessels destined for the merchant marine (Bathe, 1967; see also Chapelle, 1935).

In the two decades between 1856 and 1875, one-third of the barks and ships that entered the fleet were "built to order"; in the next decade, the only ship and three-fourths of the new barks came directly from the shipyard Over the second half of the century, vessels (particularly barks) that were specifically designed for whaling gradually replaced some of the transfers of the earlier era (Chapelle, 1935). Only five of the 77 barks and 39 of the 240 ships that entered the fleet were built to order in the 25 years through 1850, but between 1851 and 1882 (entry largely ceased after 1882) among the 282 entrants were 48 rerigged ships, 83 new vessels and only 151 transfers.

In the years of rapid growth, any ship or bark could be transferred almost directly into whaling, and its owners could expect handsome profits. But by the early 1860s, the days of the transfer were numbered. As the editor of the *Annual Review of the Whale Fishery* noted:

> . . . the greater number of suitable vessels that have this year been fitted for the fishery, compared with those that had been fitted during the last few years; the growing determination in the minds of the merchants not to introduce into service any more such expensive vessels as new clippers and bulky ships that were never meant for whalers, but to introduce vessels of proper size, and only such as may be built expressly for the business, and that can sell at comparatively low figures (quoted in *Merchant Transcript*, 1363).

Slightly more than a decade later, the same source, emphasizing the change in the relative costs, reported, "some vessels may possibly be added to the fleet from the merchant service; but such ventures are attended by so heavy an outlay for repairs, alterations, and whaling inventories, it is not possible that many such additions will be made" (*Merchant Transcript*, 1876). Two years later the point is underscored again: "Shipbuilding has revived, and twelve whalers were built during the year, it being now apparent that at present prices new vessels can be built cheaper than merchantmen can be altered into whaleships" (*Merchant Transcript*, 1878). "The building of ships for the whaling service marks a new era in the business" (*Merchant Transcript*, 1877). It should be noted that the new vessels were added at a time, when, because of increased competition from iron and steam, the price of used wooden sailing vessels was falling and at a time when the size of the whaling fleet was rapidly contracting.

Finally, the industry benefitted from substantial improvements in whalecraft. As Charles Scammon, naturalist and former whaling captain, reported in 1876: "There has been as great a revolution in the mode of killing whales during the last twenty years, as there has been in the art of naval warfare; were it not for this, few whalers would now be afloat" (Scammon, 1874). There were a few changes in the whaleboat that was used to attack the whales. Perfected by a century of experience the boats had become standardized by mid-century: "double ended, twenty-eight to thirty feet long, six feet broad, and only twenty-six inches deep amidships. They were sheathed with half-inch cedar planking on white oak and propelled by a spiritsail or, when close to the whale, by five stout fourteen-to-eighteen foot oars or by paddles" (Morrison, 1921).

Important changes were made to the harpoon and lance. The harpoon, to which a line was attached, was intended to lodge in the whale's back and fasten it to the boat until the mammal tired and could be killed by the lance. Many whales were lost because the harpoon pulled out; thus a harpooner usually attempted to place two harpoons attached to the same line in his whale. Much ingenuity went into the design of new types of harpoon heads that would hold more successfully. The two-flued harpoon was briefly replaced by the one-flued harpoon, which, in turn, was made obsolete by a series of further improvements. The toggle iron was representative of this latter group of innovations. The head was set on a pivot and held in place by a light piece of wood. The harpoon was driven into the whale. When the whale began to run, the wood broke, the head of the iron turned on the pivot, and the whale was securely tied to the boat.

As the whale swam off, the wooden shafts of the harpoons were disengaged and fell into the water. The harpoon heads were attached to a line coiled in a tub in the bottom of the boat, and as the whale ran, the line played out so quickly that it had to be continuously wetted down to counter the effects of friction. The boat was dragged along on what the whalemen referred to as a Nantucket (or New Bedford) sleigh ride. While the whale was swimming, the harpooner—the forward starboard-side oarsman (more commonly known as the boatsteerer)—changed place with the man at the stern (the boatheader or head-a-boat), who had been handling the steering oar. It was the boatheader, usually an officer, who killed the whale.

Until the late 1850s, the boat header almost always used a wrought iron lance. In the late 1850s and early 1860s, two innovations—the steel-headed lance and the bomb lance—diffused rapidly. The name of the former is fully descriptive: the innovation involved only a change from an iron to a steel lance head. The timing of its adoption suggests that its innovation depended on a decline in the relative price of steel. The bomb lance, however, marks a major change—it was an explosive device. The lance was shot from a weapon that resembled a shotgun, and it was the last of a line of inventions intended to make lances more deadly (poisoned lances, electric lances, explosive lances) and better able to hit the whale from a distance (guns, rocket launchers). The first explosive lances were almost as deadly to the boatheader and his shipmates as they were to the whale. The guns had a very substantial kick that could break the boatheader's collarbone, throw him overboard, or swamp the boat.

Elsewhere, guns were also used to propel the harpoon, but these devices were used infrequently in the American fishery. The Greener, for example, a swivel gun mounted in the bow of the whaleboat, could only be employed successfully if seas were calm and the boat was sturdy, conditions not often found in the American whale fishery. In the American fishery, the Greener was virtually confined to Pacific bay hunting for gray whales, but there it was used very successfully.

The most effective piece of new whalecraft employed in the American fishery was the Pierce, or darting gun; an innovation that first appeared in the 1860s—a time when the fishery was already declining. The gun was normally mounted on a standard harpoon, which was thrown (or darted) into the whale in the usual way. When the harpoon head entered the whale, however, it depressed the trigger of the gun and the shot sent an explosive lance deep into the mammal. If the harpoon was properly placed, the whale was killed immediately. The Pierce gun was particularly important in the bowhead fishery of the Arctic, where the harpooned whale would often attempt to dive under the ice. If it succeeded, the whalers had to cut the line in order to save themselves and their boat. The darting gun killed the whale before it could dive (Lytle, 1984; Davis, Gallman, and Hutchins, 1989).

VI. LABOR: CAPTAINS AND GREENHANDS

A typical whaling vessel left port with: (1) a captain and at least one, and sometimes as many as five, mates, (2) a number of skilled professional mariners—their ranks always included between two and six boatsteerers, often a shipkeeper or two (men who sailed the vessel while the rest of the crew was in the boats pursuing whales), and at times a head-a-boat, a second boatsteerer, or a navigator, (3) a number of artisans—the list almost always included a cooper and a carpenter, often a blacksmith and occasionally a boatbuilder, painter, sailmaker, mechanic, machinist, caulker, coopersmith, surgeon, or a doctor as well as a second cooper, carpenter, or blacksmith, (4) some service personnel—almost every vessel had a cook and a steward and these crewmen were occasionally supplemented by a second cook or steward, a steerage steward, or a steerage master, and (5) a number of seamen—some skilled, some semi-skilled, some greenhands, and often a boy or two.

Over the 90 years spanned by the study, a ship's crew averaged 28.1 men, a bark's 24.4, and the other three classes 17.1. For all three classes the average rose over time, although the greater part of the increase was concentrated in

Table 4. Crew and Crew Per Ton: New Bedford Whalers, 1816-1900

	Average Crew Size			*Men Per Ton*		
Years	*Ships*	*Barks*	*Other*	*Ships*	*Barks*	*Other*
1816-1825	20.9	14.3	14.0	0.071	0.074	0.101
1826-1835	23.4	19.8	14.8	0.074	0.080	0.117
1836-1845	26.3	22.7	16.8	0.081	0.092	0.114
1846-1855	29.1	25.8	18.3	0.084	0.099	0.157
1856-1865	30.0	27.1	20.1	0.082	0.095	0.125
1866-1875	30.9	27.4	17.7	0.084	0.096	0.153
1876-1885	31.1	27.8	18.3	0.084	0.099	0.142
1886-1895	33.0	28.4	16.5	0.083	0.103	0.138
1896-1900	—	26.4	17.0	—	0.190	—
Average	28.1	24.4	17.1	0.080	0.103	0.131

Source: Davis, Gallman, and Hutchins (1987a, p. 361, Table 10.8).

the first 50 years (see Table 4). If attention is focused not on raw crew count, but on a measure of labor input adjusted to reflect the size of the whaling vessel (men per ton), there is still evidence of increasing labor intensity. If, however, a further adjustment is made to capture the inter-ground differences in labor requirements, there is no evidence of any further increase after mid-century. "Other" vessels were the most labor intensive, while barks used relatively more labor than ships. The difference in labor intensity between ships and barks was not independent of the ground hunted—it diminished as the distance from New Bedford increased. In the Atlantic barks employed a fourth more labor per ton than ships, in the Indian and Pacific grounds the difference was only half that large, and in the Arctic it was a mere 5 percent.

A whaleman, as Elmo Hohman put it, were he a captain or a greenhand, was "not paid by the day, week, or month, nor was he allowed a certain sum for every barrel of oil or every pound of bone captured. Instead his earnings consisted of a specified fractional share, known as the lay, of the total net proceeds of a voyage. The earnings of a whaleman thus constituted a reward not only for the performance of labor under peculiarly trying conditions, but also for the assumption of both business and physical risks. For the size of his lay, representing his wages, was directly dependent upon the business risks centering about price fluctuations, as well as upon the physical risks of storm, fire, stranding, and poor luck on the whaling grounds" (Hohman, 1926). The unitiated should keep in mind that the word lay had nothing to do with the whaleman's sex habits nor did it reflect on his lack of religious affiliation. The word lay refers only to the fractional share of the total catch to which the whaleman was entitled at voyage end. The lays were expressed as fractions (e.g., 1/16 for a captain or 1/200 for a greenhand), but they were often referred to as the reciprocal of that fraction—a 16 or a 200.

Table 5. Lays by Occupation, 1840-1858 and 1866 (All Grounds): New Bedford Whaling

Occupation	*Average Lay*	*Lay Share As Percentage of Value of Catch*	*Relative Shares: Unskilled Seamen Equal 100*	*Percentage of Change in Lay: 1840-1843 to 1855-1858*
Captain	1/15.2	6.58	1219	+17.3
First Mates	1/23.2	4.31	799	+24.1
Second Mates	1/38.4	2.60	483	+21.7
Third Mates	1/53.9	1.86	344	+19.2
Fourth Mates	1/72.3	1.38	256	+11.8
Boatsteerers	1/87.4	1.14	212	+1.1
Ship Keepers	1/115.4	0.87	161	−25.3
Misc. Skilled Maritime	1/109.4	0.91	169	−22.8
Coopers	1/52.2	1.75	324	+8.1
Carpenters	1/163.9	0.61	113	−13.8
Blacksmiths	1/171.3	0.58	108	−16.7
Misc. Artisans	1/171.2	9.58	108	−14.1
Cooks	1/140.3	0.71	132	−3.4
Stewards	1/135.9	0.74	136	0.0
Skilled Seamen	1/150.9	0.66	123	−14.7
Semi-Skilled Seamen	1/166.8	0.60	111	−8.7
Unskilled Seamen	1/185.3	0.54	100	−8.7
Boys	1/415.1	0.24	45	−33.5

Source: Davis, Gallman, and Hutchins (Tape No. 2, Labor). Tape No. 2 examines 36,640 labor contracts signed between whalesmen and the agents who organized 1,258 whaling voyages that departed from New Bedford, MA, between January 1, 1840 and December 31, 1858 and between January 1 and December 31, 1866.

Wage and occupational data are available for only a part of the period, and the following analysis is based solely on the records of vessels departing New Bedford between January 1840 and December 1858 and in 1866. Table 5 summarizes the information on stations and lays, and Table 6 provides some further information about the men who made up the crews.

If the standard is the lay of an unskilled seaman, captains did very well, first mates quite well, and the other officers not badly (depending on rank, their earnings ranged from two and one-half to twelve times as much as unskilled seamen). Among the skilled maritime professionals, boatsteerers earned twice as much, and the others, about two-thirds again as much as the most unskilled among the crew. Artisans, coopers aside, did not fare so well. While a barrel-maker earned as much as a third mate, carpenters earned only 13 percent more than a typical green hand, and blacksmiths and "others" accrued only about

Table 6. Characteristics of the Crews Of New Bedford Whalers (All Grounds): 1840-1858 and 1866

Year	*Average Labor Share*	*Illiterate In Crew (%)*	*Unskilled In Crew (%)*	*Seamen Unskilled (%)*
1840	0.309	0.211	0.292	0.538
1841	0.309	0.192	0.308	0.565
1842	0.315	0.201	0.324	0.607
1843	0.317	0.190	0.292	0.546
1844	0.317	0.220	0.335	0.631
1845	0.320	0.217	0.355	0.660
1846	0.318	0.226	0.354	0.661
1847	0.317	0.236	0.355	0.658
1848	0.317	0.253	0.343	0.654
1849	0.318	0.235	0.360	0.674
1850	0.333	0.233	0.387	0.725
1851	0.344	0.235	0.390	0.710
1852	0.344	0.223	0.396	0.726
1853	0.345	0.221	0.394	0.730
1854	0.347	0.275	0.406	0.751
1855	0.359	0.247	0.430	0.779
1856	0.362	0.265	0.426	0.773
1857	0.362	0.280	0.359	0.664
1858	0.350	0.238	0.381	0.692
1866	0.344	0.277	0.312	0.559
Average	0.332	0.234	0.360	0.665

Source: Davis, Gallman, and Hutchins (Tape No. 2, Labor). See Table 5.

one-half that differential. Cooks and stewards earned about one-third more than green hands, skilled seamen about 25 percent more, and semi-skilled seamen, less than carpenters but more than blacksmiths. The time pattern is also instructive. As time passed, officers as a group and coopers appear to have obtained greater fractions, for stewards and boatsteerers there was little change, but for all other crewmen the period seems to have been one of contracting shares.

The changes in lays coupled with shifts in the size and composition of the crew meant that labor's share of the catch was not stable. A comparison of a typical crew in the years 1840-1843 with one in 1855-1858 indicates that, despite the rising proportion of barks with their smaller crews, average crew size increased by about 9 percent. The increase was not spread equally across the ship's company. The overall increase of 2.3 men was the result of an increase of 3.5 in the number of unskilled seamen, a reduction of 2.0 in the numbers of skilled and semi-skilled seamen, and an increase of .8 in the number of professionals (mates and boatsteerers). Changes in lays and in the size and

Table 7. Relative Lay Shares by Ground: New Bedford Whalers, 1840-1858 and 1866

Occupation	*Atlantic*	*Indian*	*Pacific*	*Arctic*
Captain	100	96	93	94
First Mate	100	92	88	94
Second Mate	100	92	88	92
Third Mate	100	96	93	99
Boatsteerer	100	86	79	79
Cooper	100	105	103	103
Carpenter	100	89	88	89
Cook	100	92	89	86
Steward	100	97	93	93
Skilled Seamen	100	90	85	82
Semi Skilled Seamen	100	93	88	85
Unskilled Seamen	100	88	84	81
Average All Occupations	100	93	89	89

Source: Davis, Gallman, and Hutchins (Tape No. 2, Labor).

composition of the crew meant that labor's share of net income rose from 31 percent in the early 1840s to 36 percent eighteen years later.

For almost every occupation there were consistent inter-ground differences in the average lay (see Table 7). In general, shares were highest in the Atlantic, somewhat lower in the Indian, and lowest of all in the Pacific and Arctic. As between the two latter grounds, officers fared better in the Arctic—no doubt a reflection of the navigational difficulties there—but other occupations did significantly worse. Coopers are the one notable exception to the general inter-ground rule—their shares were lower in the Atlantic than in any other ground, but that deviation can almost certainly be explained by the limited demand for their skills on the relatively short voyages to the Atlantic fishery.

It was, however, wages, not lays that were important to the crewman. Given the extreme voyage-to-voyage variation in the catch and the long delay between the time a sailor signed on and the time he was paid, there is some question as to just what constitutes an appropriate measure of *The Wage*. For example, if interest is focused on the motivations of a crewman, the best estimate might be the wage obtained by sailors of his station returning to port in the year he signed on for his voyage. Such a measure would be a reasonable index of what he expected to earn. For present purposes, however, interest is centered on what crewmen actually earned, not what they expected. The product of his lay and the value of his vessel's catch gives the clearest indication of the earnings of a seaman who completed a voyage or who was discharged for good

Table 8. Projected Earnings by Occupation, 1840-1858 and 1866 (All Grounds; Current dollars): New Bedford Whalers

Occupation	*Projected Average Monthly Earnings*	*Percentage of Change: 1840-1843 to 1855-1858*	*Minimum*	*Maximum*
Captain	97.64	25.1	1.20	621.39
First Mate	64.15	36.5	1.20	395.43
Second Mate	38.71	30.2	1.90	232.96
Third Mate	27.33	23.1	1.03	144.99
Boatsteerer	17.26	1.7	0.48	114.56
Cooper	27.02	8.4	1.03	155.35
Carpenter	9.28	−3.7	0.24	52.72
Cook	10.37	−1.2	0.53	60.00
Steward	11.16	5.0	0.46	99.01
Skilled Seamen	10.03	−7.4	0.29	71.30
Semi-Skilled Seamen	8.76	−3.4	0.27	41.43
Unskilled Seamen	8.03	−7.8	0.19	38.66

Source: Davis, Gallman, and Hutchins (Tape No. 2, Labor).

reason, and that is the wage employed in this analysis (see Table 8). A comparison of the wage estimate with earnings in the merchant marine produces some interesting results (see Table 9) (Lebergott, 1964). For the officers, whaling was a very rewarding occupation. Captains appear to have received almost three times as much as merchant marine officers, and even second and third mates made more than twice as much as their opposite numbers in the mercantile service. A part of the difference certainly reflects risk. Even excluding vessels lost at sea or returned empty, monthly earnings for a whaling captain varied widely ranging from $1.20 to $621.39 as compared to $20 to $35 for the merchant mariners.

The high earnings of whaling officers must also have reflected the heavy responsibilities they bore. Because whalers frequently travelled through waters that had hardly been charted, their officers needed even greater maritime skills than a typical merchant marine officer. In addition, they had to have a thorough knowledge of whales—their habitats and their migration patterns—and be able to command one of the New Bedford sleighs. Although the captain had ultimate responsibility, the other officers were also required to have more knowledge and a higher level of skills than their peers of similar rank in the merchant marine.

If risk and the need for specialized knowledge and skills explain officers' wage differentials, the explanation for the other three classes of whalemen (cooks, skilled seamen, and semi-skilled seaman) about whom there is

Table 9. Wages of Merchant Men and Whalers: 1840-1858 and 1866

	Captains			*First Mates*			*Second Mates*			*Cooks*			*Skilled Seamen*			*Semi-Skilled Seamen*		
Year	*MM*	*W*	*Ratio*	*MM*	*W*	*Ratio*	*MM*	*W*	*Ratio*	*MM*	*W*	*Ratio*	*MM*	*W*	*Ratio*	*MM*	*W*	*Ratio*
1840	30.0	92.5	3.1	26.0	54.9	2.1	19.3	33.0	1.7	13.8	10.9	0.8	14.0	10.8	0.8	—	—	—
1841	30.0	71.4	2.4	21.3	45.5	2.1	—	—	—	9.8	8.9	0.9	14.0	8.5	0.6	—	—	—
1842	30.0	78.2	2.6	21.0	51.0	2.4	4.0	30.0	7.5	10.0	9.6	1.0	13.0	9.6	0.7	—	—	—
1843	30.0	81.6	2.7	18.7	50.5	2.7	—	—	—	8.3	9.2	1.1	13.0	10.1	0.8	—	—	—
1844	27.5	70.0	2.5	18.7	42.9	2.3	—	—	—	8.4	7.9	0.9	14.0	7.7	0.6	—	—	—
1845	26.7	67.0	2.5	19.3	42.8	2.2	—	—	—	11.2	7.6	0.7	14.0	7.7	0.6	—	—	—
1846	28.0	83.8	3.0	20.3	53.4	2.6	19.0	332.8	1.7	12.4	9.8	0.8	14.0	9.8	0.7	8.6	8.6	1.0
1847	25.0	83.1	3.3	31.0	50.6	1.6	21.0	31.9	1.5	20.0	9.5	0.5	14.0	8.8	0.6	—	—	—
1848	30.0	110.1	3.7	22.0	69.8	3.2	20.0	44.9	2.2	12.2	12.4	1.0	15.0	12.6	0.8	10.3	10.1	1.0
1849	—	—	—	30.0	68.5	2.3	—	—	—	15.0	12.3	0.8	15.0	11.4	0.8	—	—	—
1850	27.3	109.0	4.0	17.5	73.7	4.2	—	—	—	13.0	11.5	0.9	13.0	11.6	0.9	—	—	—
1851	—	—	—	32.0	79.4	2.5	20.0	45.8	2.3	16.5	11.9	0.7	15.0	10.9	0.7	9.6	9.4	1.0
1852	—	—	—	28.0	73.6	2.6	20.0	42.0	2.1	17.3	11.0	0.6	15.0	11.5	0.8	9.5	8.6	0.9
1853	35.0	142.6	4.1	25.7	100.0	3.9	20.0	56.2	2.8	15.0	15.0	1.0	15.0	18.1	1.2	12.3	10.7	0.9
1854	35.0	109.4	3.1	46.3	76.3	1.7	33.3	44.5	1.3	27.0	11.2	0.4	15.0	12.5	0.8	9.8	8.5	0.9
1855	—	—	—	—	—	—	37.5	40.0	1.1	26.0	9.3	0.4	15.0	9.3	0.6	8.5	8.5	1.0
1856	—	—	—	—	—	—	—	—	—	—	—	—	—	—	—	—	—	—
1857	—	—	—	50.0	69.7	1.4	35.0	39.0	1.1	25.0	9.1	0.4	15.0	7.6	0.5	—	—	—
1858	—	—	—	—	—	—	—	—	—	—	—	—	—	—	—	—	—	—
1866	—	—	—	55.0	88.8	1.6	36.0	57.8	1.6	29.3	12.5	0.4	27.0	12.2	0.5	—	13.0	10.3
Avg.	29.6	91.6	3.1	28.4	64.2	2.4	23.8	41.5	2.3	16.1	10.5	0.7	15.0	10.6	0.7	—	10.2	9.3

Note: *MM* = Merchantmen; *W* = Whalemen from New Bedford.

Sources: For Merchantmen, see Lebergott (1964, Tables A21, AA22A, AA22B); for Whalers, see Davis, Gallman, and Hutchins (Tape No. 2: Labor).

comparable information must lie elsewhere. For them, despite a range of returns as wide as those for the officers, pay levels were on average substantially less (.7 to .9) than those earned by men of allegedly similar skills in the sister service. These data appear to bear out the widely held contemporary view that the two industries drew from very different labor pools (Nordhoff, 1895; Hohman, 1968). To the extent that the occupational categories are comparable and the quality of the seamen the same, the whaleman's willingness to accept both lower average and much more variable returns must suggest something about his view of risk.

Given the ground-to-ground variation in lays and the relative wages of the cooks and seamen in whaling and the merchant marine, it may seem possible to conclude that labor markets were not particularly efficient in nineteenth century New Bedford. The data on wages, however, indicate that, at least within the industry, the labor market worked well. Although the Arctic was an exception, for whalemen in general and for the seamen in particular, despite the wide year-to-year fluctuations, there appears to have been a substantial degree of long run inter-ground wage equality (see Table 10). Equality might also be achieved in the case of the Arctic, if risk were factored in and if the data spanned a longer period of time. To the extent that the data do suggest something about market efficiency, the ability of agents and sailors to recognize inter-ground differences in productivity and to take account of those differentials when negotiating contracts that covered as much as five years is certainly amazing.

Finally, although the average labor share was rising, there is evidence that, by many measures, average crew quality was declining (see Table 6). The crew became less skilled. Between 1840-1843 and 1855-1858, although a typical vessel had added .5 officers and .3 boatsteerers, it had lost 2.0 skilled and semi-skilled seamen and added 3.5 unskilled seamen. As a result, the fraction of unskilled seamen increased by almost a third (to more than 70 percent) and the fraction of unskilled in the crew by a like amount (to 40 percent). At the same time, the percentage of illiterates in the crew rose from 20 to 26 percent. If the deterioration in quality carried over to the ranks of the skilled and semi-skilled seamen (i.e., if the definition of the ranks changed as well), it would go a long way toward explaining the decline in their wages and the relative deterioration of their position vis-à-vis their counterparts in the merchant marine.

The explanation of the observed substitution of a combination of unskilled greenhands and skilled maritime professionals for able and ordinary seamen is not completely clear. Certainly it was the new technological opportunities—opportunities that reduced the need for trained sailors to handle the work aloft—that made the substitution possible. What is not clear, however, is the economic conditions that underlay the decision to make that substitution. The implied increase in total labor cost indicates that the change was not affected in an attempt to reduce total direct wage cost, but thus far it has not been

Table 10. Relative Monthly Wages by Ground: New Bedford Whalers, 1840-1858 and 1866 (Atlantic = 100)

Occupation	*Atlantic*	*Indian*	*Pacific*	*Arctic*
Captain	100	98	111	134
First Mate	100	91	103	131
Second Mate	100	90	102	128
Third Mate	100	107	119	143
Boatsteerer	100	88	92	108
Cooper	100	104	113	132
Carpenter	100	65	74	86
Cook	100	97	108	129
Steward	100	74	82	102
Skilled Seamen	100	72	82	93
Semi-Skilled Seamen	100	110	113	133
Unskilled Seamen	100	99	89	114
Average All Occupations	100	91	99	119

Source: Davis, Gallman, and Hutchins (Tape No. 2, Labor).

possible to distinguish between two other competing hypotheses. On the one hand, there is evidence to suggest that the increased direct cost reflected a deliberate decision to adopt a policy aimed at reducing labor turnover—and thus indirect labor costs—by recruiting only those men who, because of lack of marketable skills and information about local conditions and alternative employment, were less likely to desert. Conversely, other evidence indicates that the substitution may have been only a managerial response to the industry's increasing inability to recruit workers from its traditional labor pools in the face of rising onshore competition.

VII. AGENTS

Whaling agents, often owners or part-owners of the vessels they managed, were responsible for preparing the craft for sea: seeing to the renewal of masts, spars, and rigging, replacing lost or broken whalecraft, provisioning, and hiring the officers and men. Some of these functions, particularly provisioning and the employment of crewmen, could be, and often were, subcontracted to other firms. The agent, however, kept close track of all these activities, since his profits from the voyage—a share of the net proceeds—would depend in part on how carefully the preparations for the voyage were carried out.

The agent's activities did not stop when the vessel left port. While the captain was responsible for day-to-day operations, the agent maintained as close a supervision as he could manage from a distance of as much as several thousand miles. He was responsible for assuring that credit and access to cash were available to the captain when he put in to overseas ports. Information was exchanged regularly between agent and captain. The captain and the agent agreed on dates and stations where letters would be picked up and dispatched, and letters also were exchanged at rendezvous between whaling vessels or between supply ships and whaling vessels.

Some sense of the nature of the exchanges can be obtained from the letter book of Matthew Howland, an important whaling agent. On February 3, 1858 he wrote to one of his captains, Philip Howland, mildly admonishing him over his recent record:

> . . . 25 months out with 600 bbl sperm & 130 whale is rather low but *I am in hopes* that you will come up now and *be equal* to any of them according to time—I shall expect to hear of you at Talcuahelna in March with from 800 to 1000 bbls of *sperm oil on board* (Howland, 1858).

On December 15, he composed a similar letter to Paul Green, captain of the ship *Rousseau*, pointing out that, while he did not wish to second-guess him, it was nonetheless true that, having once decided to go to the Arctic, Green should have stuck it out through the whole season instead of shifting from ground to ground. Howland argued that, had Green remained in the Arctic, the voyage would have turned out better than it actually had. He also pointed out that the longer it took to fill the vessel with oil, the longer Green and the crew would be away from home and friends (a reminder that appeared frequently in these letters). There followed an account of arrangements for the delivery of provisions to the Sandwich Islands for Green's vessel, some news of home and of the success of other Howland vessels (Howland tried to set vessels in competition with each other: "Don't let the *Reindeer* beat you!"), orders to Green to ship home any bone he collected but to keep the oil aboard, and then personal regards to the mates (Howland, 1858).

On the same day Howland wrote to Captain G.P. Pomeroy of the ship *George Howland* telling the Captain that he had made a mistake in choosing to hunt in the Kodiak area. He should have gone to the Sea of Okhotsk, where Howland had wanted him to go in the first place; but once having gone to Kodiak, he should have stayed there instead of shifting to New Zealand. He told Pomeroy to keep his expenses down (a recurring theme of these letters), quoted the current prices of oil, passed along personal news, sent regards to the first and second mates and asked who was now third mate, and, finally, asked if all the boatsteerers were *good* (Howland, 1858). Two days later he wrote Captain Valentine Lewis of the ship *Corinthian*, telling him to go to Kodiak and to move on to the Arctic if hunting off the southern Alaskan coast was poor. He gave Lewis the latitude and longitude of the good catches made by other captains that year (Howland, 1858). On December 31, Howland acknowledged a letter from Captain Robert Jones of the *George and Susan* sent by steamer from the Sandwich Islands, said he had handled the matter of Jones' insurance for him, and passed along news of Jones's wife (Howland, 1858).

In July of the next year the unfortunate Captain Pomeroy was sent a letter expressing concern over the amount of cash Pomeroy had been drawing, while a letter to Jones commiserated over the death of a mate, killed by a whale's flukes, expressed the hope the replacement was proving effective, and said: "I am pleased to learn of thy judging it proper to lower for whales [illegible] after the death of Mr. Tripp" (Howland, 1859).

In August, he wrote Lewis again, telling him to extend the length of his southern cruise between Arctic seasons in order to take as much sperm oil as possible. Howland presumably felt that changes in relative prices favored this strategy. In response to Lewis's report that the crew was agitating for more favorable lays, the agent told the captain to resist for a time (to try to reduce the demands) but eventually to consent, "because we are satisfied a good crew is cheaper at high lays than a miserable crew is for nothing" (Howland, 1859, 1860).

In letters written in 1860, he complained to Jones that the Captain was not writing frequently enough and that he, Howland, was forced to follow the voyage through the newspapers, but he complimented Lewis on the amount and quality of the oil and bone sent home, all of which, he added, had been sold favorably (Howland, 1860). In the same year, Howland also wrote to Grafton Hellman, a friend of Captain Green, who was to write the Captain to inform him that his wife had died. The letter is worth quotation in extenso:

> Now, as thee has kindly offered to do anything for us in regard to this sad affair, we would recommend, if it should appear necessary, to encourage Captain Green as much as possible to look on the bright side of things and endeavor to carry out his wishes in regard to the remains of his wife, advising him to pursue his voyage as far as his feeling will allow him, as though nothing had happened, believing that this severe bereavement which has come upon him is in the ordering of Divine Providence and might have occurred if he had been at home . . . we hope he will have no idea, and we can hardly imagine he will, of abandoning the voyage or delaying the ship in Port longer than is really necessary . . . as considerable time & money have already been expended (perhaps necessarily) on account of his wife's illness (Howland, 1860).

He went on to ask Hellman to remind Green that Green had a duty to the owners. (Green decided to complete the cruise, per Howland's request.)

Matthew Howland was not in every respect a typical whaling agent. Of the 275 agents treated in this paper, 197 managed 10 or fewer voyages. Most of these people were primarily engaged in some other line of business—sometimes more than one other line: Zenas Adams was a grocer; Gilbert Allen styled himself "merchant" (so did many others who did some work as whaling agents) and was president of the Gas Light Company (a hedge?); Baylis and Cannon were in flour, groceries, and provisions; William Blackler, a real estate operator; William Brownell, a ship chandler; Lucas and Lucas ran the Caloric Paint Manufacturing Company and also dealt in cement and bricks; Chapman and Bonney were sailmakers; William Dow was a speculator; Rodney French was involved with Colorado mining and was for a time mayor of the town; Joseph and Lawrence Grinnell (and others, as well) were oil dealers; Lawrence Grinnell was also an insurance agent; Haskell and Randall were dealers in coal; the Hathaways were in the China trade; Hathaway and Luce manufactured oil and candles; Azel Howard was in dry goods; Weston Howland was in petroleum and coal oil (another hedge?); Zeno Kelley was a watch maker, jeweler, and inventor (an exploding harpoon and a harpoon gun), and in 1863 was sentenced to four years in prison and a fine of $1,000 for engaging in the slave trade; Thomas Luce was a cooper and interested in the New Bedford Ice Company; Charles Morgan was a shipowner and iron manufacturer; John Richardson was an outfitter and manufacturer of patent medicine; Richmond and Wood were tailors; Worth and Smith sold fish; and Henry Thomas was in navigation, among many other things (Dun, 1841-1890).[4]

Even the Howlands were diversified. They invested in railroads as well as in a number of local ventures, but they were chiefly whaling agents. If the number of whaling voyages organized by the twelve firms bearing the Howland name are added together, the sum comes to 476.[5] Of those, Matthew's firm alone accounted for 121. These are fairly large numbers. Because all the New Bedford voyages analyzed come to only 4,095, the family was involved in almost one voyage in eight and Matthew, himself, in almost 3 percent of the total. The Howlands were not the only big operators: 58 other firms managed between 11 and 50 voyages each, 10 between 51 and 100, and 3 between 101 and 150 (see Table 11).

These figures leave something to be desired, if the goal is an understanding of the structure of the industry. The firms were typically individual enterprises or partnerships. The death of a partner, the elevation of a clerk or a son to a position of partner, or a squabble between partners that led them to separate would make for a name change that did not necessarily signal the end of one firm and the beginning of another. Counting firms, then, is a chancy business. The problem is compounded by the matter of family dynasties. The 12 Howland firms were separate entities, but surely the family could be counted on to help one of its members, and it is difficult to believe that they did not share information as well.

It is easy to trace the Howlands in the records, but it is not so simple to identify those firms linked together by marriage. The Rotches, for example, who were the great whaling family of the eighteenth century and who are often credited with shifting the center of the whaling industry from Nantucket to New Bedford, intermarried with no fewer than nine other New Bedford whaling

Table 11. New Bedford Whaling Agents By Number of Voyages Conducted, 1796-1914

Number of Voyages	×	*Number of Agents*	=	*Total Voyages*
1		68		68
2		31		62
3		25		75
4		14		56
5		19		95
6		10		60
7		8		56
8		6		48
9		9		81
10		7		70
1 through 10		197		671
11 through 20		31		453
21 through 30		13		326
31 through 40		12		420
41 through 50		7		268
51 through 60		2		116
61 through 70		3		198
71 through 80		2		155
81 through 90		1		88
91 through 100		2		187
101 through 130		3		361
140		1		140
160		1		160
Total		275		3,543
Agents Unknown		552		
Grand Total of Voyages				4,095

Note: This does not include all New Bedford voyages between 1896 and 1914; as many as several hundred voyages may be missing.
Source: Davis, Gallman, and Hutchins (Tape No. 1).

families and at least one from Nantucket: the Rodmans, Arnolds, Barkers, Bordens, Barneys, Hazzards, Morgans, Robesons, Thomases, and, from Nantucket, the Macys (McDevitt, 1986). The Rotches managed 32 of the voyages, their closest allies, the Rodmans, another 66, and the whole extended clan, 279.

Family was not the only way in which agent firms were connected. Quakers had dominated the industry on Nantucket as Melville has told us. When, as problems with the Nantucket harbor became more severe, the industry shifted to New Bedford, it was the Quakers who led the move. All was not pure harmony among the Friends—there were divisions in the New Bedford Meeting. Nonetheless, religious conviction was a factor linking the leaders of the chief whaling firms. For example, the Rotches and the Howlands were both Quaker families.

Many of the important New Bedford agents came originally from a whaling background on Nantucket. Their sons and the husbands of their daughters (occasionally, the daughters themselves) supplied new generations of agents. Other recruits moved up from clerking positions in established firms or moved over from related businesses—such as outfitting and provisioning—or came from the ranks of ship's officers. The frequent appearance of some familiar names on whaling crew lists suggests that some scions of agent families received training at sea.

VIII. PRODUCTIVITY

New Bedford whaling rose to prominence in the years 1820-1845, remained a prosperous industry during the 1840s and 1850s, collapsed during the Civil War, recovered somewhat, but incompletely, after the War, and then, although once again relatively prosperous, declined dramatically in importance. By the mid-1890s the industry barely existed. The real prices of whale products followed a somewhat similar pattern, although the market for whale-bone held up much better than the markets for sperm and whale oil. The total factor productivity of the industry traced a pattern that was virtually a mirror image of the profit and price developments. Productivity fell steeply between 1820 and 1835, declined much more gradually from the latter date to 1845, gradually flattened out thereafter, and then began to rise gently from the 1870s through the early 1890s (see Figure 1).

There are at least two possible explanations of the pattern traced by the productivity index. On the one hand, it has been argued that the stocks of whales were hunted down as the industry grew. Fewer whales would have meant increased hunting costs and, therefore, declining productivity. Such a scenario would explain the movements in the index down to the 1860s, but not thereafter. Moreover, it is not consistent with what is known about the pattern of hunting and the demography of whale populations.

The sperms were the whales hunted most vigorously in the period of declining productivity. Before the great nineteenth century expansion of whaling, there were probably about two million of these creatures and, in the years before 1855—at which point productivity had reached its nadir—whalers had killed many fewer than 200,000. There should have been no shortage of sperm whales, especially in view of their reproductive powers, although some grounds could have been depleted. Such depletion would have led to increased search costs. Among the baleens, the gray whales were clearly hunted down; and such overhunting may have been the fate of the Arctic bowhead as well. Neither grays nor bowheads, however, were subject to substantial hunting before the 1850s. In fact productivity was actually rising over the years in which the greatest slaughter of these animals took place (Davis, Gallman, and Hutchins, 1988).

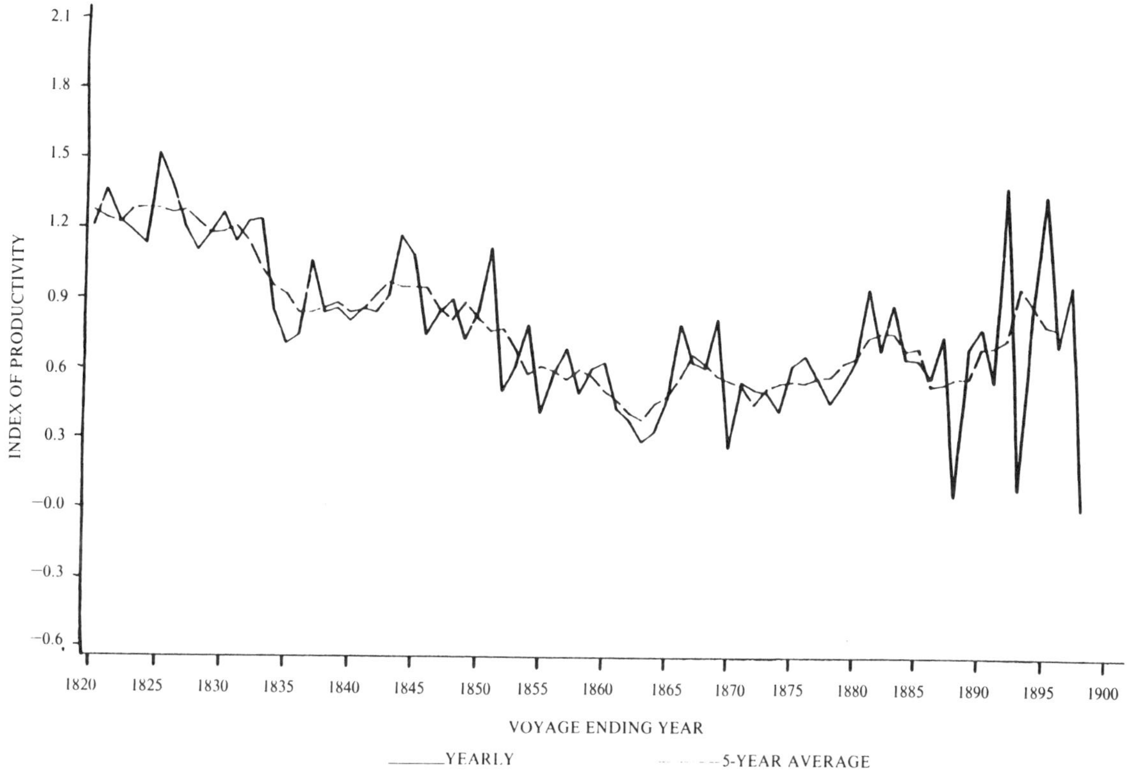

Figure 1. Index of Total Factor Productivity
New Bedford Whaling Voyages Ending 1818-1898

Moreover, indexes of lagged hunting intensity (by hunting ground and whale type) have been included in a multiple regression analysis of the productivity of the New Bedford voyages. An examination of the results of this analysis yields no hint that pressure on the whale stocks affected productivity unfavorably (Davis, Gallman, and Hutchins, 1989).[6]

On the other hand, an alternative explanation rests on the several effects of changes in the size of the industry. First, the competition among whalers for the available whales must have grown more intense as the industry expanded. That increase in intensity (more vessels searching for a fixed stock of whales) might well have had an adverse effect on productivity. In a similar vein, later, as the industry contracted, hunting pressures should have eased, and productivity might have risen again. The regression analysis when run for the full period 1820 to 1896 turns up no firm evidence that would support this hypothesis. However, a test for a more limited period spanning the 1840s and 1850s—the decades when crowding was almost certain to have been the greatest—indicates that differences in the vessel-tonnage/whale ratio were negatively and significantly associated with differences in productivity. Higher productivity was related to lower ratios, and vice versa. The suggestion is, then, that competition for whales did affect productivity, at least in the two mid-century decades.

Second, as the industry expanded between 1820 and the mid-1840s, it must have pressed on the supply of experienced whaling labor; the postbellum, contraction should have relieved the problem. It may be, then, that the swing in productivity reflects the changing quality of labor. The data show that the quality of seamen declined in the 1840s and 1850s. The agents, however, seem to have coped with this development by paying more attention to the number and quality of the officers and skilled maritime personnel. There appears to have been no change in productivity over this period that can be associated expressly with shifts in the experience levels of the seamen; but, of course, the greater part of the decline and rise of productivity took place before the 1840s and after the 1850s. It is suggestive that the regression analysis for the years 1820-1896 shows that productivity was negatively and strongly associated with changes in wage rates ashore. The analysis provides some support for the argument appearing in the literature that attractive opportunities ashore bid the best whalemen out of the industry, with unfavorable consequences for whaling productivity.

Third, the expansion of the industry must also have pressed against the supply of vessels. The 155,000 ton increase in whaling tonnage that occurred between 1820 and 1845 accounted for a third of the total increase in the tonnage of all documented American merchant vessels (U.S. Department of Commerce, 1960).[7] Until late in the period, when agents attempted to exploit the new technology, whalers were not built for the trade but drawn from the merchant marine. Because merchant vessels and whalers perform very different tasks,

Table 12. Productivity Among Leading New Bedford Whaling Agents

Name of Firm	*Number of Voyages*	*Operating Years*[a]	*Productivity Index*[b]	*Standard Deviation*	*Ratio to Avg. New Bedford Productivity*[c]
D.R. Greene	31	1833-1857	1.146	.466	1.355
I. Howland	132	1819-1861	.983	.716	1.170
C.N. Morgan	46	1826-1855	.966	.613	1.036
E.E. Jones	64	1839-1870	.965	.639	1.405
E.H. Howland	35	1843-1870	.964	.637	1.570
J. Bourne	88	1832-1883	.860	.671	1.130
J.B. Wood & Co.	49	1842-1872	.836	.654	1.269
Swift & Perry	41	1851-1880	.827	.711	1.493
H. Taber	43	1834-1880	.804	.632	1.248
G. Howland	90	1817-1871	.777	.647	.956
J.A. Parker	62	1818-1853	.738	.667	.836
Gideon Allen	48	1833-1881	.727	.875	1.283
Swift and Allen	54	1844-1883	.700	.730	1.280
T. & A. R. Nye	58	1833-1858	.695	.644	.979
C.R. Tucker	92	1835-1876	.679	.612	.980
J. & W.R. Wing	71	1853-1914	.507	.604	.929
T. Knowles	69	1849-1882	.464	.653	.803

Notes: [a] The operating years cover the full period of operation of these firms, not necessarily the years included in the calculation of the productivity indexes.

[b] The productivity indexes are multilateral total factor productivity indexes, expressed in natural logarithms (see Davis, Gallman, and Hutchins, 1989). The number of voyages included in the productivity calculations are:

D.R. Green	31	H. Tabler	38
I. Howland	102	G. Howland	85
C.N. Morgan	45	J.A. Parker	62
E.H. Jones	54	Gideon & Allen	45
E.H. Howland	80	Swift & Allen	48
J. Bourne	45	T. & A.R. Nye	75
Swift & Henry	35	J. & W.R. Wing	54
C.R. Tucker	75	T. Knowles	67

[c] The denominators of the ratios were computed separately for each agent. The voyages managed by each agent were identified by the year of return to New Bedford. The average (arithmetic mean) productivity of the entire New Bedford fleet was then computed across these years. If an agent had, for instance, four vessels returning in a given year, the productivity of that year was given a weight of four in computation of the denominator, and so forth.

Source: Davis, Gallman, and Hutchins (Tape No. 1).

vessels built for the more general trade were not well-designed for whaling. As the whale fleet expanded, this problem must have become more acute. That is, the merchant vessels best suited for whaling would be chosen first; and, as the whaling fleet continued to expand, less well-adapted vessels would have to be taken. This hypothesis has not yet been tested directly. It is worth remarking, however, that, after the 1850s boatyards began to design and build vessels expressly for whaling. At the same time, there was a spurt of innovation in whalecraft. These two developments help to account for the improvement in productivity observed after the Civil War (Davis, Gallman, and Hutchins, 1989).

Productivity varied from one voyage to the next and from one agent to another. The variation from voyage to voyage was extremely wide, as the standard deviations of the productivity indexes in Table 12 indicate. Bear in mind: these data exclude the most disastrous voyages—those that resulted in no output whatever and those that ended with the loss of the vessel. The agents, however, seem to have responded very effectively to the changing opportunities presented by the discovery of new hunting grounds and new types of whales, as well as to the shifts in the structure of demand (Davis, Gallman, and Hutchins, 1989). That they did not all respond equally successfully is demonstrated by the data displayed in Table 12. To dilute the effects of pure luck, those agents who managed fewer than thirty voyages were excluded from the calculations. Thus these data refer only to specialist agents.

Two sets of statistics appear: the raw average productivity estimate for each agent and the ratio of this estimate to the average productivity of the fleet as a whole in the years in which the agent had vessels returning to port. The productivity figures are multilateral total factor productivity estimates, expressed in natural logarithms. The range of productivity across these firms is very wide, suggesting that they were unequally skillful, a result that should not be surprising. The table also shows, however, that these agents, *as a group*, were relatively successful. Eleven of the seventeen agents exhibited productivity levels above the average for the entire fleet, in ten cases, substantially (13 percent or more) above average. Only six fell below the average, and of this group, four were within 8 percent of that figure. The specialists, then, seem to have been more successful than the nonspecialists, again a reasonable and unsurprising result.

IX. CONCLUSIONS

Jonathan Hughes cites Nushagak as an example of "institutional gridlock"—a failure of labor and management to change in the face of a new and hostile economic environment. Rising personal income reduced the demand for canned salmon, and both lower forty-eight and native fishermen found themselves increasingly on the losing side of a competitive struggle with the Japanese. It is clearly Jonathan's belief that, in the case of the salmon fishery, the industry's demise could have been prevented, or at least postponed, if only labor and management had taken a "longer view", but that the very nature of the bargaining game in which they were involved made it impossible for either party to move toward the more enlightened position.

The case of the American whaling industry was very different. Like the Alaskan packers, whalers faced a dramatic and long-term decline in demand—a decline that was accelerated by Colonel Drake's discoveries and innovations at Titusville, intensified by the continued fall in the relative price of petroleum by-products, and ended, after the steel industry proved that it could produce a product that was both strong and flexible, when there was no significant traditional market for whale products at all. Unlike the salmon packers, both agents and workers displayed great flexibility and imagination; perhaps, in Jonathan's terms, whaling agents and workers postponed the industry's demise from 1870 until the turn of the century.

No amount of flexibility or imagination, however, would have made it possible for American whalers to compete with the Norwegians in the hunt for the fast-swimming rorquals. First, the same relatively high incomes that spelled the end for the domestic consumption of canned salmon in the 1950s meant that even at the turn of the century there was little American demand for whale meat or for margarine and cooking oils made of rendered whale blubber. Second, to catch the fast-swimming rorquals it was necessary to use steam powered vessels made of steel; in the shipbuilding industry an American advantage in the construction of wooden sailing vessels was at least matched by a disadvantage in the construction of steam driven metal ones. Third, the human capital that had been built up over a century of whaling was wiped out—entirely new hunting techniques were required. The absence of domestic demand meant that even tariffs could not protect the American whalers, while the destruction of the industry's capital stock (both physical and human), coupled with a comparative national disadvantage in maritime pursuits in general, and whaling in particular, meant that, like the salmon packers, the whalemen were unable to compete in the foreign market. The whaling experience suggests that even enlightened labor and management practices may not have been sufficient to save the Bristol Bay fishery. In the words of one railroad executive, "Would good management have saved the canal boat?"

APPENDIX

The New Bedford whaling data set cited in this paper is a data set in transition: it is still being augmented and adjusted. The best way to describe it is by recounting its history and the ways in which it is expected to grow and change in the immediate future.

The New Bedford project began when Davis and Gallman, prospecting in the Baker Library Manuscript Room at Harvard for data on other industries, happened upon a manuscript prepared by one Joseph Dias relating to New Bedford whaling. Dias, perhaps a former whaling captain, had brought together a substantial quantity of evidence in a systematic way (Whipple,

1951).[8] Unlike other chroniclers, he had organized his data in a form that fit the needs of Davis and Gallman beautifully; the two were taken with the idea of a short study of productivity change in whaling. The short study of productivity change has now become a long study of many aspects of whaling.

Dias assembled data on New Bedford whaling voyages in the years from 1790 through 1907. He listed each vessel of which he had knowledge and each of its voyages, so far as he knew, giving the following information.

1. As to the vessel, he gave the name, tonnage, and rig (ship, bark, brig, schooner, sloop), as well as (often) where and when it was built and where, when, and how it ended its career. If the vessel was renamed, if it was refitted so as to alter the tonnage, or if it was rerigged (ships were not infrequently rerigged as barks), Dias indicated the changes, whenever he was aware of them. In 1865, the official method of measuring tonnage (capacity) changed, but Dias did not alter his records on that account. Because most of his vessels entered the fleet before 1865, most of his tonnages are old-style tonnages.

2. As to each voyage, Dias listed:

- the name of the agent (the organizer of the voyage);
- the name of the captain;
- the date the vessel left New Bedford;
- the date it returned;
- the amount of sperm oil brought back;
- the same for whale oil and baleen (whale bone);
- the hunting grounds hunted;
- notes on various events (substantial illness or injury to the crew or officers, the death of crewmen or officers—more often the latter than the former—attacks by South Sea Islanders or Eskimos, mutinies, and so on).

With appropriate labor and price data and some information on technology added to the Dias data, it would be possible to measure and analyze productivity differences from voyage to voyage, vessel to vessel, and time to time. Davis and Gallman decided to push ahead along these lines, recruited Hutchins, who located the necessary labor data, and arranged with the Carolina Population Center to have the data put into a SAS data set.

Dias seems to have worked with the materials assembled by Alexander Starbuck in his famous "History of the American Whale Fishery." Dias adjusted Starbuck's evidence here and there, augmented it in various ways, and extended it to the years after 1876 (the last date in the Starbuck series). Particularly important, Dias reorganized it. Starbuck lays out the data by years and ports, so that the history of any given vessel is scattered through his pages.

Dias, however, brings together all the information on any given vessel in one place, though restricting his list to voyages from New Bedford.

Where the Dias records appeared to be dubious, they were checked against Starbuck and sometimes changed. It became evident early in the project that the Dias data after 1876 were decidedly incomplete. The gaps were filled in with evidence drawn from the work of Reginald Hegarty (Dias; Starbuck, 1878; Hegarty, 1959). The voyages data set employed in this paper and in all the prior papers in this series, then, is the Dias set, corrected by reference to Starbuck and Hegarty and augmented after 1876 by data from Hegarty.

This data set is currently under revision. There are six important sources of evidence on New Bedford whaling voyages: Dias (1906), Starbuck (1878), Hegarty (1959), the W.P.A's *Whaling Masters*, the voyage abstracts assembled by Dennis Wood (1938) at one time a whaling agent in New Bedford, and notes concerning the years 1824-1830, incorporated in the Wood microfilms.[9] These six sources are now being compared and, where they differ, choices made among them. This work has been organized by Dr. Karin Gleiter, Research Associate at the Carolina Population Center, and is now virtually complete. It does not appear that the revised data set will produce major revisions in the analysis completed to date, but there will be some changes. In particular, both the copy of Dias that was employed throughout and Starbuck's work often appear to understate the amount of whalebone (baleen) returned. The correction of these errors will alter the measures of productivity somewhat and will almost certainly *raise* the level of productivity after the late 1840s (when the western Arctic grounds were opened and whalebone became an important product). The diagram shown in this paper will be affected. As it stands, it almost certainly exaggerates the decline in productivity in the 1850s and 1860s, and understates the gain in productivity thereafter.

The voyages data set has been altered in a second respect. Dias (1906), Starbuck (1878), and Hegarty (1959) appear to have assigned each vessel to the port from which it sailed, regardless of where the entrepreneurs of the voyage, the agents, were located. Thus when vessels began to shift from the East Coast to San Francisco after the Civil War, they dropped out of the New Bedford fleet, as defined by these three. The shift to San Francisco is clearly a phenomenon worth study. For this reason, the group decided to retain in the data set vessels that berthed in San Francisco but were managed by New Bedford agents. This has meant a substantial increase in the number of records in the voyages data set, records that have not yet been analyzed.

There are three sources of labor data: official records held by the National Archives, the New Bedford Public Library's collection of the Whalemen's Shipping Papers, and information assembled by the New Bedford Port Society. The last source is quite incomplete and was not employed in this project. The first two were used to obtain the number of crewmen on each voyage, for purposes of productivity analysis. Because desertion was common—especially in the 1840s and 1850s, when the industry was at its peak—it sometimes occurred even before the vessel left port, and because replacements and additions to the crew were taken on in the Atlantic islands and elsewhere, the exact size of the crew is often problematical. The two sources that were used overlap, and where they give contradictory results, the larger value was selected. No effort was made to identify the better total.

The data taken from the Free Public Library records (*Whalemen's Shipping Papers*), which cover the years 1840-1858 and 1866, were subsequently augmented and reworked. For these years evidence on stations and lays is available and this evidence was collected (see the text). The opportunity was also taken to look more closely at the estimates of the number of crewmen in these years and to make revisions where they seemed called for.

The original voyages data set did not standardize the names of captains and agents, and did not identify the owners of whaling vessels. The former task is currently being carried out. Also, the names of the owners of a large sample of vessels are being assembled from the vessel registrations (*Ship Registers*, 1940). The data on owners typically indicate place of residence, so that it will be possible to study the sources of finance of the industry. The city directories of New Bedford have been acquired for all years available (twenty volumes dated to years between 1836 and 1887). From the directories it will be possible to identify the occupations of the owners and get at another aspect of the sources of finance of the industry.

As many of the agents as could be identified have been run to ground in the field reports of the R.G. Dun credit agency (Dun, 1841-1890). Careful notes have been assembled, so that the changing credit standing of the agents can be studied. The data on agents, captains, and owners will also be used in formal productivity analysis and the data from the Dun reports will be useful in this regard, as well.

The notes on the individual voyages assembled by Dias, Starbuck, Hegarty, and Wood (the notes on morbidity, mortality, and so forth) are intriguing and will eventually be assembled in a form that will make them easier to handle.

Various other series have been brought together to promote the analysis of the whaling data: prices of whale products, estimates of the numbers of whales taken in the major hunting grounds, estimates of the size of the original populations of whales of various types in various major hunting grounds, the types of whaling gear carried on a sample of vessels, and so on (Davis, Gallman, and Hutchins, 1989).

ACKNOWLEDGMENTS

The authors gratefully acknowledge the assistance of Dr. Karin J. Gleiter, Research Associate of the Carolina Population Center, University of North Carolina, who supervised the data collection, the calculations, and the art work. The paper could not have been prepared in time for this volume without her assistance. The authors also acknowledge the Baker Library of the Harvard University Graduate School of Business and its staff for their cooperation in making the Dias and the Howland manuscripts and the R. G. Dun records available. The research has been supported in part by NSF grants BNSD-8011494, SES-8121026, by the National Bureau of Economic Research Projects Productivity and Industrial Changes in the World Economy and the Development of the American Economy, by the Center for Advanced Study in the Behavioral Sciences, and by the Division of the Humanities and Social Sciences, California Institute of Technology.

NOTES

1. Between 1820 and 1890 the United States whaling fleet accounted for about 80 percent of the world catch. Over the same period, the New Bedford fleet represented more than one-half of the American effort regardless of whether the measure of effort is vessel tonnage or catch. This paper draws heavily on Dias (1906), Starbuck (1878), and Hegarty (1959).
2. The next 8 paragraphs depend on Davis, Gallman, and Hutchins (1987).
3. The prohibition was contained in 26 Geo. III c. 60 an extension of the navigation laws dealing with the registration of vessels from the American colonies. The law was repealed in 1849.
4. On many of these pages, there are two page numbers, one in black or blue the other is red. Where there was a choice, red was chosen.
5. All of the numbers in this paragraph, Tables 11 and 12, and the rest of the paper are drawn from the Davis-Gallman-Hutchins tape. The tape does not contain a record on every New Bedford voyage—it may miss as many as 10 percent.
6. The data set includes more than 2,300 voyages, about half of the New Bedford voyages during this period.
7. The total documented tonnage in foreign trade (584,000) and whaling (36,000) in 1820 was 620,000 in 1845 the 1,095,000 total consisted of 904,000 in foreign trade and 191,000 in whaling.
8. See note 1. Joseph Diaz, Jr., then 28 years old, was captain of the whaler *Pocahantas* in 1850 when that vessel was rammed and seriously damaged by a sperm whale in the South Atlantic. Diaz managed to get his vessel to Rio de Janeiro—where it was repaired—but only after a hair-raising two-week voyage. Was this Joseph Diaz the Joseph Dias of the Baker Library manuscript? We have been unable to settle that question. Dias remains a mystery man.
9. The *Dennis Wood Abstracts* are the property of the New Bedford Free Public Library, while the notes for 1824-1830 appended thereto are apparently from a manuscript in the *Wood* microfilms by the New England Microfilming Project. These notes are particularly valuable because they appear to contain careful and complete statements of the amount of baleen brought back at the end of each voyage, information often missing from the other sources for this period. Additionally, for reasons that are unclear, Starbuck's manuscript omits many voyage dates for 1825 and in other instances provides dubious information. The notes at the end of the *Wood* microfilms thus fill some important gaps and permit some important checks to be made.

REFERENCES

Bathe, B.W. (1967). "The Clipper's Day." P 207 in *The Great Age of Sail*, edited by J. Jobe. London: Patrick Stephenson Ltd.

Chapelle, H.I. (1935). *The History of American Sailing Ships*. New York: W.W. Norton.

Chapelle, H.I. (1967). *The Search of Speed Under Sail: 1700-1855*. New York: W.W. Norton.

Chatterton, E.K. (1909). *Sailing Ships: The Story of Their Development from the Earliest Times to the Present Day.* London: Sidgwick & Jackson Ltd.

Conway, W.M. (Ed.). (1967). *The Early Dutch and English Voyages to Spitzbergen in the Seventeenth Century.* Liechtenstein: Kraus Reprint Ltd.

Davis, L., Gallman, R. and Hutchins, T. (1987a). "The Structure of the Capital Stock in Economic Growth and Decline: The New Bedford Whaling Fleet in the Nineteenth Century." Pp 396-398 in *Quantity and Quiddity: Essays in U.S. Economic History,* edited by P. Kilby. Middletown, CT: Wesleyan University Press.

Davis, L., Gallman, R., and Hutchins, T. (1987b). "Technology, Productivity, and Profits: British-American Whaling Competition in the North Atlantic, 1816-1842." *Oxford Economic Papers,* 39 (December): 738-759.

Davis, L., Gallman, R. and Hutchins, T. (1988). "The Decline of U.S. Whaling: Was the Stock of Whales Running Out?" *Business History Review,* 62(4).

Davis, L., Gallman, R. and Hutchins, T. (1989). "Productivity in American Whaling: The New Bedford Fleet in the Nineteenth Century." *Markets in History: Economic Studies of the Past,* edited by D. Galenson. Cambridge and New York: Cambridge University Press.

Dias, J. (1906). "The New Bedford Whaling Fleet, 1790-1906." Manuscript, Baker Library, Harvard University Graduate School of Business Administration, Boston, MA.

Dun, R.G. & Company Collection. (1841-90). Massachusetts 17:2, 36, 38, 40, 47, 59, 97, 116, 176, 179, 184, 206, 208, 228, 230, 249, 303, 308, 335, 353. 18: 388, 405, 412. Baker Library, Harvard University Graduate School of Business Administration, Boston, MA.

Fairburn, W. (1945-55). *Merchant Sail.* Lowell, MA: Fairburn Marine Educational Foundation Center.

Hegarty, R. (1959). *Returns of the American Whaling Vessels Sailing from American Ports: A Continuation of Alexander Starbuck's "History of the American Whale Fishery, 1876-1928."* New Bedford, MA: Old Dartmouth Historical Society and Whaling Museum.

Hohman, E. (1926). "Wages, Risk and Profits in the Whaling Industry." *Quarterly Journal of Economics,* 40 (August): 664-671.

Hohman, E. (1968). *The Amercian Whaleman: A Study of Life and Labor in the Whaling Industry.* New York: Longmans Green.

Howland, M. (1858-60). *Letter Book.* Manuscript 252, 1858-79, H864, Baker Library, Harvard University Graduate School of Business Administration, Boston, MA.

Hughes, J.R.T. (1982). "The Great Strike at Nushagak Station, 1951: Institutional Gridlock." *The Journal of Economic History,* 42:1-20.

Hutchins, J. (1941). *The American Maritime Industries and Public Policy, 1794-1914: An Economic History.* Cambridge, MA: Harvard University Press.

Jackson, G. (1978). *The British Whaling Trade.* London: Adam and Charles Black.

Jenkins, J.T. (1921). *A History of the Whale Fisheries from the Basque Fisheries of the Tenth Century to the Hunting of the Finner Whale at the Present Date.* London: H.F. & G. Wetherby.

Lebergott, S. (1964). *Manpower in Economic Growth: The American Record Since 1800.* New York: McGraw-Hill.

Lytle, T. (1984). *Harpoons and Other Whalecraft.* New Bedford, MA: The Old Dartmouth Historical Society and Whaling Museum.

Merchant Transcript. (1863).

Merchant Transcript. (1876).

Merchant Transcript. (1877).

Merchant Transcript. (1878).

McDevitt, J.L. (1986). *The House of Rotch.* New York/London: Garland.

McKay, R.C. (1928). *Some Famous Sailing Ships and Their Builder Donald McKay.* New York/London: G.P. Putnam.

Morrison, S. (1921). *The Maritime History of Massachusetts.* Boston, MA: Houghton-Mifflin.

The National Archives Projects. (1940). *Ship Registers of New Bedford, Massachusetts, 1796-1939.* 3 Vol. Boston, MA.

Nordhoff, C. (1895). *Whaling and Fishing*. New York: Dodd-Mead.

Scammon, C. (1874). *The Marine Mammals of the Northwestern Coast of North America.* New York: Putnam.

Starbuck, A. (1878). "History of the Whale Fishery." *Report of the United States Commission on Fish and Fisheries.* Part 4.

U.S. Deaprtment of Commerce. (1960). *Historical Statistics of the United States: Colonial Times to 1957.* Series Q 165 and Q 167, Washington, D.C.: U.S. Goverment Printing Office.

Whipple, A.B.C. (1951). *Tall Ships and Great Captains.* New York.

Dennis Wood Abstracts. (1938). 5 Volumes, 1831-1873. Pacific Manuscript Bureau, Research School of Pacific Studies, Australian National University.

THE HISTORY OF NATURAL RESOURCE EXPLOITATION IN THE WESTERN WORLD

Eric L. Jones

Writing about his prodigal youth as a fisheries accountant in Alaska Jonathan Hughes observed that by 1951, "the one basic ingredient, the fish, had begun to falter. The 'run' was declining, had been for years. The entire Alaskan industry was beginning to stagger. . . . The millions of salmon would be an exhaustible resource if fishing were left uncontrolled. . . . The old idea that salmon were naturally a renewable resource and a community property had been a blue-print for abuse and ultimate exhaustion. But in 1951 that was not yet clear" (Hughes, 1982, p. 5).

In the teeming runs of Alaska the prospect of an end to unrestricted fishing may not have been evident by that year. In other fisheries the problem had long been recognized. The great concern for the environment since 1970 tends to obscure the fact of earlier professional concern, amply displayed in archival sources (Dillon and Jones, 1986a, p. 31). The De Lamar Lectures at Johns Hopkins, given by E.S. Russell in March 1939, were published in *The Overfishing Problem* (Russell, 1942). Russell's references included "What

Research in Economic History, Suppl. 6, pages 235-252.

ISBN: 1-55938-150-7.

is Overfishing?" which had appeared in the *Journal of the Marine Biological Association* (1900-03). Indeed, as far back as 1863, a three-man Royal Commission, one of whose number was T.H. Huxley, had been appointed to look into the over-fishing question (Barback, 1967, pp. 80-81).

This is not, of course, to say that solutions were found; indeed, the recurrent concern suggests they were not. The exploitation of the environment, it has come to be believed, was (and is) out of control. Furthermore, there is a widespread belief that this is a western phenomenon, with its roots in a reading of the Christian view that nature exists so that humanity may exploit it.

Alternative views of the impact of the West as something less than environmentally disastrous in all respects are out of fashion, as is a further point of view which will be offered here: that the West's historical impact on the natural world was not obviously more destructive than that of other civilizations, once we allow for degree of technological opportunity, structure of relative prices, and size of population.[1] In other words, it will be urged that the environmental consequences of Western expansion confront us with common problems associated with economic growth, not peculiar moral problems.

American Indians, after all, seized the opportunities of new technologies. The adoption of the horse meant that the hunter could kill more buffalo than one woman could clean, with the result that polygyny spread and also the acceptance of "squaw men," so that more hides could be cleaned. Overhunting of the buffalo predated direct killing by white men with guns. Similarly the Navaho accepted sheep and consequently overgrazed the Southwest (Guthrie, 1971, p. 722).

Even with their own simple techniques of hunting and gathering, small populations of Indians were capable of damaging the resource base: there is archaeological evidence that they drove the sea-otter out of the Aleutian islands and that some Californian Indian communities died out because they over-harvested the shell fish on which they lived. When Indian population pressure was removed, and before the start of commercial fishing by whites, fish stocks in California rose. There were disputes among Indian groups about the removal of each other's salmon weirs. While Californian Indians eventually settled on enduring, ritualized fishery practices and controlled their own population size, the undoubtedly long saga of trial and error as they approached those norms is not historically recorded. Relatively-speaking, European people have made a rod for their own backs by leaving written records.

The clear-sighted discussion of these matters by Arthur McEvoy concludes that there was no special advantage to being a native Indian (McEvoy, 1986, pp. 19-21, 31-39). Similar problems of management had to be solved. Contrast this with the assertions about the native American as brother to all creatures, the operator and beneficiary of emotionally-loved communal property, which were made by no less influential a person than a Secretary of the Interior in a book with an introduction by John F. Kennedy himself (Udall, 1963).

Western behavior was technologically facilitated and economically motivated, too, rather than driven by a special case of the Christian ethic, as the conventional wisdom insists. To the extent that the behavior was environmentally damaging (the literature is ungenerous about offsetting effects), it was scarcely distinctive in principle, let alone unique. It was not the result of an attitude to the stewardship of the earth that has been shown to be uniquely irresponsible. The precepts of Christianity are not the only ones that are man-centered. Without further ado, the point can be made by noting that a fundamental principle of Islam, too, is that God made the resources of the earth for the use of man.

Alfred Crosby's *Ecological Imperialism* (1986) reviews the replacement of much of the isolated flora and fauna of the Neo-Europes of the Americas and Australasia by the farm crops, livestock, pests, and weeds which the Europeans disseminated. Clearly the biological consequences of settlement were extensive. But Crosby sees the *economic* outcome as a second miracle of the loaves and fishes. He points out just how many other people in the world have come to depend on food from the Neo-Europes. Despite the xenophobia of conservationists of European stock in some of the Neo-Europes and their denunciation of introduced species (except when eating them), biological *variety* there has been increased by the addition of cultivated and feral species to the native wild ones. What has really happened, a small number of extinctions apart[2] is that the *proportions* of the different populations of fauna and flora outside Europe have been altered by white settlement far more drastically than aboriginal land-use and hunting practices had been changing them.

From the economist's point of view, since high real incomes now permit so many naturalists to travel freely and internationally spot ("twitch" in the jargon) what rare species they choose, it is far from clear that there has been a net consumption loss. Not only have biologically interesting new species been acclimatised in many countries, but land use changes have widened the range of habitats. In particular they have extended the ecotone, that is the edge between different vegetational types which is so favored by birds and animals. The total number of individuals in some native bird groups has risen greatly: several North American warblers which were rare in the dense forest when Audubon was collecting specimens are now common in the woodland fringes which have been created in the northeastern United States. This is not the place to try to produce a balance sheet, although it would be possible to estimate populations of plants, birds, and animals during early white settlement from historical data combined with modern information about habitat preferences and to compare the results with modern census data.[3] We can, however, rest assured that we do not live in a natural world whose variety or interest has been significantly diminished by Western expansion. The replacement of grassland and woodland by arable and other intensive uses offering more food and breeding sites for wildlife, together with the introduction of animals, means that total biomass has also risen.

Economics has of course been concerned with assessing the costs and benefits for human individuals and society, but this is now under attack in influential quarters as "speciesism." The evolutionist Richard Dawkins (1986, p. 263) refers to "the breathtaking speciesism of our Christian-inspired attitudes." Referring to the Thylacine (Tasmanian Tiger), he says "maybe they were pests to humans, but humans were bigger pests to them; now there are no thylacines left and a *considerable surplus* of humans. . . . Stop Press: for what may, if verified, be wonderful news, see article by A.M. Douglas, *New Scientist* 24 April 1986" (Dawkins, 1986, p. 105, emphasis added). (To one's surprise, this paper turns out not to describe a recent decline in the number of human beings in Tasmania but a possible rediscovery of the Thylacine in West Australia [Douglas, 1986].)

How, then, is economics to re-orient? Are we to attempt to construct a social welfare function for the whole of living matter? The exercise of constructing a balance sheet for nonhuman organisms is foredoomed because there is no agreed method of scoring gains and losses and because of the impossibly complicated synergetic effects of interfering with ecosystems or moving organisms outside their natural habitat or range. Such effects can be bizarre and are certainly unpredictable. Consider the recent cases of the disease of babesiosis on Nantucket, brought about when *Babesia* parasites made the enormous leap to man as a host via a complex history of land-use changes and the stepping-stones of ticks, sheep, and deer: "The list of ecological-epidemiological ingredients that made this situation possible reads like the contents of a witch's cauldron," says the parasitologist, Robert Desowitz (1981, p. 147).

The charge of speciesism would challenge us to balance the books for all of what Conrad Totman has termed the "non-collaborating" organisms, involving trade-offs about which ecologists have given singularly little guidance (Tisdell, 1988, p. 378). The conventions surrounding the international migratory bird treaty—RAMSCAR—violate the principle of species equality by implying greater investments to save the rarer species, perhaps a form of speciesism in itself. Even if we had the necessary information, a Pareto-optimal ecological change is scarcely in nature. Old ideas of an equilibrium called the "balance of nature" or of populations tending toward a "climax" are now seen as somewhat misleading in a world of flux. The notion that organisms are grouped as "good" species with defined characters around which variation occurs has given way to ideas of the norms of existence as being convergence and divergence, superspecies and subspecies. We can never resolve a cost-benefit calculus for all the lower animals in their relations with one another and with our own species. It is artificial in a world of flux to think in terms of rescue operations mounted to save an individual species whose members may prey on or exclude the members of other species, unless one can state a solution to such inter-specific utility problems. With respect to the higher animals, such as birds, there have been historically compensating changes which from the individual observer's point of view may more than match any losses attributable to Western humanity's influence (Dillon and Jones, 1986b).

It is beyond dispute that there were major destructions as a part of the West's expansion. Tossed on their cockleshells amid the daunting seas of nature, the hungry mariners who set out for new worlds used what bounty they could get. The flightless Great Auk was herded onto ships over spread sails and the Green Turtle was scooped into shipboard tanks used as floating larders: the one succumbed and became extinct, while the other has earned a sheet in the Red Data Book of endangered world wildlife. The vastness of the resources of the New World was apparent to its settlers. William Parker has many times pointed out the "providential" discovery of new frontiers, new stocks, new technology to exploit them, and eventually the finding of a number of inanimate substitutes to replace animate ones: examples are the westward movement, the finding of a new stock of whales each time a species was fished out, the improvement in firearms, and the replacement of animal oils by mineral oil. Over the centuries this encouraged a generally unrestrained use of resources. The remarkable fecundity of some species which became pests was also obvious to a population growing its own food. Nature scarcely seemed endangered. Fastidiousness would have seemed silly; from the point of view of surviving and eating, it would have been silly.

There can be no surprise, and no special shame, in the initial behavior of Europeans overseas. They merely extended the traditional harvesting of wildlife, for instance by carrying the taking of colonial nesting species and egg farming from coastal northern Europe (it was also a feature of other coasts in and around the Old World) as far away as the Farallon Islands off San Francisco and the islands of the Bass Strait, Australia (Hepburn, 1853-1867; Jones, 1985). Fishing and whaling are also traditional operations in this sense: they are hunting rather than farming. What changed was the scope and scale of operations, not the principle.

On the face of things, it was reasonable for Stanley Jevons (1865) to conclude in *The Coal Question* that rising costs associated with mining at greater depths, together with the absence of substitutes for steam coal, meant that Britain's "present happy progressive condition is a thing of limited duration" (quoted in Rosenberg, 1976, p. 231). It ought to have become less respectable to hear about all-round resource depletion since Hal Williamson's (1945) paper, "Prophecies of Scarcity or Exhaustion of Natural Resources in the United States," showed, starting with apprehensions about the depletion of forests during Colonial times, how wide of the mark such fears have typically been.

The forests were depleted but in what economic sense can it be shown to have mattered? Ecologically, tree variety actually increased.

Probably most economists who have looked at the problem have taken the opposite side from the ecologists. Economists are more attuned to looking at second-order effects. Julian Simon's (1981) graphs of the nineteenth- and twentieth-century prices of coal, oil, electricity, and copper relative to wages and the consumer price index show that there has been no resource scarcity. Political upheavals apart, there are no signs of a general resource scarcity in the foreseeable future, indeed quite the opposite, since input-economizing technical change is now so rapid that raw material inputs to the world's growing output of manufactures are falling fast, with price effects that bode no good to primary-product exporting countries (Drucker, 1986). One would expect that an upcoming scarcity would be signalled by rising commodity prices; it is not signalled yet.

The dominant view that Western expansion was needlessly destructive implies that early man and non-Western cultures lived in a harmony with competing species to which we had better return if we are not to denude and foul our own habitat. Yet an environmental impact of the type the West has produced in historic times had demonstrable pre-modern precursors, just as it has modern non-Western parallels. Primitive methods produce primitive results. Robert Heizer argues strongly for a large-scale Palaeolithic impact and against the notion that the habitable world remained pristine until either the spread of Neolithic settlement in the Old World or the expansion of European civilization from the end of the fifteenth century A.D. (Heizer, 1955, p. 3; Crosby, 1986). A major human impact may have been the extinctions attributed to the hunting activities of very early humans in the Pleistocene Overkill (Smith, 1975). Aborigines are now credited with widespread habitat manipulation (for ideological reasons this is not called damage) on which white settlers capitalized. And in the modern world it was native tribes in East Kalimantan (Indonesia), engaging in slash-and-burn agriculture, who in 1982 started a fire which burned over eight million hectares of forest.

We can explain the Western use of nature more succinctly, consistently, and verifiably by reference to opportunity and the structure of relative prices than by a generalized appeal to a dishonest value system (Dwyer, 1973, p. 251).[4] As it happens, there is a wide dispersion of assertions as to which shift in theological-cum-philosophical thought brought about the supposed signal change in Western attitudes to nature. As with many literary analyses, there are severe sampling problems; it is not clear that the full range of opinion at any one date is being reported. Furthermore, a one-to-one equation is implied between certain literary pronouncements and environmentally-destructive social behavior. This is not tested, let alone demonstrated. Tracing currents of opinion is not an acceptable way of learning what actually happened in the history of the environment. The mapping of fragments of opinion from the "high culture" onto mass behavior is quite illegitimate.

Lynn White Jr.'s "The Historical Roots of our Ecological Crisis" (1967) is by far the source most often cited for the view that Christianity saddled Western humanity with the belief that nature had been created for its use.[5] Yet, neither this essay nor White's other writings on themes of technological dominance shows that Western or medieval Christian thought as such was responsible for the abuse of nature. They offer no "control" (by means of research on non-Western history) to establish that Western manipulations were more savage than those elsewhere.[6]

White's views were most famously transplanted to economic history by Landes (1969, p. 24) in that tour de force, *The Unbound Prometheus*. The term "Faustian Mastery" thus became enshrined in the standard interpretation of the Rise of the West. Landes was well aware of the ancient roots in Western culture of his Faustian ethic although he describes it in terms of an attention to means and ends which no one, surely, could regard as monopolized by the West. He also points out that the Christian Church did see the danger in a man-centered vision but he quotes Lynn White on the central shift being the replacement of animistic sprite by saint, leaving "man liberated to exploit nature as he wished" by any technology he could devise.

White claims that by destroying animism, Christianity made it possible to exploit nature in a mood of indifference to the feelings of natural objects. He goes on to assert that Christian attitudes toward man's relation to nature are almost universally held not only by Christians and neo-Christians but also by those who regard themselves as post-Christians. Since previously it had been entirely possible to fell a tree, mine a mountain, or dam a brook provided one placated the spirit in charge, the practical relevance of the rise of Christianity is unclear. As J. D. Hughes says, good intentions were not enough without scientific knowledge and technical command; people whose religion taught them that the world is a sacred place have still managed to leave their habitat a waste of erosion and deforestation (J.D. Hughes, 1975, p. 150). The romantic western notion that other peoples necessarily treat their environment tenderly is wrong. The Indian ornithologist, Salim Ali (1985) wrote of the tribal state of Bastar as it was in 1949:

> there are the traditional pre-sowing *parads* or community *battues* every year in which all the able-bodied men from tribal hamlets miles around join to beat out vast tracts of jungle and slaughter everything that moves, big or small, whether mammal, bird or reptile. These hunts are *to propitiate the spirits of the forest* and ensure a good harvest and the destructive practice continues unchecked in spite of prohibitory forest laws (p. 154, emphasis added).

In explicit contradiction of tracing the "ecologic crisis" to medieval Christianity, J.D. Hughes favors a much earlier change in Mesopotamia and

Ancient Israel, and most notably with the victory of the Greek philosophers over animism, a victory communicated to the formerly nature-worshipping and environmentally-inhibited Romans. Hume (1956) also indicts Greek philosophy. The fact that early assaults on the tree cover first of Greece and later of Rome were more limited than later assaults is as consistent with the low population densities of early classical times and the higher densities of later periods as it is with any change in attitudes. Note too that, while animism may have protected particular sacred groves of trees and the spirits inhabiting them, it did not protect the surrounding forest cover (J.D. Hughes, 1975, pp. 50-51). The Greek environment and much of the Roman empire were extensively denuded, with implications for soil depth, availability of timber, and water quality, all personally observed and reported by Plato (427-347 BC) (J.D. Hughes, 1975, pp. 70-71). There is no reason to believe that the Western world (not to mention Mesopotamia or Israel) waited for a particular interpretation of the Christian gospels before starting a widespread exploitation of environmental resources.

White offers no empirical verification that exploitative views are specific to Christianity; of the necessary corollary that religious thought of itself drives human actions; or that, ceteris paribus, exploitative actions have differed or differ among societies. Research comparing the exploitation of the natural world in the Classical Mediterranean with the later Western world, or comparing Europe with Asia, proves hard to find. Studies of environmental change during recent centuries, so common for Europe or the United States, are surprisingly sparse in non-Western histories.[7]

"The Golden Age hitherto put into the past is now placed overseas," Walter Prescott Webb once quoted (Webb, 1952, p. 10). In the environmental sphere, as it happens, one finds it placed in the past (in Antiquity), overseas (in the Far East), and in the realm of the Noble Savage, in none of them with more support than sustains other myths of a Golden Age. The evidence cited that non-Western behavior toward the environment, or behavior in the pagan West, is or was any more tender than behavior in the Christian West is thin where it appears at all. Among the authorities customarily cited, Clarence J. Glacken (1967) tells nothing about the oriental "control" that a study of the West needs if it is to establish the distinctiveness claimed for its subject. Glacken copiously demonstrates the forest clearance of medieval Europe without saying a word about the Chinese equivalent — the clearing of 670 *million* acres of forest which elsewhere has been called one of mankind's greatest acts of ecological stupidity (Borgstrom, 1972, p. 106).

The West's breast-beating about motive counterpoints the Orient as the Eden of environmental allusion, a benign mirage in which peasants husband the land in a timeless stewardship. In this sense J.D. Hughes refers to the Chinese and Japanese as "different" from Westerners. He is apparently deriving his attitude from the economic historian of the classical world, Michael Rostovtzeff, who ascribed soil exhaustion in the Roman empire, "to man, not to nature. Men failed to support nature, though they knew as well as we do, or as the Japanese and Chinese how it should be done" (J.D. Hughes, 1975, p. 134). This is at variance with the reality of Chinese agricultural history, with its colossal deforestations, erosion, silting of rivers, and infestation with waterborne parasites, and with the great phases of unrestrained deforestation in Japan (Borgstrom, 1972, p. 106; Totman, 1986).

The philosopher, John Passmore (1980) points out that the Orient was not uniform in its attitudes or behavior. In Japan, as in pre-Christian Europe, nature was accounted sacred—"can one imagine a moon-watching ceremony in the West?" (p. 26)—but he notes that this did not prevent Japan from developing an industrial civilization, "second to none in its offensiveness to ear, eye and nose" (p. 27). The putative East-West difference, nevertheless, resurfaces in that he thinks China was different from both the West and Japan. Passmore implies that pre-Communist China lacked the manipulative attitudes which he claims have been common in the West for centuries. But he belies this by noting the great agricultural engineering works carried out under early Chinese emperors, and unconsciously reduces the Chinese ideal of "conforming to nature" to absurdity by saying that it affects "even such everyday actions as the way to remove a leg from a chicken" (p. 26).

We only come to an informed appraisal of Chinese historical attitudes and behavior with the work of Yi-fu Tuan (1968, 1970). In view of the animistic bias in Chinese thought and Western humanists' uncritical lauding of Taoist and Buddhist traditions, Tuan is fortunately aware of the reality of deforestation and erosion. He cites Mencius from the fourth century B.C. on the burning of woodland to deprive dangerous animals of their harbors and gives details which show that the ancient tradition of forest care was brutally violated in practice: "the enlightened memorials to the emperor on the need for the conservation of resources are in themselves clear evidence of the follies that have already been committed" (1968, p. 184). Tuan adds that the widespread burning of woodland to encourage small shoots to grow, thus saving the labor of splitting wood, "tends to upset any residual illusion we may have of the Chinese farmer's benign attitude towards nature" (1968, p. 187).

Luckily there is also a candid assessment of non-Western ecological behavior in Bernard Powell's (1987) study of the American Indians as conservationists.[8] Pointing out that the stereotypical view of the Indians as mystics who did not pollute or litter the North American continent is shown to be wrong by the litter at ancient campsites, Powell continues: "I believe that all stereotypic views are wrong, including specifically the view that Indians have instincts or culture norms as natural ecologists, or insights into Nature denied to Whites or other races" (p. 17). He assembles evidence of extinctions at the hands of the earliest Indian arrivals: buffalo jumps where the meat of one in every four bison killed was wasted; ruinous slash-and-burn agriculture by the Maya; the destruction of soils in the Desert Southwest by salination brought about by the irrigation farming of the Hohokam; the willing destruction of the beaver, the Red Man's "brother"; and the conspicuous waste of the Potlatch system in the Pacific Northwest.

The reporting of other non-Western examples is less satisfactory. Two wrongs may not make a right, but the distinction commonly made between Western and non-Western attitudes, let alone behavior, scarcely holds. Dwyer and others tend to refer to anthropological reports of the attitudes expressed by tiny tribes such as the Tsembaga of New Guinea, who are said to keep their numbers below carrying capacity by means of rituals (Dwyer, 1973). Vernon Smith (1975, p. 742) describes how cultural restrictions on harvesting have also been used extensively by primitive peoples "at one time or another." According to Smith, the relevant sensitivity developed "sometime" after the Pleistocene extinction of the megafauna, implying that there is structure in the history of conservation that we know nothing about. The evidence Smith draws from anthropology is episodic and not very historical; the reported behavior was selective in terms of the restrictions on practices and target species adopted by any one tribal people and it is not possible to tell how long or vigorously the restrictions were in force.

Heizer (1955) offers an extensive list of tribal conservational practices (pp. 3-7). Some of the examples are open to the criticisms already levelled—it is not clear how long and how efficiently the measures were practiced. Others do, however, have a plausible ring to them. Despite the immensely localized and almost ad hoc nature of some prohibitions and the species which given peoples chose to avoid, many small-scale societies did spare female animals during the breeding season and did try to limit their catch in order to ensure stock to breed the next season. This behavior was typically ritualized, say in the form of totemic animals. The reason, according to Heizer, was "economic expediency" and not some special non-Western altruism. Similar functional behavior can be found among settled rural populations in the Western world, with different cultural accretions. It amounts to rational cropping behavior over the long term, clouded a little by the lags in adjustment to changing circumstances that one might expect ritual to impose.

What Smith refers to as the most sophisticated property-rights systems limited the physical or time access of given individuals to the resource rather than the size of the take when it came their turn. For instance, Karok fishing rights entitled the owner to use a given spot every third night and day, and to sell the right. Similar arrangements existed in the much-maligned West: in eighteenth-century Cornwall, a system of "stems" was adopted, rationing small areas of offshore waters among the seine fishermen a day at a time (Rowe, 1953, p. 272). Once more the distinction between West and non-West fails. But in both cases what was being restricted was merely individual access. There is no sign that limits were imposed on the catch and individuals had an incentive to fish harder if their time on station were restricted. These were not necessarily stock-conserving procedures, although as we shall see there were certainly measures designed to achieve that in the West as early as the middle ages.

To read increasing restrictions of rights as techniques of conservation must often stretch the evidence. Thus, Lewthwaite (1966) reports that native Tahitian reservations of large fish and turtle for the elite "have been plausibly interpreted as measures of deliberate conservation" (p. 33). Other explanations might seem simpler. Bartlett (1956), likewise, reports the existence of sacred groves in many pre-Christian tropical regions, which "except for the advance of 'civilization,' would have sufficed as sources of seed for the restoration of some species of the original flora" (pp. 709-711). While the latent function of a sacred grove may have been to make reafforestation possible, Bartlett offers no evidence that this conservational purpose was intended. The groves may sometimes have been destroyed at the behest of Christian missionaries but they were also destroyed by intrusions of other non-Western populations.

Anthropological reports from the Third World typically refer to short pre- or initial-contact periods when no great opportunity had presented itself via changes in the technology of hunting or farming. These things had, of course, changed over the longer past, making one wonder about the basis or durability of value systems in the first place. F. Spencer Chapman (*The Jungle is Neutral*) once told me that Greenland Eskimos who got hold of rifles in the 1930s began to behave toward their game "like foxes in a hen roost." It is surely best to assume that attitudes and values are malleable in the hands of economic forces in the way that Alfred Marshall was fond of describing. The very emergence of private property rights over natural resources suggests as much.[9]

Given new technologies, the behavior of native peoples toward nature (and other tribes) was scarcely restrained: foxes in a hen roost. Gunpowder and shot and steel axes were among the very earliest of trade goods in demand during contact periods. The balance of power was upset, for the Sandwich Islanders, for the Maori, for other warlike peoples. If it was upset intra-specifically, an inter-specific upset was even more likely.

Revealed preference is a better guide to the environmental behavior of non-European peoples than snapshots of their expressed attitudes at the time of contact. Early anthropological observers seemed to assume that the condition of the societies they saw had been virtually unchanged throughout time, as their informants insisted. However, the aim of oral history is "to maintain the illusion of stability in the face of change" which, looked at more closely, reveals an unexpected degree of movement (Sack, 1974, p. 201). Non-Western history was not a timeless equilibrium disturbed only by brutal white intrusions; there is every sign of earlier disturbance in the remotest corners, as, for example, with the Maoris replacing the Moa Hunters. In places there are also indications of population stress *before* the European arrival: in Mexico, on the grass plains of the United States, in parts of northern Australia, and so forth (Malin, 1956,

p. 355; Tresize, 1973, p. 27). The environment did not escape unscathed by such pressures.

The wielders of the fire-stick, the exponents of slash-and-burn agriculture, the herders of goats, and the promoters of soil salination in the early southwestern United States or the Middle East cannot be exempted from the charge of greatly modifying the habitat that was not only their own but that of all the species around them. It was for example probably forest clearance by Arab and Malay settlers in Madagascar one thousand years ago that destroyed much of the swamp woodland habitat of *Aepyornis*, the Roc, and contributed or led to its extinction. European colonists in North America and Australasia typically entered lands already made easier of access, easier to plow, and better for hunting by the recurrent native burning of the vegetation. There had already been a great deal of deforestation before they came. The extent to which the grasslands of the world were created by early, non-Western peoples may remain contentious but that they created much of them does not. Where climatic conditions strongly favor tree growth, repeated firing may not produce grasslands but may selectively favor one species of tree as the new dominant in the botanical assemblage. Heizer (1955, p. 10) gives examples from Burma, India and North America before white settlement (see also Bartlett, 1956).

The environmentalist outpourings at the end of the 1960s and during the 1970s described only the history of *Western* humanity's impact. This distorted the record of environmental change, which earlier literature had recognized. Therefore, Greenway (1967), in his classic book on the extinction of birds, wrote: "because this work is limited to discussion of the discrete populations that have disappeared during the past 280 years, the geographical perspective is distorted" (p. 29). Similarly, with respect to Australia, Frith (1973) pointed out that, "although it is generally believed that the Aborigines had little effect on the native fauna this cannot be so" (p. 9). The evidence that the aborigines in Australia had eliminated entire species does tend to be circumstantial, but even an extremely cautious writer like Calaby seems to accept their responsibility for exterminating the southern elephant seal on the Tasmanian mainland (Calaby, 1971, p. 90). The Tasmanian aborigines engaged in ring hunts, like the tribals of Bastar, the South African bushmen, and others, and this meant slaughter beyond the needs of current consumption. On the Darling river in New South Wales periodic feasts on fish supplied from extensive fish traps involved as many as 5,000 aborigines.

Hunting economies are associated with waste. Consider the elaborate procedures used by the Australian aborigines to frighten duck into their nets along the Murray river. The catch could not be adjusted nicely to provide only the meat needed; neither could it be kept down when individual hunters and fishermen dispersed from a camp or settlement in the morning. If several were lucky at the same time they would return with an overall excess. No satisfactory means of storage existed: gluttony or waste were unavoidable.

The animist hunter might believe himself to be on a spiritual continuum with his prey yet, while he might spare totemic species or the females of important prey species during the breeding season, he was not really going to stop butchering all of his little brothers. His behavior might be that of the Naskapi of Labrador who had to acknowledge the debt by making a ritual apology and preserving the dead plant or animal from profane treatment (Heizer, 1955, p. 6). The hunter's technology neither included the humane killer nor permitted a "take" in proportion to his real food needs. The moral order of hunting peoples may have been high—certainly the Australian aborigines known to Sir Hubert Wilkins were "chaste, law-abiding and kind" (Thomas, 1963, p. 8). Nevertheless, their technological order was such as to mean a lack of control over bag size and that was not admirable at all.

All told, non-Western peoples produced an amazing array of weapons, traps, nets, poisons, and deceptions for catching and despatching wildlife (Mason, 1895; Jones, 1985). One of the chapters in Mason's book on the tools of primitive peoples is titled "War on the Animal Kingdom." The evidence is abundant: for instance, mist-nets, which are indiscriminate in what they trap, originated in Japan. The current decline of a large wader (American: shorebird), the Eastern Curlew, in Australia is attributed to mist-netting in south-east Asia. Almost every village in the vicinity of wader sites in Thailand was found in 1984 to have at least one household that obtained some or all of its income by selling a variety of trapped waders (Starks, 1985, p. 30). In both Australia and Japan, these are protected species. It is not some abstract, homogeneous, "Eastern," or "Western" culture that ultimately determines behavior, it seems to be largely the level of economic, technical, and political development.

Historically, it is indeed far from clear that in West or East values determined behavior rather than changes in economic circumstances, such as the finding of new resources, the invention of new technology, or the growth of population, which all cause changes in relative prices inviting changes in the scale or direction of resource use. For example, the increased hunting of birds in northern Kenya, reported by Isack (1987, p. 96) and partly attributed by him to the arrival of Christianity and Islam, would seem sufficiently explained by population growth and the increase of sedentarism. Third World population growth also seems a sufficient explanation for the intense egging which is reducing the numbers of seabirds in Jamaica (Haynes-Sutton, 1987, p. 78) and megapodes in Sulawesi (Dekker and Wattel, 1987, p. 83). "The victory of Christianity over paganism *may* well have been, as Lynn White says, the greatest psychic revolution in Western culture; but for lack of real, as distinct from theologically postulated, power the full impact of that revolution on ecology was postponed" (Tuan, 1968, p. 181, emphasis added). However, this still implies the importance of Christian values, latent until economic capability changed, subsequently powerful in concert with this. But there is nothing to demonstrate that any other economy so endowed with fresh technological power would have produced any less impact, perhaps reshaping its official values through cognitive dissonance in the meantime. On the contrary, there is much to suggest that many others would, did, and do so respond.

It is open to us to enlarge our niche by technical change, as we are doing by economizing on metals, and to devise and enforce property rights so as to permit the often-encouragingly prompt recoveries or sustain the yields of renewable biological resources. The Western tradition undeniably includes doing these things. In 1196, Richard I, "for the welfare of his soul and of that of his father King Henry, and of the souls of his ancestors, and likewise for the benefit of his citizens of London and of the whole kingdom," ordered the removal of all weirs and fixed nets from the Thames and prohibited the erection of any others (Anon, 1921, p. 23). This was to protect fish fry, and it was followed by similar ordinances of other Christian princes, enforced by imprisonments and the burning of nets. The growth of markets, technology, and population in the West massively increased the historical scale of resource use; but Western historical behavior toward the natural world has not been shown to have been *in principle* more damaging than was behavior elsewhere. As Wright (1970) concluded, "the evidence indicates that there is a common denominator for exploitation that is independent of geography and religion" (p. 852).

Contrary to the endlessly repeated charge that, "it was an ecological catastrophe when white man arrived with his domestic animals and pests, and caused clearing, burning and overgrazing," many changes, certainly clearing and even urbanisation, have increased the complexity, variety, interest and on occasion the beauty of the human habitat.[10] As Cicero observed, humanized landscapes can also be fair: "we endeavor to create as it were a second world within the world of nature" (J.D. Hughes, 1975, p. 96). Anyone who knows the attractions of reservoirs and parks in great cities, or writings about their natural history (very different from the literature of pop ecology), will be aware of the consumption gains (Fitter, 1945; Kieran, 1971). For every land bird that is less abundant in the United States than when the Pilgrims landed, five or six species are more abundant (Jones, 1974, p. 515). Although one could never guess as much from the literature, neither Western economic growth nor environmental change has yet really caused a net loss.

NOTES

1. What will happen in the future may be different. In the late 1980s we are virtually being told in the serious press that (Western) technology will soon finish us all off. We were told this before, in graphic detail, circa 1970. The best pricking of the bubble of scientific futurology at that time was by Beckerman (1972). The dire predictions went into abeyance, as falsified predictions of the End of the World do, only to re-emerge. Even the serious press is prone to report negative

environmental changes much more than either successful clean-up operations or the biologically positive effects of many land-use changes. Yet nothing has so far appeared in this round, say about the "Greenhouse Effect," to persuade one that more is needed than the reprinting of Beckerman's paper plus international institution-building to tighten pollution controls. Hadwiger (1982) should be consulted for the career motives of ecological activists, despite his overall showing of the neglect of negative externalities by the U.S. agricultural research establishment.

Certainly there will be direct and indirect costs from atmospheric pollution but so far there seems no new reason to suppose that self-correction will not take place among rational actors aware of negative externalities and able to publicize them. Nevertheless, on the offchance that the natural scientists have not confused cycle and trend this time, or that international humanity really will prove too slow to save itself, the present essay is mainly confined to historical periods. It does not discuss the possible course of global pollution, other than to observe that this is still futurology, the heat effects may be exaggerated by temperature readings from urban "heat islands," the pollution sources are far from solely Western, and it is the Western countries which are doing most to restrict emissions. The Montreal Treaty of September 1987 limiting the use of chlorofluorocarbons exempted many of the developing nations from the limits for ten years (Anon, 1988). Nevertheless a 31-nation treaty signed only two years after the discovery of the "hole" in the ozone layer over the South Pole seems commendably prompt.

2. Greenway (1967, p. 7), gives 44 full species of birds as having become extinct, mostly since about 1680, some of which would have succumbed in the natural course of extinctions. This is a sixth of the discrepancy among authorities as to how many "good" species there actually are in the world. Cf. Austin (1962, p. 11).

3. For the dangers of this approach, see Jones (1981).

4. Dwyer (1973) thinks that only Western society regards the earth as limitless, which is simply wrong. His remedy would be teaching people to want less, which sums up the guilty anti-achievement strain in the ecological literature.

5. Note the "crisis" in the title in 1967 and the extreme statements about Christianity's guilt on pages 1206-1207. This paper has been reprinted several times; David Landes (1969) cites similar views from another of White's articles. A kindred indictment of Christianity appears in McHarg (1971). Refutations, such as that by Guthrie (1971) have by comparison been ignored.

White's main concern was certainly the unrestrained development of technological command but he is widely cited as identifying the Christian origin of the West's alleged (and allegedly unique) claim to exploit the natural environment. This has become a stereotype that students internalize and the media vaunt for purposes no doubt far from its author's imagining. It is a symbolic passage in histories of the West, and of the world, with a mythopoeic force like that often accorded to the Industrial Revolution.

6. On the other hand, Wright (1970, p. 852) did suggest using as a control the history of China, a major civilization outside the Judeo-Christian tradition and with written records.

7. The most promising title—Lester J. Bilsky's (1980) "Ecological Crisis and Response in Ancient China"—proves to be about famine.

8. For South America, it may be noted that between 1700 and 1750 a population of 300,000 Indians and Iberian settlers together virtually wiped out the entire herd of 48 million wild cattle on the pampas (Beddall, 1973, p. 905).

9. But the relationships are complicated. Private property in land could act as a deterrent to the kind of unbridled resource depletion seen on the frontier. It is not even correct to assume that the Western establishment of private property rights over tribal communalism would necessarily have meant replacing conservation by extermination: compare the report by Salim Ali, previously quoted.

10. This quotation refers to Australia (Webb, 1968, p. 223). Webb continues, "the productivity of our land still suffers." Compared with the obvious counterfactual—the persistence of pre-1788 aboriginal occupation—this customary assertion by the ecologists cannot be true.

REFERENCES

Ali, S. (1985). *The Fall of a Sparrow*. Delhi: Oxford University Press.

Anon. (1921). "The History of Trawling." *The Fish Trades Gazette* (March 19), pp. 21-69.

Anon. (1988). "Saving the Ozone." *Dialogue*, 82: 64-70.

Austin, O.L., Jr. (1962). *Birds of the World*. London: Hamlyn.

Barback, R.H. (1967). "The Political Economy of Fisheries: From Nationalism to Internationalism." *Yorkshire Bulletin of Economic and Social Research*, 19: 71-84.

Bartlett, H.H. (1956). "Fire, Primitive Agriculture, and Grazing in the Tropics." Pp. 692-720 in *Man's Role in Changing the Face of the Earth*, Vol. 2, edited by W.L. Thomas, Jr. Chicago: University of Chicago Press.

Beckerman, W. (1972). "Economists, Scientists, and Environmental Catastrophe." *Oxford Economic Papers*, 24: 327-344.

Beddall, B.G. (1973). "Letter to the Editor." *Science*, 180: 905.

Bilsky, L.J. (1980), "Ecological Crisis and Response in Ancient China." Pp. 60-70 in *Historical Ecology: Essays on Environment and Social Change*, edited by L.J. Bilsky. Port Washington: Kennikatt Press.

Borgstrom, G. (1972). *The Hungry Planet*, 2nd rev. ed. New York: Collier.

Calaby, J.H. (1971). "Man, Fauna, and Climate in Aboriginal Australia." Pp. 80-93 in *Aboriginal Man and Environment in Australia*, edited by D.J. Mulvaney and J. Golson. Canberra: ANU Press.

Crosby, A.W. (1986). *Ecological Imperialism: The Biological Expansion of Europe, 900-1900*. Cambridge: Cambridge University Press.

Dawkins, R. (1986). *The Blind Watchmaker*. Harlow, Essex: Longman Scientific and Technical.

Dekker, R.W.R.J. and Wattel, J. (1987). "Egg and Image: New and Traditional Uses for the Maleo (*Macrocephalon maleo*)." Pp. 83-87 in *The Value of Birds*, edited by A.W. Diamond and F.L. Filion. ICBP Technical Publication No. 6. Cambridge: International Council for Bird Preservation.

Desowitz, R.S. (1981). *New Guinea Tapeworms and Jewish Grandmothers: Tales of Parasites and People*. New York: Avon Books.

Dillon, P.J. and Jones, E.L. (1986a) "The Royal Australasian Ornithologists' Union Archive as a Source for the History of Science and the History of the Environment." *La Trobe Library Journal*, 10: 29-32.

Dillon, P.J. and Jones, E.L. (1986b). "Trevor Falla's Vermin Accounts for Devon," *The Devon Historian*, 13: 15-19.

Douglas, A.M. (1986). "Tigers in Western Australia?" *New Scientist* (April 24), pp. 44-47.

Drucker, P. (1986). "The Changed World Economy." *Economic Impact* 56: 6-13.

Dwyer, P.D. (1973). "Beyond Biology: Alienation and Environment." Pp. 241-252 in *Exploring the Web: Readings in Biology*, edited by J.A. Peterson. Toorak, Victoria: Sorrett Publishing.

Fitter, R.S.R. (1945). *London's Natural History*. London: Collins.

Frith, H.J. (1973). *Wildlife Conservation*. Sydney: Angus & Robertson.

Glacken, C.J. (1967). *Traces on the Rhodean Shore: Nature and Culture in Western Thought from Ancient Times to the End of the Eighteenth Century*. Berkeley: University of California Press.

Greenway, J.C., Jr. (1967). *Extinct and Vanishing Birds of the World*. New York: Dover Books.

Guthrie, D.A. (1971). "Primitive Man's Relationship to Nature." *Bioscience*, 21: 721-723.

Hadwiger, D.F. (1982). *The Politics of Agricultural Research*. Lincoln: University of Nebraska Press.

Haynes-Sutton, A.M. (1987). "The Value of Seabirds as a Socio-economic Resource in Jamaica." Pp. 77-81 in *The Value of Birds*, edited by A.W. Diamond and F.L. Filion. ICBP Technical Publication No. 6. Cambridge: International Council for Bird Preservation.

Heizer, R.F. (1955). "Primitive Man as an Ecologic Factor." *Kroeber Anthropological Society Papers*, 13: 1-31.

Hepburn, J. (1853-67). *Journals*, 4 vols. Cambridge Zoological Museum, England.

Hughes, J.D. (1975). *Ecology in Ancient Civilizations*. Albuquerque: University of New Mexico Press.

Hughes, J.R.T. (1982). "The Great Strike at Nushagak Station, 1951: Institutional Gridlock." *Journal of Economic History* 42: 1-20.

Hume, C.W. (1956). *The Status of Animals in the Christian Religion*. London: Universities Federation for Animal Welfare.

Isack, H.A. (1987). "The Cultural and Economic Importance of Birds among the Boran people of Northern Kenya." Pp. 89-98 in *The Value of Birds*, edited by A.W. Diamond and F.L. Filion. ICBP Technical Publication No. 6. Cambridge: International Council for Bird Preservation.

Jones, E.L. (1974). "Creative Disruptions in American Agriculture, 1620-1820." *Agricultural History*, 48: 510-528.

Jones, E.L. (1981). "Reconstructing Former Bird Communities." *Forth Naturalist and Historian*, 6: 101-106.

Jones, E.L. (1985). "Utilization by Man." Pp. 617-618 in *A Dictionary of Birds*, edited by B. Campbell and E. Lack. Vermillion, SD: Buteo Books.

Kieran, J. (1971). *A Natural History of New York City*. Garden City, NY: The Natural History Press.

Landes, D.S. (1969). *The Unbound Prometheus*. Cambridge: Cambridge University Press.

Lewthwaite, G.R. (1966). "Man and the Sea in Early Tahiti: A Maritime Economy through European Eyes." *Pacific Viewpoint*, 7: 28-53.

Malin, J.C. (1956). "The Grassland of North America: Its Occupance and the Challenge of Continuous Reappraisals." Pp. 350-366 in *Man's Role in Changing the Face of the Earth*, edited by W.L. Thomas, Jr. Chicago: University of Chicago Press.

Mason, Otis T. (1895). *The Origins of Invention: A Study of Industry Among Primitive Peoples*. London: Walter Scott.

McEvoy, A. (1986). *The Fisherman's Problem: Ecology and Law in the California Fisheries, 1850-1980*. Cambridge: Cambridge University Press.

McHarg, I.L. ([1969] 1971). *Design with Nature*. Garden City, NY: The Natural History Press.

Passmore, J. (1980). *Man's Responsibility for Nature: Ecological Problems and Western Traditions*, 2nd ed. London: Duckworth.

Powell, B.W. (1987). "Were These America's First Ecologists?" *Journal of the West*, 26: 17-25.

Rosenberg, N. (1976). *Perspectives on Technology*. Cambridge: Cambridge University Press.

Rowe, J. (1953). *Cornwall in the Age of the Industrial Revolution*. Liverpool: Liverpool University Press.

Russell, E.S. (1942). *The Overfishing Problem*. Cambridge: Cambridge University Press.

Sack, P.L. (1974). "The Triumph of Colonialism." Pp. 200-208 in *Problem of Choice: Land in Papua New Guinea's Future*, edited by P.L. Sack. Canberra: ANU Press

Simon, L. (1981). *The Ultimate Resource*. Oxford: Martin Robertson.

Smith, V.L. (1975). "The Primitive Hunter Culture, Pleistocene Extinction, and the Rise of Agriculture." *Journal of Political Economy*, 83: 727-755.

Starks, J. (1985). "Human Predation of Waders in Thailand." *The Stilt*, 6: 30.

Thomas, L. (1963). *Sir Hubert Wilkins*. London: Readers Book Club.

Tisdell, C. (1988). "Sustainable Development: Differing Perspectives of Ecologists and Economists, and Relevance to LDCs." *World Development*, 16: 373-384.

Totman, C. (1986). "Tokugawa Peasants: Win, Lose or Draw?" *Monumenta Nipponica*, 41: 459-476.

Tresize, P. (1973). *Last Days of a Wilderness*. Sydney: Collins.

Tuan, Y. (1968). "Discrepancies between Environmental Attitude and Behaviour: Examples from Europe and China." *Canadian Geographer*, 12: 176-191.

Tuan, Y. (1970). "Our Treatment of the Environment in Ideal and Actuality." *American Scientist*, 58: 244-249.

Udall, S.L. (1963). *The Quiet Crisis*. New York: Avon Books.

Webb, L. (1968). "The Rape of the Forests." Pp. 178-231 in *The Great Extermination*, edited by A.J. Marshall. London: Panther Books.

Webb, W.P. (1952). *The Great Frontier*. Boston, MA: Houghton Mifflin.

White, L. Jr. (1967). "The Historical Roots of Our Ecologic Crisis," *Science*, 155: 1203-1207.

Williamson, H. (1945). "Prophecies of Scarcity or Exhaustion of Natural Resources in the United States." *American Economic Review*, 35: 97-109.

Wright, R.T. (1970). "Responsibility for the Ecological Crisis." *Bioscience*, 20: 851-853.

WAS THERE A BRITISH INDUSTRIAL EVOLUTION?

Joel Mokyr

I. INTRODUCTION

In his 1970 book, *Industrialization and Economic History*, Jonathan Hughes pointed out that two schools had always existed concerning the Industrial Revolution in Britain, a gradualist school and a breakthrough or "saltationist" school. The former regarded the Industrial Revolution as the culmination of a long, drawn-out process of development, during which things kept on changing slowly, though perhaps a little bit *less* slowly than before. The latter regarded the years 1760 to 1830 as a period in which the British economy changed "suddenly and violently" using terms such as "feverish bursts" and "completely revolutionized."[1] Hughes had no doubt where he himself stood on the matter. "The present author leans towards the gradualist viewpoint . . . the longer the relevant colligation sequence used on both sides of 1760-1830, the less sudden does the Industrial Revolution seem. Seventy years ago was 1900. We cannot think of the events of the last seventy years as sudden. Seventy British years passed no more rapidly" (Hughes, 1970, pp. 44-45).

Research in Economic History, Suppl. 6, pages 253-286.

ISBN: 1-55938-150-7.

The debate outlined by Hughes is one of those interminable disputes on which professional economic historians thrive. Was the Industrial Revolution sudden or slow? In 1970, when Hughes was writing, the tide had turned in favor of the "breakthrough" school.[2] The influence of W.W. Rostow and Deane and Cole was still strong. Economic historians concerned with the Industrial Revolution associated it with economic growth, and while some disagreement remained regarding the precise timing of growth, there was no question that the view associating growth with economic change dominated the scene. Rostow's "take-off" and Gerschenkron's "Great Spurt" were the metaphors which dominated the thinking of scholars concerned with nineteenth-century european economic history. In the two decades that followed, the pendulum has swung back to the gradualists and the gradualist views of Clapham and Beales, which prevailed in the 1920s, seem to have been re-established. In a series of papers published in the past decades, Crafts, Harley, McCloskey, and Williamson showed that economic growth during the Industrial Revolution was slow, that structural changes such as urbanization and occupational change were far from complete, and that in general the British economy in 1850 was not all that different from the British economy in 1750.[3]

The new gradualist consensus has led some scholars to call for a reexamination of the entire concept of an Industrial Revolution. Some of the shriller voices calling for the excision of the concept from our textbooks and scholarly papers can be safely ignored, but the movement seems to have influenced some serious scholars as well. Eric L. Jones's recent *Growth Recurring* (1988) emphasizes again the basic theme of continuity. The argument is that some economic growth was already taking place before the Industrial Revolution, and that during it growth was proceeding at a moderate pace. Similarly, in his survey on the long-term growth of the British economy, C.H. Lee (1986, pp. 21-22) notes that "the general dilution of the revolutionary trauma has moved current perceptions of growth towards the tradition of evolutionary growth . . . the idea of discontinuity has been largely rejected or fallen into disuse."

The dispute is neither one of semantics, nor is it one of those disputes that cannot be resolved because the necessary data are not available. It is largely based on the misunderstanding created by the infusion of Kuznetsian macroeconomics into economic history by Rostow, Deane, and Cole, and others in the 1950s and 1960s which identified the Industrial Revolution with economic growth (Wrigley, 1987). The issue is primarily one of aggregation. If one insists on looking at the British economy as one unit characterized by its GNP, savings ratio, overall capital stock, and so on, economic change during the Industrial Revolution looks a pretty gradual and smooth affair. I have made this case in other places, and there is no need to repeat it here in detail.[4] Recall the statistical law that when many different components are growing at rates of widely different intensity, the movement of the total will regress to some moderate average. Disaggregating the economy into large sectors such as manufacturing, agriculture, and services does not materially alter this result. In the eighteenth- and nineteenth-century industrial growth in Europe was slow simply because "industry" consisted of many smaller subsectors, some of which were growing rapidly, others were stagnating and still others were declining. An average of these growth rates is not likely to show much discontinuous change.

Yet the intuition that something changed radically and dramatically during the seventy years Hughes spoke of is not that easily shaken off. What is wrong is its focus on *aggregate* concepts such as growth and industrialization. The main advocates of discontinuity have always been *technological* historians. David Landes (1969, p. 3) had no hesitation in stating that "the Industrial Revolution marked a major turning point in man's history." D.S.L. Cardwell referred to 1769 as the year in which Watt's separate condenser and Arkwright's water frame were patented as "annus mirabilis" although he reserved the term "revolutionary epoch" for the years 1790-1825 (Cardwell, 1972, p. 139). Arnold Pacey (1975, p.216) prefers to designate the last third of the eighteenth century as "revolutionary," on account of the acceleration in the speed of "industrial change." Bertrand Gille (1978, p. 677) points out that "a new technical system was created around the year 1780 . . . the principal industries achieved their central innovations in the years around 1780." Richard Hills (1979, p. 126) points to the jenny, the water frame, and the mule as providing "the vital impetus to launch the Industrial Revolution."[5] A possible exception would be A.P. Usher, though he explicitly used the term "Industrial Revolution."[6] A reading of more recent work in the technological history of Western Europe in this period reveals clearly that neo-gradualism has not made many inroads here.[7] To be sure, there were important inventions long before 1760, and some of the breakthroughs associated with the Industrial Revolution were not fully worked out and made economically profitable until later. Yet as Gille and others have argued tirelessly, the difference in degree is so overwhelming that pointing to Wyatt and Paul, Papin, Newcomen, and other assorted precursors simply will not change the way we think about this period any more than we are willing to give up thinking about the Reformation as starting with Martin Luther notwithstanding John Wycliffe and Jan Hus.[8]

My argument is that the Industrial Revolution as a process of economic growth was slow, gradual, and continuous. However, the Industrial Revolution as a clustering of technological changes in a wide array of industries in a short period was as violent and sudden as Gibbins and Toynbee thought. Nevertheless, we may well ask whether any of those changes were important enough to deserve the place they occupy in our textbooks and lectures. The answer is that no *single* invention may be important enough to qualify as the mainspring of the Industrial Revolution, so that if we carried out a Fogelian social savings calculation on the pivotal inventions in energy production, materials, textiles, and transportation, they would all amount to relative small percentages of GNP. However, the *totality* of inventions, improvements, modifications, and adaptations occurring in the period typically associated with the Industrial Revolution cannot be judged by a simple social savings calculation. For example, Von Tunzelmann (1978), in his assessment of the role of steam in the Industrial Revolution quite rightly compares steam power to the next best alternative, water power. However, as he points out, his computations are affected by the major improvements in water power during the Industrial Revolution, many of which were comparable in importance and effect to the great inventions of Watt and Trevithick. The revisionist view, which reduces the importance of steam power by pointing to water power as the next best alternative does not imply a corresponding diminution of the overall impact of technological change, it just spreads it around. Those who argue (e.g., Jones 1988) that the limited role of steam, the continuing importance of wood, and the survival of manual techniques in textile and sailing ships demonstrate that the Industrial Revolution was nothing but déjà vu only more so, commit something akin to a fallacy of composition.

The Industrial Revolution as a technological event will retain its connotation of discontinuity. In a fairly short period, production methods changed quickly and dramatically in a variety of industries. These changes are part of every economic history course and too well-known to need any reiteration. Yet the lingering doubt remains: if our intuition and our training so strongly suggest that nature makes no jumps, how can economic historians create a paradigm accounting for discontinuities such as the Industrial Revolution? In what follows, I propose such a paradigm.

II. EVOLUTION AND TECHNOLOGICAL CHANGE

Members of the gradualist school, who deny the abruptness of change in the British economy during the period 1760-1830, argue basically that we should think of change in terms of "evolution." Words such as "technological drift" and "remorselessly creeping change, partly by trial and error" (Jones, 1981, p. 63) conjure up evolutionary progress. A historian of technology (Hindle, 1981, p. 128) and an economist (De Bresson, 1987) have suggested making evolution the model for technological change. A recent contribution to this literature is Basalla (1988). In what follows, the potentialities of such an analogy are examined.[9] What makes the analogy particularly apt for the purpose of this paper is that a lively debate between gradualists and saltationists has been raging for the past decade or so among evolutionary biologists, parallelling to some degree the debates among economic historians.

The word "evolution" takes on two different meanings: one as a synonym of "gradual" or "continuous" and one as a specific dynamic model which is governed by mutations and selection. The two terms are not only different, they can be contradictory. Modern theories of evolutionary change allow explicitly for chaotic bifurcations and catastrophes leading to unpredictable new steady states (Laszlo, 1987). The idea of applying ideas from the theory of evolution to economics is of course not new, although evolutionary theories have been largely outside the mainstream of modern economic theory. Kenneth Boulding (1981) made an attempt in this direction, but his analogy between economics and biology is somewhat vague.[10] In their pathbreaking work, Nelson and Winter (1982) tried to rewrite the theory of the firm using evolutionary models. In their model, the analogue to the species is the firm, and firms compete with each other. Yet, in general, such applications have had little room for technological progress as an evolutionary process itself.[11] An explicit comparison between evolutionary biology and technological change is proposed by De Bresson (1987) who makes some of the same points below. Yet De Bresson, perhaps because he is less interested in long-term historical change, ends up concluding that "there are well-founded reasons for not adopting an evolutionary framework for an economics of technological change . . . a careful examination would lead us to drop the biological analogy" (p. 759).

The question whether analogies between evolution and *scientific* progress are useful has been the subject of a large and lively literature. Recently, Michael Ruse (1986, pp 32-35) has discussed in detail the advantages of such analogies. He distinguishes between what he calls "analogy-as-heuristic," in which the analogy between A (which is well-understood) and B (which we are investigating) suggests certain ways to approach the study of B and certain hypotheses to test, without necessarily implying that just because they hold for A they must hold for B. The stronger claim for analogies of this type is "analogy-as-justification" in which certain propositions are claimed for B because they are true for A, or else the entire analogy collapses. Biological evolution and technological change are similar enough to make such an analogy interesting and to suggest new ways of thinking about the economic history of technology. Yet they are dissimilar enough to disclaim that any immediate inferences can be drawn from Darwinist theory to issues like the Industrial Revolution. Such dissimilarities do not invalidate the use of the analogy. The use of analogies from other disciplines has a venerable tradition in economic science. The inspiration of classical Newtonian physics is of course at the base of equilibrium theory and comparative statics. The parallelisms are inevitably incomplete, and do not provide the researcher with a sharp analytical tool. Not every element in one area has an exact equivalent in the other: Where is the economic counterpart of entropy?[12]

The approach I take here is that techniques, in the narrow sense of the word—namely the knowledge of how to produce a good or service in a specific way—are analogues of species, and that changes in them have an evolutionary character. The idea or conceptualization of how to produce a good may be thought of as the genotype, whereas when the product is actually being produced, we can think of the actual technique utilized by the firm as the phenotype of the member of a species. The emergence of a new technique is thus equivalent to speciation, the emergence of a new species. The analogy is incomplete and arguing from partial analogy can be misleading. Nevertheless, something can be learned from the exercise. The basic premise is that technology is epistemological in nature. It is not something that "exists" somehow outside people's brains. Like science, culture, and art, technology is something we *know*, and technological change should be regarded properly as a set of changes in our knowledge. In recent years a new school of evolutionary epistemology has gained considerable influence.[13] These philosophers have attempted to regard changes in knowledge as propelled by mechanisms quite similar to changes in species. How does the theory of evolution apply to systems of knowledge like technology? The fundamental idea is simple. New ideas, it is argued, occur randomly, or rather blindly, like mutations (Campbell, 1987). Some cultural, scientific, or technological ideas catch on because in some way they best suit the needs of society just as some mutations are retained by natural selection for perpetuation. In its simplest form, the selection process works because the best adjusted phenotypes are also the ones that multiply the fastest. In the context of technical choice, "best adapted" means that at given factor prices, a given technique can produce a good at the lowest quality-adjusted cost. Through this selection process, the best ideas survive and in some cases they completely supplant lesser ones.

To repeat: in the paradigm I am proposing it is neither the "firm," nor the people, nor societies which are the analogue to species. Rather, the *techniques* play this role. Natural selection picks viable (or "adaptive" as biologists would call them) ideas for survival in a Darwinian fashion. The traits of a new technique can be summarized in a small number of variables most of which can be summarized by the economist's notion of social saving, that is, the difference in total social costs (including costs external to the firm like pollution) between producing the same goods with the old technique and producing them with the new. Lower production costs, higher durability, and safer production processes are well-defined adaptive features. Other factors could matter as well: some techniques might survive because they are attractive by criteria other than strict economic calculus, such as their aesthetic features. Given a relatively small amount of information such as factor prices and the valuation that society places on matters such as noise, clean air, virgin forests and so on, techniques can be ranked by their adaptiveness thus defined.

Consider first how a static technology is similar to a hypothetical world of unchanging species. In the absence of progress, technological information is passed from generation to generation in unaltered form. The intergenerational transmission of technological DNA occurs through training, usually of apprentices or sons by people possessing the information. Although random noise may be accompanying this information, there are mechanisms that eliminate these disturbances. Any specimen which displays different characteristics is maladjusted and dies out. The competition for resources amongst living creatures is analogous to competition in the marketplace, and natural selection assures stability.

Technological change occurs through the emergence of new ideas. They may occur perfectly randomly, or "blindly" (unforeseen by the players themselves) or systematically with a large stochastic component. Like mutations, new ideas represent deviations from the displayed characteristics, and are subjected to a variety of tests of their performance against the environment. Again like mutations, most are stillborn or do not survive infancy. Of the few that do, a minority actually is reproduced, that is, transferred to other specimens. If the new technique is adaptive, it will generate new converts, or it will simply allow its bearers to reproduce faster so that eventually it can gradually replace the old technology. The analogy is not far-fetched; like technological progress, evolution is widely understood to mean an increment in knowledge (Bartley, 1987, p. 23).

The evolutionary model does not assure that only the fittest will survive. Evolutionary biologists have long ago ceased to attach credence to the Spencerian notion of the survival of the fittest as either incorrect or a tautology. Geographical isolation can create niches in which more primitive forms survive side by side with more efficient species. When isolation is then removed, the equilibrium is upset, and less efficient species may become extinct. Similarly, different techniques can coexist if in some way the less efficient producers control a specific resource on which they have property rights and which allows them to survive and reproduce without competing head-on with other producers. The strikingly large differences in agricultural productivity found in similar and adjacent regions may be explained in this way. Neither the dodo nor primitive manual production could survive the opening-up of the world.

The analogy between Darwinian evolution and technological change should not be pushed too far because technological progress is basically non-Darwinian in nature.[14] Technology is information acquired by learning, not genes. It is thus a culture as customarily defined (Cavalli-Sforza and Feldman, 1981, p. 10). Cultural transmission such as science, art, and technology, involves the passing-on of acquired (learned) traits to the next generation (Boyd and Richerson, 1985). In biological evolution the transmission of acquired traits would be "Lamarckian" and does not occur. The intergenerational transmission of information in technology occurs, after all, through the conscious training and teaching of apprentices, descendants, and students. Yet this training is not independent of what the parent has learned during his lifetime. Moreover, technology can change through the lateral transmission of information: firms and workers, unlike animals belonging to a species, learn from each other and imitate each other. Epistemologies do not have an equivalent to DNA and do not change through mutations in the genes and chromosomes. Strictly speaking, biological mutations are nothing more than copying errors in the act of passing on information from generation to generation. In cultural change, including technology, the changes occur in the actually living specimens. They are thus not copying errors in the standard sense of the word, but rather ideas and inspirations that arise in ways mostly unknown to us but which are not completely random. Unlike science and technology, biological evolution does not involve any intentionality. No conscious entity is operating in biology like the ones that are trying to make life better, reduce production costs, fight cancer, or achieve nuclear fusion.[15] New ideas tend to be affected by their environment through subtle and often subconscious mechanisms. Thus cultural and technological innovations are directed toward problem solving and therefore will prove on average more adaptive than if innovation were purely random (Cavalli-Sforza and Feldman, 1981, p. 66).

A further difference between the two involves cross-lineage borrowings. In evolutionary biology, different species do not often exchange genes, that is, information. Hybridization in the organic world can happen, but only in closely related species. We share 99 percent of our genes with primates, yet hybridization does not occur. In the history of technology, such exchanges occur all the time. Advances in metallurgy and boring technology made the high-pressure steam engine possible; radical changes in the design of clocks and ships suggested to others how to make better instruments and windmills; fuels and furnaces adapted to beer-brewing and glassblowing turned out to be useful to the iron industry; technical ideas from organ-making were found to be useful in weaving. Therefore, in biology, the main effect of the evolution of one species on others is through its impact on the environment, whereas in technology changes in different "species" affect others *both* directly through cross-borrowing and indirectly through their impact on the economic environment.

An important difference between the two is that biological evolution's *primum movens* is usually thought to be adaptation to a changing environment whereas technological change is above all a manipulation of the environment (although some non-human species such as beavers and ants do, of course, sometimes manipulate their environment). In evolutionary biology, adaptation to a changing environment by selection operating through very small mutations involves more frequently something equivalent to factor substitution. That is, it is more like a choice among existing techniques (what economists refer to as substitution) than the creation of a new and superior alternative. The distinction between substitution and technological improvement is often difficult because it is hard to know in practice whether a technique is known and available but not used or simply unknown, but the logical distinction is quite important.[16] Yet, this difference between biological evolution and technological change may not be as decisive as might be thought. Speciation is not adaptation although it is often accompanied by it (Eldredge, 1985), just as invention is not substitution although it is often accompanied by it.

This brings us to the most confounding logical difficulty in the analogy: a new species is (or eventually becomes) reproductively isolated from others. It is, therefore, usually simple to make the crucial distinction between adaptation and speciation. In technology we cannot readily define a precise line separating a new "species" (technique) from existing ones, and therefore it is inevitably arbitrary to speak of improvement *within an old* or the emergence *of a new* technique. Yet, as I will argue, despite the inevitability of gray areas, such distinctions are not only possible but essential to the understanding of technological progress. It is perhaps of some consolation that, in some views, evolutionary biologists also "have not been able to agree on a suitable definition of a species" (Bush, 1982, p. 119).

The analogy is thus imperfect, but we should not underrate the communalities either. Biological reproduction and economic activity, in the final analysis, are both dynamics of nature constrained by the finiteness of resources. Darwin himself, after all, hit upon the idea of natural selection after reading Malthus's *Essay on Population*, the quintessential statement of scarcity in a dynamic context. Without a binding constraint of population pressure, natural selection is deprived of its main mechanism, and while there can be change, it will not be Darwinian in nature (Ruse, 1986, p. 24). By analogy, technological change will be hampered in an economic environment in which firms cannot freely enter or exit an activity, or where they are constrained by traditions and institutions to a fixed share of the market. The theory of natural selection is, of course, closely related to Adam Smith's philosophical idea of an invisible hand which through competition amongst individuals struggling for their own benefit created a higher order.[17] In both technological history and evolutionary biology, the enormous differences in time scales notwithstanding, there are identifiable secular trends. Increasing specialization and diversification have produced bewildering arrays of both biological species and techniques in use. A long-term trend toward increasing efficiency and complexity can be discerned, although such progress is more easily discerned in technological history than in evolution.[18] In both, the selection process is extremely wasteful. The vast majority of new technological ideas, like that of mutations, have been totally useless either inherently or relative to their environment. Yet in technological change, it is probably true, as Hull (1988a, p. 155) points out for the cases of scientific change and biological evolution, that "the selection process cannot be made too efficient without neutralizing its effects." After all, technological change ventures into the unknown, not into the uncertain. The risks cannot be diversified away.

At the same time, the selection processes often seem oddly incomplete. Some seemingly "unfit" species cling tenaciously to life. In other cases, biologists have pointed out that random genetic drift can lead to uncertain outcomes. Mildly deleterious genes can and do become homozygous in populations by drift, notwithstanding the pressures of natural selection (Lewontin, 1982, p. 159). Although economic historians have, in the past years, made valiant efforts to show that some apparently inefficient techniques that survived despite the emergence of newer and better ones were in reality sophisticated adaptations to their environment, their efforts have not proven that long-term survival implies efficiency. The clever analogy between the Panda's thumb and the QWERTY typewriter keyboard (Gould, 1987) illustrates the obvious suboptimality of evolutionary processes in biology and technology. Not all problems are solved, and not all possible solutions are achieved. As Campbell (1987, p. 105) remarks: "The knowledge we do encounter is achieved against terrific odds."

The analogy can be extended. In biological evolution and in technological change, the number of outcomes is constrained because selection occurs at every step. Variations on unsuccessful variations in a previous generation are rarely tested. Thus, Brian Arthur (1989) maintains that when steam cars were rejected, no further improvements on them were made although it is possible that further learning by doing would have created a steam vehicle that was ultimately superior to the gasoline engine. It is this property, cumulating outcomes from a blind variation and then exploring future variations only on those paths which passed an earlier test, which prevents a divergence of experimentation to infinity and, as Campbell explains, makes the improbable inevitable. Thus, evolution is an example of change which is "path dependent," a property of technological change recently emphasized by Paul David (1987) and Brian Arthur (1989). Outcomes are never inevitable, and worlds that could have been but never were might be fruitfully contemplated, much as they may be distasteful to orthodox historians.[19]

Moreover, in both evolution and technological change, the *ex post* course is not the one taken *ex ante*. There is a large accidental component in long-term change, and the record suggests that serendipity, opportunism, and the "King Saul effect" (which occurs when the search for the solution of a specific problem leads inadvertently to a totally new opportunity set) play an important role.[20] The importance of this effect in biological evolution is still in dispute. Gould (1982a, p. 384) points out that such effects would be nonadaptive (or pre-adaptive) in nature and emphasizes their crucial role in evolution. For example, the growth of the human brain was due to a set of complex factors related to selection. But once it reached this size, it could perform in an unimagined way, bearing no relation to the selective reasons for its initial growth. Such effects are common in technological history; many major inventions were "pre-adaptive" in the sense that they were designed to solve a small local problem and mushroomed into something entirely different.

Biological species and production techniques in use are both bounded in time. Many evolutionary biologists believe today that species, like individuals, are born and die. So did undershot watermills, water-driven clocks, and Newcomen engines.[21] Similarly, species emerge out of something else. In technology, this occurs through the process of invention, in evolution primarily through a process known as "allopatric" or "geographic" speciation, that is, the creation of new species due to its geographic isolation which prevents interbreeding (Mayr, 1970). Species die in two ways: either by extinction, often due to some outside ecological shock, or by pseudo-extinction, in which the species transforms itself into something else. Both phenomena have their analogues in technological history. Above all, technological change and evolution both contain elements that make prediction all but impossible. Historians of technology can explain the past pattern of technology, but cannot predict what is to come any more than evolutionary biologists can predict the species of the future. Progress, like evolution, was neither destiny nor fluke. Yet the power of Darwinian logic—natural selection imposed on blind variation—is that we do not have to choose between destiny or fluke.

To conclude, if it is granted that a prima facie case can be established for looking at technology from an evolutionary point of view, it seems as if the gradualists would be able to find some indirect support for their position. The "neo-Darwinian synthesis" which until recently was the unchallenged paradigm among evolutionary biologists, held that evolution was slow, continuous, and gradual. Species involved from each other through infinitely small steps, each one too insignificant to be noticed. Natural selection, however, guided what would otherwise have been a stationary process into directed adaptive genetic change. Clearly, a gradualist view of technological history, including the Industrial Revolution, would be perfectly consistent with that view of historical change. Every change in technique is a minor improvement on the previous technology in use, and it is through the accumulation of thousands of these little changes that technological progress is ultimately achieved. This extreme gradualism, first proposed by S.C. Gilfillan in the 1930s, was at the time a much-needed antidote to the naive "great men" accounts of invention of the early twentieth century, and has steadily gained influence.

Many economic historians have implicitly chosen as their paradigm the gradual evolutionary model of change. They have argued that technological change consists of a slow drift of incremental small steps, a "steady cumulation of innumerable minor improvements and modifications with only very infrequent major innovations" (Rosenberg, 1982, p. 63; see also, for example, Sahal, 1981, p. 37; Bassala, 1988, pp. 26-63). They have not realized, however, that biologists have been far from unanimous about the gradual nature of evolution itself. In a classic but controversial work, the geneticist Richard Goldschmidt (1940) proposed a distinction between micro- and macromutations. The former accounted for changes *within* a species, and were more or less continuous and cumulative. The latter accounted for great leaps in biological evolution that created new species. Goldschmidt believed that evolution moved at times in leaps and jerks through those macromutations. He argued, probably too rigidly, that new species arose *only* by way of macromutations and not by the continuous accumulation of micromutations. Following the emergence of a new species, it follows the standard evolutionary adaptive process of micromutation. Goldschmidt remained an isolated and neglected critic of standard evolutionary theory.[22] The conventional neo-Darwinian wisdom in evolutionary biology had no place for Goldschmidt's saltationism.

Recently, however, the modern Darwinian synthesis has come under considerable critique from an unexpected corner. A number of prominent paleontologists and paleobiologists, especially Stephen Jay Gould and Niles Eldredge, have maintained that the emphasis on continuity and gradual change is exaggerated if not completely misplaced. Instead of gradual change, they maintain, the fossil records show that extended periods of history are characterized by stasis, followed by periods of short, intense evolutionary change. These periods of stasis are known as "punctuated equilibria," and because of their notion of change occurring in short and abrupt leaps, they have found much inspiration in the saltationist views of Goldschmidt.

It is significant, perhaps, that the challenge to the gradualist synthesis has come from paleontologists studying fossils. The source of their skepticism is, quite clearly, the lack of evidence for *any* change during very long periods, which supports the idea of stasis, and the lack of evidence for intermediary forms between different species as gradualism would require (Eldredge, 1985). Paleontologists are to the study of evolution what historians are to the study of technology. They observe the records of the past rather than the abstract models or experimental data of the present, and in so doing they present a unique, long-term point of view. The analogy does not end there. What the new punctuated equilibrium theorists, following Goldschmidt, maintain is that there are two forms of speciation, one that is continuous, cumulative, and adaptive, and one that creates new species by discontinuous and often nonadaptive changes. These macromutations are believed to be the result of chromosomal alterations, occurring early in the ontogeny and "leading to cascading effects" throughout embryology (Gould, 1980, p. 127).

Something similar holds for technological change. In technological history there are long periods of stasis as well as major discontinuous changes that parallel macromutations. In analogy with the macromutations suggested by Goldschmidt, I propose to refer to those inventions as *macroinventions*. Goldschmidt referred to macromutations as "hopeful monstrosities," a powerful metaphor which is remarkably apt for new inventions as well. If we merely count inventions, such macroinventions were a tiny minority. Yet their number is not crucial. Inventions do not obey the laws of arithmetic, and the importance of macroinventions, as we shall see, is far larger than their small number indicates. These macroinventions may have been few and far in between, but they were the stuff from which new "species" (techniques) were made.

The traditional neodarwinist view of evolution argues that natural selection works at the level of the individual organism, in a process known as anagenesis. The technological equivalent of that is, basically, the Nelson-Winter view that economic selection works primarily on the level of the firm. Against that, the Gould-Eldredge view of evolution is one of hierarchy; it is *not* denied that evolution works at the level of the individual, but it wishes to extend selection to higher levels as well, such as the species. The idea of hierarchy is quite illuminating in technological history. The analogue here is that natural selection works at the level of the *technique in use* (analogue: species or deme) as well as on the level of the firm (analogue: individual organism) (Gould, 1982b). Techniques may be subject to both micro- and macromutations. A hierarchy of change means that technological progress takes place both through the improvement of existing techniques and the emergence of new ones. Whether such distinctions are useful or not is a matter of judgment. An exact line marking where an old technique ends and a new one begins must always be arbitrary, though I believe that the number of truly ambiguous cases is not large.

The modern assessment of Goldschmidt's view of evolution is mixed, in part because his *magnum opus* is a difficult and contradictory book. Mayr (1988, p. 465) concedes that "hopeful monsters are at least in theory possible" but adds that recent authors are virtually unanimous that there is no evidence that saltations as envisaged by Goldschmidt and others occur (p. 414). Yet some modified version of Goldschmidt's view of macromutations has survived in modern evolutionary theory. Even without "drastic mutations," it has become clear that Gould's (1982c) interpretation of Goldschmidt as macroevolution occurring through small genetic mutations early in the ontogeny with large phenotypic effects is not incompatible with Darwinist evolution and the evidence (Mayr, 1988, p. 413). The parallel with technological change is immediate: many major technological breakthroughs occurred through rather small conceptual changes or simple ideas, yet led to drastic differences in production methods. The modern critique of Goldschmidt is most effective in refuting the exclusivity he claimed for macromutations in generating new species. It is possible that new species eventually evolve through lengthy cumulative series of micromutations. No evolutionary biologist would concur today that saltations are the only source of new species. Similarly, not *all* new techniques require macroinvention. The arch-gradualist S.C. Gilfillan chose as his case study the development of the ship, in which macroinventions were rare. The eighteenth century ship was vastly different from the early fifteenth century ship, yet with few exceptions, these changes were due to cumulative microinventions.

A macroinvention in technological history involves an invention without clear-cut parentage, representing a clear break from previous technique. For such an invention to succeed, it has to have the capability to compete and survive. The technological equivalents of a viable macromutation are first, that the new idea has to be *technically* feasible, that is to say, within the ability of contemporaries to reproduce and utilize it.[23] Second, the new idea has to be *economically* feasible, that is, at least as efficient as existent technologies. In many cases, the second condition was not satisfied even when the first was, as in the case of the first fifty years of coke-smelting during which coke produced a slightly inferior quality of iron. Third—and here there is no direct analogue in evolutionary biology—the new invention has to be born into a socially sympathetic environment. There are many cases in which technologically and economically feasible inventions were suppressed and delayed by reactionary governments or worried competitors.

Once a macroinvention occurs, and a "new species" emerges, it becomes a fertile ground for adaptive microinventions. The macroinvention itself does not need to be economically very important immediately. It is defined as a new conceptual departure, not a minor improvement on existing technology, and thus it raises the marginal product of subsequent microinventions.[24] The new technology has to be debugged, adapted to a variety of local conditions, and minor improvements through learning processes continue for a long period after the new technology emerges. But eventually these micromutations run into diminishing returns, and technology will begin to look more and more like the "stasis" observed by Gould and his colleagues in the fossil record, until and unless a new major invention occurs. It is precisely the prediction of extended periods of stasis and stagnation "punctuated" by periods of rapid and intensive change that makes the Gould-Eldredge theory of evolutionary change such an attractive paradigm for technological history. As Spengler described it, somewhat crudely, "World history strides on from catastrophe to catastrophe, whether we can comprehend and prove it or not" (1932, p. 37).[25] Technological progress was neither continuous nor persistent. Genuinely creative societies were rare, and their bursts of creativity usually short-lasting. It is as one of those bursts of creativity that we should view the Industrial Revolution.

III. THE INDUSTRIAL REVOLUTION AND MACROINVENTIONS

The Industrial Revolution can now be redefined as a period in which a large number of macroinventions occurred in a short time. The last cluster of macroinventions had occurred in the two centuries after 1300. In those years weight-driven clocks, gunpowder, movable type, spectacles, full rigging, and blast furnaces should be regarded as macroinventions. But the period 1500-1700 was one of "technological drift" with few major breakthroughs. After 1700, macroinventions begin to recur, but it is not until 1760 that they become frequent. Many of these macroinventions form the core of every elementary textbook on the Industrial Revolution.

These macroinventions constitute the fundamental discontinuity of the period of "Sturm und Drang" of the Industrial Revolution. Their initial impact on the economy as a whole was limited, of course. First, almost all macroinventions needed subsequent microinventions in order to be profitable or in some cases to work at all. Second, for a variety of reasons widely discussed in the literature (e.g., Rosenberg, 1976, chapter 11), even successful inventions were often implemented slowly. The discontinuity of macroinventions is epistemological: knowledge emerged that constituted a discrete and abrupt break with the past. How large the leap has to be to be classified as a macro- or a microinvention is ultimately a matter of taste. It seems fair to say that Watt's realization of the advantages of separate condensing was a large enough departure from the Newcomen concept to qualify for this status, but Arkwright's improvement over the Wyatt-Paul concept of spinning yarn by rollers, though critical from an economic point of view, was quite limited as a conceptual innovation. The evolutionary framework also provides an alternative to the idea of regarding the transition from organic to inorganic raw materials and from animate to inanimate sources of energy as the crux of the Industrial Revolution (Wrigley, 1987). After all, iron and steel had been in use for close to three millennia before the Industrial Revolution, and the move from waterpower to steam power, or from wool to cotton can hardly be called a change from organic to inorganic raw materials. What defines the Industrial Revolution is a clustering of separate macroinventions, not necessarily some aggregate process that affected the entire British economy.

The five macroinventions chosen as examples here all occurred between 1760 and 1800, but they are not the warhorses of the Industrial Revolution such as cotton spinning, puddling and rolling, and steam power. The criterion for their selection was not their impact on GNP or economic welfare. Although that criterion is legitimate, it is not the only one by which we can choose historical examples, any more than we should study the evolutionary history of rats rather than that of Colobus monkeys only because there are more rats in the world. In these examples, I hope to demonstrate two basic properties of a macroinvention, namely its lack of obvious parentage, and its effect in raising the marginal product of subsequent microinventions which refined and improved upon the original insight. These macroinventions are thus symmetric with evolutionary biology's macromutations, and confirm the usefulness of evolutionary paradigms in the economic history of technological change.

Gaslighting

It is not usually realized how little progress had been made before 1750 in the age-old problem of providing light in darkness. The primitive oil lamps burned rapeseed oil and similar fuels, and provided a smoky and strongly colored flame. Tallow candles, widely used because of their low price, also provided fairly low quality light. Wax candles were superior, but much more expensive. Given the rather obvious need for an improved product, it seems unbelievable that no improvements of substance occurred earlier.[26] The revolutionary nature of gaslighting was not, however, in its improvement in the way homes and public places were illuminated, but in the realization that flammable gas could be used *at all* in a controllable fire and thus for illumination. It is that insight which we should regard as the discontinuous breakthrough which had no real precedent. The macroinvention occurred a number of times independently, but it was not until after 1780 that the new "species" became viable. The first realization that some gases could burn can be traced to the Flemish physician Jan B. Van Helmont (1577-1644), but the notion that burning gas for useful purposes such as illumination and heating was an eighteenth century insight. The idea that coal could be broken up into components, one of which was a flammable gas, was expounded around 1730 by a number of British chemists. Most experiments with burning coal gas were, however, motivated by the need to get rid of the gas rather than produce it from coal and utilize the energy. The owner of a Newcastle colliery, George Dixon, experimented in 1760 with coal-gas for the purposes of illumination conducting his gas through tobacco pipes but when an explosion occurred he concluded that coal-gas was too dangerous for this purpose.

After 1760, there was a growing realization that coal gas could be used for useful purposes. In about 1780, Archibald Cochrane, the eccentric Earl of Dundonald, lit the gases above his tar ovens mostly to amuse his friends and thus "narrowly missed being the inventor of gas-lighting through failing to see the possibilities, as an illuminant, of the inflammable vapors given off in the distillation of tar" (Holmyard, 1958, p. 252). There is some question to who first put all the parts together in realizing that coal-gas could not only burn well, but that such fire could produce an immensely useful service. But in the decade in which so many other miracles occurred in European industry, the 1780s, the macroinvention was definitely made, although not in Britain. Claims for the breakthrough have been made for the Louvain Professor Jean Pierre Minkelers who was reputed to have lighted his classroom with gas in 1784, and the Würzburg Professor Johann Georg Pickel, who lighted his laboratory with gas in 1786 (Elton, 1958, pp. 260-61).

The commercial application of the invention was the acid test of survival of the new species. Here the story is well-known. The Frenchman Philippe Lebon took out a patent in 1799, in which he distilled gas from wood, cooled it, and proposed to burn the gas in a glass device known as a "thermolamp" in which gas and air were separately introduced, and the heavier by-products of the wood gas were collected in a special receptacle. Lebon conducted a number of well-publicized demonstrations in 1801 at the Hôtel Seignelay in Paris, and from then on it was abundantly clear that a radical new possibility had opened up. Although Lebon's lamp was introduced at a particularly inconvenient time and he never saw a commercial application of his idea, it is clear that in his mind the macroinvention was complete. As Elton (1958) notes, "in his few writings, Lebon anticipated nearly all the applications of gas in the hundred years succeeding his death" (p. 262). Lebon's influence on subsequent developments was decisive.

The microinventions which followed the crucial insights can be summarized briefly. William Murdock, an employee of Boulton and Watt's, had experimented with gas light since the early 1790s. His special contribution was to use coal gas rather than wood derivatives. Murdock learned of Lebon's experiments and pursued them with vigor after he moved to the Soho works in 1798. Murdock heated coal in cast iron pots known as "retorts," and separated the coal-gas from the tar in air-cooled pipes. Experimentation showed which kinds of lamps were most suitable to gas lighting, how to produce coal gas in an effective way, which grades of coal to use and so on. In 1807 some of Manchester's cotton mills and London's Pall Mall were illuminated by coal gas. Of course, gas lighting had not made much of an impact on economic welfare by this time, and the solution to many of the technical problems such as centralized production, distribution to individual customers, odorless fuels (through liming) still lay in the future. But by then the fundamental breakthrough had occurred; the rest of the history of gaslighting technology can be described as incremental and gradual improvement following the classical "Darwinian" pattern.

The Breast Wheel

The period of the Industrial Revolution, although it is so often identified with the growth of steam power, was one of rapid improvement in the most important form of pre-modern industrial power, waterpower. Changes in the utilization of waterpower during the Industrial Revolution compared to previous forms were not much less dramatic than the contrast between the Watt and Newcomen engines. It would be tempting to choose the water turbine as an example of a macroinvention, as it was a radically different concept in which the flow of water could be entirely converted into work.[27] Although the concept of the turbine was actually implicit in theoretical work carried out on the Continent in the 1750s and 1760s, the practical problems of the turbine were not resolved until well into the nineteenth century. Yet, even within the somewhat more limited confines of traditional water power, the Industrial

Revolution saw at least one breakthrough that could qualify as a macroinvention.

The traditional water wheel, invented in Roman times but fully developed and utilized in the West only in medieval times, came in two quite different forms.[28] Overshot wheels, also known as gravity wheels, received water at their summit, while the undershot wheel or impulse wheel received the water from below. From the point of view of physical efficiency, overshot wheels are more efficient, with a maximum theoretical efficiency of 100 percent, whereas undershot wheels are constrained to a maximum efficiency of 50 percent. *Economic* efficiency, of course, depended on many other factors such as cost of construction, depreciation, suitability to specific sites, the variability of the flow and so on. The long and reasonably peaceful coexistence of the two types over so many centuries suggests that neither completely dominated the other, as the overshot wheels were more costly to construct and not suitable to sites along slow-flowing rivers.

What is striking is how difficult scientists found it to make sense out of the physics of water wheels. In 1704, Antoine Parent published a pioneering paper which contained the celebrated but erroneous propositions that both types of waterwheels were equally efficient, and that both were constrained to a maximum efficiency of 15 percent (4/27). Theory was soon found to be inconsistent with practice. A number of experimental physicists and engineers discovered that gravity wheels were in fact more efficient than impulse wheels, and that both could exceed the theoretical limits derived by Parent. French scientists led in the experimental and theoretical work. Antoine de Parcieux showed in the 1750s how incorrect Parent's propositions were. In 1767 Jean Charles Borda, a French military engineer, solved the theoretical problems regarding the efficiency of the various waterwheels. His work was so revolutionary that it was not widely known or accepted before the nineteenth century.

By the middle of the eighteenth century, the over- and undershot water wheels were no longer the only two forms. A third and intermediate form, known now as the breast wheel, had made its appearance. The breast wheel differs from the other two in that it takes water from an intermediate point between the summit and the bottom, and thus constitutes in some sense a compromise between them. There is some argument as to when the breast wheel first appeared. Reti (1969) attributes its incipience to Leonardo, and a number of sixteenth century writers mention it explicitly. Yet the main sources on motive power, which describe in detail the various machines used, do not mention this type of water wheel, and if the macromutation occurred before 1700, it was not yet ready for survival in a competitive, Darwinian world. The reason is that in wheels with an intermediate water intake point, water spillage from the blades or buckets was a major problem. To prevent spillage, engineers installed a casing that held the falling water onto the wheel. This casing, known as "breast" (hence the term breast wheel) appeared for the first time in Jacob Leupold's *Theatrum Machinarum Generale* (1724) but clearly was not yet widespread, as it was absent from Bernard de Bélidor's influential *Architecture Hydraulique* (1737). Incidentally, Bélidor firmly believed in Parent's erroneous propositions and also asserted that undershot wheels were far more efficient than overshot ones. Clearly, then, the breast wheel in a viable form was little known and used before the middle of the eighteenth century.

Enter John Smeaton, one of the most versatile and creative minds of the Industrial Revolution and maybe of all times. Unlike his French colleagues, Smeaton was a thoroughly empirical and practical engineer, not a theorist, a firm believer in a methodology of systematic experimentation.[29] In the 1750s, Smeaton carried out experiments similar to de Parcieux's which showed that the efficiency of overshot wheels tended to be around two-thirds, while that of undershot wheels was about one-third. In 1759, he announced his results thus definitely refuting Parent and Bélidor's theories and firmly establishing the superiority of the gravity wheel. At that point, Smeaton realized the vast potentialities of the breast wheel: it was a gravity wheel, but one that could be constructed in most sites previously suitable only for undershot wheels. Once fitted with the tightly fitting casing, it combined the advantages of the gravity and the impulse wheels.[30] It could be legitimately objected that the breast wheel was not a genuine macroinvention since it was really a modification of an existing device. But the breast wheel, by combining the best aspects of two quite different ways of producing the same thing (water power), was a fundamentally new departure. Once conceived in a viable form, the breast wheel, like all macroinventions, increased the marginal product of incremental improvements. Of those, by far the most important was John Rennie's sliding hatch (developed in the 1780s), which allowed the water to be introduced at varying points of the wheel, thus adapting the breastwheel to varying water levels. The sliding hatch gave the breast wheel a flexibility that neither of its precursors had. The breast wheel, in Cardwell's words, was turned from a "rather charming instrument of rustic economy" into a "thoroughly industrial engine."

The Jacquard Loom

Before the Industrial Revolution, the weaving of patterned fabrics could be carried out in two ways: by printing on a white piece of cloth, or by brocading, that is, weaving the pattern directly into the warp. The latter technique was far more expensive and confined to more upmarket fabrics like silk. The draw loom was developed in China, and required a second worker, the drawboy, seated on top of the loom, who selected and pulled the warp threads through which a particular weft was going. The draw loom reached Europe in the late Middle Ages and was in widespread use in France and Italy in the seventeenth century. Some improvements simplifying the work of the drawboy were introduced, but none of these were able to dispense with the drawboy itself. The old drawloom remained a clumsy instrument: the preliminary task of tying up the cords pulled by the drawboy was very complex and could take a couple of weeks, and changing from one pattern to another was thus very expensive. An error by a drawboy would result in irreversible flaws in the fabric and a waste of the costly materials. Moreover, the task of drawing was extremely arduous, and serious physical disorders developed among these workers (Usher, 1954, p. 289).

The need for some kind of automation was acutely felt. The idea of how to bring it about occurred first to the son of a French organ maker, Basile Bouchon, in 1725. The novelty of the idea was that it applied the kind of binary logic which operates organs to the automation of weaving. The pattern of warp threads to be pulled was entered on a perforated strip of paper, with wooden rods probing the holes. Outside the holes, the rod is pushed by the paper, moving a wire attached to a pulley which pulled the desired wires. Clearly, the idea of storing information on perforated paper and then letting the machine "read" this information appears in retrospect as one of the most important and radical insights in the history of technology. It delivered accuracy as well as flexibility, as the cards were not only free from human error but could be easily replaced by a different "program" and produce a different design. As it happened, however, Bouchon was far ahead of his time, and the macroinvention resulted in a technique which, for the time being, was only marginally viable. In subsequent decades a number of French engineers tried to improve the automatic draw loom. Another inventor, Jean Baptiste Falcon, replaced Bouchon's perforated paper with a set of separated perforated cardboard cards (1728). In both the Bouchon and the Falcon design, the drawboy was still necessary since he pressed the probes against the perforated paper or card, and pulled the cords selected by the machine (rather than selecting them himself) but his task was vastly simplified and errors all but eliminated. The great French engineer and inventor of automata, Jacques de Vaucanson, proposed using a cylinder with holes punched in it.[31] The important insight of Vaucanson was that the cylinder could be probed by flexible needles. Vaucanson also simplified the mechanism by attaching the warp threads directly to a hook which was manipulated by the needles and thus dispensed with the drawboy altogether.

The primitive prototypes designed by Falcon were actually put into production but did not spread rapidly. Usher may be right in claiming that the difficulties that arose were details of design rather than of principle. These looms did not dispense with the drawboys altogether, and the cost of redesigning the looms and retraining the labor force had to be weighed against limited benefits. Vaucanson's automatic loom never became practical, primarily because not enough information could be crammed onto the cylinder.

The final breakthrough occurred in 1804, when a Lyons silk weaver, Joseph Marie Jacquard, designed the loom which bears his name. Similarly to gaslighting and the breastwheel, the actual novelty of the critical invention can be questioned. Jacquard did little more than combine Vaucanson's idea of flexible rods with Falcon's endless chain of cards, and its originality is thus limited.[32] But clearly minimizing his achievement by pointing to precursors ignores the standard evolutionary test of species viability, or in our terms, economic feasibility. Macroinventions in conceptual form occurred often enough—Leonardo Da Vinci alone was responsible for dozens of them. But the Industrial Revolution was the period in which macroinventions that worked were realized, and this is what counts. The difference between the Jacquard loom and its predecessors was that it was a macroinvention destined for survivability and perpetuation. Its success was enormous, both in France and in Britain, where it soon spread from silk to worsted and other fabrics.

It is important to separate the economic significance of the Jacquard loom from its technological significance. Its inclusion in our list of macroinventions derives from its technological novelty, although survivability also requires economic feasibility. There is no question that the Jacquard loom was very different from the traditional drawloom, not only because it eliminated the drawboy but also because the pattern could be changed in a few minutes, and the Jacquard could produce figures, effects, and colors unattainable by drawlooms (Rothstein, 1977, p. 282).

Above all, a device had been created that stored information in a binary code and then released it during the production period at will. In their original form, Falcon's perforated cards survive in player pianos and the street organs of Amsterdam and Jacquard Looms were preceded by the musical boxes and toys Vaucanson designed with so much flair. The Jacquard loom inspired Charles Babbage in the design of his famous Analytical Engine as well as Richard Roberts' multiple spindle machine, which used a Jacquard-type control mechanism for the drilling of rivet holes in the wrought iron plates used in the Britannia tubular bridge (Rosenberg and Vincenti, 1978, p. 39).[33] It also inspired the American Herman Hollerith in the 1890s to use punchcards to store the information in the 1890 U.S. Census.

Chlorine Bleaching

One of the most awkward, at least to the modern eye, of the pre-industrial processes was that of bleaching. Before the Industrial Revolution, the bleaching of textiles was carried out by repeated washing and rinsing, followed by long exposure to the sun, spread out on bleaching fields. It is not widely realized today how land-intensive textile production was at that time. Moreover, the process was very slow: bleaching often took months to complete and because it required acid substances, it depended on the supply of large quantities of buttermilk and for that reason was located in large part in the dairy farming regions of the Low Countries. At a later time, buttermilk was replaced by diluted sulfuric acid.[34]

The lack of progress in bleaching should not be very surprising, given the nonexistence of a science of chemistry at that time. This, of course, did not mean that there was no chemical industry, but what it meant was that all progress in that industry was serendipitous and unsystematic, and that many subsequent insights were simply unimaginable at that time. A good example is artificial fertilizers, developed in the nineteenth century following the work by Von Liebig and others. Nevertheless, it is by now recognized that by applying the anachronistic standards of the twentieth century, the role of scientists in the Industrial Revolution has in some ways been underestimated. The tale of chlorine bleaching is a good illustration of the importance of scientists in the development of new technology (Musson and Robinson, 1969, chapter 8). The story begins with a brilliant eccentric Swedish apothecary and chemical pioneer, Carl Wilhelm Scheele (1742-86), who, among other things, was the first to discover the existence of oxygen. Though pre-modern in his adherence to the soon-to-be-discarded phlogiston theory, Scheele made many important discoveries, among them the existence of chlorine (1774). A French chemist, Claude Berthollet, had been experimenting with bleaching agents for a while with a variety of acids for bleaching purposes, and suggested in 1785 the use of chlorine as a bleaching agent. Berthollet was a close associate of Lavoisier, and was in the "modernist" (anti-phlogistonian) camp. Subsequent to his basic discovery he showed precisely how to use chlorine with textiles, preventing damage to the fabric and using chemical agents to prevent yellowing. Yet neither he nor Scheele ever realized that chlorine was an element and not a compound.

The use of chlorine gas as a bleaching agent raised enormous interest all over Europe, but especially in sun-starved Britain where the cotton industry was conducting its experiments in mechanization in these years.[35] Interestingly, James Watt himself played an important role in the introduction of chlorine bleaching into Britain. Watt was a first class chemist, and his father-in-law was a Glasgow bleacher. In 1786, Watt and Boulton visited Paris and Berthollet demonstrated his technique to them, and within a short time it was clear to both contemporary chemists and manufacturers that chlorine bleaching was a truly revolutionary idea. It is now fully understood why: whereas the acids used in traditional bleaching basically removed insoluble substances in the fibre, chlorine bleaching works through oxygenation of the color products which can then be washed out. The discontinuity was thus fundamental in nature: the chemical process at work was changed radically and suddenly. The authorities on the subject go as far as to state that "in the last quarter of the eighteenth century, no greater advance was made in the finishing sections of the textile trade than in the art of bleaching" (Clow and Clow, 1952, p. 186).

Eventually "grassing" disappeared completely for cotton, and cotton goods could be bleached within a week.

Like all viable macroinventions, the breakthrough, once completed, led to a series of improvements and adaptations, which turned a revolutionary idea into a major industrial event. Chlorine gas was awkward to handle, it had to be monitored very carefully so as not to destroy the cloth, was dangerous to those who handled it, and could not be transported. Moreover, it had to be dissolved in water to be used. One attempt to solve this problem was made by a number of manufacturers in Javelle, France, who produced a liquid called "Eau de Javel" in which the chlorine was absorbed in potash, but the bleaching liquid thus produced was found to be more useful for paper bleaching than for textiles. The final necessary step to be taken to make chemical bleaching economically feasible was undertaken by the Scottish bleacher Charles Tennant, who in 1799 saturated slaked lime with chlorine producing calcium hypochlorite, which was marketed as "bleaching powder." This solved the transportation problems which had been pestering the producers of Eau de Javelle. Although bleaching powder took a few years to replace earlier forms of chlorine bleaching, its success was phenomenal.[36]

Chlorine bleaching was a major leap forward not just in that it involved a recently-discovered, unexplored substance discovered by scientists in a field which was undergoing its most profound and far-reaching revolution ever. It was also a breakthrough because it was a harbinger of a new method for the generation of inventions which eventually came to dominate many industries. Many of the macroinventions during the Industrial Revolution, including the three discussed above, involved ingenuity, imagination, and inspiration. For the most part, however, they involved little formal training or schooling in abstract science. In the chemical industry, from the very start, there was little room for tinkerers. Experiments had to be accurate, well-designed, and systematic. Scheele and Berthollet were very different men from Arkwright and Cort. Their failure to understand the nature of chlorine and the difference between bleaching by acid and bleaching by oxidation is barely relevant. Berthollet not only had the crucial insight that chlorine could be used in bleaching; he continually improved and debugged his invention, keenly aware of its commercial possibilities, yet remained himself uninterested in personal material gain.

Ballooning

From a purely evolutionary point of view, ballooning is the most discrete technological leap of our five examples. After all, before the Industrial Revolution, people did light their houses, used water power, wove silk into patterns, and bleached their cottons and linens. Human flight had been the subject of dreams for millennia, perhaps because people first looked at birds and wondered "why not me?". But some ill-fated attempts aside, it had never happened.[37] The main reason why it never happened was precisely that man wanted to emulate birds exactly, and that all attempts to fly were based on attempts to equip the aviator with birdlike wings in an age when the physics of flight was completely unknown. Joseph Montgolfier was the son of a paper manufacturer from Annonay in Southern France. His success resembled that of his contemporary Berthollet in that he was able to work out his invention despite a fundamental error in his scientific thinking. Montgolfier was familiar with the discovery of hydrogen by Henry Cavendish in 1766, which was known to be substantially lighter than air. His reasoning was that if one filled a closed sphere with this substance, it would rise. Yet the hot air balloons were not based on this principle, but on the principle that when air is heated it expands, reducing its specific weight. Montgolfier did not realize this, and thought instead that the fire produced some gas which, too, was lighter than air.[38] There has never been any question that the idea first emerged in his mind. What is unusual in the case of ballooning is that the development stage, during which the invention moved from a crude idea inside the inventor's head into a device that worked, was so short. The timetable is quite revealing in this regard. The original idea occurred to Joseph in November 1782. A few small, private experiments in the winter of 1782 and the spring of 1783 were followed by the famous and well-publicized public Annonay demonstration on June 4, 1783. In July 1783, Etienne, Joseph's more practical and worldly brother, departed for Paris to present the world (that is, France) with the new invention. In Paris, their cause had been taken up by a physicist by the name of Jacques A. C. Charles, who admitted to have been inspired by the Annonay experiment, but suggested to use the newly discovered gas hydrogen for balloons. In August 28, 1783, the hydrogen Charlière was launched from the Champ de Mars. Eyed by an immense crowd, the balloon disappeared in the clouds and eventually crashed twelve miles north of Paris, where it was attacked by baffled peasants with pitchforks. On September 19, 1783, Etienne Montgolfier carried out his demonstration at Versailles, in front of a crowd of courtiers and nobles, with the King himself following the flight with field glasses. The balloon carried a sheep, a goat, and a rooster (who all survived the flight). Ballooning had become a rage, and the question of manned flight had become one of "when," not "whether."

The first person to actually fly was a man named Pilatre de Rozier, a scientifically inclined daredevil, who flew a number of test runs in October 1783, though the balloons remained tied to the ground. The first public demonstration of manned flight took place on November 21 in which Pilatre shared the honor with the Marquis d'Arlandes, an infantry major, using a Montgolfier-type hot air balloon. The two intrepid adventurers were the first ever to experience free human flight and lived to tell about it. On December 1, the first manned hydrogen balloon took off from the Tuileries, with half the population of Paris watching, journeying for about forty kilometers from Paris. Charles himself, with one of his engineers, made the flight. A year after Joseph Montgolfier's fateful contemplation of the siege of Gibraltar, human flight had become a reality.

The subsequent history of ballooning is of course of limited interest to economic historians. The balloon remained of interest for popular amusement and adventurers. New records were set and feats were achieved, which made for good newspaper copy and lit the popular imagination. Some attempts were made to utilize aerostatic devices in the French Revolutionary Wars, but the consensus is that these devices had more psychological than real long-lasting military effect. The balloon's economic significance never became great. It survived, largely as a direct consumption good for fairs and feasts, but it remained a rare and unusual species. Then why bother? In part, it is to underscore the point made here that the years 1750-1800 were exceptionally rich in macroinventions. In part, however, the interest in macroinventions does not need to be determined only by material criteria. From an evolutionary point of view, ballooning represented a major breakthrough. Whether or not it had a major impact on the construction of the heavier than air machines built 120 years later is still unclear. But maybe its ability to gather huge crowds, entertain them, and fill them with a feel of awe and wonderment at technology and its achievements is sufficient by itself. The same point was made recently by MacLeod (1988, p. 202).

IV. CONCLUSIONS

Macroinventions come in two variants. One, which may be termed radical macroinventions, is the totally new insight, constituting a genuine intellectual breakthrough into unchartered waters. Ballooning, chlorine bleaching, and gaslighting all clearly fall into that category, and it is this variant that corresponds most closely to Goldschmidt's idea of macromutations. A second type of macroinvention has equally important implications for the technological status quo, but has clear-cut parentage and precedence. Its importance derives from hybridization, and these inventions may be termed hybrid macroinventions. They are made by a novel arrangement and combination of well-known elements. The novelty is in the combination and the solution of the problems of making the different pieces compatible. The biological equivalent would be the creation of nectarines by crossing plums and peaches, or the "geep," a cross between a goat and a sheep currently envisioned by genetic engineers. The breastwheel clearly belongs to this type. Other inventions made during the Industrial Revolution belonging to this class are Crompton's Mule and Cort's puddling and rolling process.[39]

The distinction between micro- and macroinventions matters because they appear to follow different laws. Microinventions, overall, result from an intentional search for improvements, and are guided, at least to some extent, by the laws of supply and demand. Macroinventions are more difficult to understand, and seem to be governed by genius and luck as much as by anything else. Often they are based on some fortunate misunderstanding, in which an inventor stumbles on one thing while looking for another, or arrives at the right conclusion for the wrong reason. What we can infer, with some speculation, is what kind of societies tend to be conducive to the generation and successful completion of macroinventions.[40] To return to the Industrial Revolution, we can now reassess the debate trying to downgrade its importance in the economic development of the Western world. It is beyond question that technological change did not start with the Industrial Revolution. As noted above, the period between 1500 and 1700 was not a period of spectacular macroinventions, but one of steady progress on a variety of fronts, and it is well-described by gradual drift and slow but certain progress. These microinventions were running into diminishing returns by 1700. On a wide front of activities, from the iron industry to navigation to spinning, further gains were becoming increasingly difficult to attain. Had it not been for the burst of macroinventions we identify with the Industrial Revolution, progress would have all but ceased and technological stasis would have set in, as it did in China two centuries earlier. Without the macroinventions of the Industrial Revolution, we would have a world of almost perfectly designed stagecoaches and sailing ships. Once the macroinventions had taken place, a huge set of new opportunities for microinventions was opened, but those should not mislead us into falsely believing that they alone mattered.

Was the Industrial Revolution a solely British affair? It is striking that of the five inventions chosen, three were unquestionably French and another was a joint effort. Of course, the five cases chosen are not a random sample, and to some extent the small representation of British macroinventions is a result of my attempt to avoid the well-known cases of weaving, spinning, steam, and ironmaking. Yet it should drive home the point that the occurrence of macroinventions in a particular place was not a sufficient condition for the far-reaching economic and social changes we associate with the years of the Industrial Revolution in Britain. France was the birth place of chlorine bleaching, the Jacquard loom, as well as other inventions of comparable import.[41] Britain, however, was clearly more successful in adapting the new techniques to manufacturing. It is precisely at this stage that the difference between macro- and microinventions was crucial. Britain's strength was not in its originality, its inventiveness, or its ability to convert its science into new technology, though it had its share of all these.[42] Where its real advantage lay was in the incremental, the modifying, and the adaptive small invention. Von Tunzelmann (1981, p. 151) puts it well when he states that "technological Darwinism" (i.e., microinventions) allowed the British mechanic to scoff at French theorists. As the engineer John Farey remarked in 1829, "the prevailing talent of English and Scotch people is to apply new ideas to use and to bring such applications to perfection, but they do not imagine as much as foreigners."

It may thus well have been that Britain's advantage in technology stemmed from a second layer of creative talent. Right below the geniuses of Watt, Smeaton, and Trevithick came a large group of mostly unknown men who produced the microinventions which turned the great breakthroughs into cost-saving and growth. Such layers were far thinner in other countries, and it was there that Britain had its edge on the others. By the time of the Industrial Revolution, Britain had a class of skilled mechanical artisans unlike any other country. Alfred Marshall (1919, pp. 62-63) made the point well: "The British inventor had access to a great variety of highly skilled artisans . . . thus every experiment cost him less; and it was executed more quickly, and far more truly, than it could have been anywhere else." It is, perhaps, reasonable to characterize the difference between England and France as one of comparative advantage: whereas France had a comparative advantage in creating macroinventions, Britain's comparative advantage was in improvement and implementation. It is thus ironic but not paradoxical that the Industrial Revolution in Britain fed on technical breakthroughs many of which were imported.

In their enthusiasm to dethrone the myth of the Great Man, the technological incrementalists, from Gilfillan to Eric Jones, may have lost sight of the importance of the discontinuous and revolutionary inventions, which by themselves perhaps did not reduce costs that much, but which opened new opportunities for the microinventions that did the actual work. Without Berthollet there would have been no Tennant, and without LeBon no Clegg. The two types were thus more complements than substitutes. The incrementalists are like the classical Darwinians, believing that there are no leaps, all is gradual and smooth. Here, I hope, the notions of the punctuated equilibrium theorists may provide an unexpected rescue for the Industrial Revolution from those who would claim against all evidence that there was nothing new under the sun and that everything that happened between 1760 and 1830 had precedents.

ACKNOWLEDGMENTS

The original idea for this paper arose in a conversation with Charles Calomiris. His comments and those of Paul David, Sarah Maza, Cormac O'Grada, William N. Parker, and Harold Perkin on an earlier version are deeply appreciated.

NOTES

1. Hughes's example for the "breakthrough" school was H. De B. Gibbins (1895, p. 156).
2. The most eloquent example, perhaps, is Hartwell (1971, chapter 3).

3. For a survey on this point, see Mokyr (1985). Earlier statements like this abound; for example, Musson (1978, p. 149) flatly states that by 1850 Britain was not a very different economy than it had been in 1750. In one respect, this is patently false: Britain's population size had tripled in that period.

4. See Mokyr (1985, pp. 5-6). For a similar discussion of these issues, see McCloskey (1987, pp. 623-625).

5. Oswald Spengler wrote (1932) that the emergence of inventive man must have been sudden "like everything else that is decisive in world history," and explicitly renounced evolutionary accounts of history. "Such a slow, phlegmatic alteration is truly appropriate to the English nature," he added somewhat unfairly, "but it does not represent nature" (p. 36).

6. There is little in Usher (1954) to indicate where he stood on the issue. In his earlier book (1920), Usher seemed to side squarely with the gradualists. The crucial statement anticipates the argument made here: "The Industrial Revolution was thus a revolution in every sense of the word, except that of suddenness of transition. But the extraordinary character of the transformation must in itself be sufficient to convince one that such changes in the matters of daily life could not take place suddenly. Particular machines can be brought to public attention within a brief span of time . . . but the Industrial Revolution was more than any such formula could possibly imply" (p. 271).

7. Cf. Paulinyi's (1986) statement: "The perception [denying the revolutionary character of the innovations of the Industrial Revolution] bewildered me . . . because in no book on the history or philosophy of technology is it doubted that the technological changes which took place approximately between 1760 and 1860 introduced a new era" (p. 261).

8. Jones (1988) goes as far as saying that "industrial revolution studies rest on the assumption that the histories of industrialism and economic growth are the same thing" (p. 14). Although there are some scholars who subscribe to this interpretation, it seems a rather futile way of studying the problem.

9. Some of the material that follows appears in Mokyr (1990). For some elaboration see also Mokyr (1991).

10. In his words, individual phenotypes are "members of both biological and social species, including economic goods" (Boulding, 1981, p. 24) and mutations are any process by which the parameters of the system of ecological interaction change. The species, in Boulding's analogy, is the commodity, with production corresponding to birth and consumption to death (p. 33).

11. In a formidable new work, Foster (1987) develops a concept of *homo creativus*, as an alternative to *homo economicus*. In his work, evolutionary dynamics are made quite explicit, but his book is not directly concerned with Darwinian mechanisms of natural selection in models of long-term historical change. Another economist directly interested in evolutionary models is Guha (1981). In Guha's view, economic growth is not *analogous* to evolution but part of it, and technological and other exogenous changes lead to changes in society which adapts to changes in the environment in the same way species do. Society is thus the analogue of a species struggling for survival. Guha's view is somewhat similar to Ruse's Darwinian epistemology, which maintains that science develops because natural selection tends to encourage intelligence and creativity. This somewhat eccentric approach cannot explain very well widely observed long periods of scientific and economic stagnation, and will not be pursued here.

12. Some writers go beyond analogy and maintain that the basic underlying dynamic structures of change in natural and social phenomena, from physics to life forms to social change obey similar general laws of motion. For a statement in that spirit which seems complementary to the position taken here, see Laszlo (1987). These issues are dealt with in detail in Mokyr (1991).

13. Some of the seminal papers are Campbell (1987) and Toulmin (1967). For an application to science, see Hull (1988a) and Ruse (1986, chapter 2).

14. Gould (1987) remarks that "comparisons between biological evolution and cultural or technological change have done vastly more harm than good" and calls such analogies a common

intellectual trap (p. 18). Given the past record of Social Darwinism and Sociobiology, there is some justification for suspicion of facile comparisons. Yet, with a few exceptions, the analogy between technological change and biological evolution has not been pursued and it is my contention here that it is one of those analogies for which Gould has written elsewhere that "analogies are useful but limited; they may reflect common constraints but not common causes" (Gould, 1981, p.328).

15. As Hull (1988b, pp. 468-74) argues convincingly, this difference in no way invalidates the analogy.

16. Some other differences which allegedly invalidate the analogy are that biological evolution is very slow and irreversible, whereas cultural (and technological) change are rapid and bidirectional (Gould, 1981, p. 325). The velocity issue strikes me as specious, since there is no way to put the two processes on a similar scale. As far as reversibility is concerned, Gould is of course correct in claiming that cultural changes are not coded in our genes. But technological information was written down, in the medieval parchments of Friars Roger Bacon and Theophilus, the great Renaissance engineering manuals of Agricola and Ramelli, the technical papers of John Smeaton, and the thousands of modern journals of applied science and engineering. Technological progress can be reversed, and there are cases in which it has been; yet the preponderance of historical evidence is that it shares with biological evolution its irreversibility.

17. Gould (1980b, pp. 97-102), who points this out, adds caustically that "Darwin may have cribbed the idea of natural selection from economics, but it may still be right" (1980c, p. 68).

18. In fact, there is some dispute on whether evolution is progressive at all, and it is argued that precisely because scientific change is progressive that the analogy breaks down, and evolutionary epistemology is not an appropriate tool to study the history of science. The same objection applies, mutatis mutandis, to technology. Biological evolution is not teleological; it does not lead to any specific goal, unless one takes the view that the human race is the final objective of biological evolution. Technological progress, however, has led to something that we may term an "achievement": the liberation of a substantial portion of humanity from the shackles of subsistence.

19. An interesting feature of path dependency is inertia, resistance to change, which is observed in both biological evolution as it does in technological progress. Mayr (1988, p. 424) explains that variability is limited because "genes are tied together into balanced complexes that resist change." Successful speciation requires the breaking up of the previous cohesion and its replacement by new ones. Genetic cohesion is similar to what is known as technological interrelatedness (Frankel, 1955; David, 1975, pp. 245-46). Attempts to introduce one piece of modern machinery in an otherwise obsolete plant or a modern locomotive on outdated tracks and switches are usually doomed for reasons of "technological cohesiveness." The constraints this cohesion places on technological systems is less severe, because technological systems are far less complex than biological systems.

20. Young Saul, it will be recalled, went to search for asses and found a Kingdom (Samuel I, 9-10). The classic examples in technological history of this effect is William Perkin's discovery of aniline mauve while trying to make quinine and T.A. Edison's accidental invention of the phonograph while trying to perfect a device that recorded telegraphic impulses on paper discs.

21. Ruse (1986, p. 52) maintains that this part of the analogy fails as far as scientific progress is concerned because scientific theories rarely become extinct. Yet scientific theories are superseded, of course. One could argue over whether Galenian medicine and Phlogiston physics did not "vanish without a trace." De Bresson (1987) argues that, unlike biological species, no invention is lost and that technical knowledge is cumulative. But techniques are often totally abandoned or else preserved only in musea or enclaves (like the Amish, say). Distaff-and-spindle spinning, or using the Roman neckstrap horse harness are not less extinct than dinosaurs even if the information itself is retained.

22. See Gould (1980, p. 124). For a particularly scornful and misleading analysis of Goldschmidt's views, see Dawkins (1986 pp. 223-252).

23. Thus Leonardo's many radical and revolutionary technological ideas, many of which were potential macromutations, failed because the materials and workmen of the time were incapable of carrying them out.

24. As Usher (1920, p. 274) points out, it should not surprise us that the "subordinate" invention yields larger returns than the "principal" invention.

25. It is interesting to note that Spengler quoted the Dutch biologist Hugo De Vries, a convinced saltationist as the analogy of his historical theory.

26. The first major improvement in the oil lamp was made by the Frenchman Aimé Argand in 1782. Argand's lamp burned oil through a circular burner, using a flat wick in a perforated burner, with air rising from the center. The whole was covered by a glass chimney. Daumas (1979) points out that "this type of lamp could just as well have been invented one or two centuries earlier" (p. 461).

27. In a standard waterwheel, the water does not move relative to the buckets or vanes, whereas in the water turbine the power is derived from the fast-flowing water through the curved passages inside the turbine.

28. Much of what follows is indebted to the pathbreaking work of Reynolds (1983).

29. Cardwell (1972, p. 84) has maintained that Smeaton's empirical methodology was a good method of getting the best out of existing machines but that it usually does not lead to radically new improvements. The present example will prove an exception to that rule.

30. The traditional overshot wheel rotated in a direction opposite to the flow of the tail water, which made its operation difficult when the pond into which the water flowed was partially flooded. In those cases the only option was to construct an undershot wheel. The breast wheel rotated in the same direction of the flow of the water.

31. The exact date of Vaucanson's invention is in dispute. Usher (1954, p. 292) suggests 1747, Patterson (1957, p. 166) suggests 1745, but both Gille (1978, p. 718) and Payen and Pilisi (1979, p. 610) insist that it is a much later invention and date it to 1775.

32. Jacquard actually found, after a long search, a prototype of Vaucanson's machine which he repaired and reconstructed. It has thus been argued that he added little that was new, and that much of the extensive credit and honor he received was undeserved, a view nowadays rejected by most technological historians.

33. In his autobiography, Charles Babbage remarked that the analogy between his Analytical Engine and the Jacquard loom was "nearly perfect." A silk-woven portrait of Jacquard hung in Babbage's drawing room. See Babbage (1864, pp. 117, 164) and Hyman (1983, p. 166).

34. The use of diluted sulfuric acid was suggested in 1754 by the Scottish chemist Francis Home and reduced the time needed for bleaching by a substantial margin.

35. Watt wrote to Berthollet in February 1787 that he had mentioned his invention to the Prime Minister, and that Mr. Pitt realized that the invention was a matter of importance (Musson and Robinson, 1969, p. 265).

36. No less a chemist than Justus Von Liebig assessed that "for this new bleaching process [Tennant's bleaching powder] it would have scarcely been possible for cotton manufacturers in Great Britain to have attained the enormous extent it did in the nineteenth century" (cited by Clow and Clow, 1952, p. 194).

37. A grisly catalog of these attempts is provided in Hart (1985, pp. 196-208). Of these, the most famous is the flying monk, Eilmer of Malmesbury (White, 1978, pp. 59-73), who jumped off the top of a tower with wings attached to his arms (1010) and broke his legs. The Arab Al Djawari, at about the same time, was not so lucky and was killed after jumping off a mosque with wings made of wood. In the sixteenth century at least three documented flight attempts ended in death while others resulted in grievous injuries. In medieval China, manned kites were tried to defy gravity, but Marco Polo, for instance, related that the only aviators were fools or drunkards, as no one in his right mind would take the risk.

38. The inventing of the balloon provides us with a rare opportunity of observing how a macroinvention is born. In his old age, Joseph Montgolfier told a friend how the stimulus to produce the first balloon came about. He had been interested in the long siege of Gibraltar by the Spanish and French troops. As Gibraltar was impregnable by land and sea, Joseph wondered, could it not be taken by air? Looking at the smoke and small particles flying up in his grate, it struck him that a machine could be made to rise by the expansive power of heat on air. He took some cloth, stretched it around a frame, and heated the air with some paper. The primitive contraption promptly rose to the ceiling (Gillispie, 1983, p. 17).

39. This classification also holds for macroinventions made later in the nineteenth century. Thus, Perkin's aniline dye and Diesel's engine were clearly radical macroinventions, whereas the steamship, the typewriter, and the sewing machine are examples of hybrid macroinventions.

40. See Mokyr (1990) for a complete analysis.

41. Among the other macroinventions generated in France during and after the Industrial Revolution, we might mention the Leblanc soda process, Appert's invention of food canning, Fourneyron's water turbine, Robert's continuous paper machine, Thimonnier's sewing machine, and Philippe de Girard's wet process flax spinning.

42. The Swiss calico printer, Jean Ryhiner, remarked in 1766 that "for a thing to be perfect it must be invented in France and worked out in England."

REFERENCES

Arthur, B. (1989). "Competing Technologies and Lock-in by Historical Small Events: The Dynamics of Allocation under Increasing Returns." *Economic Journal*. 99(1): pp. 116-131.

Babbage, C. (1864). *Passages From the Life of a Philosopher*. London: Longman Green.

Bartley, W.W. (1987). "Philosophy of Biology versus Philosophy of Physics." Pp. 7-45 in *Evolutionary Epistemology, Rationality, and the Sociology of Knowledge*, edited by G. Radnitzky and W.W. Bartley, III. La Salle, IL: Open Court.

Basalla, G. (1988). *The Evolution of Technology*. Cambridge: Cambridge University Press.

Boulding, K. E. (1981). *Evolutionary Economics*. Beverly Hills/London: Sage.

Boyd, R. and Richerson, P.J. (1985). *Culture and the Evolutionary Process*. Chicago: University of Chicago Press.

de Bresson, C. (1987). "The Evolutionary Paradigm and the Economics of Technological Change." *Journal of Economic Issues*, 21(2): pp. 751-761.

Bush, G. L. (1982). "What Do We Really Know About Speciation?" Pp. 119-128 in *Perspectives on Evolution*, edited by Roger Milkman. Sunderland, MA: Sinauer.

Campbell, D. T. ([1960] 1987). "Blind Variation and Selective Retention in Creative Thought as in Other Knowledge Processes." Pp. 91-114 in *Evolutionary Epistemology, Rationality, and the Sociology of Knowledge*, edited by G. Radnitzky and W.W. Bartley, III. La Salle, IL: Open Court.

Cardwell, D.S.L. (1972). *Turning Points in Western Technology*. New York: Neale Watson.

Cavalli-Sforza, C. C. and Feldman, M. W. (1981). *Cultural Transmission and Evolution: A Quantitative Approach*. Princeton, NJ: Princeton University Press.

Clow, A. and Clow, N. L. (1952). *The Chemical Revolution*. London: The Batchworth Press.

Daumas, M. (1979). "Domestic Comfort and Sanitation," Pp. 453-472 in *A History of Technology and Invention*. Vol. 3: The Expansion of Mechanization. 1725-1860, edited by M. Daumas. New York: Crown.

David, P. A. (1975). *Technical Choice, Innovation, and Economic Growth*. Cambridge: Cambridge University Press.

David, P. A. (1987). "The Hero and the Herd in Technological History: Reflections on Thomas Edison and the 'Battle of the Systems'." Unpublished paper, Stanford University.

Dawkins, R. (1986). *The Blind Watchmaker*. New York: W.W. Norton.

Eldredge, N. (1985). *Time Frames: The Rethinking of Darwinian Evolution and the Theory of Punctuated Equilibria*. New York: Simon and Schuster.

Elton, A. (1958). "Gas for Light and Heat." Pp. 258-276 in *A History of Technology*, Vol. 4: *The Industrial Revolution, 1750-1850*, edited by Charles Singer et al. London: Oxford University Press.

Foster, J. (1987). *Evolutionary Macroeconomics*. London: Allen and Unwin.

Frankel, M. (1955). "Obsolescence and Technological Change." *American Economic Review*, 45(2): 298-319.

Gibbins, H. deB. (1895). *The Industrial History of England*. London: Methuen.

Gille, B. (1978). *Histoire des Techniques: Technique et Civilisations, Technique et Sciences*. Paris: Editions Gallimard.

Gillispie, C. (1983). *The Montgolfier Brothers and the Invention of Aviation*, Princeton, NJ: Princeton University Press.

Goldschmidt, R. B. ([1940] 1982). *The Material Basis of Evolution*. New Haven, CT: Yale University Press.

Gould, S. J. (1980a). "Is a New and General Theory of Evolution Emerging?" *Paleobiology*, 6(1): 119-30.

Gould, S. J. (1980b). *Ever Since Darwin*. New York: W.W. Norton.

Gould, S. J. (1980c). *The Panda's Thumb*. New York: W.W. Norton.

Gould, S. J. (1981). *The Mismeasurement of Man*. New York: W.W. Norton.

Gould, S. J. (1982a). "Darwinism and the Expansion of Evolutionary Theory." *Science*, 216(23): 380-387.

Gould, S. J. (1982b). "The Meaning of Punctuated Equilibrium and its Role in Validating a Hierarchical Approach to Macroevolution." Pp. 83-104 in *Perspectives on Evolution*, edited by R. Milkman. Sunderland, MA: Sinauer.

Gould, S. J. (1982c). "The Uses of Heresy." In *The Material Basis of Evolution*, by R.B. Goldschmidt. New Haven, CT: Yale University Press.

Gould, S. J. (1987). "The Panda's Thumb of Technology." *Natural History*, 1: 14-23.

Guha, A. (1981). *An Evolutionary View of Economic Growth*. Oxford: The Clarendon Press.

Hart, C. (1985). *The Prehistory of Flight*. Berkeley: University of California Press.

Hartwell, R.M. (1971), *The Industrial Revolution and Economic Growth*. London: Methuen.

Hills, R. L. (1979). "Hargreaves, Arkwright and Crompton: Why Three Inventors?" *Textile History*, 10: 114-126.

Hindle, B. (1981). *Emulation and Invention*. New York: New York University Press.

Holmyard, E.J. (1958). "The Chemical Industry: Developments in Chemical Theory and Practice." Pp. 214-229 in *A History of Technology, Vol. 4: The Industrial Revolution, 1750-1850*, edited by C. Singer et al. London: Oxford University Press.

Hughes, J.R.T. (1970), *Industrialization and Economic History: Theses and Conjectures*. New York: McGraw-Hill.

Hull, D.L. (1988a). "A Mechanism and its Metaphysics: An Evolutionary Account of the Social and Conceptual Development of Science." *Biology and Philosophy*, 3: 123-155.

Hull, D.L. (1988b). *Science as a Progress*. Chicago: University of Chicago Press.

Hyman, A. (1982). *Charles Babbage: Pioneer of the Computer*. Princeton, NJ: Princeton University Press.

Jones, E.L. (1981). *The European Miracle*. Cambridge: Cambridge University Press.

Jones, E.L. (1988). *Growth Recurring: Economic Change in World History*. Oxford: Oxford University Press.

Landes, D. (1969). *The Unbound Prometheus*. Cambridge: Cambridge University Press.

Laszlo, E. (1987). *Evolution: The Grand Synthesis*. Boston: New Science Library.

Lee, C.H. (1986). *The British Economy Since 1700*. Cambridge, Cambridge University Press.

Lewontin, R. C. (1982). *Human Diversity*. New York: Scientific American Books.
MacLeod, C. (1988). *Inventing the Industrial Revolution*. Cambridge: Cambridge University Press.
Marshall, A. (1919). *Industry and Trade*. London: Macmillan.
Mayr, E. (1970). *Population, Species, and Evolution*. Cambridge, MA: Belknap Press.
Mayr, E. (1988), *Toward a New Philosophy of Biology*. Cambridge, MA: Belknap Press.
McCloskey, D. N. (1987). "Continuity in Economic History." Pp. 623-625 in *Palgrave Dictionary of Economics*, Vol. I. London: Macmillan.
Mokyr, J. (Ed.). (1985). *The Economics of the Industrial Revolution*. Totowa, NJ: Rowman and Allanheld.
Mokyr, J. (1990). *The Lever of Riches: An Economic History of Technological Change*. New York: Oxford University Press.
Mokyr, J. (1991). "Evolutionary Biology, Technological Change, and Economic History," *Bulletin of Economic Research*, forthcoming.
Musson, A.E., and Robinson, E. (1969). *Science and Technology in the Industrial Revolution*. Manchester: Manchester University Press.
Nelson, R.R. and Winter, S. (1982). *An Evolutionary Theory of Economic Change*. Cambridge: Belknap Press.
Pacey, A. (1975). *The Maze of Ingenuity: Ideas and Idealism in the Development of Technology*. New York: Holmes and Meier.
Patterson, R. (1957). "Spinning and Weaving." Pp. 151-180 in *A History of Technology, Vol. 3: From the Renaissance to the Industrial Revolution, 1500-1750*, edited by C. Singer et al. London: Oxford University Press.
Paulinyi, A. (1986). "Revolution and Technology." In *Revolution in History*, edited by R. Porter and M. Teich. Cambridge: Cambridge University Press.
Payen, J. and Pilisi, J. (1979). "Weaving and Mechanical Finishing." Pp. 599-618 in *A History of Technology and Invention, Vol. 3: The Expansion of Mechanization, 1725-1860*, edited by M. Daumas. New York: Crown.
Reti, L. (1969). "Leonardo Da Vinci the Technologist: The Problem of Prime Movers." Pp. 67-100 in *Leonardo's Legacy: An International Symposium*, edited by C.D. O'Malley. Berkeley: University of California Press.
Reynolds, T. S. (1983). *Stronger Than a Hundred Men: A History of the Vertical Water Wheel*. Baltimore: The Johns Hopkins University Press.
Rosenberg, N. (1976). *Perspectives on Technology*. Cambridge: Cambridge University Press.
Rosenberg, N. (1982). *Inside the Black Box: Technology and Economics*. Cambridge: Cambridge University Press.
Rosenberg, N. and Vincenti, W. G. (1978). *The Britannia Bridge: The Generation and Diffusion of Technological Knowledge*. Cambridge, MA: MIT Press.
Rothstein, N. (1977). "The Introduction of the Jacquard Loom to Great Britain." Pp. 281-290 in *Studies in Textile History*, edited by V. Gervers. Toronto: Royal Ontario Museum.
Ruse, M. (1986). *Taking Darwin Seriously*. Oxford: Basil Blackwell.
Sahal, D. (1981). *Patterns of Technological Innovation*. Reading, MA: Addison-Wesley.
Spengler, O. (1932). *Man and Technics*. London: Allen & Unwin.
Toulmin, S. E. (1967). "The Evolutionary Development of Natural Science." *American Scientist*, 55(4): 456-471.
Usher, A. P. (1920). *An Introduction to the Industrial History of England*. Boston: Houghton Mifflin.
Usher, A. P. (1954). *A History of Mechanical Inventions*. Cambridge, MA: Harvard University Press.
Von Tunzelmann, G.N. (1978). *Steam Power and British Industrialization to 1860*. Oxford: Oxford University Press.

Von Tunzelmann, G.N. (1981). "Technical Progress during the Industrial Revolution." Pp. 143-163 in *The Economic History of Britain Since 1700*, Vol. 1, edited by R. Floud and D. N. McCloskey.

White, L. (1978). *Medieval Religion and Technology*. Berkeley: University of California Press.

Wrigley, E.A. (1987). *People, Cities and Wealth*. Oxford: Basil Blackwell.

INSTITUTIONAL INHERITANCE AND EARLY AMERICAN INDUSTRIALIZATION: AN ESSAY IN HONOR OF J.R.T. HUGHES

Rick Szostak

Jonathan Hughes has in many works (esp. 1977) emphasized the continuity between the pre- and post-Revolutionary legal structures in America. As Chief Justice Waite said in 1877, independence had "changed the form but not the substance" of government. (Hughes, 1977, p. 4). The institutional structure in which the early American economy operated was largely inherited from the English. As Hughes has noted, this raises the interesting question of to what degree America's success in terms of economic development was due to her having previously been an English colonial possession.

In earlier works, I have shown that England's success in being the first nation to have an Industrial Revolution was in large part due to its superiority in internal transport (Szostak, 1985, 1989). The possession of a network of both waterways and all-weather roads was not sufficient for industrialization to occur, but was necessary; it both allowed and induced the creation of factories and an increase in the rate of technological innovation. The reason, in turn, why England possessed a superior system of transport in the mid-eighteenth century, was

Research in Economic History, Suppl. 6, pages 287-308.

ISBN: 1-55938-150-7.

that while geographical advantage may have played some part England possessed a superior institutional structure. Private companies were able to get Acts of Parliament passed which gave them two important rights: the right to expropriate land (with compensation) and the right to charge tolls. This flexible framework proved much more successful than the attempts of, for example, the French government, to centrally finance and administer transport improvements.

The previous paragraphs, taken together, raise two interesting questions about American development. First, were transport improvements encouraged by the institutional framework in the United States as they had been in England? Second, if so, did they have a similar impact on economic development? Answers to these questions will provide much insight into the broader question of to what degree America's economic success during the 19th century was due to her institutional inheritance from England. If the United States were a former French or Spanish colony, would she have fared so well?

The first section discusses the degree to which early American transport developments resulted from the same institutions which had allowed England to construct at an earlier date the best transport system in the world. English industrialization relied on turnpikes and water transport. The earliest stages of industrialization in America also predate the railway. Therefore, this paper will concentrate on turnpikes, river improvements, and canals. The second section discusses the role played by these transport improvements in allowing and inducing America to industrialize. While the role of transport in economic development has been discussed before, a number of causal links between the two have received little attention in the literature. Besides, the literature on American transport has eschewed comparison with the experience of other countries. The similarities between English and American experience will be highlighted throughout this paper. The intention is to synthesize and re-evaluate the existing literature, rather than to provide dramatic new evidence.

It should be recognized at the outset that the United States possessed no peculiar geographic advantages which made it especially susceptible to transport improvement. Indeed, relative to Europe, the United States provided a forbidding landscape, especially for canal construction. As Goodrich (1961) noted, "America was a land of greater distances, higher mountains, severer climate, and much sparser population" (p. 4). Providing the new nation with a network of both allweather roads and navigable waterways would be no simple task.

I. ENGLISH INSTITUTIONS AND AMERICAN TRANSPORTATION

The naive view of transport improvements is that they are called forth as needed. Once trade has risen to a level to justify the expenditure, turnpikes or canals are naturally constructed. Thus, transport itself plays no causal role in development. Simple economic theory tells us otherwise. Transport improvements create many benefits which can not be captured by those who invest in them. Thus, the market, left to its own devices, would tend to undersupply transport services. Capital market imperfections or legal restrictions on organizational forms may severely limit the ability to raise the funds necessary (we must remember that investments in transport are among the largest investments in early nineteenth-century America). Roads and canals not only require huge sums of money but the purchase of land along the route to be followed. Every landowner along the route has the incentive to charge the promoters the full value of the route for his piece of property, for each section is essential to the whole. Without some means of forced sale, many worthwhile projects will perish in the face of intransigent landowners. In a land of new settlement a further problem arises; it may be socially desirable to build transport links into unsettled land to induce settlement. Projects of this sort tend not to interest private investors, for returns in the first years are quite low, and thus will generally require public funds.

None of these problems are either new or insurmountable. Institutions can be created which either alleviate or solve each problem; allow much of the gain from improvement to be captured by the investors, allow the requisite capital to be raised (perhaps with government subsidy), and allow the expropriation of land. In the long run, the constant pressure of economic forces will generally result in institutional change. A delay of decades or centuries in institutional response is quite possible, however, and often observed. Differences in the rate of institutional response can explain the differential development of countries in similar circumstances.

A perusal of Jackman (1916), or other standard works on English transport, show that there were centuries of slow legal change which resulted in the institutional structure necessary for the turnpike, river improvement and canal booms of the late seventeenth and eighteenth centuries. The countries of continental Europe, scurrying to catch up to England, only created successful institutions well into the nineteenth century. If the United States had been a former colony of any other nation, it would have had to create an institutional structure conducive to transport improvement. As a former colony of Britain, and one which had maintained colonial institutions, it had the necessary framework ready at hand when its citizens turned their attention to the state of the roads and waterways in the late eighteenth century. A potential delay of decades or more was thus avoided.

Transport improvements were so costly that no individual could be expected to finance them. The first essential institution, then, was the corporation. As in England, the corporate form in the United States was rare, bestowed only by legislative act, until well into the nineteenth century. Davis and North (1972) noted that the costs of incorporation were so high at the time that very few enterprises outside of transport attempted incorporation. A logical extension of this argument would be that if incorporation had been even more difficult, many of the transport projects we see would not have been undertaken. The corporate form had first been provided in England to municipal authorities for the performance of public works. Its application to inter-city transport was not without difficulty, but by the end of the seventeenth century turnpike and river improvement acts had become fairly standard. While the cost of obtaining an Act of Parliament was often a large portion of the capital invested, it was much easier for transport projects to be incorporated than for other enterprises. In the United States, the acts creating turnpikes, for example, from the beginning have a great uniformity, and it is easier for such enterprises to gain incorporation than for others.

The second necessity was the power of eminent domain. Not all governments were equally willing to sanction the expropriation of land. The Ancien Regime government in France, for example, proved quite reluctant to take land from unwilling members of the aristocracy. The English government, supposed by some to be the ultimate defender of private property rights in the eighteenth century, proved quite willing to exercise its power of eminent domain. The standard Acts establishing turnpike trusts bestowed the rights of expropriation upon these private bodies. Methods of establishing appropriate compensation were similar in all acts, and these appear to have favored the landowners (see Ward, 1974). Hughes (1983, pp. 144-145) noted that American states and municipalities exercised the right of eminent domain right from Independence. Not surprisingly, when states began creating corporations to build roads and waterways, they followed English tradition and bestowed this right on them.

Turnpikes

Colonial America had, like an earlier England, relied on locally organized statute (forced) labor to construct and maintain roads. As with England, any expansion in interregional trade must quickly show the disadvantages of such a system. Untrained and unmotivated, and only available a few specified days per year, forced labour was unequal to the task of maintaining roads in a state to support year-round wheeled traffic. To spare the United States from the high cost of packhorse transit,[1] a means had to be developed for raising funds to properly care for the main roads. The English solution was the turnpike trust. From their start in the late seventeenth century, these trusts had provided England with a network of all-weather roads by the mid-eighteenth century (see Pawson, 1977). The typical trust involved subscriptions from all men of substance in the locality. Funds were borrowed to finance construction (or improvement of the existing roadway). Payment of the interest on the sum borrowed, as well as funds for maintenance, were provided by tolls. The trusts almost never were a good financial investment. However, over a period of decades in England, men of money continued to combine in support of these local improvements.

The American experience is virtually identical. The inappropriateness of statute labor to the main roads was recognized soon after independence (though statute labor was maintained in some localities till the nineteenth century). "Apparently Great Britain had shown the way through the dilemma by a series of turnpike acts" (Kirkland, p. 37). The nomenclature utilized in the United States was slightly different; they were styled private companies rather than trusts. As we shall see, the essential fact that they were not expected to make money remained unchanged. Massachusetts and Maine passed special laws governing pikes, but all other states created each company separately. "In each case the English turnpike acts, with the reservation already noted, set the pattern of details" (Kirkland, p. 41).

These companies provided an interesting partial solution to the problems discussed earlier. Rights of incorporation and expropriation of land were essential. Moreover, the tolls allowed a local company to expropriate some of the benefits bestowed upon outsiders.[2] The subscription of all local men of substance meant that some of the gains these would receive from appreciation in land values or increased trade flows were also captured. Klein (1987) noted that it must have been obvious to investors from very early on that turnpikes would provide an extremely low return. He then proceeds to analyze the interesting question of why the free rider problem did not prevent the private provision of this public good. Social pressure usually acted to ensure that enough of those who stood to gain participated. In first England, and then the United States, the much maligned turnpike managed to raise sufficient funds from those who stood to benefit to build much improved roads.[3] The poor profitability of turnpikes is often interpreted as a sign of their limited economic importance. Rather, it should be seen as a reflection of an imaginative institutional solution to the public goods problem.

The other potential solution is government finance. Hughes (1977, p. 68) described turnpikes as a mixture of public and private finance. However, the role played by governments was quite limited. While Pennsylvania gave some support to turnpikes, and some southern states may have, the turnpikes of Maryland, New York, New Jersey, and New England were almost entirely privately financed (Klein, 1987, p. 2). The emphasis on private investment in turnpikes was to characterize much of future American transport history (Fishlow, p. 472). The investment that fledgling state governments undertook in canals in the 1820s and later had disastrous effects on their credit rating. Total investment in turnpikes was four times total investment in canals. It would seem impossible for states to have financed this much greater investment decades before the canal boom of the 1820s. This is especially so given the appropriability problem; canals often earned decent returns but turnpikes almost never did.

The lack of funds among state governments of the time was only one reason why government finance could not solve the public goods problem. The federal government did toy with a national transport plan in the first decades of independence but eventually decided it was unconstitutional. This may have been a blessing. The prototypical national transport organization was that of France. Throughout the eighteenth century, the French government lavished vast sums on a national system of roads. Bureaucratic inefficiency and a desire for monuments meant that France ended up with a handful of very good roads (which deteriorated quickly through lack of maintenance) and a lot of roads unsuitable to wagons. In the nineteenth century, the French government slowly decentralized decision making. It would not have a truly national road network until the middle of the century. The local decision making inherent in turnpikes proved to be far superior at maintaining roads in the eighteenth and early nineteenth centuries.

River Improvements

T.S. Willan (1964) has shown that a number of relatively unheralded river improvement companies possessing virtually the same form as turnpike trusts had, in the century before 1750, doubled the length of navigable waterway in England. The much heralded canal boom of the 1750s in England should be viewed as the conclusion to over a century of effort. English canal companies joined rivers only recently made navigable, were organized along similar lines to the river improvement companies, and employed no new technology.

The United States has not produced a T.S. Willan. While canals have their chroniclers, and even lowly turnpikes have received the attention of historians, river improvements have been virtually ignored. Yet, there clearly were some important projects. The late eighteenth century saw considerable improvement to the Merrimack and Connecticut Rivers. At the turn of the century the Connecticut River company recouped a $45,000 expenditure through tolls (Kirkland, 1948, p. 67). After the improvements to the Merrimack, the lower valley around Lowell industrialized, and the river carried increased amounts of raw material in one direction and finished goods in the other (pp. 64-65). The James River also saw improvement (Taylor, p. 42). Between 1815 and 1860, even the federal government devoted six million dollars to river improvements in various states.[4] Fishlow has noted that the length of navigable American rivers was six times that of canals at the end of the canal era (p. 485). At the present time, we do not know how much of this river mileage was natural and how much was due to improvement. European experience should tell us that the problems of rocks, trees, silt, flood, excess current,[5] winding course, and so forth affected most rivers. We know that river improvements were essential to the development of some American rivers. We must suspect that they were a much more common phenomenon.

Canals

It is unnecessary to describe in detail the canal booms of either England or the United States. Economic historians are much more familiar with the Bridgwater or Erie Canals than with turnpike or river projects. Again, the form of the Acts of state legislatures look similar to the previous Acts of the English Parliament. They created corporations with the right of eminent domain and the right to charge tolls. However, with canals there is an important difference for there was a much greater degree of public finance in the United States. The British government had financed some road and canal construction, mostly for defence purposes in Scotland, but this was a negligible proportion of total investment. In the United States, Goodrich (1961, p. 6) calculated that just over one-fourth of canal finance before the Civil War was private. This difference has led Hughes (1977, p. 67) to argue that transport development in nineteenth-century America followed a colonial rather than English model.[6] We will in what follows show that the difference is not as great as it might first appear, and explain why U.S. behavior deviated from English behavior.

Despite many schemes, the United States possessed only 100 miles of canals in 1816. These did not have a record of success to attract further investment in a capital-poor country (Taylor, p. 32). As with England 70 years earlier, the United States in the 1820s needed one successful canal project to start a canal boom. This example was provided by the Erie canal, financed by the state of New York. The Erie provided not only an example of a successful canal but of the potential of state-financed canals (Cramner, p. 158). It was followed by a number of canal projects. Pennsylvania devoted huge sums to ridiculous projects aimed at competing with the Erie. Ohio built some good and some poor politically-inspired canals; Indiana's record was much worse (Taylor, p. 47).

State ownership was not the whole story, though. Goodrich has noted that there were a few small private canals and a number of mixed enterprises.[7] The Delaware and Raritan, which linked Philadelphia and New York, was private. A number of canals which facilitated the transport of east Pennsylvania coal to Philadelphia and New York were privately financed. Not surprisingly, these private canals generally provided a respectable private rate of return. Mixed enterprises fare less well. It is among the entirely state-financed canals that the greatest horror stories lie. Goodrich has calculated that at least 20 percent of canal finance was devoted to projects for which the costs exceeded the benefits to society. If we were to limit our attention only to socially beneficial projects, then, the role of private investment would be significantly greater than 25 percent. Moreover, we should recognize that government finance did not and could not come from the paltry tax revenues of the time. The purchase of bonds, mostly by foreigners, was in part due to the guarantee of payment by the states, and partly due to a recognition by private investors of the potential of canal investment.

Some of the public involvement was simply due to the (often wasteful) competition between state governments. Capital market limitations also contributed (Taylor, p. 48). However, there was an overriding economic reason for greater government involvement in the United States. The United States was a new land with a low population density.[8] Many of the canal projects were "built before demand." That there were two types of canals was recognized at the time; revenue canals could be built by either government or private hands; developmental canals would require government finance (Cramner, p. 157). In the mixed enterprises, government involvement was often just enough to entice private investors. The role of government, rather than being a break with the past, should be seen as an adaptation of English institutions to the needs of the new world.

While there were many poor decisions in the history of canal construction, the important question is one of why the United States was successful where so many other countries failed (Goodrich, p. 255).[9] France had devoted huge sums to canal projects but did not have the network of waterways we see in the United States. The mixed nature of many projects in the United States must have served to protect them to a great extent from bureaucratic meddling. This can only be part of the answer.

An element of great importance to American success was that it was the state rather than federal government that played the active role. This is a digression from our main theme but a topic worthy of discussion. I have maintained elsewhere (Szostak, 1985) that the difference between French and English approaches to transport improvement is better seen as a difference between centralized and decentralized decision making than as public versus private. It was the ability of local people in England to push for a particular project which suited local needs, and to then supervise construction and maintenance, which led to English superiority. In the United States, while the role of the states led to some wasteful competition (especially in Pennsylvania), it provided a couple of advantages. First, an omnipotent national government could have delayed such hefty expenditures for budgetary reasons, but individual states faced the spectra of losing the race if they did not move quickly. Given that social benefits were high on many of these projects, the net effect was positive. Many of the projects for which social returns were less than cost were the feeder lines built in New York, Pennsylvania, and Ohio to gain the political support necessary to build the main lines (see Fishlow, 1971, p. 480). If a national plan had been necessary, political reality would have required much expenditure in states which did not otherwise build canals.[10] There were serious errors in the selection, planning, and execution of the state canals. Such errors could only have been larger if distant federal politicians and bureaucrats made the decisions.[11] Within the individual states, private interests were better able to influence the decisions of public enterprise.

II. THE EFFECTS OF TRANSPORT IMPROVEMENTS IN EARLY NINETEENTH-CENTURY AMERICA

Once we recognize that countries that are similar in terms of major economic indicators can have widely different levels of success in terms of transport development, we must recognize that transport improvements can play an important dynamic role in stimulating development. Transport gets a peculiar treatment in the literature. Nearly all textbooks on American economic history have a chapter on transport. Yet when the determinants of such matters as technological change or the emergence of factories are discussed, transport disappears from the picture. Fishlow's (1971) attitude is indicative. He recognizes that the role of transport is in a simple sense enormous. "The cumulative contribution made by the transition from the common road through to the railroad is so large and so obvious as to defy accurate calculation" (p. 514).[12] Later, however, he maintains that the cost savings from the transport improvements he discussed had no great impact on manufacturing as transport costs were a small part of the final price (p. 528).

This section describes how improvement to road and water transport affected the improvements in technology and organization in early nineteenth-century America.[13] The European experience will be used to see if any of the causal links observed there appear in the United States. The links we will be concerned with are not those which have been analyzed in the usual social savings calculations. While these calculations were a necessary antidote to overly romanticized views of the impact of railways, it must be remembered that they could not and did not estimate all the possible effects of transport improvements. Fishlow (1971), after revising upwards Fogel's estimate of the social savings of railways, writes: "Such direct benefits are but one aspect, albeit the most easily quantifiable, of the consequences of the 19th century transport revolution" (p. 520). He speaks of effects on location (regional specialization), migration, technological dissemination, and the achievement of economies of scale and division of labor. "The magnitude of such indirect effects is virtually impossible to calculate in a dynamic process in which transport innovation was but one important element. Nevertheless, they should not be forgotten" (p. 527). The desire of new economic historians to measure the importance of economic relations wherever possible is laudable and necessary. However, the cost is too high if it means we ignore that which is difficult to quantify. Lebergott (1984) correctly noted that the important decisions regarding industrialization were made by a handful (hundreds) of entrepreneurs and inventors. The impact on them of any variable may be lost in national averages. The key to understanding industrialization is to understand what caused this "handful" of people to act in new and different ways.[14]

It would be especially ironic if the research on railways had the effect of turning the interest of economic historians away from transport, for what it should have done was highlight just how good a job turnpikes, rivers, and canals could do. Yet these earlier innovations have received relatively little attention. Fishlow (1971) suspects that most turnpikes may not have repaid the cost of construction (p. 517). He is willing to credit canals with a higher social return on average than railways, but still feels that most of the canals may not have been socially profitable (p. 518). This accords with Ransom's earlier conclusions.[15] One reason (beyond those previously discussed) for the low level of these estimates is that they are based on the role of these innovations in a world being taken over by railways. The concern here is only with how they compared with what existed before. In the case of turnpikes, the view is also colored by the low private return. Having already recognized that these projects were not expected by investors to have a high private rate of return, we should have a more charitable view of their impact.[16]

It is also important to realize that turnpikes were not just a poor substitute for water transport due to higher cost per ton mile, but were rather an important complement. Railways for the first time gave the world a mode of transport suited to both the inexpensive transport of low-value goods and the speedy carriage of high-value goods. Before the railways, water transport served the needs of bulky goods, while roads were necessary for the speedy carriage of goods with a higher value/bulk ratio, including most finished goods, as well as the transmission of people and information.[17] It is, therefore, a mistake to deprecate the achievement of roads simply because cost per ton mile is higher, for roads served different segments of the market from water transport. This is a point long recognized by transport historians but overlooked by many economic historians.[18]

Fishlow (1971) attributes the "failure" of turnpikes to the slight cost advantage they possessed over common roads (p. 474). Davis et al. (1969) felt that pikes could not succeed because their costs were too high to compete with water or encourage new trade (pp. 277-278). Yet, even Fishlow recognizes a drop in transport cost of 50 percent (and the gain from replacing packhorses with wagons could be even greater). While short-distance traffic might choose toll-free roads, longer distance traffic did find it advantageous to use pikes (pp. 474-475). Thousands of investors would not choose to lose money over a period of decades on projects which did not produce significant social benefits. Taylor (1951) speaks of significant expansion in domestic trade from at least the 1820s and attributes much of this to transport improvement (p. 173). If pikes could cut costs by half, and river and canal improvements by even more,[19] this is not an untenable conclusion.

Methods of Distribution

Our understanding of industrialization has been limited by our overconcentration on production alone, with little attention paid to associated activities such as supervision, inventory-holding, and distribution. The entrepreneurs who would make the important decisions were profit-maximizers, and their decisions were affected by a variety of influences. In England, the completion of a network of turnpike roads resulted in the creation of a system of regular professional carrier services. This in turn allowed the replacement of face-to-face sales with sale by catalogue and sample. This not only allowed the entrepreneur to devote his attention to production but required the production of a standardized good. In the United States, as well, we see the emergence of regular professional carrier routes in the early nineteenth century.[20] While regular and professional carrying is possible even when packhorses must be relied on, its occurrence in such situations was rare. The large drop in cost associated with roads suitable to year-round wagon utilization induced a great increase in such services.

Chandler (1977) described in detail how changes in distribution could influence production decisions. Believing in the revolutionary role of the railroad, he does not recognize that changes in distribution had begun earlier with turnpikes. He speaks of the competition wholesalers received from travelling salesmen in the 1840s (p. 217). Yet travelling salesmen had always been an important part of the American scene (Taylor, 1951, p. 13; Hughes, 1977, p. 77). Their importance increases in the early part of the century as producers cease to make face-to-face sales.[22] Chandler (1977) speaks of local peddlers being replaced by stores well into the railway era (p. 217). However, Taylor (1951) notes perceptively that the spread of the local retail store predates the rise of the factory (p. 216).

Travelling salesmen and local retail stores both mean the same thing. Producers no longer sell their goods directly to consumers.[23] Sale by sample and catalogue must begin. Standardized goods must be produced. It is recognized in the literature that the new technology which came to characterize American manufacturing could not have come into place without a large market for standardized goods (Rosenberg, 1971), but we have a poor understanding of how that situation emerged. Rosenberg went so far as to attribute the new technology to a difference in tastes, the last refuge of an economist looking for an explanation (p. 247). Only rarely has the role of distribution in fostering new technology been recognized, as in Hounshell's perceptive discussion of the clock industry. "The national market created or tapped by the Yankee peddlar system cannot be overlooked as an important supporting factor in the mechanized, quantity production of wooden clocks" (Hounshell, 1984, p. 54). How the timing of changes in distribution may have been crucial to the development of the American system of manufactures will be discussed later in this paper.

Market Size

The United States is a large nation, and many have noted the various advantages which sprang from potential access to large markets and numerous raw materials.[24] Not all large nations have succeeded as well as the United States, however. The United States was the first country of continental proportions to develop, and this was largely a result of transport improvements (Fishlow, 1971 p. 468). The nineteenth-century American market was dominated by rural households (Hughes, 1983, p. 164). American farmers were wealthy by world standards, but this potential could only be tapped as transport links were built. In England, market widening was not essential for factory production in most industries, as large markets already supported large firms. In a new land like the United States, transport improvements could play a vital role by connecting existing farmers with industry and opening up vast new areas for agricultural exploitation.[25]

America became much more self-sufficient in manufactured goods, at the expense of English industry, during the nineteenth century. A survey of American economic history texts yields a number of different explanations for this. While all may possess a grain of truth, they all fall far short of providing us with the last word on this course of events. The role of artificial protection is often cited. For example, Lebergott (1984 p. 125) has argued that the trade disruption surrounding the War of 1812 was the seminal event, providing American producers with a few years freedom from foreign competition. If we are to accept this argument, we must forego the traditional opposition of the economist to tariffs. We must admit that the static advantage of free trade can be severely outweighed by the dynamic advantages of protectionism. Perhaps in the absence of tariffs (or significant trans-oceanic transport costs, which amount to the same thing), America would not have industrialized. Or, perhaps there were advantages as yet imperfectly delineated by historians which would have made of America an industrial giant even if placed in direct competition with Europe from the beginning. The degree of protection (natural plus tariff), if any, necessary for American industry to get on its feet is an interesting historical question the study of which could shed light on the proper role for trade policy in development. In any case, American industry soon "grew up." One crucial factor in the success of American industry was the transport network discussed above. Before the development of this network, the United States could be characterized as a series of coastal enclaves tied to each other and Europe through shipping. Producers in one enclave would have only a very slight advantage over European producers in exporting to other enclaves. With road and water improvements, American manufacturers gained access to a large internal market. They were thus able to achieve any possible economies of scale. No other land of new settlement could boast such a network. Only in the United States had a large national market emerged. Integration of the American economy was the key which allowed American industry to move from cottages to small factories, and the substantial drop in cost involved allowed it then to compete with English imports.[26]

Were producers being exposed to significantly wider markets? If so, we would expect to see increasing regional specialization as producers were able to enter markets previously dominated by inefficient local production. On a grand scale, the work of North and Davis (1972, p. B5), Ransom (1976), Taylor (1951, p. 169), and others all testify to the role played by transport improvements in causing specialization to occur between the east and midwest. By logical extension, those regions of the eastern United States most suited to industry must have been winning out over those areas less suited.[27]

Speed

One of the disadvantages of factory production is that the investment in fixed capital and need for a regular work force make steady operation a requirement and thus necessitate the holding of inventories.[28] This disadvantage can be mitigated by transport improvements; optimal inventory size decreases as the reliability of access to materials improves. The emergence of reliable and trustworthy professional carriers with regular schedules will be very helpful here. Another factor which will encourage factory production is an increase in the speed of transport. Among other things, this will allow quick re-ordering of supplies when shortages appear. The English experience of great drops in travel times after turnpikes are introduced is duplicated in America. The trip from Boston to New York took over 6 days in 1784, 74 hours in 1800, and only 33 hours in 1833 (Taylor, 1951, p. 142; Kirkland, 1948, p. 56). Chandler has emphasized how transport improvements can affect production processes via the concept of throughput. It is important to recognize that major gains in both speed and reliability of transport had taken place decades before the railway.

Information Flows

It is obvious both that transport improvements must encourage information flows, and that these in turn must encourage the adoption of new methods of organization and technology. The difficulty of measuring information flows should not dissuade us from discussing them. Information is carried either by the written word or through personal contact. In England, the post office quickly responded to better roads by expanding service. While Taylor (1951) criticized the U.S. Post Office for only slowly improving speed and service, due largely to the reticence of Congress (pp. 149-150), the number of post offices expands dramatically from 75 in 1790, to 903 in 1800, 4500 in 1820, and 13,468 in 1840 (Pred, 1973, p. 80). Postal revenue per capita increased from one cent in 1790 to five cents in 1800, 12 cents in 1820, and 27 cents in 1840.

The period after the turnpike boom in England sees a blossoming of provincial newspapers. These papers were an invaluable source of commercial information. The number of newspapers published in the United States grew from 92 in 1790 to 235 in 1800, 512 in 1820, and 1404 in 1840 (Pred, 1973, p. 21). Circulation increased from 4 million to 147.5 million. While many factors were involved in the tremendous growth of newspapers, ease of delivery as well as access to newsprint must have played an important role. Through letters and newspapers, then, the American businessmen had much greater access to information in 1840 than a half century earlier. Through improvements in passenger transport, face-to-face contact was enhanced to a similar degree.

It is widely recognized that the transmission of technology at the time required personal contact, and the same would be true for organizational innovation. In England, as road travel became less expensive, quicker, and more comfortable, the amount of passenger traffic increased enormously. We see the same result in America. Taylor (1951, p. 27) noted that turnpikes were a boon to passenger traffic. Horseback gave way to coaches for personal travel between 1796 and 1812—the heyday of turnpikes; the number of such vehicles increased threefold (Kirkland, 1948, p. 48). The emerging stagecoach lines played an even greater role in encouraging personal travel (Kirkland, 1948, p. 48).[29]

Information flows within a particular industry also depend, naturally, on how concentrated the industry is. It has already been shown how important regional specialization is; however, urbanization is also important. Smolensky (1971, p. 397) discussed the role of falling transport costs in inducing urbanization. The number of cities in excess of 2,500 increases from 24 in 1790 to 90 in 1830.[30] The first truly industrial cities in the United States emerge in the 1820s (Davis et al., 1969, p. 266). Taken together, we can see that American entrepreneurs and inventors would have much greater interaction in the 1820s than would have been possible just a couple of decades earlier.

Factories

The first factories in the United States emerge after decades of road and river improvement and the earliest phase of factory development is associated with the canal boom of the 1820s.[31] Long before railroads, some entrepreneurs had found it worthwhile to gather their workers into centralized work places.[32] In 1815, American industry was dominated by household production; within decades this was replaced by centralized production. The proximate cause, as noted by Lebergott (1984, p. 133), must be that factory production was less costly than household production. If this had always been so, however, why had household production dominated for so long, when Americans could readily observe factory production in England from colonial times? The answer is that factory production had only become the least expensive mode of production in the nineteenth century, and this transformation was largely due to the improvements in road and water transport of the late eighteenth and early nineteenth centuries.[33] Imagine an entrepreneur in 1820 who wants to produce textiles, or boots, or ironware. He is deciding whether to put the work out to households or set up a centralized workplace. He no longer has to worry about face-to-face sales of output, so he can contemplate supervising production (at a time when reliable and trustworthy middle management has yet to emerge). He can rely on reliable transport services to deliver a variety of supplies when he needs them. He faces a wider market. He can locate in an urbanized setting, where the availability of a labour pool, repairmen, and various services will enhance the possibility of his factory succeeding.[34] He has access to better information on market conditions,[35] and organizational and technological developments elsewhere. All of these factors serve to make the factory look more attractive.[36]

There is one other factor discussed before which may play a bigger role than all the above, for it goes beyond allowing the factory to emerge, and actually induces its emergence. As sales by sample replace direct sale, it becomes necessary to produce a standardized good. As Nussbaum (1968) recognized long ago, domestic production is incapable of producing a standardized product.[37] To take advantage of the new distribution system it was necessary to gather workers where they could be supervised.

Technology

At the beginning of the nineteenth century, the United States is borrowing technology from Europe. Even at this stage, it is essential that the United States possess technicians capable of modifying foreign technology to local conditions (Rosenberg, 1972, pp. 62, 83-4). Early on, American technology diverges from that of Europe. Before mid-century, the American system of manufacture has become something for Europeans to attempt to emulate.[38] Why did the United States prove so good at both adapting foreign technology and developing its own during this period? Social attitudes favorable to tinkering may be a partial explanation, but we must remember that this technological precocity only becomes marked in the nineteenth century.

Sokoloff (1988) has found a high correlation between patenting activity and access to navigable waterways in early nineteenth-century America. Counties on navigable rivers or canals had levels of patenting per capita well over 50% higher than other counties, after controlling for region, urbanization, and labor force distribution (p. 837). While favoring a Schmooklerian demand-led explanation of technological innovation himself, Sokoloff recognizes that there are various avenues of causation which could underlie the strong correlation which he obtained.

Again, transport improvements usher in a new world in which technological innovation is more likely. Access to important raw materials was essential for some technological developments.[39] New technology almost never erupts from one mind. Thus the increased interaction allowed by improvements in information flows, including regional specialization and urbanization, is crucial. As Adam Smith long ago noted, market-widening is necessary for increasing division of labor. Division of labor means that the potential for mechanizing a particular task is more likely to be recognized, and that the gains from doing so will be greater. The emergence of factories makes some innovations easier to visualize, and others more viable. As Allyn Young said, it does not pay to make a hammer to hit one nail. Moreover, the interaction between workers and supervisors could be a valuable source of innovation (Landes, 1986, p. 615). Much of the new technology in early nineteenth-century America emerged from competition among specialized machine-making firms (Rosenberg, 1971, p. 252). Such firms only emerged after transport improvements and regional specialization allowed them to supply a number of producers with machinery less expensively than those producers could build themselves.

These and other indirect links between transport and technology were found to be of great importance in my analysis of eighteenth century English industry. Although it is impossible to trace the development of American technology to show here the extent to which the same forces were at work, we can, however, look briefly at the most famous stream of technological development, and try to discern why, given the many similarities between English and American experience, American technology diverges so much from that of England.

As Hounshell (1984) pointed out, the phrase "American system of manufactures" has often been misinterpreted in the literature. It is often associated with an emphasis on the production of interchangeable parts. However, attempts at interchangeability had previously been made in Europe, and were rarely successful in early nineteenth-century America. Rather, the real distinguishing feature of American industry during this period was the willingness of a number of firms to invest in special-purpose machinery which would perform a specific task in the manufacture of a particular product. From this starting point would eventually evolve the mass production techniques of the twentieth century.

It is obvious that such a system of manufacturing could only develop if a large market for standardized goods existed. While a necessary condition, it is clearly not sufficient, for English manufacturers had access to such a market for decades. It is often remarked that one of the difficulties faced in European attempts to copy American technology is that Europeans had to compete with the previous system centered on skilled craftsmen. David has noted that a technological path, once begun, tends to become self-sustaining. American industry, by evolving in a certain direction, created an institutional structure conducive to further developments along the same lines. The advantages of the new technology increased gradually through time.

If America had been less successful in developing her transport network, industrialization must have occurred at a slower pace. Early industrialists, facing different market potential, would have been less likely to diverge from European methods of production.[40] That is, if America had not been ready for the American system in the early nineteenth century when modern industry first emerges, it may never have happened.[41] History often appears inevitable ex post, but America's success was not inevitable. Her institutional inheritance from England was crucial in shaping her destiny.

Conclusion

After the English Industrial Revolution we enter a new world. All countries which industrialize after England were aided by the English example. Thus, factors necessary for English industrialization might not be required by any follower nation. It is therefore impressive that American experience decades later is similar in so many ways. Nineteenth-century history is full of failed attempts to transfer English technology to lands which could not support it. The United States was ready for new technology and methods of organization, however. Much of the reason for this is the institutional legacy of Britain, and the resulting turnpikes and canals.

NOTES

1. Six horses pulling a wagon could transport eight times as much as they could carry on their backs. Long-distance wagon traffic would only be possible at reasonable cost with a road surface free of holes and mud.
2. Charging tolls may seem straightforward. The introduction of tollbooths on previously public routes had occasioned riots in England in the first decades of the innovation, and in France when it was attempted after the Revolution. Social acceptance and legal enforcement were necessary. In England, local people were often exempted from the tolls. In the United States, the same solution was adopted (Klein, 1987). Toll-evasion was always a problem, but the English example provided partial solutions.
3. Kirkland (1948) comments on the effects of pikes on road quality. Methods of construction and maintenance were well known; they simply had to be applied. Roads were straightened, grades were lowered, and roads were widened to permit two-way traffic (p. 39). We will see later the effect this had on wheeled transport.
4. See Taylor (1951, p. 67). While the Constitution prevented the federal government from launching a national transport plan at that time, it did from time to time devote funds to particular projects.
5. The steamboat, introduced from 1811, made two-way navigation possible on many rivers, especially in the west, where floating rafts downstream had been all that was possible previously. Mak and Walton (1972) concluded that the transformation of the midwest into America's agricultural heartland was due to improvements in river transport. Freight charges on the Hudson fell 90 percent between 1814 and 1854 (Taylor, p. 136).
6. "Where the new republic developed a surprising novelty was its use of government for social control objectives in its internal economic development" (Hughes, 1976, p. 162). While the

degree of public support for canals was new, the canal companies in other ways resembled their English forbears.

7. According to Goodrich (1961), private investors again did not just consider their potential dividends from the canal, but their private gain as landowners and shippers. He does not discuss what social pressure might have been brought to bear on these investors.

8. Low population density meant that inexpensive transport was even more important for the development of industrial establishments which required access to a large market.

9. Chevalier, visiting the United States in 1835, marvelled that the United States could establish a network which European countries with three to four times the population could not (Segal, 1961, p. 216).

10. The southern experience will be discussed later. It is likely, given the makeup of the southern economy, that canal projects there might have had a significantly lower return than those in the north. While presidential vetoes to national transport plans were based on the perception of extra-constitutionality, there were also fears of expense and corruption (Taylor, 1951, pp. 19-20).

11. While individual states were driven by economic motives, the federal government might well have emphasized military motives. Difficulties in transporting men and supplies during the War of 1812 had indeed caused much interest in Washington in transport improvement. The Canadian case is perhaps instructive. There had been much agitation in Canada for canals around the rapids on the St. Lawrence. The British government, fearful of invasion, would not support a canal along the U.S. border, and instead wasted millions on the economically useless Rideau Canal in the 1830s. The first St. Lawrence seaway was thus delayed till almost mid-century.

12. Others go even further. "In the case of the American economy, there can be little doubt that the evolution of a satisfactory transport network was one . . . necessary condition" for economic growth (Davis, Hughes, and McDougall, 1969, p. 276). They note that the U.S. market was fragmented at Independence, and that the seaboard possessed few raw materials.

13. There is widespread agreement in the literature that, while the full flowering of American industry occurs later, the all-important first stages of industrialization occur before 1850. Lebergott (1984) notes that American industry was in its infancy when Talleyrand visited in 1796, but its manufacturing prowess was clear to all a half century later (p. 124). The earliest factories, and the beginnings of the emergence of the American system of manufacture both predate the railway.

14. We must not lose sight of what the purpose of economic history is. Whatever counterfactual is constructed, it turns out that the world went on much as before. As GNP rarely grows more than a couple percent per year in historical settings, this is perhaps not surprising. Yet the main purpose of economic history must be to explain why growth or development (however defined) occurs faster at some times and places than at other times and places. Until we can properly explain what caused these differentials, we should be wary of calculations that show that one potential cause had an insignificant impact. Our inability to find factors which played an important role may be more a reflection of our inability to measure the appropriate causal links than an indication of the way the world works.

15. "While I have conveyed my personal skepticism concerning the contribution of the canals to growth, I would be the first to admit that such a judgment remains to be confirmed (or refuted) by further research" (Ransom, 1977).

16. Estimates for the contributions of road and water improvements in England are limited even more severely by lack of data. Hawke and Higgins (1983) make a seat of the pants estimate that the social savings of early nineteenth-century canals is of the same order of magnitude as for later railways (pp. 196-198). Albert, however, feels that the social rate of return on turnpikes was considerably above 40 percent and the returns on canals probably even higher (pp. 193-196).

17. Another advantage of road over water transport is that it can be extended everywhere. Loading and unloading could occur anywhere. Also, the smaller size of wagons meant it was better suited to small consignments. Departure times could be more frequent. Not only was road traffic quicker, but it was more dependable as it was less subject to flood, drought, or congestion.

18. "Highway transport did not play an important role in the interregional movement of goods and people until after the evolution of the motor vehicle" (Davis et al., 1969, p. 290). Decades earlier, Taylor (1951) noted that turnpikes predominated where water alternatives were poor, most canals carried no passengers, valuable goods were carried by land when water transport was time-consuming, and that road transport saved on transhipment costs, allowed merchants to deal with only one carrier, and had a much more reliable schedule (pp. 153-156).

19. With the completion of the Erie Canal the cost per ton of shipping from Buffalo to New York dropped from $100 to under $9.

20. Kirkland (1948) notes that the romantic stagecoach has tended to divert attention from the more important freight traffic. Boston had 67 different stage coach lines in the 1820s (chapter 2). English law governing common carriers was replicated exactly in the U.S. (Hughes, 1977, p. 78).

21. The four-wheeled wagon, with its great cargo capacity, came to dominate American road transport in the early nineteenth century, replacing the two-wheel cart in the two decades after 1812 (Kirkland, 1948, pp. 56-57).

22. Taylor (1951) provides examples of such sales (pp. 239-240).

23. Chandler (1977) speaks of middlemen as the traditional mode of distribution for millenia (p. 245) but; in fact, face-to-face sales were more the norm.

24. The role of transport in tapping raw materials is so obvious as to require little discussion. Segal, (1961), for example, described how canals opened up access to Pennsylvania anthracite, and this coal was the basis for much industrialization of the 1820s.

25. Fishlow (1971) feels that the biggest impact of transport on industry was to indirectly increase the size of the agricultural market it could reach by encouraging settlement.

26. Some enclaves might seem large enough to have supported one or two "factories." Monopolistic competition could prevent firms from achieving the efficient scale. Access to a wider market would cause them to face a more elastic demand, and then expand production. We have discussed and will discuss other ways in which transport improvements aided the shift to centralized production.

27. The debate on why the South sees far less industry and much smaller industrial establishments than the North during the antebellum period is far from having achieved a consensus. The traditional view that small local markets, due to a combination of unequal income and poor transport had severely constrained southern industry, has been challenged by Atack (1977), who doubts that southern manufacturers suffered from an inability to achieve economies of scale. Bateman and Weiss, (1975), however, have suggested that southern manufacturers may not have been aware of industrial possibilities. It is unclear to what degree a national transport plan would have led to more equal industrialization. Transport improvements are not sufficient to generate industrialization. It may be that the peculiarities of the Southern situation not only made it less suited to industrialization but less suited to the task of transport improvement. A better understanding of why the South failed to construct a transport network like the North might provide significant insight into the broader question of the southern lag in development.

28. The domestic system was inherently more flexible as I have argued elsewhere (Szostak, 1985).

29. One response to improved road surfaces was to develop improved stagecoaches which could provide an improved ride. See Taylor (1951).

30. See Hughes (1983, p. 184). He describes this period as "even before the first real boom in internal improvements," despite the turnpike construction of the period.

31. The emergence of factories in England of the 1750s and 1760s also followed decades of road and river improvement, and occurred simultaneously with the first canal boom.

32. It is not just the huge works like the Boston Manufacturing Co.'s mill at Lowell. A number of entrepreneurs find it worthwhile to gather handfuls of workers under one roof. Some, but far from all, of these establishments are attached to a water wheel or steam engine.

33. This line of argument echoes that applied to England in Szostak (1989). The scale of operation of many of these centralized work places remained small throughout the nineteenth century. Atack (1986) has suggested that these were complementary to larger establishments, rather than substitutes.

34. A factory relying on division of labour suffers much more from machine or worker breakdown than the more flexible domestic production.

35. And thus, depending on the line of production, may wish to be better able to respond to changes in fashion. A factory could alter production over night. With domestic production, it could take months.

36. Only painstaking research in business history can test the empirical importance of these factors to individual enterprises. The theoretical case is clear.

37. Taylor (1951, pp. 217-218) discusses the pressure for standardization in the early 19th century, but does not recognize what has caused this pressure, nor that only factories are capable of producing a standardized product.

38. As Hughes (1983, p. 151) has noted, the United States came to rival European industrial production by the end of the nineteenth century only because industrial output grew much faster than in Europe. Some of this was due to faster population growth. Temin (1971) has noted that at least for textiles between 1815 and 1833, the annual rate of growth of 16 percent is more due to the drop in final price, and this must have resulted from organizational and technological change.

39. Coal is an obvious example. The transformation of the American iron industry to coke-smelting is closely tied to access to different types of coal. The adoption of the steam engine so important in allowing industrial enterprises freedom of scale and location is also dependent on access to inexpensive coal. Chandler (1972) has previously described the role of improved access to Pennsylvania anthracite in American industrialization in the 1830s and 1840s.

40. Early America may have suffered from a shortage of skilled labour, and this may have affected the direction of technological change. Such a constraint would be less binding if industrialization had occurred more slowly.

41. And then what? According to Chandler, among the reasons for the emergence of managerial capitalism first in the United States was the previous evolution of the America system of manufacture.

REFERENCES

Atack, J. (1977). "Returns to Scale in Antebellum United States Manufacturing." *Explorations in Economic History* 14: 337-359.

Atack, J. (1986). "Firm Size and Industrial Structure in the United States During the Nineteenth Century." *Journal of Economic History* 46: 463-476.

Bateman, F. and Weiss, T. (1975). "Comparative Regional Development in Antebellum Manufacturing." *Journal of Economic History* 35: 182-208.

Chandler, A. D. (1972). "Anthracite Coal and the Beginnings of the Industrial Revolution in the United States." *Business History Review* 46: 141-181.

Chandler, A. D. (1977). *The Visible Hand.* Cambridge, MA: Belknap Press.

Cramner, H. J. (1961). "Improvement Without Public Funds: The New Jersey Canals." In *Canals and American Economic Development*, edited by C. Goodrich. New York: Columbia University Press.

Davis, L. E., Hughes, J.R.T., and McDougall, D.M. (Eds.). (1969). *American Economic History.* Homewood, IL: Irwin.

Davis, L. E. and North, D. C. (1972). *Institutional Change and American Economic Growth*. Cambridge: Cambridge University Press.

Fishlow, A. (1971). "Internal Transportation." In *American Economic Growth*, edited by L.E. Davis, J.R.T. Hughes, and D.M. McDougall. Homewood, IL: Irwin.

Goodrich, C. (1961). "Conclusion." In *Canals and American Economic Development*, edited by C. Goodrich. New York: Columbia University Press.

Hawke and Higgins (1983). "Britain." In *Railways and the Economic Development of Europe 1830-1914*, edited by P. O'Brien. London: Macmillan.

Hounshell, D. (1984). *From the American System to Mass Production 1800-1932*. Baltimore, MD: The Johns Hopkins University Press.

Hughes, J.R.T. (1976). *Social Control in the Colonial Economy*. Charlottesville, VA: University Press of Virginia.

Hughes, J.R.T. (1977). *The Governmental Habit*. New York: Basic Books.

Hughes, J.R.T. (1983). *American Economic History*. Glenview, IL: Scott, Foresman.

Jackman, W. (1916). *The Development of Modern Transportation in England*. Cambridge: Cambridge University Press.

Kirkland, E. (1948). *Men, Cities, and Transportation*. Cambridge, MA: Harvard University Press.

Klein, D. (1987). "The Voluntary Provision of Public Goods: The Turnpike Companies of Early America." Paper presented at the EHA meetings, San Francisco, CA.

Landes, D. (1986). "What Do Bosses Really Do?" *Journal of Economic History* 46: 585-624.

Lebergott, S. (1984). *The Americans: An Economic Record*. New York: W.W. Norton.

Mak, J. and Walton, G. (1972). "Steamboats and the Great Productivity Surge in River Transportation." *Journal of Economic History* 32: 619-640.

Nussbaum, F.L. (1968). *A History of the Economic Institutions of Modern Europe* New York: F.S. Crofts.

Pawson, E. (1977). *Transport and Economy: The Turnpike Roads of Eighteenth Century Britain*. London: Academic Press.

Pred, A.R. (1973). *Urban Growth and the Circulation of Information: The United States System of Cities 1790-1840*. Cambridge, MA: Harvard University Press.

Ransom, R. (1964). "Canals and Development: A Discussion of the Issues." *American Economic Review* 54: 365-376.

Ransom, R. (1971). "A Closer Look at Canals and Western Manufacturing," *Explorations in Economic History* 8: 501-508.

Rosenberg, N. (1969). "Technological Change." In *American Economic History*, edited by L.E. Davis, J.R.T. Hughes, and D.M. McDougall. Homewood, IL: Irwin.

Rosenberg, N. (1972). *Technology and American Economic Growth*. New York: Harper & Row.

Segal, H. H. (1961). "Canals and Economic Development." In *Canals and American Economic Development*, edited by C. Goodrich. New York: Columbia University Press

Smolensky, E. (1969). "Industrial Location and Urban Growth." In *American Economic History*, edited by L.E. Davis, J.R.T. Hughes, and D.M. McDougall. Homewood, IL: Irwin.

Sokoloff, K.L. (1988). "Inventive Activity in Early Industrial America: Evidence From Patent Records, 1790-1846." *Journal of Economic History*, 48: 813-850.

Szostak, R. (1985). *The Role of Transportation in the Industrial Revolution: A Comparison of Eighteenth Century England and France*. Ph.D. Thesis, Northwestern University.

Szostak, R. (1989). "The Organization of Work: The Emergence of the Factory Revisited." *Journal of Economic Behavior and Organization*.

Taylor, G.R. (1951). *The Transport Revolution 1815-1860*. New York: Holt, Reinhart, and Winston.

Temin, P. (1969). "Manufacturing." In *American Economic History*, edited by L.E. Davis, J.R.T. Hughes, and D.M. McDougall. Homewood, IL: Irwin.

Ward, J.R. (1974). *The Finance of Canal Building in Eighteenth Century England.* London: Oxford University Press.
Willan, T.S. (1964). *River Navigation in England.* London: F. Cass.

EXPERIMENTAL METHODS TO ADVANCE HISTORICAL INVESTIGATION: AN EXAMINATION OF CARTEL COMPLIANCE BY LARGE AND SMALL FIRMS

Brian R. Binger, Elizabeth Hoffman, and Gary D. Libecap

I. INTRODUCTION

A distinguishing characteristic of Jonathan Hughes' work has been his concern with the effects of incentives on behavior. In this paper, experimental methods are used to examine the compliance problem encountered in cartelization efforts. While the link between the work of Jonathan Hughes and experimental methods in economics may seem to be quite distant, these two strains of research have similar philosophical bases. Hughes' longstanding attention to the effects of incentives on behavior is quite consistent with the approach of experimental economics, which uses laboratory methods to explore the effects of institutions and incentives on behavior.

The experiments are built around an historical cartel case, involving quota restrictions imposed by the states of Oklahoma and Texas on crude oil

Research in Economic History, Suppl. 6, pages 309-324.

ISBN: 1-55938-150-7.

producing firms (see Wiggins and Libecap, 1987). One of the distinguishing characteristics was that the bargaining parties did not behave symmetrically with regard to quota compliance, support for cartelization, or government intervention. Instead, there were sharp differences in behavior among the contracting firms. In particular, large firms generally supported the quotas and small firms generally opposed them. Analysis of the case suggests that differences in firm size among contracting parties—differences which may arise as a result of historical accident, secondary effects of property rights distributions, or overt political decisions—are important determinants of the success of cartelization efforts. Moreover, government policy will be influenced by both supporters and opponents of quotas.

This paper begins by briefly outlining the historical case in Section II and the model of compliance by firm size in Section III. Section IV outlines the experimental design, Section V discusses the experimental results and their implication for understanding the historical events outlined in Section II, and Section VI discusses conclusions.

II. OIL CARTELIZATION IN TEXAS AND OKLAHOMA 1926-1935

Between 1926 and 1930, an unprecedented clustering of oil discoveries in Oklahoma and Texas led to dramatic increases in crude oil production and a corresponding fall in crude oil prices. During that time, some of the largest oil fields ever found in North America were brought into production, including the huge East Texas and Oklahoma City fields. By 1931 Oklahoma and Texas accounted for over 60 percent of U.S. crude oil supplies.

Prices fell due to competitive extraction from common pool reservoirs. Under the rule of capture, property rights to oil were assigned only upon extraction. Because firms were granted access to the reservoir through leases from landowners, the number of firms on a reservoir was determined by the fragmented nature of surface land ownership, implying that large numbers of small firms often competed on each field through intense drilling and rapid production. In July 1926, prior to the major discoveries, the nominal midcontinent price for 36 gravity oil was $2.29. By July 1931 it had fallen to $.18 per barrel. This dramatic fall in price was far greater than the fall in the consumer price index and led some crude oil producing firms to contract to restrict output and fix prices.

Despite an obvious need, however, private efforts to restrict output were unsuccessful. After trying private contracting, some, but not all firms turned to the state governments of Texas and Oklahoma to complete and enforce agreements. Yet, in eight years of bargaining only an imperfect cartel was ever assembled. With ease of entry into the industry and the proliferation of very small firms, the problems of organization and enforcement were large. At no time during the period 1926-1933 was a cartel stabilized with output firmly fixed. Instead, output remained well beyond the collusive profit-maximizing level throughout the period.

Government efforts at output control led to the setting of production quotas by the Texas Railroad Commission and the Oklahoma Corporation Commission, beginning in 1928 in Oklahoma and 1930 in Texas. Moreover, the national guard was used in both states to temporarily close the Oklahoma City and East Texas fields during periods of major production increases beyond quota limits. The closing of the East Texas field in August 1931 contributed to a rise in price to $.92 a barrel by April 1932. But, with the removal of military control, production once again rose and prices fell to $.25 a barrel by May 1933. Tighter controls were achieved in September 1933, with the imposition of the NRA code and federal enforcement through restrictions on interstate shipments of oil. By December 1933 crude oil prices had risen to $1.00 per barrel. This about restored the real price of oil to 1926 levels.

While no oil producers in Oklahoma and Texas were "large" by the standards of industrial concentration (larger firms typically had only 1-5 percent of the market), there were considerable differences in firm size, determined largely by lease size and the willingness of landowners to consolidate leases. In the United States, mineral rights are reserved to surface landowners and production rights are given to crude oil producing firms through leases. When landownership is fragmented, as it is in East Texas, leases will be small, leading to many small leases on even a large oil field. Many leases on that field were under 5 acres and a large proportion of the leases on the Oklahoma City field were under 50 acres.

Leases could be consolidated, but the leasing and producing strategies of both landowners and small firms limited the possibilities for consolidation. Because crude oil is migratory, large landowners feared migration to other areas, while small landowners wanted to encourage migration to increase their share of field rents. Both of these motivations led landowners to prefer not to lease to a firm with production on a neighboring lease and to encourage lessees to produce as rapidly as possible. Large landowners wished to capture as much of the oil as possible before it migrated under someone else's land, and small landowners tried to capture as much migratory oil as they could. To enforce rapid production by lessees, production, and development schedules generally were specified in leases, and violation could lead to cancellation of the lease.

Another factor contributed to lease fragmentation, despite benefits to firms from consolidation. There was a long-standing populist distrust of large out-of-state firms in Texas. Large firms were the integrated firms with production from multiple leases across many fields and across various states. They also had pipelines, refineries, and retail outlets for oil products. Small independent oil producers typically produced from one lease only and, hence, did not have production on other fields or in other states. They relied on local independent refineries and oil well service firms. For these reasons, small independents were viewed as having close ties to the community and larger firms were viewed with suspicion. This, combined with the fact that small firms tended to take the lead in developing new oil fields, affected the political climate with respect to quota definition. The large firms called for and benefited most from cartelization efforts, but the political power of the small firms led to a call for equal treatment of small and large firms. Hence, quota definitions were expressed as across-the-board percentage reductions from an output which was arguably competitive. Furthermore, as part of the initial prorationing legislation in 1930, high-cost (mostly small) firms were exempt from prorationing restrictions.

Thus, while cost considerations favored larger firms, land fragmentation and political support for small firms ensured the continued survival of thousands of small producers. The result was that there were considerable differences in production across firms in Texas and Oklahoma. For example, for the first quarter of 1931, Humble produced 6.5 million barrels, Gulf produced 5.7 million barrels, Mid Kansas produced 3.9 million barrels, Shell produced 3.5 million barrels, and Texaco produced 3.0 million barrels. These were all large, integrated firms with production in several states. In contrast, smaller firms ranged in size from 100,000 down to as low as 100 barrels over the same time period (*Oil Weekly*, May 29, 1931).

Given the persistence of such differences in firm size and market share, there were sharp differences in behavior among firms according to size. On the Oklahoma City field, a committee of six large firms was formed to fix field quotas for state-wide prorationing of production among all Oklahoma fields by the Oklahoma Corporation Commission. The committee members—Skelly, Barnsdall, Phillips, Tidal, Carter, and Wirt Franklin—were among the largest 25 firms in the state, based on 1929, first quarter production (*Oil Weekly*, December 12, 1929). By 1933 the state-wide prorationing committee had 14 members, 11 of which were top 25 operators (*Oil Weekly*, January 2, 1933).

In order to obtain at least verbal support for prorationing from the low-cost small firms (who feared being pushed out of the market by output restrictions), prorationing shares were determined as percentage cutbacks from the current (probably competitive) output levels. This system at least maintained current market shares.

Larger firms consistently supported enforcement of prorationing rules. No top 25 firm in Oklahoma was identified as challenging in court or cheating on prorationing quotas. Moreover, lawyers from Texaco with a 1.9 percent market share and Skelly, with a 1.4 percent market share in the third quarter of 1930 assisted the Oklahoma Corporation Commission in legal challenges to prorationing (*Oil Weekly*, September 12, 1930).

In contrast, very small Oklahoma City firms repeatedly cheated on the prorationing quotas set by the Corporation Commission and fought in the courts for more lenient production rules. Court challenges of Oklahoma regulations were initiated in 1930 by C.C. Julian, Capital, Champlin, Marco, Plains, Century, and Oil, Inc., where all but Champlin (with a 0.7 percent market share) had shares under 0.15 percent for the first quarter of 1931 (*Oil Weekly*, September 13, 1930, October 24, 1930; *Oil and Gas Journal*, January 9, 1931). These small firms were also involved in rampant cheating. This led the governor to order periodic military occupation of the Oklahoma City field to force compliance.

Not only did larger firms comply, but they tended to produce below their authorized quotas. Prorationing did not successfully bring output to near monopoly levels and large firms unilaterally cut production below their authorized quotas. Major firms such as Carter (market share 4 percent in the second quarter of 1930) and Prairie (5 percent) informally adopted Sunday closings, where wells were shut and drilling halted (*Oil Weekly*, January 31, 1930). By September 1931, voluntary underproduction on the Oklahoma City field equalled 3,600,000 barrels of crude oil. Of that, 71 percent was by 4 large firms: the Indian Territory Illuminating Oil Company, the state's largest with a 6 percent market share in the first quarter of 1931, Phillips (3 percent), Skelly (1.5 percent), and Wirt Franklin (1 percent) (*Oil Weekly*, September 25, 1931).

The record of differential support for prorationing based on firm size is repeated in Texas. A trade group of Texas' largest firms, the Midcontinent Oil and Gas Association, established a Central Prorationing Committee to assist the Railroad Commission in bringing East Texas into compliance with state-wide prorationing rules. The committee also lobbied the Texas legislature for strict enforcement of quotas, but there was opposition by representatives of very small East Texas firms (*Texas Senate Journal*, 1931, pp. 418–452). The railroad commission delayed prorationing controls on East Texas until 1931, because of small firm resistance. The legislature also delayed enactment of a state-wide market demand prorationing law until November 1932, two years after the discovery of the East Texas field. Despite the urging of larger firms, neither the Railroad Commission nor the Texas legislature was willing to confront the large number of small East Texas operators who opposed controls. Moreover, when prorationing was finally enacted it followed the lead of Oklahoma in adopting an across-the-board percentage reduction from current output levels, thus maintaining market shares.

As in Oklahoma, large firms supported the Railroad Commission's quotas and engaged in private enforcement. For example, Gulf (8.6 percent of the market in the first quarter of 1931) refused to purchase oil produced in excess of Railroad Commission rules (*Oil Weekly*, May 29, 1931). Further, only large firms paid the assessments levied by the Railroad Commission to cover the costs of policing output controls in East Texas (*Texas Senate Journal*, 1931, pp. 15-23). Large firms also lobbied for federal enforcement, including Shell (5.4 percent in the first quarter of 1931), Atlantic (0.7 percent), Magnolia (3.3 percent), Sun (2.3 percent), Phillips (1.8 percent), Standard of Indiana (1.5 percent), Empire Fuel and Gas (0.6 percent), and Sinclair (0.6 percent).

In contrast, small firms routinely violated prorationing rules and challenged them in court. In July 1931, small firms overturned the Railroad Commission's regulation of crude oil production on the East Texas field (*MacMillan* v. *Railroad Commission*, 51 F. 2nd, 400). Texas Governor Sterling responded by placing the field under martial law in August 1931, closing it for 19 days while new quotas were implemented. With the removal of martial law, small firms drilled additional wells and increased output while larger firms held back. Small firm resistance to output controls continued with the adoption of NRA controls which raised prices to $1.00 by May 1933. Published lists of dozens of cheating firms reveal that only small firms violated quotas. Federal enforcement was further weakened when, in 1935, a group of 26 small East Texas firms successfully obtained a court ruling overturning NIRA section 9(c), which prohibited interstate shipment of oil produced in excess of state quotas (*Panama Refining* v. *Ryan*, 293 U.S. 388).

These differences in firm behavior were an important part of cartel efforts to enforce quotas for domestic crude oil production. In the next section we present an extension of the Cournot-Nash model which shows how arrangements similar to those tried in Texas and Oklahoma can lead to strictly differential incentives for individual firms. We then create in the laboratory an environment with incentives similar to those faced by small and large firms in such a naturally-occurring environment. In this way we can test whether this model can generally be used to predict firm behavior under such quota systems.

III. A COURNOT-NASH MODEL OF CARTEL COMPLIANCE BY LARGE AND SMALL FIRMS

To develop a model that is consistent with the evidence presented in the previous section, we extend the basic Cournot-Nash model to allow for heterogeneous, quantity-constrained firms and an imperfect set of quota restrictions, which do not bring total output to the collusive, profit-maximizing level. Under such quotas, firms of varying size may have different incentives to expand or contract production from their quota assignments.

Consider an industry of n firms with a linear, downward-sloping demand curve and constant marginal cost. Applying the usual competitive, monopoly, and symmetric Cournot equilibrium economic models, a competitive industry will produce a quantity such that price equals marginal cost, the joint-profit maximum occurs at one-half the competitive quantity, and the symmetric Cournot equilibrium is at $n/(n + 1)$ times the competitive quantity. Figure 1 illustrates these three equilibria for a duopoly.

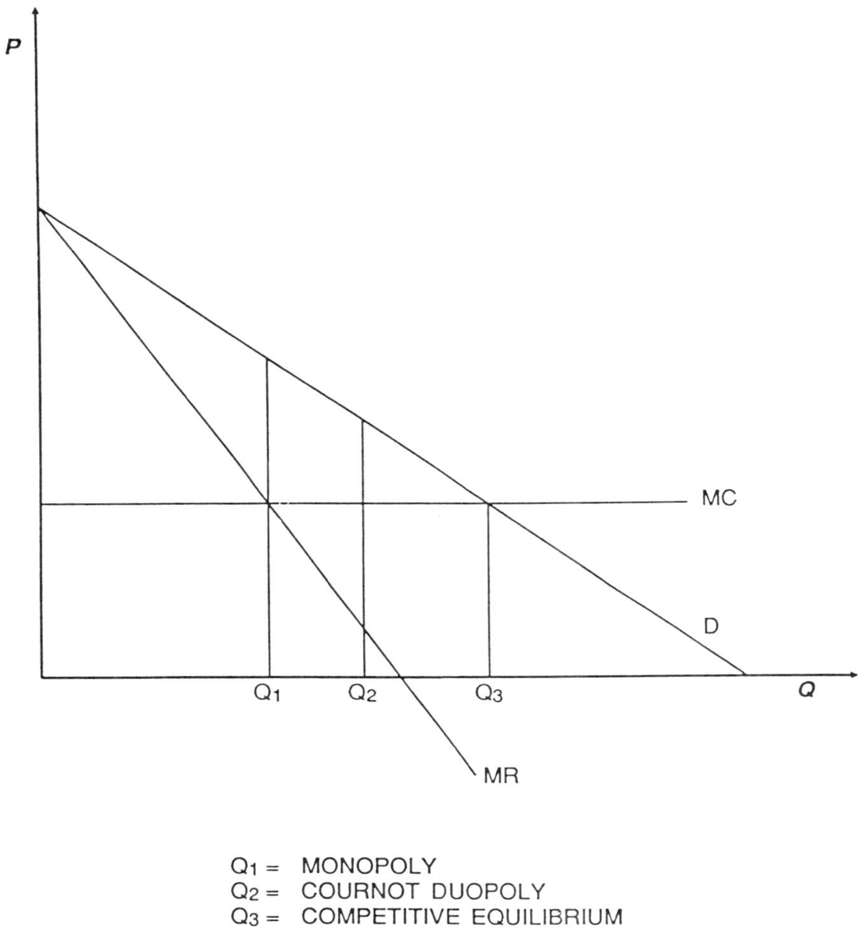

Figure 1. Equilibrium Output Predictions for a Monopoly, a Duopoly, and a Competitive Industry

Now, suppose that L firms are "large" and s firms are "small" ($L + s = n$) and there are many more s firms than L firms. The incentives are now different for L and s firms, even if the Cournot-Nash behavioral assumption that firms take other firms' outputs as given is maintained. For example, the large firms may take total small firm output as given and then reach the Cournot equilibrium for the large firms on the residual demand.

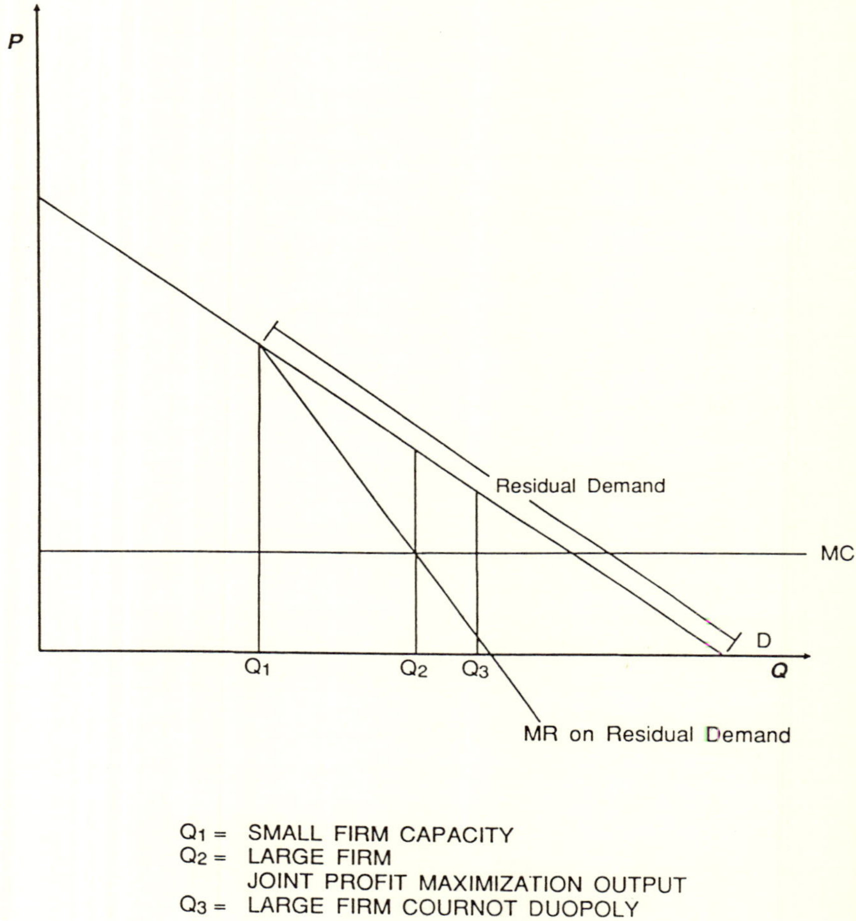

Figure 2. Cournot Equilibrium for Heterogeneous, Capacity-Constrained Firms

This is an extension of the usual symmetric Cournot-Nash equilibrium model to heterogeneous, quantity-constrained firms and is illustrated in Figure 2 for the case of two large firms. Suppose the many small firms each produce at capacity. This strategy would be optimal if there were so many small firms that no one small firm could have any discernable effect on market price. It would also be optimal if a symmetric Cournot-Nash equilibrium implied a firm output in excess of small firm capacity: since the small firms are constrained, they cannot expand to the symmetric equilibrium output. In that case, their individual profit-maximizing output is their capacity. Total small firm capacity is shown as point Q_1 in Figure 2. That leaves the rest of the demand curve for the large firms. Joint-profit maximization for the large firms occurs where marginal cost equals marginal revenue on the residual demand curve and the Cournot-Nash equilibrium is at two-thirds the difference between the quantity such that price equals marginal cost and small firm capacity. This simple model extends to the case of more than two large firms. The large firm Cournot-Nash equilibrium will be at $L/(L + 1)$ times the difference between long-run competitive equilibrium and small firm capacity. To approximate conditions in Oklahoma and Texas, suppose cartel restrictions involve proportional reductions from competitive output levels. Additionally, suppose each firm's quota is set so that small firms are not producing at capacity, but large firms are producing more than their residual Cournot-Nash outputs. Under those circumstances, small firms have an incentive to expand back to capacity. Large firms, in contrast, make higher profits by actually reducing output. The result is that small firms have an incentive to cheat on the cartel agreement, while large firms have an incentive to support cartel enforcement and to reduce output even further.

If the behavior of oil-producing firms in Oklahoma and Texas in the 1930s can be rationalized with the model developed above, then it provides a possible explanation of the firms' differential compliance with prorationing agreements. However, observing that a model rationalizes a behavior in one particular historical context does not constitute a test of that model. While there might be disagreement about what constitutes a "test" of a model, the predictive power of a model is greatly enhanced if it rationalizes behavior from different, but comparable, data sets. One way to provide additional data is in a controlled laboratory environment. The next section presents the results of a set of laboratory experiments designed to parallel the essential features of both the model and the historical case under consideration.

IV. EXPERIMENTAL DESIGN

In recent years, laboratory experimental techniques have come to be used in economics for a variety of purposes,[1] such as testing the predictions of economic theories in a controlled environment, studying the properties of various exchange institutions, designing and testing the implementability of new allocation mechanisms, and studying the behavior of individuals in various market settings. One of the basic tenets of experimental economics is parallelism (Smith, 1982): the environment created in the laboratory should parallel as closely as possible a naturally-occurring environment under study.

Parallelism includes such diverse elements as the rules governing the operation of an exchange institution and the saliency of the incentives facing the economic agents. If a laboratory experiment is carefully designed to parallel the naturally-occurring economic environment, then insights gained in the laboratory can arguably be applied to that naturally-occurring environment.

This was our objective in designing a laboratory experiment to test the predictions of the model developed to explain the behavior of oil-producing firms in Texas and Oklahoma in the 1930s. The basic experimental design parallels both the simple outline of the model developed in section III and the essential features of the 1930s prorationing arrangements. We sought to ascertain whether "firms" in the laboratory, which faced incentives similar to those faced by the historical oil-producing firms, behaved in a fashion similar to those actual firms. Finding that they did, we conclude that the model does provide a reasonable rationalization for the observed behavior.

The experimental design replicates the simple example used to develop the Cournot-Nash model with heterogeneous, quantity-constrained firms in the previous section. For each experiment, 12 subjects were recruited from economics principles classes at the University of Wyoming and were told only that they would participate in an economics experiment. They were paid a $4.00 participation fee upon arriving. Further payments depended on their profits from the experiment. Each experiment was conducted in a large lecture hall and the subjects were asked to spread themselves around the room, to face the front, and not to speak to any other subject. When all subjects had arrived they read through the instructions which are reproduced in the appendix. Then the monitor read them again and answered any questions.

These instructions told the subjects that at the beginning of the experiment they would each take a 10 question, general knowledge quiz and that the two subjects who got the most right answers would earn the right to be large sellers.[2] The other 10 subjects would be small sellers. Each seller would then be given private information indicating the maximum number of units he or she could offer for sale each trading period.

The task each trading period was for each seller to indicate a number of units he or she wished to sell that trading period. Each unit sold cost the seller 301 francs and each seller was given a buyer's demand schedule which indicated the selling price for every possible market quantity. Market quantity was determined by summing the units offered for sale by all 12 sellers. There were 2000 francs for every U.S. dollar. Each small seller received a 4000 franc capital payment at the beginning of the experiment and any seller who went bankrupt would be asked to leave.[3] Each seller was given private information about its own capacity: each large firm had a capacity of 200 units and each small firm had a capacity of 20 units.

In mathematical terms, this experimental design incorporates a linear demand curve of

$$P = 601 - Q,$$

and constant marginal cost of 301. Letting price equal marginal cost:

$$301 = 601 - Q.$$

Thus, the competitive quantity is 300 units and the joint profit maximum is at 150 units. If each small firm were to produce its capacity of 20 units, the residual Cournot equilibrium would be a total of 200 units offered by the small firms and 66 or 67 offered by the 2 large firms together.

For the first 10 trading periods sellers were privately told how many units they were to offer. In periods 1-5 the small sellers each offered 10 units and the large sellers each offered 100 units. These offers implied a market quantity of 300 units, a market price of 301 francs and 0 profits. These first 5 periods were designed to parallel the competitive situation in Oklahoma and Texas immediately following the discovery of the Oklahoma City and East Texas fields. At the beginning of period 6 it was announced that each seller would reduce output by 20 percent so that all sellers could make profits. Small sellers were privately told to offer 8 units and large sellers were privately told to offer 80 units in periods 6-10. These offers implied a market quantity of 240 units, a market price of 361 francs and total profits of 14,400 francs. Periods 6-10 were designed to parallel the equal percentage reduction prorationing agreements proposed and periodically enforced by the Texas Railroad Commission and the Oklahoma Corporation Commission.

In periods 11-20, sellers could offer any number of units they wished up to their individual maxima of 20 or 200. Then, at the beginning of period 21 it was announced that sellers would be in "a restricted output mode." They were told to treat the amount offered in periods 6-10 as a restricted output maximum. They could offer less than or equal to 8 or 80. Periods 26-35 were again unrestricted output (up to capacity), periods 36-40 were restricted output, and periods 41-50 were unrestricted output. There were a total of 50 periods, but sellers were not informed in advance of the total number of periods to avoid possible end-game effects. The sequencing of restricted and unrestricted output periods was designed to parallel the periods of enforcement and nonenforcement of the Texas and Oklahoma regulatory agreements.

The next section analyzes the data for both restricted and unrestricted output periods between periods 11 and 40. The residual Cournot-Nash equilibrium prediction differs for the restricted and unrestricted output periods. During the restricted output periods, small sellers should produce their restricted outputs of 8 each and large sellers should cut back to 74 each. During the

Table 1. Cheating by Large and Small Firms

	Small Firms		*Large Firms*	
	Number	*Percent*	*Number*	*Percent*
All Unrestricted Output Periods	1247/1800	69	131/360	36
Periods 41-50 Only	446/600	74	41/120	34

unrestricted output periods, small sellers should produce their maxima of 20 units each and large sellers should cut back to 33 or 34 each. A weaker prediction is directional: during unrestricted output periods, small sellers should produce more than 8 and large sellers should produce less than 80.

V. EXPERIMENTAL RESULTS

Table 1 presents the number and percentage of times that small and large firms offered more than 8 or 80 units, respectively, across all experiments and all unrestricted output periods, and for periods 41-50 only. Table 1 indicates that the directional prediction is generally supported by the experimental evidence. Overall, small firms cheated 69 percent of the time during unrestricted output periods, while large firms cheated only 36 percent of the time. Moreover, when we consider only the last 10 periods, after subjects had had a chance to learn what strategies to play in the game, the results are even stronger. During the last 10 periods, small firms cheated 74 percent of the time, while large firms cheated only 34 percent of the time. Thus, while large firms do occasionally cheat and small firms do not always cheat, the differential incentives are leading small and large firms to behave generally in the directions predicted by the model.

Table 1 indicates that the basic prediction that differences in firm size and incentives lead to differences among firms in compliance with cartel agreements appears to be strongly supported by the experimental evidence. This finding suggests that studies of compliance with cartel quota arrangements need to take account of such differences among firms if we are to understand both compliance and the formation of government policy. For example, it is not surprising in light of this evidence that government regulatory policy is often inconsistent, setting prices or quotas on the one hand and then providing inadequate enforcement on the other. The large firms may lobby for quotas while the small firms constitute a large bloc that opposes those same quotas.

VI. CONCLUSION

This paper has outlined and illustrated a new methodology for conducting empirical tests of models developed to explain historical phenomena.

Whenever we try to explain history we face the danger of succumbing to the *post hoc ergo propter hoc* fallacy. When we use standard economic theory that has already been tested under a variety of conditions, we can be fairly certain that we are applying a principle with wide application. However, in many instances standard economic theory does not explain what we observe historically and we are led to develop new explanations which seem to "fit the facts." Generally, however, we cannot take the next logical step of testing our newly developed model with a different set of data. This is what we have attempted to do in this paper.

Wiggins and Libecap (1987) developed a model of cartel compliance, which was consistent with historical events in domestic crude oil production in Texas and Oklahoma in the early 1930s. We have shown with our experimental test that they developed a general model of compliance by firm size which does not depend upon the particular historical circumstances they were studying. Not all historical explanations lend themselves to the kind of clean experimental test we were able to conduct. When they do, we feel that experimental tests should take their place along side econometric analysis and the counterfactual as a tool for future economic historians.

Finally, in the tradition of Jonathan Hughes, we have brought differential incentives to the forefront of an analysis of cartel compliance. We have shown that different size firms have different incentives to comply with output restrictions and behave in accordance with those differential incentives.

APPENDIX

Instructions General

This is an experiment in the economics of market decision making. Various research foundations have provided funds for this research. The instructions are simple and, if you follow them carefully and make good decisions, you might earn a considerable amount of money which will be paid to you in cash.

In this experiment we are going to simulate a market in which you will be participating with several other sellers in a sequence of market days or trading periods. Attached to the instructions you will find a cost schedule and a buyers' demand schedule. These describe to you the value of any decisions you might make. All prices and costs are expressed in francs. There are 2000 francs for every U.S. dollar.

Specific Instructions

During each market period you will offer units of a fictitious commodity for sale. In some periods you will be told how many to offer and in others you will be able to choose how many to offer. You will also be told the maximum number of units you may offer for sale in any one trading period.

Each unit that you sell during a trading period you obtain at a cost of 301 francs. Total costs for different quantities you might sell are listed on your separate cost schedule. Profits in each market period (which are yours to keep) are computed by taking the difference between your revenues from selling the number of units you offer for sale and your total cost.

Suppose, for example, that you offer two units for sale and your cost per unit is 301 francs. If everyone else were to offer two units, the market quantity would be 24 units (2 units times 12 sellers). Looking at your market demand schedule, you can see that if the market quantity is 24 units, the price is 577 francs. To find your profit, multiply the number of units you offer for sale times the market price to find total revenue, find the total cost of the number of units you offer for sale on your cost schedule, and then subtract the total cost from the total revenue:

$$\text{Total earnings in francs} = \text{total revenue} - \text{total cost} =$$
$$2(577) - 2(301) = 1154 - 602 = 552 \text{ francs}$$

Notice that if the market quantity becomes larger than 300 units, the market price becomes less than 301 francs and all sellers lose money.

The blanks on your record sheet will help you record your profits. In each trading period, record the number of units offered for sale in column 2 and the total cost of those units in column 6. Once market quantity and market price are determined, record market quantity in column 3 and market price in column 4, and your total revenue (column 2 times column 4) in column 5. You should then record your profit (column 7) as the difference between column 5 and column 6. Keep track of your cumulative profits in column 8. Subsequent periods should be recorded similarly.

Preliminary Arrangements

Before we begin this experiment you will all take a 10 question general knowledge quiz. There will be a 10 minute time limit for completing the quiz. The two participants who get the most correct answers on that quiz will have earned the right to sell large quantities of the commodity. The other 10 participants will only be able to sell small quantities. If more than two participants score equally highly, those participants will take a second, more difficult 10 question general knowledge quiz to break the tie. There will be a 5 minute time limit for completing the tie-breaking quiz.

The 10 sellers who will only be able to sell small numbers of units will each receive a 4000 franc capital payment at the beginning of the experiment. If any seller's cumulative profits (plus capital payment for those 10 sellers) goes below zero, that seller will be asked to leave.

Market Organization

The market for this commodity is organized as follows. At the beginning of each trading period, each seller will write the number of units he or she is selling that trading period on a slip of paper and hand it in. The experimenter will add the units offered by all sellers and display the total number of units offered by all sellers on the blackboard. That number will then determine a market selling price along the attached buyers' demand schedule. Once the selling price is determined, sellers will compute their revenues, costs, and profits for that trading period.

For the first 10 trading periods, sellers will be told how many units to offer for sale. For the next 10 trading periods they may offer any number of units they wish, up to the maximum allowed each participant. Then, after the twentieth trading period, the experimenter may occasionally dictate how many units to sell for some number of trading periods. Otherwise, sellers may continue to offer any number they wish, up to the maximum allowed each participant. During the experiment, sellers are not to speak to or communicate with one another in any way.

You are free to make as much money as you can. Remember that small profits each trading period add up over time.

ACKNOWLEDGMENTS

The authors thank Joel Mokyr, participants at the 1988 Cliometrics Society annual meetings, members of Vernon Smith's graduate seminar in experimental economics at the University of Arizona, and two anonymous referees for helpful comments. Phillip K. Lowrey provided invaluable research assistance. Research funds were provided by the State of Arizona through the University of Arizona Economic Science Laboratory and the National Science Foundation.

NOTES

1. For discussions of the uses of laboratory experiments, see Hoffman and Spitzer (1985b), Plott (1981), and Smith (1982).

2. The general knowledge quiz was given because previous research by Hoffman and Spitzer (1985) indicates that experimental subjects who do not believe that they have earned a differential property endowment do not behave as if they have the right to that endowment. We wanted to make sure that large sellers considered that they had earned the right to make a substantial amount more money than small sellers. Otherwise, if large sellers reduced output, we could not be sure it was a result of the incentives in the experiment.

3. No seller went bankrupt in any of the 6 experiments.

REFERENCES

Hoffman, E. and Spitzer, M.L. (1985a). "Entitlements, Rights and Fairness: Some Experimental Evidence of Subjects' Concepts of Distributive Justice." *Journal of Legal Studies*, 14(2): 259-298.

Hoffman, E. and Spitzer, M.L. (1985b). "Experimental Law and Economics: An Introduction." *Columbia Law Review*, 85(5): 991-1036.

Libecap, G.D. and Wiggins, S.N. (1985). "The Influence of Private Contractual Failure on Regulation: The Case of Oil Field Unitization." *Journal of Political Economy*, 93(4): 690-714.

Plott, C. R. (1981). "Industrial Organization Theory and Experimental Economics." *Journal of Economic Literature*, 20: 1485.

Smith, V. L. (1982). "Microeconomic Systems as an Experimental Science." *American Economic Review*, 72: 923.

Wiggins, S.N. and Libecap, G.D. (1987). "Firm Heterogeneities and Cartelization Efforts in Domestic Crude Oil." *Journal of Law, Economics, and Organization*, 3(1): 1-25.

INDEX